# BUPPIES, B-BOYS, BAPS & BOHOS

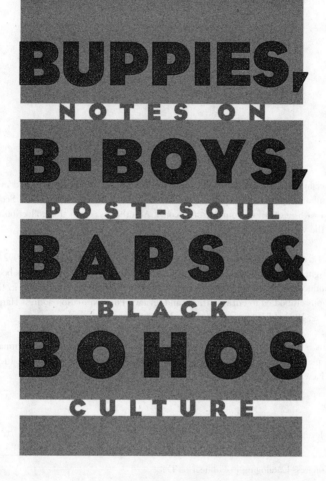

# BUPPIES,
## NOTES ON
# B-BOYS,
## POST-SOUL
# BAPS &
## BLACK
# BOHOS
## CULTURE

# NELSON GEORGE

HarperCollins*Publishers*

"Rapping Deejays" and "Standing in the Shadows of Motown" originally appeared in *Musician* magazine, and are reprinted with permission. The liner notes to "The Best of Gil Scott-Heron" are reprinted with permission from Arista Records. All other essays in this collection previously appeared in the *Village Voice*.

HarperCollins books may be purchased for educational, business, or sales promotional use. For information please write: Special Markets Department, HarperCollins Publishers, Inc., 10 East 53rd Street, New York, NY 10022.

FIRST EDITION

*Designed by Jessica Shatan*

Library of Congress Cataloging-in-Publication Data

George, Nelson.
    Buppies, B-boys, Baps & Bohos : notes on post-soul black culture / Nelson George.—1st ed.
    p.   cm.
    ISBN 0-06-016724-6 (cloth)
    1. Afro-Americans—Music—History and criticism—20th century. 2. United States—Popular culture—History—20th century. 3. Popular music—United States—1971–1980—History and criticism. 4. Popular music—United States—1981–1990—History and criticism.
    I. Title. II. Title: Buppies, B-boys, Baps & Bohos.
    ML3479.G44   1992
    306.4´7´08996073—dc20            92-53347

93 94 95 96 97 ❖/RRD 10 9 8 7 6 5 4 3 2

*For Richard Wright and James Baldwin,*

*who taught me it was all right*

*for little black boys to write*

*about how they saw the world*

*with no apologies and no fear.*

# CONTENTS

# PREFACE

This book is about the culture of African-Americans who've come of age since the demise of the civil rights movement in the late '60s. And, since I am one of those folks, it's also inevitably about me and my experiences living in and reporting on a world created by the struggles of previous generations. In the essays in this book, I report on, hang out with, and take measure of rappers, filmmakers, crack dealers, mainstream politicians, schoolteachers, mulatto beauties, followers of the Five Percenter religion, Afrocentric activists, retro-nuevo musicians, and one second baseman. All of us live in slightly different worlds, but crucial to the shaping of all our experiences and attitudes have been the values of the white American mainstream that our parents fought to be a part of, the anger that Malcolm X and others expressed about the white system's injustices, and the daily battles to survive and thrive in the space in between.

Media savvy but with a shallow music-video sense of history, leaning toward black nationalism but enticed by capitalism's assimilationist lure, the people I've interviewed, applauded, or criticized don't fall into neat slots along traditional political, class, or economic lines. But I believe they can—as the title of this book suggests—be put together in a way that suggests certain categories or contours that now define the post-soul African-American world. My generation, and the younger people coming up after us, frustrate our elders, terrify (and influence) the world around us, make headlines, make mistakes, make money, and make plans.

This is very much a book about change—about going from Aretha Franklin to Janet Jackson, from Berry Gordy to Prince, from Muhammad Ali to Michael Jordan. During the decade-plus these pieces cover, the black aesthetic (a term that refers not just to musical style but to a whole way of being) has evolved with blinding speed. Most of the rules I learned as a child in the '60s and '70s have been corrupted or rewritten. Hip hop, just to take the most obvious example, has spread from the urban underground, where I found it in my early story on Kurtis Blow, to white—or at least well-heeled—suburbia. During this same period, breakthrough black superstars made more money than ever before in history—most of it helping to subsidize multinational corporations that reconfigure black artistry into reproducible formulas. The decay of vocal personality and local musical traditions that marked r&b after 1975 is a negative benchmark of this period, just as the empowerment of black filmmakers has been a positive one.

The title essay and timeline outline my view of the key people and events that molded the post-soul era. The timeline appears here as it did in the March 17, 1992, issue of the *Village Voice* (where many of these pieces also first appeared, either as features or as part of my column, "Native Son"). It's a flexible document, though, that could be added to and subtracted from as time goes on. The first section, "B-Boys," provides a selective survey of my writings on hip hop, the crucial innovation by black youth of the '80s. The piece that opens that section was one of the first, if not the first, on the subject of rapping deejays to appear in any national music magazine. "Media Impressions" is a mirror that reflects a black columnist writing for a white publication about other blacks working in mass media. In an age of instant interpretation, I did my best to add to the information overload.

Soul music was the backdrop for my childhood, and the emotional honesty and craft of soul musicians still warm me like no other art form. Much of my adult life has been spent looking for contemporary artists who can challenge the masters, as "Soul Culture: Trad and Retro-Nuevo" documents. "To Be a Black Man"—subject self-evident—ends with the single most popular column I've ever written, a piece that speaks to the rage even the most mild-mannered African-American male feels too often.

New York City is my home, my heart, my inspiration, and my headache. Crippled by congestion, corruption, and plain ol' bad habits, the "Big City of Dreams" (see part five) still stimulates my mind like no place I've been and no place I expect to go.

This volume does not contain all my essays, and not even all my favorites. It does, I hope, add up to an argument about a generation's way of coping and being, of how the past and present conspired to mold a nation of buppies, b-boys, baps, bohos, and all of us in between.

BROOKLYN, NEW YORK

JULY 1992

# ACKNOWLEDGMENTS

Shout outs to my agent, Sarah Lazin; HarperCollins editor, Wendy Wolf; my *Voice* editors, Bob Christgau, Joe Levy, Doug Simmons, and Mike Caruso; my publicist, Von Alexander, and my able aide, Michelle Pierce; my HarperCollins publicist, Andrew Malkin; my Fort Greene homies Chris Rock and Bill Stephney; the Italian restaurant crew of Darnell Martin and Ann Carli; my Compton guide, Katrina Forteno; the original investor, Melissa Clark; my longtime running buddy, Pam "Blondie" Lewis; my nieces, Ebony and Amber; my mother, Arizona B. George; and all the folks subjected to my pen all these years.

# INTRODUCTION

It might have been when mobile DJs began rocking Kraftwerk's "Trans-Europe Express" in 1977 or when WBLS's slogan shifted from "the total black experience in sound" to "the total experience in sound" to "the world's best-looking sound." Or when dressing down to dress up became the new Saturday-night aesthetic of high school teens. Another clue was when Richard Pryor's blues-based life experience humor gave way to Eddie Murphy's telegenic, pop-culture–oriented joking. Neither you nor I knows exactly when it happened. But we know what happened. Over the last 20 or so years, the tenor of African American culture has changed. I came up on the we-shall-overcome tradition of noble struggle, soul and gospel music, positive images, and the conventional wisdom that civil rights would translate into racial salvation. Today I live in a time of goin'-for-mine materialism, secular beat consciousness, and a more diverse, fragmented, even postmodern black community. The change was subtle, yet inexorable.

At *Billboard* magazine in 1982, I pushed to update the title of the "Soul" chart. Prince wasn't soul, nor was Kurtis Blow or Run-D.M.C. The direction of black music, one of the truest reflectors of our culture, had changed profoundly, as it always does. After much discussion the chart was renamed "Black," which outraged many white retailers and black musicmakers. Too ethnic. Too limiting. Too damn black. Where "soul" was once universally accepted, the new era had yielded no new all-purpose catchphrase for the black mood—we couldn't very well call it the funk-disco-hip hop-soul-crossover chart. This diversity said a lot about the new African American mentality desegregation has spawned. In October 1990 *Billboard*'s chart was recast as "Rhythm & Blues," a supposedly nonracial compromise that was actually an anachronistic evasion, the kind of back-to-the-futurism that signals a whole population overwhelmed by the complexity of the present.

As a musical genre, a definition of African American culture, and the code word for our national identity, soul has pretty much been dead since Nixon's reelection in 1972. But what's replaced it? Arguing in these pages in 1986, Greg Tate tried to establish a "new black aesthetic" as a defining concept. He had a point, though I'd argue there was more than one aesthetic at work. For better and worse, the spawn of the post-soul era display multiple personalities.

Group self-definition is always tricky. It's too easy to turn people into caricatures or distort the complexity of individual experiences. Still, it's clear to me that four new African American character types have been crucial in shaping this country over the last 20 years—types that began germinating in the '70s and blossomed in the '80s. There is the Buppie, ambitious and acquisitive, determined to savor the fruits of integration by any means necessary; the B-boy, molded by hip hop aesthetics and the tragedies of underclass life; the Black American Princess or Prince a/k/a/ Bap, who, whether by family heritage or personal will, enjoys an expectation of mainstream success and acceptance that borders on arrogance; and the Boho, a thoughtful, self-conscious figure like "A Different World"'s Cree Summer or Living Colour's Vernon Reid, whose range of interest and taste challenges both black and white stereotypes of African American behavior.

The B-boy has rightfully been the most celebrated and condemned of these figures, since he combines the explosive elements of poverty, street knowledge, and unfocused political anger. B-boy style has flowed far from its ghetto base and affected language, clothes, music, and damn near everything else. In fact, these other postsoulers often respond consciously to his challenge. But they ain't no joke either. The four types first came together in *She's Gotta Have It*, a film that managed to accommodate B-boy Mars Blackmon, Boho Nola Darling, Bap Greer Childs, and embryonic Buppie Jamie Overstreet.

The post-soul era hasn't just been about style or aesthetics, but cash money too. Economics is very much a part of my framework. There is a bigger spread between black rich and poor than at any point in this nation's history. The debate over the role of capital in our race's advancement has taken a new twist, with neocons in media if not grassroots ascendancy. Economic clout has granted many black cultural figures an unprecedented level of financial control over their art. Once Berry Gordy was the patron saint of black capitalism, but Godfather Bill Cosby, singer/conglomerate Michael Jackson, TV host/producer Oprah Winfrey, and a legion of others enjoy total product control—though, significantly, not distribution control—over their hunk of culture. That's an undeniable result of genuine integration. There is wide disagreement, however, whether this black media elite has really uplifted the race or is just another example of American capitalism's savvy taste in window dressing.

Which brings us back to our search for the source of this transition—for the single event that first engaged all these aesthetic, class, and economic issues. After considerable equivocation, I've decided that my starting point is a renegade work that, like many pivotal expressions throughout history, has only been encountered by a small percentage of the folks it affected. It was the creation of a man who'd lived as a Boho, a Buppie, and a B-boy, with a little Bap arrogance on the side. Twenty years after its release, this work's children stroll our streets alienated from if not ignorant of the old soul verities.

## SWEET STUFF

When Melvin Van Peebles's *Sweet Sweetback's Baadasssss Song* came out in 1971, nothing like it had appeared on an American movie screen before. The depiction of a Watts-based male hustler's act of rebellion against brutal police and subsequent flight to freedom "was an important moment in the evolution of black cinema which involved redefinition and initial statement of a willingness to act against one's fate in America," according to veteran black filmmaker St. Clair Bourne. Film historian Gladstone Yearwood has written that *Sweetback* "stands as a milestone in contemporary black cinema because of its popular impact, its example of economic independence, its fine use of cinematic language and its creative incorporation of the Afro-American expressive tradition." Risking his directing fee from the politically correct civil rights–era comedy *Watermelon Man* and $50,000 borrowed from that remarkably open-minded capitalist Bill Cosby, Van Peebles made a film that both challenged the industry and foreshadowed the ongoing conflicts between street culture and mainstream taste. After a Boston theater cut out nine minutes of the film and the Motion Picture Association of America gave it an X rating, Van Peebles made like a lawyer for 2 Live Crew: "Should the rest of the community submit to your censorship that is its business, but White standards shall no longer be imposed on the Black community."

*Sweetback* initially opened in only two theaters—one in Atlanta, one a Detroit venue that specialized in zombie triple features—and never received national distribution worthy of its controversy. Yet *Sweetback*'s ghettocentric style, outsider perspective, and financially independent spirit still reverberate in two crucial African American artistic movements—hip hop and black film. *Sweetback* defied the positive-image canon of Sidney Poitier, dealing openly with black sexuality, government-sanctioned brutality, and the arbitrary violence of inner city life. Its refusal to compromise still sparks black artists from Ice Cube to Matty Rich.

At a 1980 colloquy on the film, Van Peebles explained his narrative strategy. "The reality is that our people have been brainwashed with the 'hip' music, the beautiful color, and the dancing images flickering across the screen. This is what they know as cinema. And that's where we must begin. We obviously cannot dwell there; but it's a point of departure. . . . That's what revolution is! It isn't everybody standing up here on an intellectual high. And it is not meeting people and starting from where they are not. It is starting from where they can see."

With a change here and there, Van Peebles's rap could be the spiel of a hardcore hip hopper in *The Source* talking about his rhymes and videos, though what the rap generation owes *Sweetback* has been absorbed secondhand through the blaxploitation films that *Sweetback* spawned. Those films, which took Van Peebles's aggressive hero and made him/her either a cop or a traditional gangster, live more on home video than in dim memory for the hip hop generation. *Superfly* and *The Mack*, criminal-minded chronicles of a cocaine dealer and a pimp respectively, inform the imagery and music of Big Daddy Kane, N.W.A, the Geto Boys, Ice Cube, Public Enemy, and hundreds of lesser rappers. Blaxploitation set standards for ghettocentricity the rap generation matches and single-mindedly exceeds, reaching levels of profanity, sexism, and violence that these '70s flicks only suggested.

What's more, their funk-soul-disco soundtracks were composed by some of the most visionary minds of post-soul black pop. From veteran soul performers like Curtis Mayfield, James Brown, and Marvin Gaye to more broad-based producer-instrumentalists like Willie Hutch, Norman Whitfield, and Maurice White to Miles Davis and his student Herbie Hancock, these composers created a motherlode of riffs, sounds, and vocal harmonies that today underpin thousands of sample-heavy hip hop recordings. The new level of ambition that seized black pop between 1971 and 1974 was in large part inspired by the access of so many producers and artists to film. While as a genre blaxploitation may strike us now as narrow and negative, the music created to support these films wasn't. Black pop's longer tracks, more complex horns, strings, and percussion, refinements in synthesizer technology, and jazz-inflected vocal harmonies all got their start in

Hollywood. So *Sweetback* trickled down to the current generation.

For black filmmakers, *Sweetback* is a vital memory of what could be, and its bastard child blaxploitation is a bitter reminder of what to avoid. No one had plotted a feature film with an uncompromised black viewpoint and put it into theaters without mainstream Hollywood involvement since the days of Oscar Micheaux, and Van Peebles's achievement wouldn't be duplicated with similar impact for 15 years. But for independent filmmakers as diverse as Halie Gerima, Charles Lane, Julie Dash, and Warrington Hudlin, blaxploitation was what kept African Americans from focusing on the variety of black perspectives they were exposing at film festivals, art houses, and, following the formation of the Black Filmmakers Foundation in 1978, discos, art galleries, and parks. This community of politically committed and historically aware filmmakers was eclipsed in the black community by blaxploitation even after the blaxploitation era ended.

Unlike the black theater, dance, and literary worlds, all sustained by a committed interracial following and regularly covered in the black and white press, black independent filmmaking received little recognition until 1986. Hollywood's dominance over African American viewers seemed unshakable. After blaxploitation dried up, Richard Pryor and then Eddie Murphy were the only African Americans with star status, while no directors, writers, or producers entered Hollywood's closed circle. During the current explosion, black filmmakers have embraced Van Peebles's legacy and disavowed blaxploitation. Van Peebles, who's finally gotten his props as a pioneer, represents what a lot of these filmmakers say their work is—rebellious, sociologically important, entrenched in the black psyche. Yet the content and/or marketing of many of these films shared more with the low-brow, commercially calculated productions of blaxploitation than with the renegade artiness of *Sweetback*. By denying this, the new directors imply that to acknowledge any connection with blaxploitation is to celebrate everything about it—to ghettoize your work, and to recall with fear and loathing how quickly and easily the earlier black film boom was deflated.

The great thing about rap for its early audience was that it created homegrown heroes with larger-than-life personas. Shaft, Truck Turner, and Nigger Charlie were disposable Hollywood fictions. Grandmaster Flash, Afrika Bambaataa, and Kurtis Blow were stars of the ghetto and from the ghetto. Similarly, the circumscribed world of independent film has its own heroes, such as MacArthur fellow Charles Burnett, whose *Killer of Sheep*, one of the select films stored in the National

Archive, is regarded by many as the black masterpiece of the '70s. But in the current commercial climate, most black directors, like the early rappers, can't be sure whether this is their 15 minutes of fame or the beginning of a career. With the taste of hype lingering on their tongues, it'll be hard for them to swallow when the film colony decides, maybe in a fiscal quarter or two, that Hispanic films are the next big thing.

Though the saga of post-soul culture hinges on the way two fringe movements, hip hop and black film, came up from the underground, other equally important strains reflected the unending debate over authenticity, co-optation, and redefinition that desegregation's new opportunities and contradictions intensified. Are blacks selling out our culture to corporate America? Is our media elite using its new clout to promote the best aspects of the race or just pandering to black folks' worst instincts? What do they owe their core audience? Aside from dollars, what is gained by reaching a white audience? Looking over the last 20 years, it's apparent that when confronted by crossover, assimilation, and white standards of success, most African Americans have said, "Well, I guess they're all right by me." Even our most nationalist pop culturalists, people like Chuck D and Spike Lee, work within the established systems of capitalization and distribution. Both, for example, maintain total creative control over their work, but the only revenue stream that flows directly into their accounts is merchandising money.

So despite the rise of Afrocentric consciousness, I find that many young-gifted-and-black post-soulers practice integration without anxiety. Buppies, Baps, and Bohos have come of age since the end of the struggle against blatant segregation. Through busing or family migration, many attended predominantly white schools and took their access to mainstream opportunities for granted. That's not to say they're Uncle Toms or even that they're out of touch with the masses of unassimilated African Americans, but both dangers lurk. Their experience, especially if it was not formed by ghetto life or some romantic ghettocentric identification, makes race consciousness less central to their being. "The Cosby Show," along with figures such as Bryant Gumbel, Oprah Winfrey, Michael Jackson, and Governor Doug Wilder epitomize this view. Bill Cosby's landmark sitcom embraced the middle-class achiever culture closest to the traditional civil rights agenda. Cosby's Dr. Cliff Huxtable and his lovely lawyer wife, Clair, represented the upside of crossover, with Lisa Bonet's Denise giving voice to the relatively color-blind children of this race-neutral environment. The boho vibe Bonet suggested was made explicit in the music, speech, and dress of her husband Lenny Kravitz, Tracy Chapman, Cree Summer, and the Black Rock Coalition. Looking back to the dawn of the '80s, Prince can now be seen as the "new breed leader" he always postured as, a figure emerging from the frozen North to announce that multiculturalism was coming, that explicit sexuality was no big thing, and that black-is-beautiful was just nostalgia. Along with his doppel-gänger Michael Jackson, Prince successfully blurred ethnicity, escaping from standard definitions of blackness (and black male sexuality too) as he reaped both healthy artistic tension and megabucks.

Most of us aren't simply B-Boys, Buppies, Baps, or Bohos. We are some combustible compound—I used to describe myself as a B-boy intellectual. But in the two decades since Van Peebles's film, all of us have seen African American culture evolve (or, as some old jacks argue, devolve) from gospel-and-blues rooted with a distinctly country-accented optimism to assimilated-yet-segregated citified conscious-ness flavored with nihilism, Afrocentrism, and consumerism. The soul world lingers on, but for the current generation it seems as anachronis-tic as the idea of a National Association for the Advancement of *Col-ored* People and as technologically primitive as a crackly old Motown 45. Our aesthetic metamorphosis is not always a bad thing—Dr. J begets Air Jordan, Zora Neale Hurston begets Alice Walker. But it's not always good either—PCP begets freebase begets crack. Mostly, it just is, and there ain't no stoppin' it now.

VILLAGE VOICE, 1992

# A CHRONICLE OF POST-SOUL BLACK CULTURE

## 1971

■ **MELVIN VAN PEEBLES**'s *Sweet Sweetback's Baadasssss Song* premieres in Detroit in March, signaling a new direction in African American film and culture. Directed guerrilla-style in Watts, it ridicules **SIDNEY POITIER**'s ultra-assimilated image, instigates Hollywood's blaxploitation era, and projects rebellious black heroism in visual terms that will echo in pop music iconography 20 years later. It will impact the black intelligentsia more directly than the working-class blacks who will frequent blaxploitation flicks.

■ **MUHAMMAD ALI**, back fighting after being stripped of his title for refusing to violate his vows as a Muslim minister and register for the draft, has his comeback derailed by defending champ **JOE FRAZIER** at Madison Square Garden. Despite this defeat, Ali's religious commitment and boastful, poetic arrogance bridge '60s activism and '80s style.

■ **AL GREEN**'s "Tired of Being Alone" is the first hit for the last of the great soul singers. The central fixation of Green's music—physical lust versus spiritual love—is a tension that new styles will abandon.

■ **SLY & THE FAMILY STONE**'s dark, murky, bitter *There's a Riot Goin' On* presages minimalist hardcore rap both lyrically and sonically.

■ *Shaft*, directed by **GORDON PARKS, SR.**, is the first Hollywood blaxploitation film, complete with fly threads, **ISAAC HAYES**'s Oscar-winning score, and a cameo by blaxploitation regular **ANTONIO FARGAS**.

■ Two new magazines address two complementary post-civil rights constituencies: **BLACK ENTERPRISE**, the bible of the burgeoning new class of white-collar blacks, and **ESSENCE**, which targets collegiate black women. Both document more subtle issues than the soul-era periodicals *Ebony* and *Jet*.

■A feature-length documentary, *Soul to Soul*, contrasts footage of IKE & TINA TURNER in West Africa with scenes of African performers in the U.S.

■THE REVEREND JESSE JACKSON forms People United to Save Humanity in Chicago. PUSH will confront economic and educational issues and serve as Jackson's platform.

# 1972

■Bubble-lettered GRAFFITI pieces by Phase 2 (Lonny Wood) are displayed at United Graffiti Artists' Rozor Gallery Show. Soon Twyla Tharp will use a graffiti backdrop for a Joffrey Ballet premiere of her *Deuce Coupe*.

■*Trouble Man*, starring ROBERT HOOKS, has a doowop-jazz title song and an excellent score by MARVIN GAYE.

■Washington, D.C., security guard FRANK WILLIS reports a robbery-in-progress at the Watergate Hotel that will bring down the Nixon administration.

■THE TEMPTATIONS's "Papa Was a Rolling Stone" goes to No. 1. This Norman Whitfield production is a prime example of the cinematic funk that pervaded black pop during the blaxploitation era.

■ISHMAEL REED's *Mumbo Jumbo*, an innovative novel with 104 bibliographical citations, scores of photos and illustrations, and a plot about Third World art being "liberated" from Western museums, uses jump cuts and soundbites as if Reed were a film director or hip hop DJ.

■*Superfly*'s depiction of a glamorous cocaine dealer so concerns civil rights leaders that the NAACP distributes leaflets asking the producers to reshoot the ending so that the dealer dies. RON O'NEAL's charismatic Priest is a rebel with a capitalistic cause surviving in a world of sneaky partners, corrupt cops, Mafia thugs, and cartoonish nationalists (a staple of blaxploitation). GORDON PARKS, JR., utilizes cutting-edge fashion and CURTIS MAYFIELD's hit-filled score to reach the wide black audience *Sweetback* never attracted. *Superfly*'s seminal blaxploitation will spawn two sequels, one scripted by ALEX HALEY. In defense of the film O'Neal says, "The heroin pusher is the scourge of the black community. But we're talking about coke, which is basically a white drug. Since coke is not physically addictive, people do not steal and rob to get it. There are no coke junkies."

# 1973

■THE INCREDIBLE BONGO BAND releases the pioneering hip hop record "Apache," which will be popularized along with the same band's "Bongo Rock" by a Bronx mobile DJ named Kool Herc.

■HUSTLER'S CONVENTION by Lightnin' Rod (a/k/a the Last Poets) is a moralistic blaxploitation film on record that's performed in the urban storytelling tradition hip hop will overturn.

■*The Mack*, one of blaxploitation's most popular films, features costar RICHARD PRYOR at the height of his wicked comic brilliance and WILLIE HUTCH's "Brothers Gonna Work It Out," later a Public Enemy title.

■ENTER THE DRAGON, Bruce Lee's first big-budget film, costars black martial artist Jim Kelly, indicating the importance of black ticket buyers to the makers of kung fu flicks and their prospective impact on combative young urban males.

■*Black Caesar* stars FRED WILLIAMSON and is backed by a slamming JAMES BROWN score. Its title character, a Harlem drug chieftain, recalls the real-life Nicky Barnes.

■The Census Bureau reports that INTERRACIAL MARRIAGES rose 63 percent during the '60s. Although marriages between white men and black women declined from 25,913 to 23,566, the number of unions between black men and white women grew from 25,496 to 41,223.

■NEW YORK YOUTH GANG activity reaches a high of 315 gangs and over 19,000 members: The Black Spades of the South Bronx are the biggest. One prominent member goes by the street name Afrika Bambaataa.

■PAM GRIER begins her reign as black America's first female action hero. In *Coffy* she's a nurse who hides razor blades in her Afro and takes on drug dealers. She goes on to star in *Sheba Baby*, *Foxy Brown*, and *Friday Foster*.

■With its extravagant costumes and overwrought performing style, LABELLE is a turning point in blending the soul-gospel tradition with a flamboyant black gay style. Patti Labelle, Nona Hendryx, and Sarah Dash develop a strong feminist and gay male cult.

■*The Harder They Come*, starring reggae star JIMMY CLIFF, turns into a midnight hit that helps popularize Jamaican dance music in the U.S., while showing the effects of American western movies in the Third World. In the next decade the sound systems and criminal posses it depicts will be transplanted to the mainland. With its blend of advocacy, rebellion, and music, this film will stand as both the best rock movie and the best blaxploitation movie of the decade.

■A bounty of African American mayors: THOMAS BRADLEY in Los Angeles, MAYNARD JACKSON in Atlanta, COLEMAN YOUNG in Detroit.

■At icebound Shea Stadium, O. J. SIMPSON not only breaks JIM BROWN's rushing record, but becomes the first running back in NFL history to gain more than 2,000 yards on the ground in one season. The contrast between the two men is significant: Brown is a nationalistic black capitalist sympathetic to the dying black militant movement, Simpson a staunch integrationist whose apolitical avoidance of controversy will set a standard for post-'60s black sports stars.

# 1974

■RICHARD PRYOR's *That Nigger's Crazy* LP, a seminal piece of Africamericana, brings the N-word aboveground.

■MUHAMMAD ALI regains the heavyweight title by using "rope-a-dope" to KO GEORGE FOREMAN in Zaire. Ali and his Flavor Flav, Drew Bundini Brown, dub the fight "the rumble in the jungle."

■The Joint Center for Political Studies reports that 2,991 blacks hold elective office in 45 states and the District of Columbia, compared to 1,185 in 1969. Prominent among them are Newark mayor KEN GIBSON and Brooklyn's feisty Congresswoman SHIRLEY CHISHOLM.

# 1975

■DJ KOOL HERC hosts shows at Hevalo, a club located at 180th and Jerome, where he specializes in the short "break" sections of records. The dancers who follow him will come to be called "B-boys" or "break boys." He also plays parks with a sound system he labels "The Herculords."

■GRANDMASTER FLASH, a/k/a Joseph Sadler, builds a rep as a DJ by playing at a park at 169th Street and Boston Road. Grand Wizard Theodore travels from the Bronx down to Times Square's Downstairs Records to buy records for Flash. Among the jams he selects are "white boy records" such as Aerosmith's "Walk This Way."

■MUHAMMAD ALI avenges his earlier loss to Frazier in a titanic fight he titles the "thrilla in Manila."

■ARTHUR ASHE wins at Wimbledon, crowning his pioneering career as tennis's first black male star. Like SIDNEY POITIER, Ashe embodies white (and black) fantasies of the perfectly assimilated African American, though in reality he's politically active. His smooth upward mobility is a prototype for Baps and Buppies to come.

■*Cooley High*, directed by MICHAEL SHULTZ and written by ERIC MONTE (who created TV's "Good Times"), is a sleeper hit that provides warm, humane portraits of young men growing up in the Chicago projects and exploits the nostalgia value of old Motown.

■From the gay club underground a/k/a discos comes a long-playing orgy called "Love to Love You Baby" by a black singer named DONNA SUMMER. Summer's success helps call attention to the increasing public influence of homosexual taste on the music mainstream. Paradise Garage DJ LARRY LEVAN is a crucial disco figure.

# 1 9 7 6

■*Rocky*, with its prominent black characters and action format, shows Hollywood how to tap into the black action market. Leads like FRED WILLIAMSON and JIM BROWN give way to second bananas CARL WEATHERS and MR. T of the *Rocky* films.

■A year before *Star Wars*, producer-conceptualist GEORGE CLINTON is already in space as the sci-fi motif of Parliament's *Mothership Connection* frames extraterrestrial funk of the highest order. Spearheaded by keyboardist BERNIE WORRELL and bassist BOOTSY COLLINS, Clinton and the P-Funk mob carry the banner for a raw black music aesthetic.

■*Sparkle* is noteworthy for CURTIS MAYFIELD's neo-soul score, a plot that echoes the Supremes' real-life soap opera before *Dreamgirls*, and a superb young cast that includes Irene Cara, Philip Michael Thomas, Lonette McKee, and Dorian Harewood.

■NTOZAKE SHANGE's *For Colored Girls Who Have Considered Suicide When the Rainbow Is Enuf* fuses a rich poetic language with feminist politics, part of the wave of African American literature by women that brings long seething tensions between black men and women to the fore. It remains a staple of black college theater to this day.

■STEVIE WONDER releases *Songs in the Key of Life*, a sprawling double album packed with great songs. At a time when most black pop is either sappy crossover or disco drivel, Wonder's gift for melody earns him the "genius" designation.

■JULIUS "DR. J" ERVING joins the mainstream when the National Basketball Association absorbs four American Basketball Association franchises. Dr. J and other brothers liberated from obscurity—David Thompson, George McGinnins, George Gervin—spark a revolution in style that eventually changes the NBA and elevates black schoolyard style to an art form. Soon the slam dunk will be as much part of our sporting culture as the grand slam.

■AFRIKA BAMBAATAA DJs his first party at the Bronx River Community Center, supported by the Zulus, a new-style gang more into music and dance than crime.

■NICKY BARNES, a/k/a "Mr. Untouchable," leader of Harlem's largest heroin ring, hands out turkeys on the corner of 126th Street and St. Nicholas for Christmas, a scene that will appear 15 years later in *New Jack City*.

# 1977

■*Roots*, a miniseries based on ALEX HALEY's book about tracing his family tree to Africa, airs for eight consecutive nights on ABC, earning the highest ratings of any network program in history and generating a long-term interest in Africa among American blacks.

■Yale student WARRINGTON HUDLIN makes *Street Corner Stories*, a film about working-class black men who hang out mornings at a New Haven diner that becomes a festival favorite in America and Europe.

■CHARLES BURNETT has a similar success with the landmark black independent film *Killer of Sheep*, a neorealistic tale of an impotent slaughterhouse worker in Watts.

■KRAFTWERK's trance dance, "Trans-Europe Express," is a left-field black hit that influences many young DJs.

■Queens party promoter RUSSELL SIMMONS, 19, sees his first rapper, Eddie Cheeba, rhyming over the beat from Parliament's "Flashlight" at Charles's Gallery on 125th Street.

■A year after his turkey triumph, NICKY BARNES is convicted of narcotics trafficking and gun possession, ending the reign of one of the biggest old-school dope kingpins and setting the stage for younger gangsters and synthetic drugs.

# 1978

■The Black Filmmaker Foundation is founded by a collective of businessmen and filmmakers including WARRINGTON HUDLIN.

■DISCO FEVER, the first home of hip hop, opens in the South Bronx, a long throw home from Yankee Stadium.

■Proto–B-boy LEON SPINKS beats MUHAMMAD ALI in a New Orleans shocker. Spinks ushers in a new generation of black athletes who battle drug abuse and the media.

■A typical uptown "Super Disco" is presented at the Audubon Ballroom. GRANDMASTER FLASH, THE FURIOUS FOUR (Melle Mel, Keith Keith, Kid Creole, Mr. Ness), and LOVEBUG STARSKI are on the bill.

■For several months this year the VILLAGE PEOPLE, a collection of gay male stereotypes fronted by soul-styled black vocalist Victor Willis, are the country's hottest group. Many straight folks don't get the joke. For many black gays the Village People are a welcome affirmation of their existence in a culture that wants to ignore them.

■Where the Village People are pop-corny, SYLVESTER's "You Make Me Feel Mighty Real" is the kind of gay gospel dance music that will later inspire house.

■The Supreme Court rules AFFIRMATIVE ACTION can result in reverse discrimination. The civil rights movement is over and conservative backlash has begun.

■MICHAEL SCHULTZ is the first African American director to land a Hollywood film without a racial theme: *Sgt. Pepper's Lonely Hearts*

*Club Band,* an ill-conceived Beatles homage starring the Bee Gees and Peter Frampton that damages the careers of all involved.

■MICHELE WALLACE's *Black Macho and the Myth of the Superwoman* is published to amazing hype (she makes the cover of *Ms.*) and scathing criticism. For all its faults, the book is crucial for its criticisms of the civil rights movement, which open the discourse on male-female relations in the African American left while giving black feminism greater media visibility.

■Former community activist MARION BARRY is elected mayor of Washington.

■A study finds that 45 percent of all NEW YORK CITY HIGH SCHOOL STUDENTS use "some psychoactive drug."

■Model-turned-disco diva GRACE JONES celebrates the bisexual and campy black gay aesthetic New Year's Eve at Studio 54.

# 1 9 7 9

■Reviving interest in ZORA NEALE HURSTON, the Harlem Renaissance writer who has become the patron saint of black feminists, grows with the publication of *I Love Myself When I Am Laughing,* essays edited by ALICE WALKER with an introduction by literary scholar MARY HELEN WASHINGTON.

■A Howard Smith Scenes column on the FABULOUS FIVE, a graffiti group led by Brooklynite Frederick Brathwaite (later known as Freddy Love and then Fab Five Freddie), leads to a show of the group's work in Rome.

■THE FATBACK BAND's "King Tim III (The Personality Jock)" is the first rap record. But Tim, who spiels in the older black radio style, is not part of the Bronx hip hop crowd. He's hired when the Fatback Band see DJ Hollywood hosting shows at the Apollo and, instead of making a deal with the original old-school rapper, try to do it on their own—a major goof.

■CHIC's "Good Times" joins MFSB's "Love Is the Message" as one of the mobile DJs' favorite grooves. Unlike many early hip hop favorites, these songs were black radio hits that DJs and rappers adapted to their purposes.

■SYLVIA ROBINSON, owner of the troubled All Platinum Records, attends a show at the Harlem World disco on 116th Street, across from the mosque founded by Malcolm X. Robinson hears DJs rapping over records and sees the reaction. She organizes the SUGAR HILL GANG, who has the first rap hit with "Rapper's Delight" on her brand-new Sugarhill label. Again these are not real rappers—one member is a bouncer at Disco Fever—but they at least bite rhymes from real rappers. "Rapper's Delight" uses the music from "Good Times"; Chic requests and is granted writing credit on later pressings.

■EARVIN "MAGIC" JOHNSON leads his Michigan State team past his great rival Larry Bird of Indiana State in the NCAA final. Johnson's blend of height (he's 6-9) and playmaking ability changes basketball.

■*Billboard* does a story on "DISCO RAPPERS"—"a spinner who talks in a lyrical, rapid fire, streetwise dialogue over the pulsating rhythm track, began in the black discos of New York." The article notes that "Rapper's Delight" is No. 41 on the disco chart and "King Tim III" is No. 42, and that Spoonie Gee has "Spoonin' Rap" in stores. The story is picked up by the U.K.'s *New Musical Express*, which notes that the "deejay who raps docs not appear to be a million miles removed from the ancient Jamaican art of toasting."

■RICHARD PRYOR's *Live in Concert* opens. Pryor's genius as mime, storyteller, and observer of human life has never been better documented.

■THE BLACK FILMMAKER FOUNDATION presents films by independent black filmmakers around New York in parks, museums, and nightclubs.

■CHARLES LANE's A *Place in Time*, a silent comedy shot in black and white, is shown at Othello's disco on Eighth Avenue.

■The QUINCY JONES–produced *Off the Wall* elevates MICHAEL JACKSON to adult stardom, its seven million sales the most ever by a black male. People begin remarking on how Jackson's face is changing.

■DARRYL DAWKINS breaks two backboards within a month, hastening the introduction of flexible rims.

■*Billboard* reporter ROBERT FORD, JR., and ad executive J. B. MOORE write and produce KURTIS BLOW's "Christmas Rappin'," which gets picked up by Mercury. The first rap artist on a major label is managed by CCNY schoolmate RUSSELL SIMMONS.

■As the decade ends PCP, a/k/a angel dust, is the street drug of choice.

# 1980

■In January members of the HIGH TIMES CREW are arrested at a Washington Heights subway for "fighting"—that is, breaking. They are photographed by Martha Cooper for the *New York Post*, the first known photos of break dancing.

■MOLEFI KETE ASANTE publishes *Afrocentricity* with Chicago's African World Press. Over the next decade this brief overview will spearhead the challenge to a Eurocentric history.

■Trumpeter WYNTON and saxophonist BRANFORD MARSALIS play with Art Blakey's Jazz Messengers. Wynton's chops, sense of history, mastery of the classical canon, and well-tailored suits will make him jazz's first truly "cool" figure in a generation.

■NELSON GEORGE's "A Consumer Guide to Rap Records" is rejected by *The New York Times*'s Arts & Leisure section because "it's just too far off the beaten track" and "just seems too specialized."

■MAGIC JOHNSON leads the Lakers to the NBA title with an amazing sixth-game win over DR. J's 76ers. Magic plays center for an injured Kareem and is named the series's most valuable player.

■"Mr. Magic's Rap Attack" airs on WBHI from 2:00 to 5:00 A.M. Saturday nights. At several stations over the next decade, MR. MAGIC will play a crucial role in creating the hardcore rap audience.

■RICHARD PRYOR critically burns over half his body while freebasing cocaine.

■SUGAR RAY LEONARD loses to and then defeats Roberto Duran, who surrenders with the famous last words "no más."

■WLIB switches from an all-music format to a news-talk format.

■KURTIS BLOW releases his gold single "The Breaks." Futura 2000 bombs (a/k/a paints) a subway car in tribute.

■RICHARD PRYOR and Gene Wilder star in the Sidney Poitier–directed STIR CRAZY, which earns $101 million.

■PRINCE establishes his off-center sexuality, multiracial identity, and eclectic musicianship with *Dirty Mind*. He also wears black panties on stage.

■Richard Goldstein's lengthy *Voice* cover story on GRAFFITI notes: "Graffiti's sensibility has a musical equivalent in 'rap' records—another rigid, indecipherable form that can sustain great complexity."

The piece also discusses two then unknown artists, Keith Haring and Samo a/k/a Jean-Michel Basquiat. The *Voice* centerfold features six whole-car designs photographed by Henry Chalfant.

# 1 9 8 1

■The Rock Steady Crew dancers perform at the home of the downtown avant-garde, the KITCHEN. Graffiti artists, rappers, breakers, and even roller skaters perform at the ROXY ROLLER RINK. ABC's "20/20" does one of the first national television reports on the new rap phenomenon.

■Six-month-old PROFILE RECORDS spends $750 to make Dr. Jeckyll (Andre Harrell) & Mr. Hyde's (Alonzo Brown) "Genius Rap," which moves 150,000 12-inches.

■Young EDDIE MURPHY revitalizes "Saturday Night Live" with a slew of crazy characterizations, including black pimp Velvet Jones, children's show host Mr. Robinson, and exercise guru Little Richard Simmons.

■"The Adventures of GRANDMASTER FLASH on the Wheels of Steel" is the first record to capture the mixing and scratching techniques of hip hop parties.

■*Dreamgirls*, MICHAEL BENNETT's homage to Motown, opens on Broadway to rave reviews and spawns JENNIFER HOLLIDAY's No. 1 single "And I Am Telling You I'm Not Going," a phlegmy retro-soul success in an era of self-conscious black pop crossover.

■FRANKIE SMITH's gruff "Double Dutch Bus" goes gold, feeding the idea that rap records are a silly fad.

■CHARLES FULLER's Pulitzer prize–winning A *Soldier's Story* opens at the Negro Ensemble Company. This mystery of murder and intraracial strife features a brilliant cast that includes ADOLPH CAESAR, CHARLES BROWN, and the then little-known DENZEL WASHINGTON.

■Blacks constitute 11.2 PERCENT of those EMPLOYED and 22.3 PERCENT of those UNEMPLOYED according to the National Urban League's "State of Black America" annual report.

# 1 9 8 2

■The Saturday morning cartoon characters the SMURFS inspire a dance and numerous records, each with a different spelling to avoid lawsuits.

■Capping a long campaign led by STEVIE WONDER, DR. MARTIN LUTHER KING's birthday finally becomes a national holiday.

■Junior's "Mama Used to Say" is the first in a decade-long stream of BLACK BRITISH SOUL RECORDS to break through on black American radio.

■British promoter COOL LADY BLUE's weekly hip hop event at Negril brings uptown kids downtown and rap music to white hipsters.

■AFRIKA BAMBAATAA & SOUL SONIC FORCE's "Looking for the Perfect Beat" comes out on Tommy Boy.

■HERBIE HANCOCK's "Rockit" features the scratching of old-school DJ Grandmixer DST. It is one of the first collaborations between an established musician and a hip hop spinner.

■Under the banner of GRANDMASTER FLASH & THE FURIOUS FIVE, Melle Mel and Duke Bootee cut "The Message," the first commercially successful political rap single.

■ALICE WALKER's *The Color Purple* is published to critical acclaim. Many black men hate it, but QUINCY JONES vows to turn it into a film.

■BELL HOOKS's *Ain't I a Woman*—which analyzes African American women in the context of male sexism, white female racism, and the interaction of all women—introduces a significant new voice in feminist thought.

■LOUIS GOSSETT, JR., wins the supporting actor Oscar for *An Officer and a Gentleman*.

■In the concert film *Richard Pryor Live on the Sunset Strip*, the comic graphically describes the attraction of FREEBASING.

■RICHARD PRYOR renounces the use of the word "nigger" in *Ebony*.

■BILL STEPHNEY, Hank and Keith Boxley (a/k/a SHOCKLEE), William Drayton (a/k/a FLAVOR FLAV), Andre Brown (a/k/a DOCTOR DRE), and Chuck Ridenhour (a/k/a CHUCK D) hang out at Adelphi University's WBAU, playing hip hop records and making their own.

■GEORGE CLINTON's dance jam "Atomic Dog" is the last hit by the P-Funk leader. Its success with young audiences foreshadows the vitality of P-Funk's music throughout the rest of the decade for the hip hop generation.

■North Carolina wins the NCAA title against Georgetown with a jumper in the final seconds by freshman MICHAEL JORDON.

■Oakland A's outfielder RICKEY HENDERSON steals 120 bases.

■MICHAEL JACKSON's *Thriller* reaches record stores in time for one of several Christmas pushes and goes on to sell more than 40 million worldwide. With his ongoing plastic surgery, androgyny, and prodigious performing talent, Jackson embodies the compromises, contradictions, and triumphs of the black crossover mentality.

■TROUBLE FUNK's "Drop the Bomb" brings Washington, D.C., go-go beats to rap.

# 1983

■RICHARD PRYOR is budgeted $40 million by Columbia Pictures president Guy McElwaine to fund Indigo Films. Pryor's company—to be run by his buddy, Jim Brown—will specialize in black films. Some of that money goes toward a three-picture deal with ROBERT TOWNSEND— one of his proposed projects is similar to *Hollywood Shuffle*; some goes toward a script about Charlie Parker that will, years later, be made by Clint Eastwood; and GEORGE JACKSON puts in time there as a vice-president of production. But no films are made under the Indigo deal, though Pryor produced the autobiographical *Jo Jo Dancer* and his third concert film, *Richard Pryor Here and Now*, during the production company's brief history.

■Representative HAROLD WASHINGTON is elected mayor of Chicago after a racially charged campaign. The crusadelike mobilization of the city's blacks makes Washington one of the few big-city black mayors with a clear racial mandate.

■JEAN-MICHEL BASQUIAT moves beyond his roots in graffiti to national prominence with a show at Los Angeles's Larry Gagosian Gallery.

■Harvard undergrad REGGIE HUDLIN directs a short about a son who sneaks out to a party against his father's wishes. It's called *House Party*.

■JESSE JACKSON goes to Syria to free American hostages and becomes a hero.

■Youth muggings at DIANA ROSS's free Central Park concert make headlines and are blamed for a midtown crime spree.

■**LORENZO CHARLES** wins the NCAA for North Carolina State with the dunk, a shot once banned from college basketball.

■Led by **DR. J** and **MOSES MALONE**, Philadelphia wins the NBA title in four games.

■**EUZHAN PALCY** debuts with the female coming-of-age film *Sugar Cane Alley*.

■**SPIKE LEE** directs a "White Lines" video on spec for Grandmaster Flash with **LARRY FISHBURNE** in the lead. Sugarhill turns it down.

■**FLASHDANCE** introduces the feature film as full-length music video and hastens the burnout of breaking.

■**EDDIE MURPHY**'s comedy helps *Trading Places* make $90 million.

■Al Pacino's Tony Montaña, the violent Cuban protagonist of Brian DePalma's **SCARFACE**, written by Oliver Stone, emerges as the patron saint of coke dealers.

■Black scholar **HENRY LOUIS GATES, JR.**, discovers the 1859 manuscript *Our Nig*, by Harriet Wilson, which he documents as the first novel written by a black woman in the U.S. Aside from spurring black women writers, this literary archaeology catapults Gates to a prominence that will make him one of America's best-known scholars.

■**CHARLIE AHEARN**'s *Wild Style*, the first realistic depiction of the emerging B-boy culture, is released. The independent film includes appearances by old-school rapper Busy Bee and artist/scenemaker Fab Five Freddie.

■**STYLE WARS**, a documentary on breaking and graffiti, airs on PBS.

■Ex-bodyguard and Rocky opponent **MR. T** has his season of fame on NBC's "The A Team." Some believe his gold fetish sparks the rope-chain craze.

■**JESSE JACKSON** announces his candidacy for the Democratic presidential nomination.

# 1 9 8 4

■The February 13 *Washington Post* reports that in a private conversation with black reporter Milton Coleman, **JESSE JACKSON** called New York "Hymietown" and Jews "Hymies." For 13 days Jackson denies the comments; then he apologizes. The Nation of Islam's Louis Farrakhan calls Coleman a "traitor" and a "Judas," issuing what some interpret as a threat against the reporter's life. This incident has two important repercussions: It weakens Jackson's support among many whites and strengthens the Nation's among blacks alienated from the American system, particularly the hip hop generation.

■JOHN EDGAR WIDEMAN publishes *Brothers and Keepers*, an eloquent depiction of assimilated and underclass African America in which one brother becomes a college professor while the other goes to jail for murder.

■Attending the Grammys with teen model Brooke Shields and kiddie star Emmanuel Lewis of TV's "Webster," MICHAEL JACKSON wins eight awards for *Thriller*.

■Despite police reports that BREAK DANCING has decreased gang violence, the San Bernardino City Council votes to impose a fine for public dancing because it interferes with mall shopping.

■UTFO'S "Roxanne, Roxanne," produced by FULL FORCE, ignites a battle royal over this young woman's virtue. First 14-year-old ROXANNE SHANTE disses back with "Roxanne's Revenge." Full Force recruits its own pinup girl, who replies with "The Real Roxanne." The Roxanne series is an example of the verbal battles that proliferate in hip hop and a harbinger of the female bashing to come.

■MARVIN GAYE's father shoots him dead.

■Georgetown beats Hakeem Olajuwon and Houston for the NCAA title to cap a season in which Georgetown emerges as black America's team. Led by black coach JOHN THOMPSON, Georgetown plays a combative style epitomized by center PATRICK EWING, target of racist insults around the country, and relentless skinhead power forward MICHAEL GRAHAM. In a historic NCAA semifinal versus Kentucky, the Hoyas force the Wildcats to shoot 9.1 per cent in the second half. "Starter" athletic wear bearing the Hoyas's pit bull–like logo becomes an integral part of urban style.

■JESSE JACKSON, who had already bowed out of the race for president, delivers an inspiring speech that is the highlight of the Democratic convention. It soon becomes available on home video.

■Wearing a trendsetting hi-top fade, CARL LEWIS wins four gold medals at the Los Angeles Olympics.

■CHAKA KHAN's "I Feel for You" samples Stevie Wonder's "Finger-tips—Pt. 2" and is sprinkled with a MELLE MEL rap. The promo clip is adapted from a Norma Kamali fashion video and showcases breakers SHABBA-DOO and BOOGALOO SHRIMP.

■PRINCE's masterful *Purple Rain* soundtrack elevates him into a pop icon and sets up the hit movie, which exploits his sexuality and blurred racial identity. The Time's MORRIS DAY and JEROME BENTON seem primed to be the '80s Abbott and Costello, but by the time the movie opens, Day has split Prince's camp. So have two other original Time members, bassist TERRY LEWIS and keyboardist JIMMY "JAM" HARRIS, who begin producing full-time.

■GRANDMASTER FLASH & THE FURIOUS FIVE split with Melle Mel and then Sugarhill to sign with Elektra.

■Rappers RUN-D.M.C., KURTIS BLOW, WHODINI, THE FAT BOYS, and NEWCLEUS, and break crews the MAGNIFICENT FORCE, UPTOWN EXPRESS, and DYNAMIC BREAKERS, bring in $3.5 million in 27 dates on the Swatch Watch–sponsored Fresh Fest tour, which spreads hip hop across America. Run, Whodini, and the Fat Boys all garner gold records. Run-D.M.C.'s onstage ingestion of Olde English Malt Liquor makes it the official B-boy brew.

■The Los Angeles r&b station KDAY converts to the country's first rap-only format.

■In a year prominent African Americans picket the South African embassy to jump-start the U.S. antiapartheid movement, Anglican bishop DESMOND TUTU wins the Nobel Peace Prize.

■Syracuse University student VANESSA WILLIAMS is the first black Miss America. Three months later, when nude photos of her are published in *Penthouse*, she's stripped of her title, which goes to another black woman, runner-up SUZETTE CHARLES of New Jersey.

■Beat Street dancer/actor ROBERT TAYLOR makes the cover of *Newsweek*.

■One hundred BREAK DANCERS perform at the Olympic Games closing ceremony.

■"The Cosby Show" brings a proudly bourgeois black family to American households. Cosby, one of TV's leading commercial pitchmen for several years prior to the show, creates a vision of black life that annoys many, charms millions, and goes on to reach the No. 1 spot. LISA BONET's character, Denise, becomes the nation's first black boho pinup girl.

■SADE's "Hang On to Your Love," a huge U.K. hit, introduces the integrated Brit-soul band here and makes its Nigerian-British lead singer a multiculti fashion trendsetter.

■CHARLES BARKLEY brings buck-wild style to the Philadelphia 76ers and eventually assumes the team's leadership mantle from Erving. Where Dr. J embodied a jazzy elegance, Barkley represents B-boy bodaciousness.

■AUGUST WILSON's *Ma Rainey's Black Bottom* opens at the Cort Theater with ex-con CHARLES DUTTON a featured player.

■The *Wall Street Journal* hails RUSSELL SIMMONS, 26, as "the mogul of rap."

# 1 9 8 5

■The best balladeer of his generation, LUTHER VANDROSS, releases his most accomplished album, *The Night I Fell in Love.*

■WHITNEY HOUSTON's debut album, *Whitney,* synthesizes the pop-soul tradition of Dionne Warwick and the MOR schlock of previous Arista hitmakers Barry Manilow and Air Supply.

■Run-D.M.C.'s *King of Rock* cover features the band's signature black fedoras, which become one of pop culture's most distinctive trademarks. Sixteen-year-old L.L. COOL J writes the lyric to "Can You Rock It Like This."

■WILLIAM "REFRIGERATOR" PERRY, a 310-pound Chicago Bears tackle, scores a touchdown as a running back on "Monday Night Football," which transforms him into a hulking, grinning endorsement machine.

■JEAN-MICHEL BASQUIAT and Andy Warhol collaborate on a gallery show that mates new street and old Pop hype, elevating Basquiat's public profile while trivializing his work.

■THE FAT BOYS jiggle through a Swatch Watch spot.

■The UZI submachine gun emerges as the drug dealer's weapon of choice.

■Boogie Down Productions, the brainchild of ex-homeless teen KRIS PARKER (KRS-One) and homeless shelter counselor SCOTT LAROCK, release the original hardcore classic, *Criminal Minded.*

■Harlem resident and Phillips Exeter student EDMUND PERRY is shot dead by undercover officer Lee Van Houten. Police allege Edmund and his brother Jonah assaulted the cop. On January 22, 1986, Jonah is cleared of all charges.

■*Krush Groove* stars RUN-D.M.C., THE FAT BOYS, KURTIS BLOW, and RICK RUBIN in a scenario based on RUSSELL SIMMONS's career. The feature has a black director, MICHAEL SCHULTZ, a black cinematographer, ERNEST DICKERSON, and a black producer, DOUG MCHENRY. On October 25 *Krush Groove*, budgeted at $5 million by Warners, opens at 515 theaters and leads all releases by grossing over $3 million nationally in its first week, though there are several incidents of violence at New York–area theaters, where it makes $1 million anyway. Its combination of opening-week success and opening-week violence will be seen again in black film.

■Philadelphia representative WILLIAM H. GRAY III becomes chair of the House budget committee.

■FISHBONE, a gaggle of black San Fernando Valley musicians, disdain the clichés of contemporary r&b for a bawdy mix of ska, punk, reggae, and funk that reflects the rising boho sensibility.

■DWIGHT "DOC" GOODEN, barely 20, wins 24 games for the New York Mets.

■LOUIS FARRAKHAN addresses 25,000 at Madison Square Garden.

■*The Color Purple*, directed by Steven Spielberg, starring WHOOPI GOLDBERG and OPRAH WINFREY, and produced by QUINCY JONES, makes $94 million. Whoopi's career will feature a long succession of bad scripts, while Oprah, whose syndicated talk show is already challenging Phil Donahue, will establish herself as a multimedia force, starring in the film adaptation of *Native Son* and turning GLORIA NAYLOR's feminist fiction, *The Women of Brewster Place*, into an ABC miniseries. No woman will capitalize on the African American vogue of the late '80s better than Oprah and none worse than Whoopi.

# 1986

■The mass marketing of freebase cocaine, a/k/a CRACK, will change first the American drug business and ultimately American life. After its introduction, black youth culture becomes increasingly nihilistic and materialistic.

■A 26-piece BLACK ROCK COALITION big band plays the Kitchen.

■ANITA BAKER's *Rapture* displays her voice in all its husky, jazzy vitality, defying the standard dance-oriented formulas for female vocalists.

■THE LATIN QUARTER, midtown's only hip hop club, is the site of funky music and many a chain-snatching.

■JANET JACKSON's *Control,* one of several expertly crafted albums written and produced by JIMMY JAM and TERRY LEWIS, establishes her as brother Michael's female counterpart. The video for "What Have You Done for Me Lately" is choreographed by Paula Abdul and helps popularize the snake dance.

■PEPPER JOHNSON does the wop dance on the field after his Giants win the Super Bowl.

■Uptown Records, owned by ANDRE "DR. JECKYLL" HARRELL, develops an r&b–styled rap epitomized by HEAVY D. & THE BOYZ. The first two videos on this MCA-distributed label are directed and produced by WARRINGTON and REGGIE HUDLIN.

■EDDIE MURPHY mentions the "Black Pack" at a press conference for *The Golden Child,* listing its other members as ARSENIO HALL, ROBERT TOWNSEND, KEENEN WAYANS, and comic/writer PAUL MOONEY.

■RUN-D.M.C. and Aerosmith record "Walk This Way," a breakthrough record and video that confirms Run-D.M.C.'s trailblazing status.

■Perhaps the best rap tour ever begins featuring four platinum-level acts—RUN-D.M.C., WHODINI, L.L. COOL J, THE BEASTIE BOYS. The Beastie Boys' *Licensed to Ill* goes on to sell four million copies in the U.S. for Def Jam, a standard unsurpassed in rap until 1990.

■MICHAEL JORDAN scores 63 points in a nationally televised playoff game against defending champion Boston Celtics.

■LEN BIAS, 22, is killed by freebase days after being named the Boston Celtics' No. 1 draft choice.

■The Black Filmmaker Foundation hosts the New York premiere of SPIKE LEE's *She's Gotta Have It.*

■Paul Simon's GRACELAND, a controversial and innovative use of

South African music, is released six months after the historic compilation of South African pop, THE INDESTRUCTIBLE BEAT OF SOWETO.

■MICHAEL GRIFFIN is hit by a car on the Shore Parkway after being chased by a gang of white youths in Howard Beach, Queens. This racist outrage introduces several figures to the six o'clock news—the Reverend AL SHARPTON and attorneys C. VERNON MASON and ALTON MADDOX.

■A Long Beach, California, rap concert headlined by Run-D.M.C. is halted by a brutal riot as black and Latino gangs bumrush the show. This incident incites "RAP CAUSES VIOLENCE" rhetoric and is the first national inkling that Southern California's gang problem is out of control.

■SCOTT LAROCK is shot dead outside Highbridge Gardens Homes in the South Bronx.

■D.J. JAZZY JEFF & THE FRESH PRINCE's "Parents Just Don't Understand" is a huge crossover pop hit. The duo is booed when they perform the song at the Apollo, signifying rap's hard-soft split.

■"The Cosby Show"'s MALCOLM JAMAL-WARNER hosts a "Saturday Night Live" with special guests Spike Lee and Run-D.M.C.

■In November, LARRY DAVIS, accused executioner of drug dealers and would-be rapper, shoots six cops and escapes. While he's on the run, copies of his demo circulate around the rap business, but when he's caught in the South Bronx a month later, no record deal is forthcoming.

■MIKE TYSON knocks out Trevor Berbick in the second round to take the WBC title.

■GREG TATE's visionary article, "New Black Aesthetic," appears in the *Village Voice*.

■X, an opera composed by ANTHONY DAVIS with a libretto by THULANI DAVIS, debuts at the New York City Opera, an important moment in the mythologizing of Malcolm's legacy.

■GEORGE WOLFE's play *The Colored Museum,* a humorous critique of black cultural truisms that reflects a new mood of self-examination in the black intelligentsia, opens at the Public Theater to rave reviews.

# 1987

■Black quarterback DOUG WILLIAMS leads the Washington Redskins to triumph in the Super Bowl.

■Def Jam's *Less Than Zero* soundtrack contains **L.L. COOL J**'s "Going Back to Cali," which seriously damages his hardcore rep, and **PUBLIC ENEMY**'s "Bring the Noise," which opens with **MALCOLM X**'s voice saying, "Too black, too strong."

■Wappingers Falls teen **TAWANA BRAWLEY**'s sordid tale of being raped by six white men is seized upon by the **MASON-MADDOX-SHARPTON** team to attack the state's criminal justice system. Huge holes appear in Tawana's account, but the trio refuses to address the details and she never tells her story either in open court or in the mainstream media. The case profoundly weakens Sharpton and company's impact with moderate blacks, but doesn't deter their grassroots following.

■**JEEPS** with booming systems become a new urban status symbol.

■**AUGUST WILSON**'s Pulitzer prize–winning *Fences* opens at the 46th Street Theater with **JAMES EARL JONES** in the lead.

■**TONI MORRISON** publishes *Beloved* to tremendous acclaim and takes her place as the nation's preeminent African American novelist—a position formerly occupied by Richard Wright, Ralph Ellison, and James Baldwin.

■**ROBERT TOWNSEND**'s *Hollywood Shuffle*, a satire on Hollywood's mistreatment of blacks, continues the black film momentum Spike Lee began.

■**TERENCE TRENT D'ARBY**, an American expatriate living in England, gets superstar hype from Columbia after major success in the U.K.

■*Black Athena*, by white Oxford don **MARTIN BERNAL**, argues that Egypt rather than Greece was the cradle of Western civilization, and documents the obfuscation of the Afro-Asiatic roots of world culture by white historians. Black scholars around the world have made this case for years, but Bernal's pedigree suddenly gives the argument credibility in European academic circles.

■"I Cram To Understand U (Sam)," by 16-year-old **MC LYTE**, is one of rap's first female hardcore records.

■**BIG DADDY KANE**'s "Raw" and his hi-top fade are state-of-the-art hip hop style. Cold Chillin' Records joins Warner Bros., bringing uptown legends Kane, **BIZ MARKIE**, and **MARLEY MARL** into the Burbank fold, another sign of hip hop's embrace by the once-hostile record industry.

■Amid rumors of drug abuse, **BOBBY BROWN** splits from New Edition and is replaced by **JOHNNY GILL**.

■EDDIE MURPHY's "Comedy Express" appears on HBO, introducing many to ARSENIO HALL, ROBERT TOWNSEND, CHRIS ROCK, MARSHA WARFIELD, and BARRY SOBEL.

■MIKE TYSON wins a 12-round decision over James "Bonecrusher" Smith in Las Vegas to capture the WBA. A few days later, Tyson invites actress ROBIN GIVINS to dinner in Los Angeles and she comes, along with her mother, Ruth Roper.

■A harbinger of the increasing quality of non–New York hip hop: Three of the four finalists in the New Music Seminar's DJ COMPETITION are from outside the Apple—Philadelphia's Cash Money, Los Angeles's Joe Cooley, and Mr. Mix of Miami's 2 Live Crew.

■On the cover of Boogie Down Productions's *By All Means Necessary*, KRS-ONE poses with an Uzi, an homage to a famous photo of MALCOLM X with a rifle taken after the firebombing of his Queens home. On the album KRS-One talks about "jimmy caps," an endorsement of condoms as a tool for AIDS-related safe sex. The Fab Five Freddie–directed video for BDP's "My Philosophy" uses images of Louis Farrakhan and Malcolm X as symbols of empowerment.

■MAGIC JOHNSON's Lakers best Larry Bird's Celtics for the NBA title.

■T-SHIRTS with the slogans "Black by Popular Demand" and "It's a Black Thing, You Wouldn't Understand" spread across the nation from predominantly black colleges.

■BLAXPLOTATION FILMS like *The Mack* and *Superfly* reach a new generation as VCRs become more common in black households.

■ICE-T's debut album, *Rhyme Pays*, gives nationwide exposure to L.A.'s gangsta rap—a style influenced by gang culture and the sensationalistic books of ICEBERG SLIM and DONALD GOINES.

■Kids on subways are seen reading copies of THE AUTOBIOGRAPHY OF MALCOM X, Elijah Muhammad's MESSAGE TO THE BLACKMAN, and the rap magazine WORD UP!

■Dodgers executive AL CAMPANIS is fired for telling "Nightline" that blacks "may not have some of the necessities" to manage major league teams.

■GEORGE JACKSON and DOUG MCHENRY produce *Disorderlies*, a horrid film matching the Fat Boys and Ralph Bellamy.

■NEW YORK NIGHTLIFE shifts as the Bronx's Disco Fever closes, Union Square opens for the hardcore, and Nell's becomes an in spot for black hipsters.

■The robotic half-human hero of ROBOCOP provides a new street name for vicious police.

■MIKE TYSON defeats Tony Tucker in a 12-round decision to win the IBF championship, uniting all three belts and becoming the first undisputed heavyweight champ since LARRY HOLMES.

■Built around actor/coproducer TIM REID and utilizing the skills of black writers and directors, the CBS sitcom "Frank's Place" is widely hailed for its humorous yet realistic depiction of black southerners.

■PBS's six-part civil rights movement documentary EYES ON THE PRIZE introduces a new generation to historic figures of the civil rights movement, including MALCOLM X and the BLACK PANTHERS.

■GARY BYRD, a proponent of Afrocentricity, makes his afternoon talk show on WLIB a forum for Tawana Brawley's advisers, revealing the gulf between African American and European American reality.

■The gleeful misogyny of EDDIE MURPHY's concert film *Raw* (with an opening skit written by Keenen Ivory Wayans, photography by Ernest Dickerson, and direction by Robert Townsend) helps take rap's anti-woman invective to a new level.

■BARRY MICHAEL COOPER coins the phrase "New Jack City" to describe the violent teen culture of Detroit in a *Voice* cover story.

## 1988

■The slammin' blend of rap rhythms and r&b harmonies Barry Cooper has already labeled "New Jack Swing" is instigated by TEDDY RILEY, who produces and/or arranges hits for Bobby Brown, Keith Sweat, Al B. Sure!, Heavy D., Kool Moe Dee, and his own band Guy. Riley's sound breathes new life into r&b, influencing its two top production teams, Jimmy Jam Harris and Terry Lewis and L.A. & Babyface, and dominating playlists at black radio stations reluctant to play rap.

■Singing B-boy BOBBY BROWN's "My Prerogative" establishes him as New Jack Swing's breakout star and propels his *Don't Be Cruel* to sales of five million copies.

■MICHAEL JORDAN wins the NBA all-star game MVP trophy before a hometown crowd. Amid the Nike commercials featuring Jordan and Spike Lee and the game itself, the CBS broadcast sprinkles shots of MIKE TYSON and ROBIN GIVINS huddled at courtside. That evening they get married at a local church.

■Patrolman EDWARD BYRNE is shot dead in Queens by drug dealers. HOWARD "PAPPY" MASON, a large new jack drug dealer, is convicted of ordering the murder.

■TRACY CHAPMAN's self-titled album follows the hit single "Fast Car."

■LIVING COLOUR, led by Black Rock Coalition cofounder Vernon Reid, debuts on Epic with *Vivid*. After much touring and groundwork, "Cult of Personality" becomes an MTV staple.

■Dennis Hopper's cop movie *Colors* unintentionally spreads L.A.'s gang culture across the country. ICE-T adds credibility with the chilling title track and DAMON WAYANS's loopy gang-banger provides humor by dry humping a stuffed rabbit during a robbery.

■RUN-D.M.C. star in the Rick Rubin–directed *Tougher Than Leather*, a movie so stupid it alienates hip hop fans and, effectively, ends the band's reign.

■Teenager JOHN SINGLETON meets SPIKE LEE in Los Angeles after a screening of Lee's new *School Daze*.

■EDDIE MURPHY tells the Oscar audience that black people are underrepresented in the film industry.

■JESSE JACKSON wins the Michigan caucus, but the excitement level of this mainstream campaign is more subdued.

■KEENEN WAYANS's blaxploitation parody, *I'm Gonna Git You Sucka*, establishes his raw comic style and features memorable turns by Damon Wayans, Chris Rock, Ann Marie Johnson, Jim Brown, Isaac Hayes, and blaxploitation's own Antonio Fargas.

■Alan Parker's MISSISSIPPI BURNING rewrites the civil rights movement.

■MAGIC JOHNSON's Lakers are the first NBA champs to repeat since 1969, making courtside seats at the Forum, coach Pat Riley's *GQ* look, and "Showtime!" part of our national lore.

■PUBLIC ENEMY's masterpiece *It Takes a Nation of Millions to Hold Us Back* appears on Def Jam. Rick Rubin exits Def Jam and starts Def American Records in Los Angeles, taking Andrew Dice Clay with him.

■The Seoul Olympics are dominated by FLORENCE "FLO JO" JOYNER's fingernails (displayed while she wins the 100- and 200-meter dash) and JACKIE JOYNER-KERSEE's determination (seen in her long jump and heptathlon triumphs). Ben Johnson bests Carl Lewis in the 100 and is then disqualified for steroid use.

■DANNY GLOVER and Mel Gibson costar in *Lethal Weapon*, which earns $65 million.

■"Yo! MTV Raps," hosted by FAB FIVE FREDDIE, airs Saturdays and garners the highest ratings in the network's history.

■On the cover of ERIC B. & RAKIM's *Follow the Leader*, the duo sport Dapper Dan–designed Louis Vuitton outfits and more gold than Fort Knox.

■In August MIKE TYSON breaks his right hand on Mitch "Blood" Green's face outside Dapper Dan's, where the champ is stopping off to pick up a custom-made "Don't Believe the Hype" jacket. When not busy in the street, Tyson knocks out Michael Spinks in 91 seconds.

■At the Dope Jam concert at the Nassau Coliseum, a young man is stabbed to death over a gold chain. In the wake of this tragedy, and the media's attacks on hip hop, a group of performers and industry figures organized by Jive vice-president Ann Carli and journalist Nelson George work on an anti–black-on-black violence record. The group calls itself the STOP THE VIOLENCE Movement after a song written by KRS-One.

■JEAN-MICHEL BASQUIAT dies of a heroin overdose.

■MIKE TYSON, ROBIN GIVINS, and RUTH ROPER appear on "20/20" with Barbara Walters with the champ looking drugged as Givens calls their marriage "torture." Later it is revealed that Tyson was prescribed Thorazine and lithium prior to the taping.

■Producer/director DEBBIE ALLEN takes over "Cosby Show" spinoff "A Different World," pumping new relevance into this look at black college life by highlighting three crucial characters: JASMINE GUY's Whitley, the ultimate Bap; KADEEM HARDISON's Dwayne Wayne, a humorous blend of Bap, Boho, and B-boy; and CREE SUMMER's Freddie, Bonet's heir apparent as America's favorite Boho.

■Los Angeles musician and Lisa Bonet's husband LENNY KRAVITZ is signed by Virgin. His retro-nuevo rock and hippie costumes find a cult audience, making him and Bonet the first couple of boho African America.

■ROBIN GIVINS in Los Angeles and MIKE TYSON in New Jersey file divorce papers. She claims Tyson beat her; he claims she tricked him into marriage with a false claim of pregnancy. Givens becomes a target of rap ridicule as the ultimate gold digger.

■With George Bush's election GENERAL COLIN POWELL is named head of the Joint Chiefs of Staff. Because he's so good at running press conferences about invasions of Third World countries, he's mentioned as a potential vice-presidential candidate.

■JESSE JACKSON and other prominent blacks call for the word *black* to be replaced by *African American* in an effort to reinforce identification with the Motherland.

# 1989

■On Martin Luther King Day, the STOP THE VIOLENCE Movement releases "Self-Destruction," which will go on to sell over 500,000 copies and raise $600,000 for the National Urban League. On the same day, for the fourth time in a decade, there's a black riot in Miami triggered by the shooting of a black suspect by a white or hispanic officer.

■Sixty percent of BLACK STUDENTS IN HIGHER EDUCATION are women, the highest female-to-male ratio of any racial group.

■N.W.A's gangsta masterpiece *Straight Outta Compton*, along with a slew of other records by Compton-based acts, turns this obscure city into the nation's newest symbol of urban decay.

■ONE-THIRD OF BLACKS live in households with incomes below the poverty level and 45 percent of all black children live in poverty-level homes.

■The NEW YORK TIMES does a long front-page story on the increasing interest in Afrocentric education in the black community.

■"Yo! MTV Raps," now also a weekly show hosted by DOCTOR DRE and ED LOVER, pulls in huge ratings and spreads hip hop culture.

■The Love Ball brings VOGUING aboveground at an AIDS benefit.

■SOUL II SOUL's "Keep on Movin'" and NENEH CHERRY's "Buffalo Stance" intensify the trans-Atlantic impact of U.K. black music.

■RONALD BROWN is voted chair of the Democratic Party.

■EIGHT HARLEM TEENS are charged with raping a white jogger in Central Park.

■*Do the Right Thing* premieres at Cannes to the praise and outrage of American critics. It will eventually earn $27 million, make many top 10 lists, win an Oscar nomination for best screenplay, and elevate SPIKE LEE to the top rank of world filmmaking. Several reactionary journalists, including *New York*'s David Denby and Joe Klein, *Newsweek*'s Jack Kroll, and the *Voice*'s Stanley Crouch, predict the film will cause violence.

■ARSENIO HALL begins his rule of late night cool by bringing urban slang ("Let's get busy!"), an eager smile, and cutting-edge musical guests to mall America.

■YUSUF HAWKINS, a 16-year-old black shopping for a used car in Bensonhurst, is shot dead after being chased by a crowd of Italian American youths.

■Priority Records receives an FBI letter criticizing N.W.A's "Fuck tha Police." As they tour during the summer and fall, they are dogged by a police fax campaign urging local departments to get the show canceled.

■BILLBOARD reports growing efforts to repress musical acts that "swear, engage in erotic posturing and sing lyrics touting violence."

■TERRY MCMILLAN's love story of a middle-class teacher and a working-class construction worker, *Disappearing Acts*, becomes a Buppie favorite.

■Twentieth Century–Fox agrees to release EUZHAN PALCY's anti-apartheid *A Dry White Season*, starring Marlon Brando and Donald Sutherland.

■The tastelessly funny, racially edgy comedy of KEENEN IVORY WAYANS's "In Living Color" debuts on Fox. Brother DAMON emerges as the show's star and ROSIE PEREZ brings new jack dance to regularly scheduled TV. The black rock band Living Colour sues Wayans for copyright infringement.

■In a close election, DAVID DINKINS is elected mayor of New York.

■The Los Angeles Raiders's ART SHELL becomes the first black head coach of the postwar era.

■**I DREAM A WORLD**, an album of photos and minibios of African American women, is a publishing surprise with six-figure sales, mostly to black middle-class families.

# 1990

■Designer **PATRICK KELLY**, a shrewd self-promoter who uses overall jeans, big round buttons, and toy black babies to market his flamboyant fashions, dies of AIDS.

■One in four **BLACK MEN IN THEIR TWENTIES** are either behind bars, on probation, or on parole. The 610,000 black men between ages 20 and 29 who are involved with the criminal justice system outnumber the 436,000 blacks of the same age enrolled in higher education.

■D.C. mayor **MARION BARRY** is caught smoking crack with model Rasheeda Moore in an FBI sting at the Vista International Hotel. The FBI videotape airs regularly on national TV.

■**REGGIE HUDLIN**'s *House Party*, starring the rap duo Kid 'n Play and comic Robin Harris, earns $26 million and makes the director and brother-producer **WARRINGTON** hot properties.

■Waterbury, Connecticut's **GARY FRANKS** is the first black Republican elected to Congress in 50 years.

■**M.C. HAMMER**'s scintillating performance of "U Can't Touch This" on "Arsenio" helps mushroom the record's sales and confirms rap's new visual orientation.

■**CARTER G. WOODSON**'s 1933 classic, *The Miseducation of the Negro*, is reprinted by the Africa World Press, influencing the likes of KRS-One.

■**NELSON MANDELA** visits America, provoking a brief outpouring of brotherhood and African American pride. In celebration of his Harlem speech, "Black Bart Simpson Meets Mandela" T-shirts are sold on 125th Street.

■**ICE CUBE** splits with N.W.A and records the ferocious *Amerikkka's Most Wanted* in New York with the Bomb Squad.

■**SHELBY STEELE**'s *The Content of Our Character* wins a National Book Critics Circle Award. While his neocon ideas about racial harmony strike many as naive, Steele's emphasis on black responsibility and self-determination seems like common sense across the political spectrum.

■BIG DADDY KANE steals JIM BROWN's woman in a video. Off-camera, the ex-football and blaxploitation star mentors Kane and many gang-bangers in Los Angeles.

■*USA Today* reports on the rising crossover appeal of black fashion—twisted braids, dreadlocks, hi-top fades, L.A. Raiders gear, banana head-bands, African beads, baggy clothes—which it calls AFROCENCHIC.

■Rapper WILL SMITH stars in NBC sitcom "The Fresh Prince of Bel-Air." QUINCY JONES is the executive producer.

■The Oscar-winning *Driving Miss Daisy* makes over $100 million, spotlighting MORGAN FREEMAN's magnificent acting, but disturbing blacks with its Reaganite feel-goodism.

■VANILLA ICE's "Ice Ice Baby" video makes a decent dancer and wack rapper hip hop's Fabian.

■SPIKE LEE edits the October *Spin*, interviewing EDDIE MURPHY and AL SHARPTON and assigning AUGUST WILSON an incisive essay on African American aesthetics.

■ST. IDES MALT LIQUOR, which has almost twice the alcohol content of the average beer, uses rap to market its brew, including a TV spot with Ice Cube.

■CHARLES BURNETT's *To Sleep with Anger* stars executive producer DANNY GLOVER. Glover's presence gets the director his first commercial feature opportunity, but doesn't guarantee blacks' attendance. Despite glowing reviews Burnett claims his tale of black Los Angelenos haunted by deep South superstitions is mismarketed.

■Hip hop media assassin HARRY ALLEN appears on "Family Feud" wearing a white kufi. His family loses to a white midwestern clan.

## 1991

■Michael Bivins, a minor member of New Edition, introduces his post–New Jack Swing philosophy in BELL BIV DEVOE, a group he forms with two other New Edition members, which he says is "Smoothed out on the r&b tip with a pop feel appeal to it." BBD also popularize Timberland gear hip among nonhikers. Two other Bivins–managed groups, ANOTHER BAD CREATION and BOYZ II MEN, go platinum. Boyz II Men's album is called *Cooleyhighharmony*.

■COOLEY HIGH is released on videocassette.

■DR. DRE of N.W.A beats DEE BARNES of Fox-TV's "Pump It Up" in a Los Angeles nightclub before hundreds of witnesses. Dre blamed her when an N.W.A interview was followed by an Ice Cube rebuttal. Barnes sues for millions as N.W.A gloats about the beating in interviews.

■"Family Matters"'s STEVE URKEL becomes the first hip black nerd in history.

■CORNEL WEST's *The American Evasion of Philosophy: A Genealogy of Pragmatism* focuses attention on the eloquent ideas of this Princeton philosopher.

■*New Jack City*, directed by MELVIN VAN PEEBLES's son, MARIO, produced by George Jackson and Doug McHenry, and scripted by Barry Michael Cooper, opens to shootings at several theaters nationally and a riot at an overbooked Westwood venue. It makes $48 million, boosting the careers of Ice-T, Wesley Snipes, Chris Rock, and everyone else involved. Blaxploitation smartly updated for the '90s, it starts this year of black film on an optimistic note.

■ROBERT TOWNSEND's *The Five Heartbeats* ends the optimism as the actor/director's tribute to '60s r&b vocal groups suffers from poor marketing, weak reviews, and the indifference of young blacks. The dichotomy between *New Jack City*'s youth appeal and *The Five Heartbeats*'s failure bodes poorly for adult-themed black films.

■BILL DUKE's *A Rage in Harlem* adapts Chester Himes's cartoony novel of '50s Harlem with verve as ROBIN GIVENS shocks her critics with her steamy, assured performance.

■JENNIE LIVINGSTON's *Paris Is Burning* documents the wellspring of vivacious style that is black transvestite life.

■A four-CD JAMES BROWN package with extensive liner notes and discography gives the Godfather his props.

■Nineteen-year-old MATTY RICH releases a hardcore rap 12-inch disguised as a movie called *Straight Out of Brooklyn*. Though he criticizes

Spike Lee, Rich acts in a Spikean manner by dissin' his elders and opening his own Brooklyn store.

■**Fab Five Freddie**, a downtown scene icon, appears in a Colt 45 ad with blaxploitation sex symbol **Billy Dee Williams**.

■**Spike Lee**'s *Jungle Fever*, a tale of dysfunctional families, is cannily packaged as an interracial love story. Sam Jackson's crackhead son and Ossie Davis's blindly religious preacher father embody the generational conflict rife among African Americans. This generation gap is further illustrated when Amiri Baraka leads protests against Lee's film of Malcolm X's life in a nasty scene of artistic agitators from the '60s and '80s trading low blows.

■L.A.'s **Kday** is sold and its rap format discontinued.

■**John Singleton**'s *Boyz N the Hood* opens to more violence than *New Jack City* and almost unanimous critical acclaim. The film overcomes its nasty opening weekend to gross $55 million and turns Ice Cube into a household name. At 23, Singleton, like Rich, is part of the hip hop generation, and his film balances traditional Hollywood storytelling with a raw, male-dominant viewpoint. Larry Fishburne's strong, righteous father is an Afrocentric fantasy of child rearing.

■N.W.A's *Niggaz4Life* goes to No. 1 on the *Billboard* chart after two weeks.

■**Michael Jordan** leads the Chicago Bulls to the NBA title over the Lakers. And, maybe more culturally important, splits Coke for Gatorade.

■**Mayor Dinkins** is jeered by angry youths in the aftermath of the Crown Heights riot while rappers X-Clan lead protests against the police.

■Disney uses anachronistic, **Graffiti-Style** bubble letters for the logo of the Charles Lane–directed flop *True Identity*.

■Virginia's black governor, **Doug Wilder**, announces his candidacy for the Democratic presidential nomination. Unlike Jesse Jackson, this mainstreamer plans a conventional campaign with neoliberal themes of tight budgets and efficient management.

■*Newsweek*'s cover story on Afrocentrism asks, "Was Cleopatra Black?" Eleven years after **Dr. Asante** coined the word, the battle over multiculturalism in general and Africa's contribution to world culture in particular is the nation's hottest educational issue.

■Neocon CLARENCE THOMAS, nominated to succeed civil rights warrior Thurgood Marshall, is confirmed as the second black to serve on the Supreme Court by the smallest margin in history after he's almost derailed by law professor Anita Hill's charges of sexual harassment. Never has America seen so many real-life Buppies on TV. Unfortunately, they're all Republicans.

■PUBLIC ENEMY's blacker-than-thou posture seems to attract, not alienate, young white listeners as the rappers tour with their thrash-metal allies Anthrax.

■Dancehall toaster SHABBA RANKS has the No. 1 black album in the country, a first for a Jamaican artist. The upsurge in grassroots popularity of Jamaican-style rapping symbolizes the long-overdue breakdown of tensions between African Americans and West Indians.

■G. Heileman is forced to withdraw its POWERMASTER malt liquor, which was to contain 31 percent more alcohol than Colt 45, in the wake of intense criticism from the black community and health activists. Like Uptown cigarettes before it, PowerMaster is stopped before it can be marketed to the black consumers targeted by its manufacturer.

■MAGIC JOHNSON's announcement that he's HIV-positive awakens millions of sports-loving heterosexuals to the reality of AIDS.

■Black Filmmaker Foundation cofounder Warrington Hudlin begins producing EDDIE MURPHY's *Boomerang*. With brother Reggie directing, this marriage of the first family of black independent film and Hollywood's biggest box-office black star is as potentially important as Lee's *Malcolm X*. While Lee documents crucial history, the Hudlin-Murphy match will test whether black indie filmmakers can graduate to big-budget, mass-market moviemaking while retaining their identity.

# B-BOYS

# RAPPING DEEJAYS

In the clubs and on the street the rappin' king lays on
   over the beat.
Now if your name is Annie get up off your fannie
If your name is Clyde get off your backside
If your name is Pete you don't need a seat
Cause I'm Kurtis Blow and I'm on the go
Rockin' to the rhythms in ster-e-ereo

—FROM "RAPPIN' BLOW" BY KURTIS BLOW

If you ask anyone who is not black, not under 20, and not a resident of Harlem or the South Bronx who started the rapping deejay style, they will undoubtedly cite the Sugar Hill Gang's "Rapper's Delight." To anyone who follows popular music by studying the trade publications and their top 100's, that would seem a logical answer, since the Sugar Hill disc was the first and only rap record to cross over at that time. Slightly more insightful music fans might suggest that the veteran funk/r&b group the Fatback Band had something to do with it, since their single "Kill Tim the III" first appeared on Billboard's soul chart at about the same time "Rapper's Delight" made its debut.

Well, so much for what charts in major publications can tell you about what is really happening musically in America. Because in either case you would be very, very wrong.

A much more accurate idea of where rapping deejays began can be found any Saturday night at a South Bronx disco called Club 371. There, if you're lucky, a local legend named DJ Hollywood will be orchestrating a merger of black street wit, the latest dance hits, and turntable technology to drive a crowd of tough-to-please New York dancers into total ecstasy. The crowd is composed of young adults and teens, college students and low-on-the-ladder office workers, blacks and hispanics, who smoke their herb, search for some companionship, and in general get loose. Dreams of upward mobility may spin in their heads, but the reality is that more of them end up in Attica than in that suburban house with its regulation two cars and 2.3 kids.

A terrible school system, an addictive welfare system, and a government that lets drugs pour into the community have, along with twin turntables, somehow conspired to make these young people come up with their own distinctive brand of entertainment. All in all, the situation doesn't differ greatly from the one that sparked England's punk rock movement. Lower-class kids have always wanted and created their own insular thing. London youths of the mid-'70s plugged in their guitars, just as the generation before had, but said something different this time. Meanwhile in Harlem the plastic disco of Studio 54 was ignored, and the music was transformed into a uniquely black and streetwise form closer to home.

The deejay raps over the instrumental sections or breaks of popular dance records reminiscent of Jamaican deejays talk over the heavy dub instrumentation of reggae. Most of the youngsters who do this in America are ignorant of the Jamaican precedent, yet the raps serve the same purpose in both these African-derived cultures. Whether it's heard in a park in Brooklyn or a junkyard in Kingston, it is rhythmic music and the spoken voice unconsciously creating a potent echo of Africa.

Unfortunately the rapping deejays are looked down upon by older and more middle-class blacks, who see them not as a continuation of tradition, but as perpetrators of old stereotypes. One black writer with access to a major music publication told me he'd never write about them "because they don't deserve the ink."

His condescending attitude is hardly isolated and to my mind reflects a wish by some to coat black culture with a superficial "high-mindedness" and "art," European concepts that seem to take any form of expression out of its context, mount it, and drain away its relevance to everyday life. The rappers make no claims that they are artistic or are presenting "positive images" to black America. They talk about what they feel and know, simple as that.

Like their antecedents, the jive-talking air personalities of r&b radio such as Dr. Jive and Jocko, the rappers are crowd-pleasers whose rapport with their audience is remarkable. The rapping deejay cited by his contemporaries as developing the current rapping approach is Hollywood, a hefty 24-year-old with gold chains around his neck and a short, razor cut hair style. When he was at the peak of his popularity a few years ago he could command and guide a crowd with the dexterity of a James Brown. My first encounter with Hollywood came in 1977, at a concert held at the City College of New York's Harlem campus. I knew of his reputation and of Club 371. Tapes of his performances were becoming valued items among young Harlemites and his style was already being copied by mobile deejays around town, but I wasn't prepared for what would happen live. Harold Melvin & the Blue Notes, Evelyn King, and Brainstorm were on the bill. Hollywood was to provide between-the-acts entertainment. Instead, the headliners were only interludes between his performances. Two thousand black and hispanic youths were totally under his control.

With MFSB's "Sexy" grooving underneath him, Hollywood scat-rapped à la Eddie Jefferson. "Hip, hop de hip be de hop, de hip hop, hip de hop. On and on and on and on. Like hot butter on what . . . ?" Hollywood then cut the music, leaving the crowd room to shout "Popcorn" right on time. The huge college gym had become a gigantic disco, and people were dancing everywhere.

Performances like this inspired a whole slew of deejays to follow his lead. DJ Starski, Grandmaster Flash, Kurtis Blow, and Eddie Cheeba (blow is a slang term for cocaine; cheeba for marijuana) are the best among the many deejays who followed Hollywood's lead before establishing their own rapping personas. All of them are from either Harlem or the South Bronx and all are very proud of their inner-city roots.

Their raps deal on a street level like many a classic blues lyric; the rapping deejays celebrate the ribald and raunchy, always with a sense of humor. The bravado of the blues style also runs through the raps of almost every deejay.

The stuff of pop culture makes up a very important part of the rapping deejay's repertoire. The origin of Starski's name is obvious. In "Rapper's Delight" there is a long section devoted to the seduction of Lois Lane in which Superman is characterized as "a fairy" who "flies through the air in his red and blue pantyhose." This kind of pop culture fun and games has been practiced by George Clinton and Bootsy Collins quite successfully for several years now. Rapping deejays are also masters of the everchanging American language of slang. A phrase such as "people in the back, if you're not the whack" is nothing if you don't know what "the whack" means. The best definition possible is that if you don't know what it means you probably are "the whack," or maybe even "whacked,"as in "That dude is whacked."

Some of the rappers' imagery mixes slang and pop culture so thickly that it takes some study to understand what's going down. In "Rapper's Delight" the term "Death OJ" is used. In current slang "death" means something good, while "OJ" is a reference to a big car: Erstwhile football star and all-around adman O.J. Simpson does Hertz commercials featuring Ford and Lincoln Mercury cars. If we add "death" to Ford and Lincoln Mercury cars (leaving out any disrespectful reference to Pintos), we come up with the "Rapper's Delight" character driving off in a Lincoln Continental. How's that for musicology?

As for the future of rapping, I think it will become a prerequisite for all black club jocks (and many whites) to be fluent in some form of the language. The kids who enjoy rapping now will stay with it as they grow older, just as those in the doo-wop generation still treasure their memories and records. The early rap records will be collector's items, while independent labels will continue to feed the desire for new product.

MUSICIAN, 1980

# RAPPIN' WITH RUSSELL

## Eddie Murphying the Flak-Catchers

The offices of Rush Productions are two cramped little rooms on Broadway in the 20s, which on any given afternoon are filled by the loud voices of black men and women. They are mostly young, real street, and real anxious. On this day in January a graffiti artist sits in one corner of the outer room with hopes of painting an album cover. Over on a beat-up couch is a girl in striped pants and a Run-D.M.C. T-shirt waiting for her old man, one of the 22 street-oriented acts managed by Russell Simmons' Rush Productions, to find out when his next gig is. Three young dudes dressed in the B-boy-style—untied Adidas sneakers, jeans, sheepskin coats, and Cazals—are leaning against a wall joking and eyeing the girl waiting on the rapper. The token white is Bill Adler, a former *Daily News* reporter who is the company's full-time PR man. Behind him, shifting through papers and cradling a phone on her shoulder, is Heidi Smith, once Russell's lone overworked office staffer and now one of several overworked office employees.

I stick my head in the other room, seeking Russell. Instead, sitting behind Russell's desk in front of the bright orange-and-red mural that says "RUSH" in letters the size of subway car graffiti, I find the king of rap himself, Kurtis Blow. I congratulate him on his recent marriage and the birth of his son, known affectionately around Rush as "Joe Blow." I also praise his production of the Fat Boys's album, which will soon go gold. I tell him that I'm writing a piece on Russell, he tells me that's all right but I really should be doing his life story. I say I'll think about it and ask where Russell is. I'm supposed to be accompanying Russell and Kurtis Blow's producer, Robert "Rocky" Ford, to a meeting with Cannon Films about a rap movie. After urging me again to consider writing his life story, Kurtis tells me they are over at this putrid Chinese restaurant that Russell loves because they make screwdrivers strong, the way he likes them. I run into them in the street. "Yo home piss," says Russell, "You ready to serve these Israelis or what?" Rocky and I laugh and just look at him. This is the man the *Wall Street Journal* calls "the mogul of rap?"

At 27, an age when most of his black business contemporaries have designer suit tags branded into their breastbones, Russell promotes street music and makes no apologies. The staccato, crashing drums, the gritty, uncompromised words about life in Kochtown, and the down-playing of melody that marks the music of Blow, Whodini, Run-D.M.C., L.L. Cool J, and the other acts he manages are his lifeblood. He loves all this loud, obnoxious aural graffiti. As far as I can tell—and I've known Russell about six years' worth of headaches, triumphs, and late-night phone calls—he never intends to do anything else but make street records, chain smoke, talk fast, and uninhibit the inhibited.

Russell is hyped for the meeting. He's puffing on a Kool, bouncing around in shiny black penny loafers, and rubbing his bald spot comically for me. Russell's about five foot ten and 165 pounds, with the complexion of a ripe squash and a generally sunny disposition. He's the kind you can tell your worst joke to and get a laugh. I wish I could do justice to the rapid-fire monologue he delivered in the cab up to Cannon's East Side offices, but without a tape recorder it's hopeless. The gist of it was that we were about to see Russell act like Eddie Murphy in *Beverly Hills Cop*. That's why he asked us along. We're gonna be the reasonable Negroes and he's gonna be the bad nigger, sort of a mercenary '80s version of mau-mauing the flak catchers. Russell wants to make a point: he's not some dancer shuffling for a (pardon the expression) break. He wants respect and Cannon has already showed a lack of it. Cannon sent a writer uptown to hang out and get a feel for the scene. The writer listened to Russell's ruminations on rap and shook his head affirmatively when Russell emphasized that he wanted no part of another *Beat Street*—all fake dialogue, gospel singers at the Roxy, and other disagreeable Hollywoodisms. The writer, a white Californian who told Russell he sees a black about once every three months in his neighborhood, said, "Yeah," "Un huh," and "I understand your concern." And still wrote a jive treatment as much about a white girl trying to break into the music business as the uptown scene. In addition, Cannon, in a full-page *Variety* ad, announced that their rap movie would be shot in, of all places, Pittsburgh! Thickening the plot, a black production company from Los Angeles had approached Russell, guaranteeing him considerable creative input and serious profit participation. "All the VCR money. You hear me, Nelson," he shouted in the cab. Unfortunately, the brothers had a shaky reputation and short bread. We knew Cannon wasn't the classiest studio in the world—the bulk of its films were substandard 42nd Street fodder (one upcoming project is called *Godzilla vs. Cleveland*). Cannon had, however, committed several million to the project and would undoubtedly make a profitable, chintzy flick.

But Cannon's minions had already lost Russell's good will and in the meeting he truly Eddie Murphyed them. He talked loud and fast and was contemptuous of the film's portly producer, a man who bragged, "I dined with Hepburn last night" and then called Kurtis Blow Curtis Brown. Russell responded by emphasizing how important his acts were in the music business, and basically, with just slightly more subtlety, that he really didn't need them. "I've been working for ten years to make this music mean something," Russell said at one point. "You can come in with one film and ruin everything I'm trying to build." To say the least, ye olde film producer was surprised at Russell's impertinence. So was I. From my pragmatic post as "reasonable

Negro" Russell was alienating folk who'd definitely make a rap film, if not the one he wanted made, in exchange for a maybe situation. Russell calmed down after a while—even listened to them a little bit. However, the spirit of Murphy had seized Russell's soul, and with a gleeful smile, he chortled later with Andre Harrell a/k/a Dr. Jeckyll about serving them at the meeting, then complained that Rocky and I had been too good at our assignment. We almost stopped him from having fun.

The next day Russell signed a deal with the black production company and was rewarded with the wooing of Michael Schultz, the black director who handled *Cooley High*, one of Russell's favorite films, to supervise the project. In turn he delivered Run-D.M.C., Blow, Whodini, and the Fat Boys, whom he doesn't manage. By denying all that top rap talent to Cannon he would certainly hurt their project and, as blaxploitation films used to advertise, "stick it to the man."

Russell is a product of that generation of blacks who spent early '70s Saturdays enthralled by the white-bashing activities of Shaft, Super Fly, Trouble Man, Coffey, etc. At times he seems to fantasize about being as cold-blooded promoting raps as they were kicking ass. And if you think about it, Eddie Murphy, another product of the blaxploitation generation (remember Murphy's film critic Adbul Rahiem championing the virtues of Isaac Hayes's *Truck Turner*?), is nothing but an intentionally funny version of those bad-ass heroes in *48 Hrs.* and *Beverly Hills Cop*.

Unfortunately, for Russell being bad-ass isn't enough anymore. Since that meeting rap has exploded yet again. Run-D.M.C., the Fat Boys, and Whodini have all sold over 500,000 albums and Blow's *Ego Trip* is in the ballpark. Their videos are on MTV. Russell's acts are being swamped with endorsement and film offers. And, perhaps most profitably, the record industry itself is finally giving up the only kind of respect it can understand—money offers.

But therein lies the rub. You could call Russell a "mogul." It is to some degree an apt description, since he certainly has a deep economic stake in rap's present and future. But "mogul" also suggests someone who dominates an industry, and Russell, for all his influence, is at the mercy of many elements he does not control. Unlike the big tickets of pop culture—your George Lucas, Michael Jackson, Grant Tinker–level mogul—Russell doesn't have the financial clout or emotional distance to manipulate. You see, Russell really is his audience. He lives the B-boy life, and the values are found in his records. Unlike Afrika Bambaataa or Russell's brother Joey, a/k/a Run of Run-D.M.C., who are part

of a vanguard of rap innovators, Russell is one of the few products of
the rap generation to become an important businessman. He doesn't
battle other rappers or spinners for record sales. Instead he engages
wily, older businessmen in treacherous battles for survival. Russell's not
going bald 'cause it's been easy.

At least the business side hasn't. Life for Russell has never been that
rough. His background belies the stereotype that rap music is the pure
product of ghetto life. Both he and his brother grew up in the middle-
class Queens neighborhood of Hollis, an area of homeowning, upwardly
mobile dreams that has flourished since the '50s on the premise that life
in two-story dwellings with furnished basements is superior to that in the
tenements and projects of Brooklyn and Harlem. The parents of Hollis
(and St. Albans and Ozone Park and Jamaica) were beneficiaries of the
post–World War II striving for integration and the opening of civil service jobs to minorities. Russell's father, Daniel, supervises a Queens
school district and teaches black history at night. His mother, Evelyn,
works for the Parks Department. Back in 1976, when Russell enrolled at
City College's Harlem campus, where he'd earn 112 credits toward a
sociology degree, he seemed headed in the same direction.

What was always surprising—at least to me when I attended St.
John's University in the late '70s—was how fascinated with street culture the children of Hollis were. I came from Brownsville, an area that
could easily have been Melle Mel's model for "The Message"; I knew
"the ghetto" was nothing to romanticize. Yet here were kids like Russell who grew up in their own houses, with access to cars, furnished
basements, both parents, and more cash than my friends ever knew,
acting (or trying to act) as cool as any street kid. Russell's embrace of
street life, and, ultimately, his movement into it as a businessman,
occurred in the CCNY lounge. There he fell in with a group of aspiring
party promoters, including a brash Music & Arts senior named Curtis
Walker who used to sneak over to CCNY when he should have been in
school. Calling themselves "The Force," throughout 1976–77 they
gave parties in Harlem at Small's Paradise and the now defunct
Charles Gallery. Walker, assuming the streetwise persona of Kurtis
Blow, began rapping over records, influenced by the work of an older
man, Pete "DJ" Jones, whose style was similar to that of boasting radio
jocks like Frankie Crocker, and by D.J. Hollywood, a young rapper who
gigged regularly at a Bronx club called 371 and encouraged call-and-
response interaction with partygoers. It is Hollywood who originated
the "hip hop de hippy hop the body rock" that led to the rap-breaking-
graffiti scene being labeled hip hop.

In New York in the mid-'70s, rappers and their deejays were the nightclub equivalent of synthesizers in the recording studios. While synthesizers began replacing musicians in the studio, effectively cutting production costs, black discos with teen and young adult audiences used rap acts to replace bands. "They were a lot cheaper and they drew the same kinds of crowds," says Russell. "Lots of times, we'd give shows with rappers and get bigger crowds than if we had a guy with just records. The more exposure you got it seemed like the bigger your name got. The more fliers and stickers and posters that you could get your name on, the more popular you'd become as a rapper." "There was so much competition by then [1977] in rapping and deejaying uptown, Russell and I went to Queens, the boondocks, and started promoting there," remembers Kurtis Blow. Moving to Queens broadened rap's base in the city, reaching teens like Russell who were removed from ghetto life but not immune to the invention and flamboyance of its style.

Still, rap and Russell didn't hit their stride until he started promoting rap shows at the Hotel Diplomat on West 43rd Street in 1977. The Times Square location meant that the shows could attract black teens from the outer boroughs as well as Harlem. Coinciding with this move was the brief mating of Blow and Grandmaster Flash with Kurtis on the mike and Flash on the turntables. To promote this superstar hip hop do, 15,000 fliers were distributed and another couple of thousand stickers plastered in subways by Russell. "We had two thousand kids come see them that first night at the Diplomat," Russell recalls. "You know, people were standing outside Xenon's waiting to be picked to go in like Studio 54. And down the block you had B-boys coming down the street to go to the Diplomat two doors away." The Diplomat's shows truly helped widen rap's audience (people like Hollywood, Eddie Cheeba, and the Furious Five all eventually appeared there). Yet there was danger surrounding these shows. "We went through a lot of security companies," Russell says. "They worked one show and then the next security company would come. They'd work one show and that was it. It was like that rough. The Diplomat had bulletproof box offices. We stayed back there for most of the night. And Kurtis," Russell starts to laugh, "would always come in the box office and stand around. When it was time to go on stage, he'd run up there and perform and come right back in."

The insular, occasionally violent world of rap was changed forever in the summer of 1979 when first the Fatback Band's "King Tim III" and, most profoundly, the Sugar Hill Gang's "Rapper's Delight" hit the streets. The success of "Rapper's Delight," by three kids with only a tenuous connection to the original rap scene, shocked the established rappers. "There was a show in October or November in the Armory in Queens," Blow remembers. "We had, like, four thousand kids. All the original rappers were there and 'Rapper's Delight' was a big hit. Starski said on the mike, 'Yeah, y'all know we're still gonna be on the moon.' We all resented it. Everybody hated it. Now I see that they opened the doors for us and I'm grateful now. But at that time I was so furious."

I first met Russell and Kurtis in the offices of *Billboard* in the summer of 1979. *Billboard* staffer Rocky Ford and J.B. Moore had brought them up to the office to talk about making a rap record. Rocky had written the first piece in the established media about rap, a funny little story in *Billboard* prior to "Rapper's Delight," and, with help from me, then a St. John's University student working part-time at the *Amsterdam News* and free-lancing for *Billboard*, had been researching the rap scene. He and Moore had decided to work with Kurtis, because compared to Grandmaster Flash, Starski, and the other original rappers, he was the most clean-cut and articulate. And he had Russell, someone who knew the rap scene and was itching to learn the record business. Looking back on it now I know that Russell's presence was as important as Kurtis's talent in getting them to invest their then meager resources in a record about Santa Claus in Harlem. "Christmas Rappin'" would eventually sell nearly a million copies.

Six years ago Russell was even more frantic than he is now, partly because he was doing a lot of drugs (he says solemnly that those days are over) and partly because he was just one overactive, anxious young man. Every meeting with him was like being injected with a thousand cc's of adrenaline. His energy fascinated me, though our friendship had its rough spots. One night he left me stranded in Long Island following a Kurtis Blow gig at some Hempstead dump. Another time he took me to the Disco Fever in the days before it became a musical tourist trap and left me in a room full of coked-up stickup kids and rappers.

What redeemed our friendship was that despite his occasional lapses, Russell was the only guy on the rap scene who seemed to have any long-term goals. He was serious where his contemporaries just wanted to party. Everybody wanted to make records. But did everybody realize what promotion and marketing to the nonrap audience would entail? Did they realize that if rap was successful they'd be approached by record industry pros, people who didn't give a fuck about anything except their ability to make a quick buck? Russell did. In fact, it used to drive him crazy. He'd call me or Rocky at any time of the day or night to complain about how someone was trying to serve him or his artist. In his early twenties Russell was trying to woo finicky reporters, get his money from small-time concert promoters, and make the major labels pay attention to him. His paperwork was sloppy. He slept in the recording studios. He told his skeptical parents he'd made the right decision in leaving school. He was happiest when he talked about the music he wanted to make. Not the "pop-rap" Ford & Moore were making for Kurtis, but "beat" records that captured the feel of clubs like the Fever.

It wasn't until Russell teamed with ex-jazz bassist Larry Smith, creator of "The Breaks"'s bass line and Ford's childhood chum, that he had someone who could translate his beat fanaticism into music. Together they made two recordings that would change New York street music: Jimmy Spicer's humorous, Jimmy Castor-influenced rap "The Bubble Bunch" and Orange Krush's "Action," which featured Allyson William's sensual shouting. The key to both was the "bubba bubba tap" rhythms of drummer Trevor Gale, a chucky bass drum stop that has become standard for rap music (e.g., "It's Like That").

Another child of "Action" and "Bubble Bunch" is L.L. Cool J's "I Need a Beat," the first record on Def Jam Records, an indie label started by the record producer Rick Rubin that Russell is now a partner in. The drum machine is slow and, as Russell says, "sleazy," the cymbal is hot, and the other instruments serve to intensify the rhythm. It's a record for dancers who know that the spaces between the beats aren't really spaces, but sounds of pleasure where your body—suspended in action, chilly in motion—awaits its guidance to slide over a few soul-satisfying inches. It is a statement of principle that says Russell and Rubin are going right for the core B-boy audience.

Def Jam is also very much a product of Russell's economic frustrations. Executives at the major companies have refused to believe in rap or the long-term creativity of its makers. When Blow signed with Mercury in 1979, I assumed every label would have at least one rap act within two years. Instead, rap acts have come and gone from the roster of the corporate music machines because these organizations, very often advised by their black executives, have shown no interest in or outright contempt for the music.

Epic's rap history is illustrative. Back in 1980 the company released a seven-inch (seven-inch!) single by D.J. Hollywood featuring a cooing girl chorus, then didn't promote it. Hollywood is a legend in this city, yet rap's pioneer was quickly forgotten at Black Rock, headquarters on

West 52nd Street. When Epic briefly distributed Aaron Fuch's Tuff City rap label in 1983, they had Davy DMS's "One for the Treble," a beat-box record by an ex–Kurtis Blow spinner and prolific hip hop songwriter-musician. It was an instant B-boy classic, as fresh as Run-D.M.C.'s "It's Like That." Yet "One for the Treble" sold about 80,000 copies for Tuff City while "It's Like That" did approximately 250,000 for Profile. The difference? Epic didn't see the potential in the music and couldn't be bothered with what it saw as an experiment. Subsequently Run-D.M.C.'s debut album sold over 500,000, a genuine RIAA gold record, because Profile president Cory Robbins and Russell worked the 12-inches "It's Like That"/"Sucker M.C.'s," "Hard Times"/"Jam Master Jay," "Rock Box," and "30 Days" with the zeal of a major label; promoted Run-D.M.C.'s black hats and leather to give them an iconic image (cf. Jackson's glove and Cyndi Lauper's hair); and reached out to the substantial hip white audience that—very much like reggae's white aficionados—identify with its raw, outlaw attitude. Arista did (eventually) get behind the English label Jive and its efforts to win a U.S. audience for the rap duo Whodini. As a result, Whodini's Larry Smith–produced *Escape* went gold. Representative of Jive's commitment is that Whodini has had four videos in support of two albums while Blow, with five albums at PolyGram and a steady seller of 100,000 to 300,000 units, just got his first for his current single "Basketball."

Russell's dream has been for all his acts to be signed to one label that he controlled. Under the aegis of PolyGram's late black music vice-president, Bill Haywood, it almost happened. But after Haywood's death in 1983, the remaining executives, white and black, didn't understand the music or deal. Jimmy Spicer's "Bubble Bunch" and Orange Krush's "Action" were released on Mercury. The failure of both commercially outside the New York area definitely hastened Russell's hair loss. After those records, the arrangement died of corporate malnutrition. As a result, Rush's acts are now strung across the roster of several, mostly independent, labels: Profile, Jive, Mercury, Disco Fever, Nia, and now Def Jam. As a result, most of the acts live from record to record. When Russell brags, "None of our records have ever lost money," he doesn't mention just how essential that situation has been to his economic well-being.

Ex-indie Sugarhill Records, now distributed by MCA, once dominated the rap market with an enviable in-house set-up: a two-story building in Englewood, New Jersey, contacts to record distributors going back over a decade (Sugarhill owners Joe and Sylvia Robinson once owned All-Platinum and control the Chess catalogue), a brilliant house band that will one day be regarded as the Booker T. & the MG's of the early '80s. While Russell was still building his roster of rappers, Sugarhill Records, with the Sugar Hill Gang, Grandmaster Flash & the Furious Five, Spoonie Gee, and Sequence defined the music's cutting edge. The grooves were varied and, except for streaks of unabashed sexism, the raps were always clever. But the across-the-board acceptance of Grandmaster Flash & the Furious Five's "The Message" in 1983 ended up hurting the label. In its wake Grandmaster Flash exited to Elektra Records after a lawsuit over money and creative control. So did many key musicians, such as "Message" cowriter Duke Bootee, who signed with PolyGram, and Reggie Griffin, who signed with Qwest Records and arranged Chaka Kahn's "I Feel for You." Only the brilliant Melle Mel, with his caustic, biblical attack on racism and corruption, and commanding delivery, remains a vital sales and creative force for Sugarhill.

Sugarhill's loss was Russell's gain as young rappers who might have gravitated to the Jersey label instead turned to Rush Productions. For a time it looked as if Afrika Bambaataa's space-rap sound, through his liaison with Tom Silverman's aggressive Tommy Boy label, would succeed Sugarhill's. But after "Planet Rock" and "Looking for the Perfect Beat," innovative recordings coproduced by Arthur Baker and Jon Robie and heavily influenced by Kraftwerk, Bambaataa's been a commercial bust. His collaborations with Material, Johnny Rotten, and other "new music" types have given him a high media profile, but his terrible misuse of James Brown on "Unity" illustrated why Bambaataa hasn't tapped the hip hop soul in almost two years. As a result, the most significant rap hits of the past two years have been in some way connected to Rush Productions. He and Smith coproduced both Run-D.M.C. albums; Smith produced Whodini and Blow produced the Fat Boys. The hottest rap 12-inch of 1985, UTFO's "Roxanne, Roxanne," was produced by the Brooklyn band Full Force, who've written for and played on the last two Kurtis Blow albums and whose manager, Steven Salem, once shared office space with Rush.

It's an incestuous little world that Russell works in, one he feels has values and attitudes that aren't understood by outsiders. To him that's the reason rap and New York street music in general haven't yet been embraced by the music industry mainstream. Significantly, Russell doesn't call his music "rap" or "street" but "black teenage music." He sees his records not as part of a genre but a statement from a new generation—a generation, coincidentally, that puts great stock in machismo.

To Russell, for example, the reason there are so few female rappers "is that the most progressive forms of music are too hard-edged for women. What do heavy metal and wrestling say about women? I ask that because rap has the same kind of audience and feeling to it. But you'll never hear any of our artists rapping about getting over on a woman in a vulgar way. You can listen to all the records I've been involved in and not hear that stuff about busting out young girls in them. We already have this bad image with black program directors about the country, so I'm very careful about what I say. I'd do a record like 'No Sell Out' [a rap record on Tommy Boy using excerpts from Malcolm X speeches] if I could make it work. A good track could support any idea. But I'm not gonna lecture the audience. I'm not a teacher. I make music based on the ideas my artist gives me. If Run wants to do 'Hard Times' or 'It's Like That' I'm gonna help them make it work. The only thing I ask is that it have an edge. Teenage music is rebellious."

To his taste, most mainstream black pop is "too polished, too slick." "I like real sounding music, real sounding instruments—even our drum machines sound hard, and I like loud music. Music feels good loud," he says, explaining why on "Rock Box" and most of the *King of Rock* he employed black rock guitarist Eddie Martinez to such crunching effect. "I can't help it if it's called rock 'n' roll. It's still B-boy music. It still has breaks, it still has def beats. The difference between white teenage music like Quiet Riot or AC/DC and black teenage music right now isn't that big."

Russell has been very open-minded about building bridges between the uptown scene and the more progressive white rock clubs. Before it was fashionable he was hanging out at Disco Fever and Danceteria, rapping with Melle Mel at 1:00 A.M. and Malcolm McLaren at 4:00 A.M. So when he looks you in the eye and says excitedly, "I want to produce Devo," you don't bust out laughing, but ask, quite respectfully, why? "I believe I could make Devo def. Hear me, I'd make Devo def. I love all those sounds they make. Don't like the songs. But I could fix them and make them def."

Looking ahead five years Russell hopes he'll "be able to pay for this loft I want and have four or five major stars. I'll be involved in black teenage music if I still understand it. I might not be able to still make it. I at least hope I'll understand what's good about it enough to hire someone who does." Russell stops, pauses a minute, then adds, "I want to make successful black heroes, like what I've tried to do with Run-D.M.C. and Kurtis. I didn't say 'positive' because that's a trap. It's got to be real."

"Russell Simmons is a bloodsucker," a prominent record producer tells me in late February. "That's the feedback I'm getting on him, man. They say he's unorganized and that his artists would be better off somewhere else." Then the producer laughs. "You know what that means, man, it's character assassination. They are after him. He has a thing going. When it was that street level, selling 12-inches on indie labels, they left him alone. But now rap is selling LPs. Run-D.M.C. and Whodini have broken in the rock and black markets. The Fat Boys are a novelty act that works. So now the industry is coming after him just like they did to George Clinton, Gamble & Huff, and every black music entrepreneur. If his shit isn't together they'll take everything that isn't nailed down."

By March my friend has proved prophetic. Larry Smith, another Queens native who has explored the darkest corners of the South Bronx with Russell, has signed his publishing to Jive's Zomba Music for a large advance. Unfortunately, Russell has promised that publishing to another company as part of another deal, putting Russell in an embarrassing, potentially litigable position. Aggravating the tension is that Larry agreed to produce the soundtrack for Cannon's rap film. The two are still friends, and outside the Beacon Theatre where Run-D.M.C. recently headlined they could be seen embracing. For Larry they were good business moves, which didn't prevent them from taking the smile off Russell's face. They were a signal to him that his rap kingdom was hardly secure.

There were more lessons to come. While negotiating with a major record label for a production deal he made the tactical error of including a group in his proposal he has a business relationship with but no papers on. The company does some checking and the next thing Russell knows that group is cutting its own deal. In the world of rap 'n' roll neither the record label nor the group was wrong. They were trying to do the best they could for themselves. Russell left a loophole, the kind he can't afford anymore.

Russell is taking all this with surprising calm. He understands his mistakes and is trying to tighten his operation. In the last six months he's added a number of administrative staffers, and he's seeking larger offices. Andre Harrell has quit his day job as a time salesman at WINS to become vice-president of Rush with an eye toward nailing down some of the endorsements the company is being offered. Russell may be a bit shaken by the wheeling and dealing swirling around him, but that only brings out the Eddie Murphy in him. I mention one of the people in the industry who question Russell's business acumen.

"That guy can only suck my dick when he sees me," he tells me with a conspiratorial chuckle. "I'm invaluable to the success of his company. He never says that to my face. I'd serve him." We laugh, and I tell him to save that crap for the next Run-D.M.C. album.

As *Billboard*'s black music editor, I interact daily with sleaze, stars, star-fuckers, and a few honest businessmen and musicians. All of them are out to make money. So is Russell. But in Russell there is a love of music, at least his particular brand of it, that is real. Like another middle-class hustler with good ears, Berry Gordy, Russell Simmons is trying to build something that will last. I'm not totally convinced it will happen. So much rests on the durability and continued evolution of a decidedly radical musical style. One of Russell's favorite sayings comes from Dr. Jeckyll: "Inside of every suppressed black man is an angry nigger." I suspect that as long as Russell believes that and promotes music that sounds like it, homeboy will be all right. Even if he is from Queens.

VILLAGE VOICE, 1985

# CPT TIME

The city of Compton, known as Comptown or CPT to its younger residents, is a 40-minute ride from West Hollywood and the larger-than-life billboards of Sunset. Its main thoroughfare is the Harbor Freeway, a long, ugly, winding piece of Southern California eight-lane that'll drop you off in what's currently America's most notorious ghetto. As if on cue, a left turn takes you right into two police cars parked in the middle of the street. Gang-bang aftermath? Naugh, this isn't *Colors*, just a minor traffic accident, but in car-conscious Cali even a small automobile infraction draws a crowd of enforcers.

Rolling down Wilmington Boulevard, the car crosses an expanse of dirt. Here are the train tracks featured in those N.W.A videos, and huge electric towers right out of a *Godzilla* flick. In a couple of blocks you hit a residential area with a car or two in the parking spaces, one of them usually a late-'70s or early-'80s model. Middle-aged blacks, a great many of them retirees who've been in Compton for at least one or two decades, live here in single-story houses and a few mobile homes. In the residence of Dee Dee Forbes, the shades are drawn, the fans are going full blast, and "The Young and the Restless" is on the tube. Mrs. Forbes, a humorous parent of two and grandmother of seven, moved to Compton from Louisiana in 1952. There were jobs in the factories here then and whites in the Los Angeles area weren't as interested in lynching you as down South, she recalled. By the end of the '50s her nine brothers and sisters had all followed her west to the land of long shopping strips, relative integration, and a pleasant, relaxed lifestyle. In the '70s, though, the local industrial economy slowed down, and whites began exiting. Gangs, a part of Los Angeles life since after World War II, grew bigger and bolder. Given the rural southern and western roots of its residents, guns, be they hunting rifles or old army revolvers, were common in Compton. With time, weapons got bigger and deadlier. But in Mrs. Forbes's view, it was the mass marketing of crack that turned parts of Compton from hardworking to violent. Mrs. Forbes's neighborhood was usually quiet, in large part because there weren't many teens around. Any children you saw playing in a front yard did so "only when one of their grandparents can sit out there with them."

"Where you going?" she asked when it was time to leave. "Don't just be driving around out here. It's dangerous out there." Just then Buddy, one of her grandchildren, drove up for a visit. A handsome six-footer with a greasy Cali-styled high-low, he's congenial and curious about New York. Turns out the young man, who looks to be about 23, has been running drugs since he was 16. He works long hours and has had innumerable run-ins with the law and rival dealers. But Buddy keeps on. Says one of his cousins, "He won't quit until he's made enough for a BMW."

At about 2:00 P.M. on a weekday in Compton there aren't many people on the street, but then, pedestrians are hardly an L.A. norm. Clusters of people, mostly men 30 years and up, hang around variety and liquor stores, looking much like the displaced African Americans you see in every other poor black 'hood in America. Just like Harlem Hospital on our uptown landscape, south central L.A.'s Dr. King Hospital on Wilmington Boulevard is a testament to self-inflicted genocide. It's commonly believed that the army sends doctors to train in its emergency room because of all the mini-AK47 victims received there.

Despite that sad fact, and the nihilistic image of CPT promulgated by such rappers as Eazy-E, N.W.A, Ice Cube, and Above the Law, on this day I saw no drive-bys and very few young men who fit the "gangsta, gangsta" rhetoric. But there was one tense moment. As I cruised by a beat-down house near the Watts Tower, a brother wearing a Raiders cap, a drippy jheri curl, no shirt, and black jeans stepped out of the shade of his porch and into the sun to stare back at me. To a media-conscious outsider, he seemed a walking stereotype from either *The Source* magazine or *Colors*. In reality he could have been wondering why this fool in the car was playing him so close. My knee-jerk reaction to the kid illustrates how the image of Compton has been dominated by Eazy-E and L.A.'s quasifascist county police chief Daryl Gates, both of whom use its depressed streets to justify their self-righteous paramilitary posturing.

What hasn't yet happened for Compton, or for most of contemporary African America, is the emergence of voices that convey the relationship between, say, a homestanding Grandma Forbes and the drug-dealing grandson Buddy within the context of a town like Compton. Maybe John Singleton will be the man. The bespectacled 23-year-old is a homie from black L.A. with a USC film school degree, representation from the powerful Creative Artists Agency, and a three-picture deal with Columbia reportedly worth nearly half a million. Singleton's good fortune can be traced to *Boyz N the Hood*, a screenplay whose title comes from an early N.W.A single, but whose sensibility is more *Manchild in the Promised Land* meets *Cooley High*.

*Boyz*, which takes place in Watts as well as parts of Compton, is about a bookish kid with a bad temper named Tre Styles, his separated parents, and a slew of friends living and dying in black L.A. The film begins with Tre at age 10, then jumps to when he's 17. We meet his nationalist father the mortgage broker, a virginal girlfriend with an eye on Spelman College, a football hero sweating his SAT score, and a whole bunch of crack dealers who range in personality from Ice Cube's evil to Flavor Flav's tomfoolery. A scene where kids battle over a football within spitting distance of a dead body captures the blend of the commonplace and the macabre that envelops everyday life in places as schizophrenic as Compton.

Singleton, who is touted by some as "L.A.'s Spike Lee," expects to be shooting this script in September. There's always a chance that the heat on him may cool—Hollywood is profoundly fickle. But to me it looks like he's got the youth and understanding to challenge Compton's knucklehead rappers on their own turf—to illuminate not just the town's sicknesses, but its soul.

VILLAGE VOICE, 1990

*Dee Dee and Buddy Forbes are pseudonyms.*

# TAKE BACK THE MIKE

**T**he rap panels at this year's New Music Seminar, just like those at every previous NMS, will be remembered—if anyone remembers anything once the schmoozefest is done—for voices raised in angry debate. Here's Tim Dog and his uptown posse, whose massive N.W.A dis "Fuck Compton" is selling briskly in New York and L.A., shouting at C & C Music Factory's Freedom Williams for complimenting N.W.A's production technique—and intimating that their audio smarts separate them from most New York groups. Or radio executives who do play rap clearly explaining the economic underpinnings of their programming decisions only to be confronted by angry questioners who insist that they play Brand Nubian, as if that one record constituted a hip-hop litmus test. Or Harry Allen inviting himself onto a rap panel, only to be dissed first by gay activist Jim Fouratt and then, quite effectively, by MC Serch for hypocrisy in his criticism of white rappers.

Despite the NMS's attempt to deemphasize hip hop—for the first time, the seminar declined to sponsor the annual DJ Battle for World

Supremacy, which drew about 500 onlookers to the China Club—the rap panels still generated the week's highest decibels. The subtext of all this fury was that New York, while rap's birthplace, is no longer its commercial crucible, and the homeboys aren't having it. In an article in *The Source's* new trade-magazine subsidiary, *Break Beat*, Tommy Boy president Monica Lynch wonders, "Has New York Fallen the Fuck Off . . . Or What?" The answer is not a total yes—the combined sales of Public Enemy, KRS-One, Heavy D., De La Soul, and others are still significant. But pop-rap (Vanilla Ice, Hammer), Compton rap (N.W.A, Ice Cube, DJ Quik), and dirt-rap (2 Live Crew, Too Short) mush the Apple in the face on the national tip. For two years in a row New York underground Gods—last summer Poor Righteous Teachers, now Brand Nubian—have proven as untranslatable outside the Northeast as, say, hi-NRG disco records were a decade ago.

The comparison is apt—the same purist snobbishness and cosmopolitan arrogance that detailed that wave of dance music nationally has seized the local rap mentality. As Ice Cube pointed out at one panel, Los Angeles radio has always played a varied menu of regional rap. New York, in contrast, has grown increasingly incestuous, self-important, and nostalgic. A botched old-school hip-hop-in-the-park event at 98th and Amsterdam was attended primarily by young blacks and whites who yearned for the glory days. The reality is that this city's victory in launching a worldwide phenomenon in no way guarantees its continuing dominance—what was once an urban cult is now a multinational commodity. It can't go back to what it was before. Run-D.M.C.'s *Raising Hell*, the record that proved to radio programmers, video outlets, and record labels that rap was marketable, ended that era. Just as Hollis and Long Island superseded the Bronx and Harlem musically, Los Angeles and Oakland have surpassed New York commercially. If rap is an art form, then New York should be happy making records it considers artistic and be satisfied with that. But if the bitching brothers and sisters at NMS still think they're in a business as well, they aren't going to get paid grabbing their groins and yelling, "New York is fat!" Sunbelt rappers listened to New York's dopest stylists and built off what they heard; to compete, New Yorkers are going to have to learn to listen back. If the city continues looking to the past instead of fighting for the future, the motherfucking saga will definitely continue—elsewhere.

# MICHAEL BIVINS
## Boy to Man

**E**ight years ago, when New Edition first played New York dressed in chintzy stage clothes and singing with all the verve of scared cats, I wouldn't have bet a penny on their future. Yeah, they could dance. But their untrained voices and ersatz Motown songs, courtesy of two then obscure Boston writer/producers named Arthur Baker and Maurice Starr, made these five youngbloods from Roxbury's Orchard Park projects seem like nothing but a novelty act. I remember watching them on "New York Hot Tracks" and shaking my head. Was this what the grand tradition of black harmony groups had come to?

That rhetorical question has been answered in the affirmative. Displaying a kind of durability, personal growth, and musical smarts few anticipated, New Edition begins this still young decade as one of black music's most important institutions. And like the bench player who turns out to be a great manager, the most visionary member of this quintet has turned out to be the guy initially considered least likely to succeed. Michael Bivins was a short kid with a bit of a speech impediment whose main vocal contribution on their first two albums was spoken bits on ballads and an occasional rap. Ralph Tresvant and Ricky Bell had better voices, Bobby Brown more charisma, and Ronnie DeVoe better looks. In press clips from the 1983–85 period, when New Edition–mania gripped pubescent black girls, Bivins's distinguishing trait is his insistence that he is a businessman. "I handle promotion and publicity," he says proudly in several fanzine pieces, which at the time seemed like a sweet way to make the kid sound interesting.

Wrong again. Bivins's Biv Entertainment—slogan: "There's no business like Biv business"—now produces or manages three of the hottest nonrap acts in black music: Bell Biv DeVoe, Another Bad Creation, and Boyz II Men. But what's even more impressive than the hits is the vision suggested by the approach of the music and the imagery of the groups. As performer and as entrepreneur, Bivins seems to be in one of those rare grooves where he's in sync with the ever-evolving psyche of black youth and, as in the case of the best crossover, spreading this culture to whites without condescension or compromise.

The sales of BBD (3.5 million on MCA), ABC (2 million on Motown), and Boyz II Men (1 million on Motown) invite comparisons with influential early-decade explosions led by Berry Gordy in the '60s, Gamble & Huff to start the '70s, and Prince's Minneapolis sound inaugurating the '80s. But though there's a musical unity to his hits, Bivins's success isn't tied to a particular locale or easily definable sound. Instead he promulgates a rude, hyperactive attitude that respects r&b harmony and rap energy, yet isn't as formulized as new jack swing quickly became nor as political as rap. Bivins's work doesn't have a radical thought in its head, but it's thick with rap's celebration of self, a giddy enthusiasm for women's body parts that's straight out of funk, and an enticing, slangy hipness.

The roots of Bivins's rise go back to 1987–88, the period surrounding the release of New Edition's N.E. *Heartbreak*, much of it produced by Jimmy Jam and Terry Lewis. Bobby, who'd split the group after some bitter disputes over direction with Bivins, made *Don't Be Cruel*, which five million copies later established him as the quintessential B-boy love man, while his replacement Johnny Gill was primed by Motown as the new jack Teddy Pendergrass. Meanwhile Ralph, for whom people had been predicting solo stardom since he was 15, was finally making his own record. Ronnie, Ricky, and Mike looked like the odd men out. But as old jokes that they'd all end up working for the Boston MTA resurfaced, Jam & Lewis, two gents who know a bit about redefining performers' careers (see Janet Jackson for reference), convinced them to record as a trio. This was seen as a joke by a lot of industry folks now kissing their ring. Why the hell were they wearing all that Timberland crap? And what exactly did "Smoothed out on the r&b tip with a pop feel appeal to it" mean?

Well, the little girls understood. Employing some big names (Bomb Squad principals Hank and Keith Shocklee and Eric Sadler) and talented newcomers (Dr. Freeze, Howie Hersh, Carl Bourelly), BBD enjoyed a string of kinetic, hedonistic, cleverly arranged singles that beautifully balanced Bell's thin yet committed vocals against Biv and DeVoe's sly spoken asides. Rarely on "Poison," "B.B.D. (I Thought It Was Me)?" "She's Dope," or "Do Me!" do the brothers rap hip-hop style. Instead they interject or chant, supported by Boyz II Men's four-part harmonies and fluid rhythm tracks that are hip-hop influenced but have a colorful musicality all their own. The "me and the crew used to do her" line in "Poison" irritates me, but otherwise this is a visionary record. Writer Dr. Freeze, a/k/a Elliot Straitel (who also penned Color Me Badd's "I Wanna Sex You Up"), has an understanding of drama and a cluttered yet controlled sound that obviously affected Bivins.

I say that because "Poison," the first single and title track from BBD's album, is the model for all the best moments on Another Bad Creation's *Coolin' at the Playground Ya' Know!* and Boyz II Men's *Cooleyhighharmony*. Unlike their goody-goody Motown labelmates the Boys, ABC are the Little Rascals of black pop. Watching this Georgia-born sextet scamper through their videos, sporting fresh cuts, Starter sports gear, and well-rehearsed scowls while singing the teeny-pop "Iesha" or kiddie-funk "Playground," I always imagine that this is Bivins's revenge on Maurice Starr. Instead of making them into the pseudo–Jackson Five of Starr's dreams (see New Kids on the Block for further reference), these kids are baaaaaad little dudes with beepers and the whole nine— in other words, like Bivins and the New Edition crew were offstage. Though thankfully not as naughty as BBD, ABC's two monster successes, written by Biv and the young producer/arranger Dallas Austin, have the same mercurial quality. It's short-attention-span music for a generation reared on the kinetic cutting of video—which in the case of both these groups was handled by black filmmaker Lionel Martin.

The same fast, intense style also fires up Boyz II Men's massive single, "Motownphilly," a hooky, densely arranged tribute to the rich r&b vocal group traditions of those two towns that features one of Bivins's trademark spoken-word bridges. But the strange thing about the most musically gifted of Biv's groups is that this Philly-based quartet is far and away the most boring. To possess real pipes is to face the challenge of using them creatively. But counterpointed against the munchkins' young leads, Boyz II Men's backing harmonies on ABC's "Iesha" are more fun than the mostly faceless singing on their own album. Boyz II Men are savvy enough to have a concept—*Cooleyhighharmony* is based on Michael Schultz's fine 1975 film, *Cooley High*— but not inspired enough to manifest it in any exciting way (see Take 6 and Sounds of Blackness for ongoing reference). And though they all sing better than Ricky Bell or Bobby Brown, not one of them is as individually engaging. Moreover, Bivins's eye for imaging, so deft when employed on the other two groups, fails him here. A fashion note, Mike: Pastels will never work on brothers.

With Bell Biv DeVoe, Another Bad Creation, and Boyz II Men, Michael Bivins proves a prime creator/reflector of '90s African Americans. The new decade is still defining itself, still finding a voice that's clearly not the '80s (though it might be the '70s). I believe the eclectic styling and sound of Biv's artists is a sign of what's to come. Check out "Word to the Mutha!," a cut on the BBD remix album WBBD—Boot City! that collects the entire New Edition posse, including Gill and Brown, on a high-spirited boastfest of singing, rapping, and talking about how large they are. Gill's gospel classicism, Brown's new jack attitude, and Tresvant's love-man tenor sound fine bouncing off the spunky rap-singing of their initiated groupmates. There is a synthesis at work on this track, and all the Biv business, that holds a key to a new direction in black popular music. I still look forward to New Edition's next album. But while I'm waiting, I think I'll lay money down on a pair of Timberland boots, just to keep up.

VILLAGE VOICE, 1991

# SCARFACE

**M**urder was at an all-time high when I visited Houston last August and the Sunbelt metropolis was paranoid. The week before, at a televised town meeting on crime, there was talk of an under-18 curfew (which has since been imposed). Everyone in town seemed to have a story of a recent rip-off—a car stolen, a home burglarized, a 9mm aimed at a chest. On the radio, morning men told bad jokes ("Two peanuts were walking down the street. One was a salted") before spinning the local anthem, "My Mind Playing Tricks on Me."

Way before New York paid attention, the Geto Boys were ruling the Southwest and it wasn't simply because the track was fat. Houston, and the entire state of Texas, was reeling from the pressure of unemployment, tri-racial polarization (black, white, hispanic), and crack, all of it intensified by damn near tropical heat. In the notorious Fifth Ward, where black folks live in Trenchtown shacks that make South Bronx buildings seem comfy, always plentiful guns were being squeezed off with a crazed rapidity only "My Mind Playing Tricks on Me" could explain. No words of Afrocentric unity were uttered. No dreams of upward mobility offered comfort. People were too afraid of everyone else—the police, their neighbors, local and imported gangs—to believe civic-pride rallying cries could stem the violence. The voices of Bushwick Bill, Willie Dee, and Scarface, especially Scarface, flowed through Houston's breathy humidity as heads nodded, community activists squirmed, and people cleaned the gun sights on their 12-gauges before Sunday dinner.

Scarface a/k/a Brad Jordan dominates "Tricks" with his matter-of-fact verses of self-delusion, schizophrenia, self-hate, vulnerability, self-destruction, and selfishness. His drug dealer narrator lives life in a cold sweat of paranoia. He kicks out his woman for dipping into his stash (or did she?), can't find solace in prayer or his family, and nightly sees himself (or is it other dealers?) lurking around every Fifth Ward corner, driving every jeep, haunting every sleep. His restless ramblings suggest a dude ready to squeeze off all right . . . on himself. (Something of a Geto Boy tradition. Last year, in an alcohol daze, Bushwick Bill handed a gun to his girlfriend and begged her to shoot him. He lost an eye.)

*Mr. Scarface Is Back* (Rap-A-Lot) takes the compressed imagery of "Tricks" and spills it over 12 raps that for thematic consistency and ghetto storytelling make Ice Cube's last effort sound mumble-mouthed. I'm not a fan of genocidal hip hop—black-on-black crime with a beat mostly leaves me cold—but Scarface's creepy embrace of the psychotic in himself draws me in against my will. "I'm taking all kinds of medication," he intones at one point, "to keep my mind off premeditation." Well, whatever he's taking, it ain't working. "Today I hit a nigga with a torch, shot him in the face and watched him die on his front porch." Where N.W.A's *Niggaz4Life* is as slick and psychologically empty as a Joel Silver action flick, Scarface's solo effort has a nuanced power I associate with *Henry: Portrait of a Serial Killer* or, perverse in a different way, the oft imitated ending of Sam Peckinpah's *The Wild Bunch*.

In fact some of Scarface's stories, set in the Southwest like Peckinpah's best work, could be blaxploitation scenarios. Using an Al Pacino sample as the hook, "Mr. Scarface" tells the bloody saga of a drug dealer, underground for six months, resurfacing to reclaim his turf in a sex and buckshot filled saga that could furnish the plot for *New Jack City II*. In "Good Girl Gone Bad," a con man who pulls a fast one on our narrator is hunted down and surprised at home in bed, asleep with his son. Showing a sliver of charity, Scarface takes the con man out to the bayou to kill him and keeps the boy, relating how the child "now calls me Poppa." In "Born Killer," Scarface, down on his luck ("I'm homeless/Ain't gotta phone, so I'm phoneless") and desperate for cash, decides to rob his old bank because, "They know me real good so they don't think I'd gank." These are just a couple of the bizarre bits from an album whose song titles ("Diary of a Madman," "Your Ass Got Took," "Body Snatchers," "Murder by Reason of Insanity," "A Minute To Pray and a Second To Die") would be funny, in a sick way, if I'd never been to Houston and seen how buck-wild Scarface's natural habitat is. Yeah, my man is pushing it crazily with lines like, "Dad said always look a man in the face before you kill him." But there is a gun-crazy depression-bred fever in Houston that is spreading faster than bankruptcy. When a yuppie mainstream filmmaker like Lawrence Kasdan can feel it in Hollywood's temple of denial, then Scarface doesn't seem all that outlandish.

By not hiding behind tired gangsta rapper cop-outs ("I'm just reporting what I see, you-know-what-I'm-sayin'?") and, with much resignation and sorrow, admitting his complicity in the violence, Scarface depicts a society stripped of all pretense of morality, where rugged individualism has corroded into survival of the illest. Scarface's Houston is a place where materialism has driven some residents mad with consumer envy and the Lone Star state of mind is now nihilism.

These declarations of decadence are spewed over tracks that, while not for one minute original in use of samples, use that familiarity to offer some relief amid Scarface's sardonic salvos. Musically the best moment here is "Money and the Power," a stomping, mid-tempo groove punctuated by a deep-voiced chorus chanting the title. Direct, virile, and hypnotic, this track is one of the only times that the production (courtesy of Doug King, James Smith, Bido, Crazy C., Roland, Sam, and Scarface) is equal to the rhyme.

Given this album's high body count and Scarface's low self-esteem it's no surprise the last song is titled "I'm Dead." Martyrdom is one of rap's major themes, since it symbolically links these entertainers with slain leaders and, quite practically, illustrates how cheap black male life is these days. Unlike Chuck D and Ice Cube, both of whom have depicted themselves hung or electrocuted by a vengeful state, Scarface wakes up one morning to the sight of one black man stabbing another with a butcher knife. Nothing unusual there—until he realizes he was the victim. "I reached to touch my face," he reports calmly, "but couldn't feel my beard stubble." Like most of the album this rap is surreal, dreamy, and accepting of casual violence. Neither angry nor political, "I'm Dead," like all of *Mr. Scarface Is Back*, is a sad postcard from the nation's underbelly, a place we're all becoming quite familiar with.

VILLAGE VOICE, 1992

# COOL VS. CHILLY

### PIMPS, PLAYERS & PRIVATE EYES JUICE

We used to round up our regular crew—Rob, Gary, Bland—count up our coins, and hop the IRT into "the city" on Saturday afternoons. Our destination was Forty Deuce and the moldy Times Square theaters where for $3.50 you could see two flicks and have enough money left over for a large buttered popcorn and a pack of licorice. The selection on the Deuce spanned the gamut of male adolescent interest. One theater, maybe it was the Selwyn, specialized in kung fu movies. There always seemed to be a new Fred Williamson jammie, something like *The Legend of Nigger Charley* or *Hammer* or even *Three the Hard Way*, which also featured Jim "Slaughter" Brown and Jim "Black Belt" Kelly. Often the black action flicks were paired with some macho white boy flick: *Death Wish* with *Superfly T.N.T.* or *Magnum Force* with *Trouble Man*. Forty-second Street between Seventh and Eighth in the early '70s—before the sale of trey bags gave way to red caps and the arcade on the south side of the street became a porno emporium—was our

playground. We'd hang into the night, absorbing every nuance of blaxploitation cool we could—envying Richard "Shaft" Roundtree's lanky
leather coat, Max "The Mack" Julien's perfect H-bomb Afro, and the
way Ron "Superfly" O'Neal made bubble-bath love to Sheila Frazier.

Of course the idea that we highly impressionable ghetto boys
would imitate what we saw on the screen was crucial to the controversy
these films aroused. And, I must admit, the cultural gatekeepers were
right: Blaxploitation films did have their lingering effects. Aside from
an appreciation for sensual bubble baths, I gained a lingering attachment to turtleneck sweaters, leather pants (only recently overcome),
and calling women "baby" or "babe" that now spans decades.

In my case, these films and their soundtracks also led me to a fascination with music as drama, rekindled by *Pimps, Players & Private Eyes*
(Sire/Warner Bros.), a compilation of songs from the blaxploitation era
put together by Ice-T and his manager, Jorge Hinojosa. On most of these
10 tracks, I hear tasty strings, pungent horns, wild wah wah guitars, bad-
ass bass lines, and haunting keyboards cocooned around the voices of
distinctive soul men to create sonic scenarios of groovy danger. The
intros alone to the Four Tops' "Are You Man Enough?" (from *Shaft in
Africa*), Bobby Womack & Peace's "Across 110th Street" (the title track
from one of blaxploitation's underappreciated gems), and Curtis Mayfield's "Pusherman" (from *Superfly*) cinematically evoke the cool but
lethal world of the films they supported. The verses boldly detail the
pleasures of being "a player," and yet, in keeping with the gospel heritage of the performers, offer optimistic alternatives and escape routes.
After chronicling the pimps, hookers, and junkies of Harlem, Womack
sings of "a better way out," then warns "take my advice to live or die,
you gotta be strong if ya wanna survive." The Four Tops' Levi Stubbs, in
the middle of a lyric outlining paranoia circa 1973, tells the song's super
baaad subject (and, by implication, the listener), "Someone needs a
friend, just around the bend/Don't you think you should be there?"
"Pusherman" starts as a celebration of a coke dealer's monied lifestyle,
then flips for the vocal bridge when Mayfield suddenly mouths the sentiment, "I know I can't take it. This life just don't make it."

So each song's drama emerges both from the arrangements—sudden pauses, surprising breaks, impassioned wordless singing over
instrumental passages—and the tension between the songs' gritty subject matter and the natural leaning of these church-reared singers
toward a message of redemption. In fact, despite the fly threads,
groovy chicks, heavy dudes, and nefarious white men of these films,
many of the most notorious ended with some form of cleansing. (In

*The Mack* pimp Max Julien returns South to the church; in *Superfly* Ron O'Neal's Priest quits dealing.) In blaxploitation music this celebration/rejection friction was a by-product of a transition between the gospel core that underpinned soul and the secular citified attitude that would partially replace it in the next (now current) generation.

Marvin Gaye's "Trouble Man" (from the like-named detective flick) is easily the most complex *P, P & P* track musically and lyrically. Soft and seductive, the song swingingly blends minor chords, scat singing, big band brass, boppish piano, and soaring flutes into a sound that defies categorization. Lyrically, Gaye provides a coolly articulated defense of street life that unlike his peers, he never once apologizes for. "I didn't make it, baby, playing by the rules," he croons subtly, managing to imply a vision that the rappers who sample his music use eight lines to crudely announce. Even more laconic is Isaac Hayes's Oscar-winning "Theme From Shaft." Its terse interplay of horns, wah wah guitar, and cymbals is one of the most identifiable motifs in African American musical history. The lengthy intro, which in the film plays as Roundtree wanders the same, now ancient Times Square I first watched *Shaft* in, is as well-shaped as my man's sideburns. And Hayes's memorable incantation ("He's the black private dick who's a sex machine to all the chicks") still haunts the world of black macho, informing the perceptions of chocolate love men like Big Daddy Kane and Wesley Snipes. (Can Wes's own *Shaft*-like vehicle be far behind?) The rest of *Pimps* is split between quality soul ballads (Millie Jackson's "Love Doctor" from *Cleopatra Jones*, Willie Hutch's "I Choose You" from *The Mack*) and sub-standard stuff (O.C. Smith's "Blowin' Your Mind" from *Shaft's Big Score*, Hutch's "Theme of Foxy Brown," the Impressions' "Make a Resolution" from *Three the Hard Way*) that'll cure nostalgics of any illusions about the '70s easily waxing the '90s.

For further insight into the Clash of the Odd-Numbered Decades, check out *Juice* (Soul/MCA), the soundtrack supervised by Soul Records president Hank Shocklee and Kathy Nelson. One is immediately struck not by the obvious generation gap, but by a profound age gap between them. Blaxploitation, like soul music, was by and about adults. The true player—pimp or detective, male or female—was a person of experience. Blaxploitation's characters and musicians were products of the Southern migration soured by the lack of opportunity in the big cities. *Juice*'s four teen protagonists, and the majority of the 14 acts on the soundtrack, are blaxploitation's children whose street values are no longer challenged by the Christian church. The secular values of by-all-means-necessary survival have replaced the Ten Commandments.

The dominant personality of *Juice*'s music is, much like Tupac Shakur's hooded Bishop, a teenage male in search of respect and on constant guard to protect his shaky self-esteem, untroubled by moral constraints against verbal or physical violence. There are four r&b cuts on *Juice*—the retro-nuevo funk of the Brand New Heavies with N'Dea Davenport on "People Get Ready," the new jack swing of Teddy Riley and Tammy Lucas on "Is It Good to You," the gospel inflections of ex–GUY lead singer Aaron Hall on the "Can't Truss It" clone (check that bass line) "Don't Be Afraid," the hip hop doowop of ex–Furious Five member Raheem on "Does Your Man Know About Me." However, with the exception of the surprisingly agile Rahiem track, the arrangements lack the inventive nuance of their blaxploitation forebears.

Clearly it is the rap material and the B-boy mentality that's the true focus of the soundtrack and film. Claustrophobic, cynical, and callous, the important hip hop on this album is as cold-blooded as blaxploitation was cool and complicated. Some cuts are proudly homicidal (M.C. Pooh's "Sex, Money & Murder," Cypress Hill's "Shoot 'Em Up") or criminal minded (Naughty by Nature's "Uptown Anthem," EPMD's "It's Going Down," Too Short's "So You Want to Be a Gangster"). All chronicle a world with no pity and no escape. The one attempt at a "positive message" is the Juvenile Committee's "Flip Side," which talks of unity but is simply too weak to compete. Tellingly, in director Ernest Dickerson's clearly anti–black-on-black crime film the most arresting marriage of music and image is the house party where the wounded DJ Q stalks Bishop as Cypress Hill's "How I Could Just Kill a Man" pumps on the soundtrack. The matrix of music, fun, and danger in that sequence strikes a chord that captures hip hop's romantic embrace of violence.

The only track that manages to equal the drama, both musical and lyrical, of the best blaxploitation themes is Eric B. & Rakim's "Juice (Know the Ledge)." The thumping jazz bass, flute samples, and Eric B.'s judicious scratches give the cut a necessarily foreboding atmosphere; Rakim's rap voice is as piercing and intelligent as any soul star's, and his contrast of verses documenting his criminal largeness with a chorus that foreshadows his own death is in the tradition of Womack and Mayfield without compromising hip hop hardness. On "Know the Ledge," Rakim, a man of God (in this case Allah) and a poet, lives in the space between then and now, a tricky balancing act that, as time passes, gets more difficult every day.

# THE NEW STREET ART

**T**he Adventures of Grandmaster Flash on the Wheels of Steel" (Sugarhill 12-inch) captures the spirit and creativity of the city's summertime block parties better than any record I've ever heard. It does this by unleashing Flash's magic turntable technology and recording it for the first time, a task which took five days. Nothing on "Wheels of Steel" is new—all its techniques were developed and refined in basements and clubs around the Apple over the past five years—but for it to be documented on vinyl for the world to hear, study, and dance to, warms my heart.

"Wheels of Steel" begins with "You say one for the trouble," the opening phrase of Spoonie Gee's "Monster Jam," broken down to "you say" repeated seven times, setting the tone for a record that uses the voices and music of Chic ("Good Times"), Queen ("Another One Bites the Dust"), and the Sugar Hill Gang ("8th Wonder"), and "Birthday Party" as musical pawns manipulated at Flash's whim. He also repeats Deborah Harry's "Flash is bad" from "Rapture" three times, turning her dispassion into total adoration. When Flash Plays "Another One Bites the Dust" he puts a record on his second turntable, shoving the needle and the record against each other to produce a rumbling, gruff imitation of its bass line. As the guitar feedback on "Dust" builds so does Flash's rumble and then (throwdown!) we're grooving on "Good Times." Then "Freedom" explodes between pauses in Bernard Edward's bass line. His bass thumps and then the Furious Five chant "Grandmaster cuts faster." Bass. "Grandmaster." Bass. "Cuts." Bass. "Cuts." Bass. "Cuts . . . cuts . . . faster." But for me the cold crusher occurs about four minutes into its 5:49. During "8th Wonder" Flash places a wheezing sound of needle on vinyl in the spaces separating a series of claps. That, my friends, is art.

And Grandmaster Flash is a true street artist.

VILLAGE VOICE, 1981

# WORLD CULTURE

**R**ap records aren't primarily about the rap. They're about the intensification of rhythm, about how much beat you can stand before your mind explodes into angel dust and your legs crumble to the dance floor. And though this usually means echoes of Africa, deejays know that black folks aren't the only ones with a sense of rhythm—in a club like Disco Fever in the Bronx or in a park like the one across from my mom's house in Brooklyn, any beat by anybody has a shot. Check out "Positive Life," a Tay-ster 12-inch by Love Bug Starski & the Harlem World Crew. Starski's rap is OK—the Wolfman Jack parodies are the highlights—but the music ...

The Harlem World Crew, if that's what the band is called, begins by playing the bass line from Teena Marie's "I Need Your Lovin' " amid yells and congas. The rhythm changes and—breakdown!—it's the Police's "Voices Inside My Head," with horns carrying the melody, more Teena. A McDonald's joke and then back to the Police. Teena again. Congas. Now bells and congas suggesting the eight bars of Bob James's "Mardi Gras" that has turned his Bob James 2 album into a $50 item on the beat market. Now a single-note guitar like that for maybe six seconds mimics another deejay favorite—one of the percussive guitar riffs on Aerosmith's "Walk This Way," which may be Joe Perry's only contribution to world culture. The last section of note is a funky-drummer solo obviously inspired by the floor-tom theatrics of Harvey Mason put down behind George Benson's "On Broadway." Cut to Wolfman Jack. End.

In seven minutes Starski and crew have gone over a lot of ground, but not as much as I've heard him and other deejays cover on a good night. Rapping and its music were born on the street, but the street's ears reach beyond Central Park North. "Positive Life" won't sell as many copies as "Rapture," but because this reverse steal is done with such flair, the Starski will sleep at night. Or whenever he goes to bed.

# GRANDMASTER FLASH

## Flash Is Bad

**H**ip hop and rap have become interchangeable terms, but they are really different, though kindred, sons born of the same streetwise daddy. A rap record is a hip hop record. A hip hop record is not necessarily a rap record. Let me define my terms: Rap records are dominated by the tone and/or words of the rapper, while the music, basically variations of current hot street rhythms, can be in balance with the rapper's voice or may highlight it. However, if the music overwhelms the words it's probably not a rap record but a hip hop record. Let me give an example: The album version of "It's Tricky" by Run-D.M.C. is a rap record that uses a rock guitar as part of its rhythmic arrangement, yet the voices and the words are way out front. The 12-inch remix, on the other hand, is a hip hop record, because the mixer Shep Pettibone stuffs the track with all manner of reverb and echo while remaining surprisingly true to the original's rawness.

Where rap is a performers' music that succeeds because of attitude, articulation, and rhymes, hip hop is ruled by the producer-mixers who *hear* with the percussive instincts of a rapper, but can transfer the sound into more mainstream recordings. What you see now are producers and engineers who first worked in rap becoming part of the pop r&b scene, which they're infusing with their rap sensibilities. They program drum machines, arrange synthesizers, mix and remix in a way that makes it hip hop dance music, say in the style of Full Force's big-beat girl-group productions for Lisa Lisa & Cult Jam ("I Wonder If I Take You Home"). The dynamic works both ways; mainstreamer Larry Blackmon's designer funk on Cameo's "Word Up!" and "Candy" wouldn't be possible without rap.

Grandmaster Flash & the Furious Five, the graybeards of rap and hip hop, founded this dichotomous institution. "The Adventures of

Grandmaster Flash on the Wheels of Steel," which features Flash cutting together grooves and verbal phrases from a slew of rap and nonrap singles, is pure hip hop; it is rhythm as montage, with beats and rhymes colliding into and complementing each other. The less innovative but highly effective "Larry's Dance," a summer 1985 jam, has a rap on top, but it's the stuttering Flash-arranged beat that is most important, hence hip hop. Of course, this group's greatest record, "The Message," is also one of the greatest raps, whose ominous synthesizer arrangement accentuates its images of apocalyptic chaos—the words are the thing, hence rap.

In the days before Run-D.M.C., Whodini, and even the Beastie Boys usurped the crown, Grandmaster Flash & the Furious Five were the kings of rap. Unfortunately their reign ended when Melle Mel, the political soul and rapping heart of the Furious Five decided to stay at Sugarhill when Flash split for Elektra in 1982. While Melle Mel's career has, so far, been swallowed up in Sugarhill's legal entanglements with the IRS, Flash has made three disappointing albums that are all hip hop, no rap. That is not to say that the current *Ba-Bop-Boom-Bang* doesn't have rapping on it: A mix of old Furious Five vets and newcomers provide the voices. It does mean that those voices are thin and uncommanding; their raps about smelly underarms, designer jeans, and self-help are wack. Flash coproducer Larry Smith—a man who made great raps ("Sucker M.C.'s") and hip hop ("Five Minutes of Funk")—provides a textbook study of rap/hip hop production with beefy drum programs, cartoonish synthesizer frills, and Flash scratching in the studio. But Smith alone can't save the record from artistic failure. Smith's wall-of-sound doesn't fill the verbal void for a very simple reason. All rap is hip hop, all hip hop isn't rap, but a rap that's all hip hop is a bad rap.

VILLAGE VOICE, 1987

# RAKIM AND ERIC B.

## Hyper as a Heart Attack

**I**t is my contention that William Griffin, better known as Eric B.'s rapper, Rakim, a 19-year-old resident of Wyandanch, Long Island, with an interest in Islam, is the deffest rapper around. But before praising Rakim a digression is in order. Too many people who profess to like rap don't distinguish among its many historic and stylistic differences. Only by placing Rakim in context do you appreciate his mastery. Here it is:

**The Old School:** Either contemporaries of, or originally inspired by, the first hip hopper, D.J. Hollywood, they include Eddie Cheeba, Love Bug Starski, Grandmaster Caz, and Kurtis Blow. This generation popularized the party clichés—"Throw your hands in the air and wave them like you just don't care" and "Somebody/Everybody/Anybody scream!" With the exception of Blow none of these pioneers made the transition to record, because so much of their style was based on interplay with a live audience. A lot of old-school techniques came from glib radio jocks (particularly the early '70s WWRL crew of Gerry Bledsoe, Gary Byrd, and Hank "The Dixie Drifter" Spann). The only survivor who still has juice is WBLS's Mr. Magic, whose "Rap Attack" is a B-boy version of r&b radio.

**The Rockers:** This approach is defined by bombastic Hollis crew members Run of Run-D.M.C. and L.L. Cool J. Like most good middle-class music makers, these guys traffic in overblown rebellion for the legions who buy attitude as much as music. Run and L.L. are loud, nervous, kinetic; both sound freshest over minimalist rhythms occasionally spiked with guitars. Larger than life, almost cartoons really, they are rappers as arena rock stars.

**Velvet Voices:** If they were singers, Heavy D., Public Enemy's Chuck D, Whodini's Ecstacy, Kool Moe Dee, Melle Mel and D.M.C. would be labeled baritones or low tenors. They are authority figures who lecture (Chucky D, Melle Mel), instruct (D.M.C., Kool Moe Dee), and seduce (Ecstacy). The heightened masculinity of their timbres can make a limp rhyme hard. The most underrated is Ecstacy, who has the widest emotional range in this crew, and the most promising is Heavy Dee, whose "Mr. Big Stuff" made fat-rap fly again.

**Clown Princes:** Given the right rhyme any rapper can be funny, but Slick Rick, Dana Dane, and Beastie Boys King Adrock and Mike D. specialize in yucks. Slick and Dane started in the Kangol Crew, an unrecorded rap quartet in which they perfected upper-class British accents, slurred pronunciation, and female impersonations of "The Show" (Slick) and "Nightmares" (Dane) done over tracks rife with reference to TV themes and nursery rhymes. They're amusing in a Redd Foxx–like way, though charges of sexism are well-founded. Same thing can be said of MCA and Adrock, though the laughter usually tempers the cringing. Adrock's mousey voice is the illest instrument in rap.

**The Showmen:** Biz Markie, with his dance, skull, throat-beatboxability, and goofy glow, must be seen to be appreciated; his Apollo performance of his new single, "Pickin' Boogers," was a nose-opener. The wholesome Doug E. Fresh is still more human beatbox than rapper, yet when you combine his rhymes, sound F/X, harmonica, dancing, and Cheshire cat smile, it's clear Fresh is one of the music's most versatile live performers. No question, Doug E. Fresh is the Sammy Davis, Jr., of hip hop. Give him another great record, and he'll house all these m.f.'s.

**Cutting Edges:** Rather than loud and boastful, these voices are cool, conversational, and threatening. The overrated Schoolly D, the quick-witted King Sun ("Hey Love"), and the vet Spoonie Gee ("Godfather," a rare comeback) all have casually incisive deliveries. But the real edge, the master rapper of 1987 (damn near '86), is Rakim, a man qualified to narrate the cassette versions of Donald Goines's *Daddy Cool*, Chester Himes's *Real Kool Killers*, and the collected works of Iceberg Slim.

Rakim's intonation itself conjures wintry images of cold-blooded killers, chilly ghetto streets, and steely-eyed hustlers. There's a knowing restraint in his voice that injects danger into even harmless phrases. Eric B. and Rakim's debut single last summer, "Eric B. Is President"/"My Melody," on Harlem-based Zakia records, was as stunning a first statement as Run-D.M.C.'s "It's Like That"/"Sucker M.C.'s." The groove of "President" was gritty wop fodder while Rakim's rap (including the sandpapery comment "You thought I was a doughnut/You tried to glaze me") presented his credentials. Better still was "My Melody," in which, riding over a sleazy rhythm, Rakim devastated the mike with a boast equal parts vinegar, bullshit, and Islamic allusions.

*I take seven MC's, put them in a line*
*Add seven more brothers who think they can rhyme*
*It'll take seven more before I go for mine*
*Twenty-one MC's ate up at the same time*

On the strength of that 12-inch Rakim was a challenger for the rap king title. Now *Paid in Full* (4th & B'Way), Rakim and Eric B.'s first album, certifies that Rakim ("Taking no prisoners/Taking no shorts") uses his deadpan tone and quiet fire to dis the old school, cut the clowns, make the velvets sound velour, and cold rock the rockers. Throughout *Paid in Full* there are moments when Rakim's voice and words, complemented by Eric B.'s dictionary of James Brown beats, make mesmerizing hip hop. For example, the opening of "I Know You Got Soul" is an apology, challenge, critique, and invitation: "I shouldna left you/Without a strong rhyme to step to/Think of how many weak shows you slept through/Time's up! I'm sorry I kept you."

*Paid in Full* contains no rock 'n' roll or overt comedy cuts. On "I Ain't No Joke" Rakim slides between long sentences ("I hold the microphone like a grudge") and terse rhymes ("You're right to exaggerate/Dream and imaginate"), a strategy that speeds up and slows down his syncopation, much like a saxophonist moving through a long solo. On "Move the Crowd" the choppy snare drum and funky horn sample inspire Rakim to use short phrases that suggest a rhythm guitar. Over the "Don't Look Any Further" bassline Eric B., establishing once and for all that he's a DJ and not an MC, introduces himself on mike before leaving Rakim to talk about money or, as he puts it, wonder "How I can get some dead presidents." Unlike most current rap albums, where all five rap styles appear, Rakim undermines all the distinctions with a sinister vitality. It's such a strong personality that over the course of, say, three albums he may find himself becoming a parody. But for now when he asks, "Who can keep the average dancer hyper as a heart attack?" you know the answer.

# NATIONWIDE

## America Raps Back

**R**ecord industry types used to ask me, "How long will this rap thing last?" They don't any longer. Not when three different hip hop tours played to near-capacity crowds at sports arenas and concert halls across America last summer. Not when they can look at *Billboard*'s black album chart last November and see that eight of the top 30 albums are by rappers, including three top 10. Not when their kids ignore Marlon Jackson, the Bar-Kays, and Shalamar for the simple pleasures of U.T.F.O. and Kool Moe Dee.

Rap, and its hip hop musical underpinning, is now the national youth music of black America and the dominant dance music of urban America, with the possible exceptions of Washington, D.C., spawning ground of the hip hop influenced go-go scene, and Chicago, with its retro-disco house music. Rap's gone national and is in the process of going regional. That seems like a contradiction, but it's actually easily explained. Rap spread out from New York to attract a loyal national audience. New York rapped and America listened. Now America is rhyming back.

Over the last year and a half labels like Miami's Luke Skywalker, Houston's Rap-A-Lot, and Boston's Beautiful Sounds have emerged, independent record companies nurtured by local rap scenes and often fighting losing battles for radio play in their areas. While creatively these cities have yet to spawn Def Jam/Rush level stars, these fruitful hip hop markets will inevitably produce talent with national appeal. Dallas and Houston, Cleveland, Detroit, Philadelphia, Miami, and even Los Angeles, can, according to Def Jam promotion vice-president Bill Stephney, "outsell New York on certain records."

At last summer's raucous hip hop competition at the New Music Seminar, it was clear that there was more to rap than Uptown. Three of the four finalists in the scratching DJ throwdown were from outside

New York: Philadelphia's Cash Money, who, with MC Marvelous, cuts for Sleeping Bag; Los Angeles's Joe Cooley, who works with rapper Rodney O; and Miami's Mr. Mix, of the notorious 2 Live Crew. Though none of the out-of-town rappers made the finals, several were among the most memorable, including Detroit's Robert S., who's recorded two poorly promoted 12-inches on Epic; Philadelphia's well-regarded M.C. Breeze; and Cleveland's Bango the B-Boy Outlaw, who'll be heard on the soundtrack to Dennis Hopper's Los Angeles gang melodrama, *Colors*, in late February.

The reasons for rap's growth are easy to trace. First, there's the music; direct, raw, easy to emulate. Equally important have been New York rap tours, and not just the big arena extravaganzas of recent years. When Kurtis Blow and Grandmaster Flash hit the road in the early '80s, they helped create a new chitlin' circuit of teen appeal clubs and auditoriums. Because it was so inexpensive to book rap acts—Blow travelled with just a DJ and a road manager—dates were possible not only in small venues but, in towns like Gary, Indiana, and Lake Charles, Louisiana, a rapper could play multiple dates in one night. So the generation of rappers and scratchers now emerging first tasted hip hop up close and personal.

In each city where rap's appeal has expanded there have been key figures who've fought authorities, peer pressure, and local inferiority complexes. In Cleveland WZAK program director (and sometime rapper) Lynn Tolliver has been on point since the early '80s by fearlessly programming rap at all hours, where many other PDs try to limit it to late hours. In Philadelphia (first at WHAT and now at WUSL) DJ Lady B has been "the Godmomma" to the most impressive community of rap talent outside the Apple. Because Lady B has always played homegrown talent beside New York honchos, Philadelphians became aware of local groups and purchased their homies' records. Because of Lady B's advocacy Jive Records has invested heavily in Philadelphia hip hop in the past year, signing Schoolly D, Steady B., and Jazzy Jeff & Fresh Prince. In Miami a homeboy using the handle Luke Skywalker founded Luke Skywalker Records, which is anchored by the ultra-raunchy 2 Live Crew. Their ribald *2 Live Crew Is What We Are* was so lyrically foul several localities sought to ban it (and even got a record store clerk arrested down South for selling it), yet it was the first non–New York area rap album to sell over 500,000 units. (I don't count Whodini's three made-in-London albums since they all involved New York talent.)

Of all the regional hip hop catalysts, I've found two—Houston's

Steve Fournier and Los Angeles's Jorge Hinojosa—the most interesting because of their ambition, energy, and location. Fournier is a stocky, bearded white Texas DJ who five years ago fell in love with rap. He landed a gig at a big barn of a dance hall called Rhinestone's and, because of his "110 per cent rap" policy, the place became the Gilley's of hip hop. Recently Fournier moved to a new barn, Spud's of Houston, where he still plays to crowds as large as 2,000 seven days a week. There's very little rap played on Houston radio, so Fournier's club play constitutes the medium of most exposure for rap, not just in Houston, but in the Southwest.

But Fournier wants more. Like many non–New York rap entrepreneurs he seeks the respect of New York and acknowledgment of his area's importance to rap's future. As a result Fournier has founded the Rap Commission, a national record pool based in Houston with offices in New York and Los Angeles. Fournier, of course, heads it and acts as a conduit for rap records to reach the DJs and club jocks scattered around the country. The Rap Commission would then have the most comprehensive list to date of labels, club jocks, and radio outlets for hip hop. The idea that such an institution would be run by a white man in Texas makes many brothers here in the Apple bristle, as if Fournier's efforts were an affront to the black roots of rap. Fournier feels that's simply New York chauvinism. "Texas is centrally located in one of the biggest hip hop markets," he says. "There are tons of local groups here and I think acts like the Geto Boys, Jazzy Red, or R.P. Cola are competitive with New York and Philly but don't have the national exposure. Hey, New York is still where it was born, but the rest of the country has something to contribute."

Not surprisingly, one of Fournier's chief supporters is another non–New Yorker, young half-Bolivian hustler Jorge Hinojosa. Often described to his chagrin as "a West Coast Russell Simmons," Hinojosa has an enthusiasm and quick wit reminiscent of Rush Productions' founder. Hinojosa manages the city's best known rapper, Ice-T (whose *Rhymes Pays* on Sire has sold over 300,000), signed an L.A. rap compilation album called *Rhyme Syndicate* to Warner Bros. (it includes a 20-page comic book highlighting L.A. hip hop), and is the top rap promotion man there. (He broke Salt-n-Pepa's "I'll Take Your Man" in L.A. and worked the early Mantronik records for Sleeping Bag.)

"I never wanted to be a manager," he says, "but when I worked at Island Records Ice-T and his producer Afrika Islam couldn't get signed there. I begged Island to sign him. When they didn't I quit my job to work with him." In the early '80s New Yorkers considered Los Angeles "too soft" to be a factor in hip hop, and those horrible Cannon break-dance flicks (*Breakin'* and *Electric Boogaloo*) seemed to confirm Southern California's cotton candy approach to street music. But the tone and, as a result, the image of the city's street culture has changed profoundly. The tension between lower class black, Latino, and Asian youth in LaLa-land has created a mean streets lifestyle that embraces rap's hard edge, sometimes explosively, as in the notorious gang riot during a Long Beach rap show in 1986.

Hinojosa, aided by the heavy rap programming philosophy of KDAY's Greg Mack, has capitalized on the growing awareness that East Los Angeles has its own street culture, one equivalent to the East Coast. That the West Coast–based Warner Bros. signed Rhyme Syndicate (and recently negotiated a distribution deal with New York–based Cold Chillin' Records) is, to some degree, a byproduct of Hinojosa meetings with El Lay's once suspicious record executives.

Hinojosa, Ice-T, who was born in Newark but raised in Los Angeles, and former Soul Sonic Force member Afrika Islam formed a team, one that anticipates the future of hip hop. Hinojosa, a resident of the San Fernando Valley, is an upper-middle-class kid with business savvy; Ice-T is street, but L.A. street, with long red hair and raps that refer to West Coast scenes; and Afrika Islam, who was once a Bronx fixture but is now living and spinning in Los Angeles, brings New York expertise to Ice-T's music. As a unit they illustrate the local flair, old school style, and ambivalence that mark this phase of non–New York hip hop.

I say ambivalence because Ice-T recorded his album in New York, subconsciously confirming the idea that quality rap can only be recorded here or with New York involvement. Moreover, too many non–New York rappers "bite" the styles of Run, the Fat Boys, Slick Rick, L.L. Cool J, etc., failing to localize the music. Case in point: *Boston Goes Def!* on Beautiful Records. It contains 15 cuts from different rappers, yet there are only two specific references to Boston. A shame, since the beats, samples, and verbal dexterity of the rappers, overall, are as good as anything you'll hear on Magic or Red Alert's shows this weekend. Of the Philly crew Schoolly D is the most belligerently local. On occasion he writes quite powerfully about the violent world of *his* Philadelphia (e.g. "P.S.K.") detailing a landscape specific and personal. Moreover, he is contemptuous of New York's superstar rappers, rarely performing here or even traveling north for business meetings with Jive. If Schoolly D can consistently funnel that anger into good music—which, alas, he hasn't—then he could set the tone for a new non–New York hip hop. To date the most effective non–New

York rap record is that controversial 2 Live Crew album. To my ears it was crude on all levels; the raps were witless ("Throw the 'D'"), the elocution sloppy, and the recording quality awful. Yet its fast tempos (surely influenced by Miami's enduring disco romance), in-yo-face words, and down-home flavor made it, for a time last spring, the South's hottest rap record. And, maybe, that's the point. The rap that'll surely flow from down South, the Midwest, and the West Coast will not, and should not, feel beholden to what came before. Just as hip hop spit in the face of disco (and funk too), non–New York hip hop will have to use its own accent, its own version of B-boy wisdom, if it's to mean anything. After all, New York is already paid in full.

VILLAGE VOICE, 1988

# BOBBY BROWN

## Bad Boy Makes Good

A few years back your faithful narrator worked on *Cool It Now: The Authorized New Edition Biography* (Contemporary Books, now available in leading discount bins). In the course of compiling this quickie I discovered that these kiddie stars were no Osmonds, but worldly products of Boston's hardcore Orchard Park projects in Roxbury who identified as strongly with Run-D.M.C. as they did with their ostensible role models, the Jackson Five.

Disputes with their managers (my contractors) made writing the book a fine balancing act. A more weighty conflict, though, was growing between Bobby Brown and several members of the New Edition posse. Brown's idols were Rick James and Cameo, and when he took his nightly solo, using funk vocals and hip hop attitude, he ripped right through New Edition's bubble gum. In his heart Brown was no Jermaine Jackson to Ralph Trevsant's Michael; my man was really Larry Blackmon. So when Brown split New Edition it wasn't news to me. What did shock me was the word someone put out on the kid. The buzz was that Brown had bad habits, bad manners, and no future. A less than promising solo debut, *King of Stage*, yielded a squeaky hit, the ultra-teenybop ballad "Girlfriend," but little evidence that Brown was maturing as a musician or man.

Which is why it's pleasing to say that *Don't Be Cruel* (MCA) is *so* dope. One reason is "My Prerogative," among the most acerbic and hard-edged nonrap singles since the fall of P-Funk. "Everybody's talkin' all this crap about me/Why don't they just let me be," he snarls with an arrogance worthy of L.L. Cool J or, well, hell, even Wilson Pickett. Over stinking, smelly, plain old noisome Teddy Riley keyboard grooves, Brown delivers testimony to selfhood as fierce as anything Muddy Waters threw down. Like so much black male music, "My Prerogative" is more than a cock-strong and cunning celebration of ego—it's a plea for respect.

That Brown and Riley kick ass isn't surprising. Like Al B. Sure! and Keith Sweat, both are new jacks who fuse hip hop and r&b, the most progressive new wing of black pop. Crucial here is that Brown's sense of self is strong enough to personalize L.A. Reid & Babyface's computer-chip production. L.A. & 'Face damn near define radio's "hot" format with Peebles ("Girlfriend," not Brown's), Karyn White ("I Love the Way You Love"), Paula Abdul ("Knocked Out"), the Deele ("Two Occasions"), and a million more. But on "Don't Be Cruel" and "Roni," Brown dominates. He raps on both, injecting East Coast street vibe into the seamless West Coast grooves. Reid & Babyface clearly adapted to Brown, writing material such as "Roni," short for *tenderoni*—females sweet, sexy, and probably underage.

Even when L.A. & Babyface provide the usual clean-shaven r&b—"Rock Wit'cha" and "Every Little Step"—the effect is neither mechanical nor saccharine due to Brown's sass. The rest of *Don't Be Cruel* is not as nasty or satisfying. Of the remaining four tracks, two are worth conversation: "Take It Slow," produced by Larry White, is an old-fashioned drag that Brown chills through, though his Isaac Hayes love-man rap sputters. He's warmer and more convincing on "All Day All Night," a beat-box ballad.

Brown, now 20, has come to terms with himself and his old mates. Still, at the Garden October 27, opening for New Edition and Al B.

Sure!, Brown was petulant ("They only gave me 25 minutes! 25 minutes!"). He was sexual (took off his shirt with Rick James–like flair). And he was funny ("Everybody under 13 put your hands over your ears! This is for the adults only!"). Singing with a raw, earthy tenor, even deeper than the record, and dancing nastier (more grit than superlover Al!), Brown did serious damage. The highlight wasn't the *Don't Be Cruel* material but a sped-up, more nuanced interpretation of "Girlfriend," rescuing it from the kiddie scrap heap. When I wrote that book, Bobby Brown was a hyper kid. What I saw at the Garden was a young man with a future.

VILLAGE VOICE, 1988

# KOOL MOE DEE & L.L. COOL J

## I Versus I

At a Ladysmith Black Mambazo concert in Central Park two years back, I asked a South African brother what one especially gorgeous song was about. He told me it was about how dope they were. Not exactly in those words, of course, but several Mambazo songs celebrate the group's badness. Under those glorious, ethereal 7UP commercial harmonies, in other words, they were grabbing their dicks. I found that reassuring—maybe boasting is just in the bones of brothers. That urge traveled with us on the slave ships, inspiring the blues, spawning saxophone cutting contests, sliding into the heads of Little Richard and James Brown, and leading rappers to ejaculate mouthfuls of *I*s. Boasting is a black male essence, a verbal one-upsmanship that thrives in the dozens, that noble, street-corner endeavor. If your *I* is supreme, then what does that make my *I*? A sucker? Undoubtedly.

Hip hop is a world of *I* opposing *I* over microphones aimed like Uzis. Be it East Coast versus West Coast, Bronx versus Brooklyn, activists versus gangsters, rappers versus r&b, hip hop exists in a state of perpetual combat, constantly seeking sucker MC's to define itself against. Last summer's verbal warfare between Kool Moe Dee and L.L. Cool J raised the urge to art. Moe Dee got the party started last year with the cover art on his second album, *How Ya Like Me Now*, where a jeep has run over L.L.'s then trademark red Kangol. On that LP's title cut, Moe Dee accuses L.L. of "biting my rap style" and other heinous breaches of decorum. L.L. answers back on "Jack the Ripper," a furiously paced bit of disrespect ("How ya like me now, punk?!/ I'm gettin' busier/I'm double platinum, I'm watchin' you get dizzier"). Moe Dee came back with "Let's Go," a delightfully dishy dissertation on what L.L. stands for (lousy lover, lazy and lethargic, etc.), which should be used in English classes to illustrate alliteration. After Moe broke a copy of "Jack" at the Apollo, there was a buzz about a Wrestlemania match.

While negotiations continue, Moe and L.L. are going mike-to-mike in two other arenas: sales and artistry. Can L.L., coming off the triple-platinum *Bad* and platinum *Radio*, hold off the challenge of Moe Dee, whose breakthrough *How Ya Like Me Now* went platinum? On the sales tip, L.L.'s *Walking with a Panther* (Def Jam) has more than a million copies, while Moe Dee's *Knowledge Is King* (Jive) has moved 650,000 units, giving the boy wonder a substantial lead. On the art tip, the battle is keener. That *Knowledge*, Moe's third, is his best, isn't saying much. *How Ya Like Me Now* had two dope jams (the title cut and "Wild Wild West"), a couple of semis, and plenty of filler. Everything on the first half of *Knowledge* hits hard, along with one solid uppercut in the second. L.L.'s *Panther* misses more, but he throws more punches, 16 on vinyl, 19 on CD, 20 on cassette. The decision? Let's go round by round; I'll describe, then decide.

Moe Dee, a member of the defunct old-school crew, the Treacherous Three, reaches high levels of self-glorification. Three of the 10 tracks start with *I* ("I Go to Work," "I'm Hitting Hard," "I'm Blowin' Up"). Three others have opening lyrics that begin with *I*. Yet it's not a suffocating ego; "Knowledge Is King" and "Pump Your Fist" are jams about uplifting black folks, reflecting Moe's role in the Stop the Violence Movement's "Self Destruction," the all-star rap charity single.

His natural braggadocio and good intentions sometimes conflict: "The lust for money is out of control," he observes on the seemingly heartfelt "Pump Your Fist," yet on the desultory "Get the Picture" he boasts, "I'm rollin' over rappers like a U.S. tank/Meanwhile laughin' all the way to the bank." Brashness plus humor make the autobiographical "They Want Money" less a misogynistic anthem than a clear-eyed depiction of parasitic sisters in a pitched battle with one materialistic male (a/k/a Moe). Similar in approach, but more complex, is "The Avenue," easily the album's triumph. It begins with a repeat of "Money"'s she-devil griping, then becomes a prose painting of an uptown strip where cops and kids face off over cars and crack.

My major beef with *Knowledge Is King* is that it sounds too clean. Producers Moe Dee, Teddy Riley, manager LaVaba, and Peter Q. Harris have concocted sleek tracks that, particularly on side two, percolate without punishing. Still, as the heir to Whodini's mantle as black radio's favorite rap act, Moe continues to grow qualitatively. Yet if he really wants to blow up, the man needs more sonic versatility.

In contrast, L.L.'s *Walking with a Panther* suffers from sonic sprawl, too many sounds and too many songs. Along with Dwayne Simon of the L.A. Posse (and several cuts cowritten by Public Enemy teammates Hank Shocklee and Eric Sadler), L.L. grabs at greatness and winds up with hubris. "1–900–L.L. Cool J" has a super funky groove that's ruined by the conceit of girlies calling him for bits of purple poetry. On one song L.L. asserts he's "so bad I can suck my own dick," a line so boldly narcissistic it even shocked other hip hoppers. Similarly, the awful ballads "Two Different Worlds" (which is going to be a hit, so bet it) and "One Shot at Love," along with the up-tempo "Nitro," are oversaturation with the regal attitude that makes him the rapper that other rappers love to hate.

But let's give the kid some credit; he's conceived eight, maybe nine, jams that challenge Moe cut for cut. "Fast Peg," only three minutes long, is a vivid closeup of a sepia gun moll with "a D.C. haircut and stewardess legs" who drives around "in a kitted up Jetta. Under the seat an automatic Baretta/You know the whole blah-zay blah," and who takes a bullet for her drug dealer boyfriend. A crisp short story, it chills. "I'm That Type of Guy" is a lean, mean-spirited item that works because of his sultry spoken delivery and the sullen groove. "Brenda's Got a Big Ole Butt" is an honest story of one young man's lust for booty in which the narrator, quite up-front with ex-girlfriends and impending conquests, screws his big head off (and, at least once, uses safe-sex techniques!). "Jingling Baby," with its crazy fresh Dennis Coffey "Scorpio" sample and cute female voice on the hook, will sound great on the radio. While he's never matched the frenzy of "Rock the Bells" from his '85 *Radio,* on the wah wah guitar heavy "Clap Your Hands," his rhymes flow with that earlier energy. Other hype moves include "Def Jam in the Motherland" (propelled by MFSB's "Love Is the Message") and "You My Heart," the only good ballad.

But for some the *Panther* centerpiece will be "Jealous," the fourth L.L. versus Moe Dee bout. After the rapid fire of Moe's "Let's Go," L.L. decides, quite maturely, to utilize supple disdain. In a voice more conversational than confrontational, he refers to Moe as "dog doo doo," "a backstabber," and other not-nice things, with a smooth male chorus intoning "Jealous, jealous . . . " Firm and condescending, L.L. ends the track talking with homie E. Love about chilling with a bottle of champagne, as if Moe isn't worth his time. If only more of this nonchalant cool was apparent on *Walking with a Panther,* he'd be right. As it is, I'm afraid this judge scores the bout a split decision.

VILLAGE VOICE, 1989

# GOIN' OFF IN CALI

Universal Amphitheater, Los Angeles County, July 28, approximately 10:00 P.M. L.L. Cool J is rhyming for several thousand whites, blacks, and latinos. The stage comes complete with flashing lights, dancing girls, and guest rapper Busy Bee playing Flavor Flav to L.L.'s Chuck D. But the Crips in the house don't care where the show is supposed to be. In the arena's darkness a posse of 10 to 15 of them, their blue colors no longer camouflaged under black caps, jackets, and jeans, reveal themselves. Not long afterwards a scuffle ensues and a brother in a white Le Coq Sportif sweatsuit goes down. I don't see what or who started it, but I see the result. Four security guards carry him through a side door and lay him on the ground. He's dark-skinned, about six feet tall with short hair, but unfortunately his most distinguishing characteristic is now a large red dent in his left temple. His nose and mouth, like his once white jacket, look dipped in crimson.

Inside the arena the show proceeds. Rap crowds, despite the anarchy sometimes surrounding the music, usually manage to ignore or at least distance themselves emotionally from any violence. Tonight is no exception. This multiracial gathering remains cool even as the Crips march down toward the front of the stage, each man grasping the shoulder of the man ahead of him. A team of about 15 thick-armed security men in white T-shirts blocks them just before they reach the standing section in front of L.L. and Busy Bee. With the house lights on and security now alert, the Crips stand on chairs and flash their hand sign toward the stage as L.L. rips through "Rock the Bells."

Standing backstage as paramedics and police speak with the victim, I stare at him and feel my stomach quiver. A booking agent and vet of 10-plus years of hip hop business stands by me. "You should have been at Long Beach, at that Run-D.M.C. show," he said, referring to the infamous gig where warring gangs faced off during Whodini's set. "The group wouldn't go back on the stage," he recalls, "and I didn't blame them. I mean guys were literally being thrown out of the balcony onto the stage. I am not kidding."

The early leg of the L.L. tour, which featured Compton's own N.W.A and Eazy-E, was beset by a police fax campaign spreading the lyrics of the antibrutality parable "Fuck tha Police" to precinct houses across America. Not surprisingly, this resulted not only in angry cops and lots of no-shows, but in the usual paranoid press. In fact, however, "rap violence" is a journalistic cliché that conceals the bitter truth, especially in the City of Dreams: Rap is just another venue for the gangs' performances. The image of the Crips flaunting their strength, cocksure they could roll on the guards and, at the very least, shut L.L. up with one furious bum rush, will stick with me as a symbol of L.A.'s brutal youth culture. But every day the front page of the *Los Angeles Times*'s Metro section, which should be called "Gang Bang Digest," chronicles the open warfare in east and south-central Los Angeles. A far nastier item during my recent visit west described a Sunday service disrupted by a three-man hit squad shooting up four parishioners. There's no more apt metaphor for the hold gangs have on local youth.

Gangs are a religion in L.A., and the faithful are as contemptuous of opposing belief systems as Christians are of Islam. The church shooting is no isolated incident—it mirrors the schism between old black tradition and new jack nihilism.

"Out here four things are thought to make you a man," says anti-gang activist Ron Johnson. "Getting a girl pregnant, taking a life, surviving prison, and joining a gang. Those are real goals that Crips, Bloods, and everyone else takes seriously." Johnson, who moved to L.A. from New York four years ago, feels the level of black-on-black interpersonal brutality out there is worse than anything back east. "There is a lot of culture and history just in the air in a place like New York. There's a real nationalist cultural influence. The gangs fill those cultural gaps here."

Johnson's hope for degangsterizing L.A. is "to politicize the gangs, to make them sort of a black army." I like Johnson's heart, but I'm not sure his idea is any more practical than Tom Bradley's steel-versus-steel approach. Certainly the police can't intimidate the gangs out of existence. Gang sweeps, usually race-based teen roundups, don't address the social and economic disaster facing this grossly segregated town. Nor, it should be noted, has the uncharismatic presence of a black career public servant as mayor. The usual urban ills of crappy schools and substandard health facilities, compounded by the crack-financed gang expansion, turn black and Latin youths into both predators and prey. Spending on social programs in Cali never recovered from Proposition 14. The money for the job training necessary to move blacks into the area's high-tech aerospace or low-tech furniture industries is channeled instead into stopgap projects like building a convenient prison in the heart of the black community—or the recently completed "escape-proof" jail downtown, where five guys broke out two weeks ago.

Moreover, and this is an important lesson for the Apple, there seems to be no moral imperative, from elected officials, from the well-to-do west side, or in the press, for meaningful change in the lives of poor Los Angeles. Predictably in the state that's spawned both Ronald Reagan and S.I. Hayakawa, people who say gangs must be stopped are talking about Uzis, not classrooms. In their destructive insularity, the L.A. gangs recall the wild young men of A Clockwork Orange. But what frightens me even more is the next step of the parallel—the government's quasi-fascistic response. Gangs are viewed solely as criminal collectives when they are also self-sustaining extended families that provide self-worth and the illusion of security.

It's easy to understand why kids embrace institutions created by themselves and for themselves which stand up to threatening forces within and outside the community. That's the logic of Public Enemy's gunsight logo—one reason young black men flaunt guns is that guns really are aimed at them. But obviously, terrorizing everybody outside the clan is no way to achieve true self-worth, and that syndrome has only gotten worse since crack turned gangsterism into a growth industry. Los Angeles is not New York, as Johnson said. But don't think our gang problem won't get a lot worse. The sense of generational alienation that rap both suffers and expresses is not dying. It's multiplying, nationwide.

VILLAGE VOICE, 1989

# RAP'S 10TH BIRTHDAY

Ten years ago this past summer the Sugar Hill Gang's "Rapper's Delight" was on the radio, and, in Brooklyn's Birdel's on Nostrand Avenue, owner Joe Long was selling boxloads of 12-inches. The single was hitting so hard and fast that Sugarhill Records hadn't even made logos yet; they slapped on orange stickers with so little information it made them look like bootlegs. I remember Joe smiling and saying that "Rapper's Delight" was "the hottest thing in the street in a long time."

Ten years ago in SoHo's earth-toned Greene Street studio, accustomed to hosting John Cage and Phillip Glass, two *Billboard* magazine employees, Robert Ford, Jr., and J.B. Moore, were recording a record called "Christmas Rappin'" with a Harlem homie, Curtis Walker, a/k/a Kurtis Blow. Bassist Larry Smith (later to produce Whodini and Run-D.M.C.), Joey "Son-of-Kurtis Blow" Simmons (later Run of Run-

D.M.C.), and Blow's manager Russell "Rush" Simmons (later rap's biggest manager) were among the many then-obscure folks who stopped by to joke, laugh, and ponder the recording process. Rap records? Well, it had worked for those no-talent Sugar Gangers. Still, we wondered if anyone would buy more than one rap record.

Ten years ago, at a schoolyard in the South Bronx, Cool Herc rolled up in a van with turntables and records. A crowd of kids waited. After plugging his equipment into the base of a streetlight, Herc scratched beats from "Bongo Rock" and *Shaft in Africa* and other obscure records until well after dusk. Surprisingly few people danced. Most of the overwhelmingly male crowd hovered around the turntables, peeking over each other on tiptoes and trying to figure out which records contained which beat.

Ten years later I can see rap's triumph not simply as musical but as social. It crystallized a post–civil rights, ultra-urban, unromantic, hyperrealistic, neonationalistic, antiassimilationist, aggressive Afrocentric impulse reflecting the thoughts of city kids more deeply than the celebrated crossover icons Michael Jackson-Bill Cosby-Oprah Winfrey et al. This was music funneled through Bruce Lee, Mr. Magic, Bootsy and George "Dr. Funkenstein" Clinton, *Scarface*, Sylvia Robinson, Magic versus Bird, Jesse Jackson, Ed Koch, James Brown, *A Clockwork Orange*, Malcolm X, Pee-wee Herman, Nelson Mandela, Frankie Crocker, Michael Jordan, "Miami Vice," and the Smurfs. It emerged cartoony, antimelodic, brooding, materialistic, entrepreneurial, chauvinistic, user-friendly, genital conscious, and always spoiling for a fight.

Hip hop became the catchall for the culture of clothes, slang, dances, and philosophies that sprang up in the '80s. But rap on records—words as rhythm, weapon, metaphor—represented a new worldview just as soul music did in the '60s and disco, sadly, did in the '70s. Rap, however, isn't a music. It's a cultural black hole able to suck up r&b, rock, go-go, house and, soon, Third World rhythms without losing its combative personality. Every time I've thought its energy was flagging, new beats ("Planet Rock," "Sucker M.C.s," "Eric B. Is President," "Bring the Noise," "It Takes Two," "Me, Myself & I") made things hectic all over again.

For me rap was a professional and aesthetic inspiration. The first two pieces I sold to this paper were on DJ Lovebug Starski and Grandmaster Flash & the Furious Five, and it was rap that got me bylines at several other publications. Rap's ability to be righteously, uncompromisingly black yet speak to mixed audiences proved to me the power of undiluted African American thought, both as a celebration of our people and a critique of the whitebread mainstream.

The question is no longer, "Will rap last?" but "Who will control it?" The major labels' racial and class prejudices kept them out of rap well past the time its commercial viability had been proven. Now MCA and Atlantic, following the lead of CBS and Warner Bros., are signing every halfway decent act they can. The number one record on *Billboard*'s black album chart this fall is by D.O.C., a Los Angeles–based rapper on Atlantic. That he's number one is no surprise—he's part of the super-hot N.W.A-Eazy E posse—but that he's from Dallas and on Atlantic, considering this genre's East Coast and indie record company roots, is a sign of the new times.

It is also potentially quite troubling. One of the elements that diluted r&b in the last generation has been the majors' noisome meddling. Too many records issued—too many bad records issued—too little personalized artist development, too many folks promoting and marketing it with zip understanding of its audience or traditions, led r&b into a creative impasse that, lately, only hip hop–influenced producers have unblocked.

Equally wack, black radio has yet to fully understand this movement. Rap shows are slotted in fringe time, rarely receiving primetime airplay corresponding to its sales. Because of this I-don't-want-to-know attitude, black radio will confuse bad rap with good, because it hasn't developed the aesthetic judgment to tell them apart. These quality-blind priorities are especially dangerous when major labels push lame acts like the Fat Boys and J.J. Fad.

To proclaim the death of rap is, to be sure, premature. But the farther the control of rap gets from its street-corner constituency and the more corporations grasp it—record conglomerates, Burger King and Minute Maid, "Yo! MTV Raps," etc.—the more vulnerable it becomes to cultural emasculation.

**VILLAGE VOICE, 1989**

# GHETTOCENTRICITY

## DE LA SOUL

If Professor Molefi Asante's philosophy of Afrocentricity means placing Africa at the center of one's thinking, then ghettocentricity means making the values and lifestyles of America's poverty-stricken urban homelands central to one's being. While much hip hop of the last four years has been assertively Afrocentric, since the days of D.J. Hollywood rocking Club 371 live in the boogie-down Bronx this genre has been proudly ghettocentric. Not surprising since rap was first performed by and for children of the Bronx and upper Manhattan. It was that "hotel, motel, Holiday Inn" hedonism that sparked its spread, leapfrogging it around the Northeast, across the country and oceans, east and west.

Of the many subgenres and local scenes rap has inspired none has been as surprising or potent as the crew of hip hoppers produced on Long "Strong" Island. If you factor in the Hollis Crew, whose home turf isn't far from the Queens–Long Island border, Run-D.M.C., L.L. Cool J, Davy D, Public Enemy, EPMD, and Eric B. & Rakim have all come from home-owning, civil-service-job–working, black middle-class environments. But with the exception of some of Run-D.M.C.'s early rhymes, the specifics of that life—private colleges, malls, white girlfriends, and a certain wariness/envy toward city kids—are missing from their work. Instead, this crew has been as ghettocentric as Chester Himes's Coffin Ed and Gravedigger Jones novels. Whether these brothers were all just intrinsically hardcore or, God forbid, fearful of sounding soft, the underlying absence of any exploration of black suburbia is as characteristic of Strong Island hip hop as dope beats.

Except, of course, on De La Soul's 3 *Feet High & Rising*, which in 1989 augured a revolution. It was awesomely arty ("Da Inner Sound Y'all"), laid-back and smart, enticingly obscure to those outside the Native Tongue clique (which is why one wanted to be inside), embracing of women as lovers and equals (as on "Buddy"), and so clearly alternative even R.E.M. fans had to give it props. That record's tongue and cheekiness, combined with Pos, Dove, and Mase's dread embrace and paisley-and-daisy-profilin' anti–B-boy look, turned out hip hop style. It was hip hop bohoism as only self-consciously idiosyncratic middle-class kids have time to manufacture. Critically acclaimed, commercially successful, and fashionably large, De La Soul's debut charted a new direction in rap and, one hoped, would steer its multiracial audience away from knee-jerk ghettocentricity.

But a funny thing happened to this trio on the way to CD number two. For one thing, their stage show was tired. Producer Prince Paul's sonic collages and the band's low-energy delivery, brilliant on a Sony CD player, translated into a static, way-too-precious concert hall persona. Moreover some fool booked them on tour dates with the likes of N.W.A, rap's most influentially nihilistic posse. Crowds wearing Raider gear when it still signified hard core activity and gathered to shout "We Want Eazy!" didn't give a fuck about these Day-Glo dreads. And the dissing continued backstage. Rap stars, flunkies, and fans stepped to De La Soul all across the country because they were hippies.

So if *De La Soul Is Dead* (Tommy Boy) sounds bitter, it's no affectation. Though the samples are still incredibly clever and De La's rap style still distinctive—slinky stuttering, silly smart, thoughtfully sloppy, and much imitated—the tone of this second effort is dark, dismissive, and, yeah, more ghettocentric than expected. They spend a lot of time boasting about their fighting prowess on "Oodles of O's" and "Pease Porridge." On "Afro Connections at a Hi 5" they go after the Hollis Crew with a viciousness that suggests a long simmering feud, shouting with glee that the Kings of Rock are falling off because of their "rhythm & bullshit!" "Ring Ring Ring (Ha Ha Hey)" is about being sweated by new jack rappers with demo tapes, and while it swings, it sends out an unbecoming message of I'm large arrogance. It's the kind of song Grand Funk Railroad used to write about groupies, hardly the original insight you'd hope for from these brothers. De La Soul's emotional masterpiece is "Millie Pulled a Pistol on Santa," the sad story of a girl whose sexually abusive father works as Santa Claus at Macy's. Technically its deadpan narrative is the equal of anything on *3 Feet High & Rising*, yet the title and subject of "Millie" testifies to the dark side of the Soul.

The group's previous flower power panache isn't entirely gone. The cool rocking "A Roller Skating Jam Named 'Saturdays' " and "Bitties in the BK Lounge" are both wonderful slice-of-life vignettes that suggest that when their rap career is over, De La Soul could write skits for Keenen Wayans. Yet when you listen to the collection's most significant songs, plus the spoken word bits that fill out its 80 plus minutes (e.g.: parodies of rap and Quiet Storm radio), this project is definitely hard edged even when it's not hard core.

After 3 *Feet High & Rising*, De La Soul seemed a much needed antidote to N.W.A, the Geto Boys, and the rest of that genocidal brew spilling forth at the time. Moreover, by rejecting the ghetto as the center of their thought De La Soul suggested an alternative for black consciousness at a time the dogmas of a quasinationalist gangsterism had currency. But that De La Soul *is* dead. In order to prove their manhood to challengers who thought them soft (in all ghettocentric meanings of the word) and maybe even to themselves, De La Soul have opted for a semimacho stance at odds with their landmark introduction. It's understandable, even prudent considering the state of the world today, to drop the daisies and clench the fists. *De La Soul Is Dead* is a response to the sad, inescapable fact of 1991: The world is a ghetto.

VILLAGE VOICE, 1991

# POP LIFE

Joint-ski (not his real name) is a New York hip hopper in good standing: he's made more dope records than wack, has toured the world (all the way to Albuquerque), and, yes, has even been interviewed on "Yo! MTV Raps." He's not jumbo yet, but he's on the way to getting bigger and deffer.

Like most rappers, Joint-ski is into "fly" girls in jingling gold earrings, baggy pants, and just a bit too much eyeliner. Remarkably, he's not obsessed with light-skinned girlies—his last two women were both petite and chocolate brown. But don't get him wrong: If one of those crazy dope white models who come to the Thursday night Car Wash parties was seeking a sensual uptown experience, he'd be with it. And Joint-ski is no macho boaster, though in his heart of hearts he'd like to be. He's only 19 and he still hasn't defined his identity in hip hop or the world: Will he be Big Daddy Kane's younger brother or the latest member of the funky dread vanguard?

So Joint-ski isn't your typical rapper. But he's like a slew of other rappers in one significant respect. Joint-ski's father, a man who exited his life when Joint-ski was a kid, now wants to hang with him. "Yeah, he's been calling me," Joint-ski said quietly one evening on the street outside his record company's Manhattan office. "Tells my Moms, 'It's time we got to know each other.' She says it's just because I'm making money. I don't know. He is my father, know what I'm sayin'?"

It goes a little something like this. When these rappers were your average nappy-headed little black boys living in Brooklyn, Harlem, or the boogie-down Bronx, Pops stepped off on Mom. The reasons for these ruptured unions vary, but in the '60s in New York City fractured black families were hardly an unusual event. I know 'cause my name-sake took off, too. In my case, and I suspect in quite a few others, the culprit was the bright lights–big city syndrome that has pulled so many Southern-bred brothers out of their homes and into the streets—the same urban temptations their sons rhyme about.

Joint-ski doesn't know if that's what led his father to mess up and basically doesn't care. What's clear is that from kindergarten to young manhood Pops was, at best, a fleeting presence who'd tease with promises of time and money, and then disappear into a netherworld of unreturned phone calls and missed birthdays. Hip hop parties, and the crew of rappers, DJs, dancers, security guards, and roadies that roll with them, came to fill that male vacuum in their lives. So much of rap's sexism, nationalism, and boasting is about groups of unmentored young men coming to terms with a hostile world and defining, passionately, foolishly, nakedly, just what kind of men they should be.

Pops began calling when Joint-ski emerged from New York's pile of wannabe stars into the dollars and sense of a record deal. Pops told him he needed advice and guidance, and the benefit of "living in the world" only a father could provide. Joint-ski's mother wasn't one bit happy about this. Back when Pops skipped, he not only left his five-year-old kid, but he abandoned a woman who'd committed her life to a marriage. Since then, much of that love has been focused on nurturing and protecting her son. That Joint-ski was even considering her erstwhile husband's offer smacked of betrayal.

Yet for many rappers the deep-seated desire for their fathers' attention (and implicit rejection of their mothers' counsel) overrides all. Absence makes their hearts grow anxious. Today, several top rappers—I know at least three others—have once wayward fathers involved in managing their careers. Are they qualified? Hell, no. Do their sons crave this newfound attention? You know it.

Joint-ski, however, isn't going for it. After some agonizing, he stepped to his father and told him, face to face, "I don't know you. I don't need your friendship. I got friends."

Joint-ski's decision was practical, one made with his mind more than his heart. But don't expect to hear this tale told on CD to a dope beat. Joint-ski can't bring himself to rhyme about it. He's thinking about calling his album *It's My World*, but there are parts of his world listeners will never dance to.

VILLAGE VOICE, 1990

# 2

# MEDIA IMPRESSIONS

# CRITICAL CONDITION

The Universal Cineplex Odeon is one of the new temples of American moviegoing. Perched atop a hill in Burbank that abuts the huge Universal Studios backlot and theme park, the theater's 18 screens attract viewers from the San Fernando Valley as well as Los Angeles proper. It's the ultimate multiplex, a mass entertainment venue designed to house consumer-friendly product like *Backdraft* and *Robin Hood*. But things are changing. On line, two very Valley girls fret about whether the 10 o'clock show of *Jungle Fever* will be sold out and smile in anticipation of Ice Cube (Cube to them) appearing in the forthcoming *Boyz N the Hood.*

Later, inside one of the cineplex's main rooms, a medley of sepia-tinted future features constitutes the coming attractions: Danny Glover plays straight man to Martin Short in *Pure Luck*, Morgan Freeman backstops Kevin Costner in *Robin Hood* and, most disturbingly, Richard Pryor teams with Gene Wilder again in *Another You*. What's upsetting isn't simply that Pryor and Wilder are plowing old ground again *(Silver Streak, Stir Crazy,* and *See No Evil, Hear No Evil)*—a senior studio executive once told me Hollywood was in the "pulp" business—but that Pryor looks like a zombie. In the clip, he rarely speaks—mostly we see the great comic in various bits of wide-eyed gasping and excitement, or, in a recurring image, blowing a feeble sax. He looks skinny, his face drawn and caked with makeup, and there's not a spark of energy behind his eyeballs. Amid all the hoopla about black film '91, the appearance of the most brilliant African American comedy star of all time in what may be his swan song shouldn't go unnoticed.

At 50, Pryor, who last month had triple-bypass surgery in Los Angeles after a decade of poor health, seems never to have truly recovered from his freebase-induced flame-up in June 1980. He's still made films and indulged in the flip-flops from woman to woman that have scarred his personal life. But what of stand-up comedy, the realm where he did his greatest work and remains peerless? Since his last album, 1983's *Here and Now*, he has neither recorded nor toured, though in the late '80s he slid onto the Comedy Store stage on occasion to do a set or two, sending waves of unfulfilled anticipation through the comedy underground.

But in the last decade, a time when his art should have expanded, he—like Sly Stone, his peer in artistry and drug addiction—became a fond memory for over-30s and a tragicomic legend for new jacks. In their new biography of the comic, *If I Stop I'll Die* (Thunder's Mouth), novelist John A. Williams and his journalist son Dennis chronicle Pryor's life in a brisk, thoughtful, but far from comprehensive 219 pages. Though the Williamses' book is not the close study Pryor's complicated career warrants, its narrative helps us focus on the key postfire failures that now obscure their subject's legacy.

One, simply put, is that Pryor let greed overcome his self-respect. He did the ghastly *Superman III* for $4 million, and, for nearly as much, consented to do *The Toy*, in which a white millionaire bought Pryor's black character for his son—the most embarrassing role played by a brother since the cooning days of Willie Best. Over and over (*Brewster's Millions, Critical Condition, Moving*) he took big bucks to portray jittery, insecure, high-strung protagonist-victims far removed from the complexity of his onstage routines—just as Eddie Murphy was developing his cocksure persona, too. Pryor's estranged black manager David Franklin tells the Williamses, "You can put a pound of shit here and a pound of gold and Richard, for some reason, will take the shit every time." With the exception of the self-directed, autobiographical *Jo Jo Dancer: Your Life Is Calling*, Pryor has never attempted a cinematic equivalent of his profound monologues.

The '80s were a tragedy for Pryor not just as an artist, but as a symbol of African American empowerment in Hollywood. His relationships with the two most important blacks in his business life, Franklin and Jim Brown, both ended in bitter disappointment. Pryor's stewardship by Franklin was a historic one—the pairing of a black superstar with a rising young member of the race's professional class was initially hailed as trendsetting. Though the association finally ended in a flurry of lawsuits over financial mismanagement, the Williamses are sympathetic to the view that Pryor chafed under Franklin's close scrutiny, particularly his disapproval of the star's drug abuse.

Ex-football and movie star Brown was both Pryor's best friend and the president of the comic's landmark Indigo Productions. In 1982

Columbia Pictures gave Pryor unprecedented power—Pryor got $40 million to make four films with total artistic control. (The script for one, *The Charlie Parker Story*, was later directed by Clint Eastwood as *Bird*.) It was a deal no African American filmmaker had before or since. The only results: his third concert movie and *Jo Jo Dancer*. By December 1983 Brown was fired, and within two years Indigo had evaporated back into Columbia's corporate ledgers. Some of the brightest lights in today's black Hollywood—actor-director Robert Townsend, producer George Jackson—worked with Indigo. It's not inconceivable that the company could have incubated the current boom all by itself. Alas, Indigo, like so much of Pryor's Hollywood experience, is more about what might have been than what was accomplished. At the end of the biography, the Williamses express the fear that, given Pryor's recent track record, he'll be mistaken for a clown by those unaware of his earlier artistry, much as Louis Armstrong was during his later years. In truth Pryor may have become just that—a man who's lived longer than his genius.

VILLAGE VOICE, 1991

# UP FROM INTEGRATION

**W**alking through the hallway of East Flatbush's Meyer Levin Junior High School in the early '70s, I received an unwelcome compliment. I had a bathroom pass, probably from Spanish or math. So I was out sightseeing: peeking in classrooms for friends, making faces at teachers, and looking at the trophy cases from the days when Meyer Levin was dominated by Eisenbergs, Rubins, and Dubinskis.

I was tapped on the shoulder by a "hall lady," one of the white-haired local residents who habitually directed patronizing smiles and a judgmental air at us dark "bus-pass kids." She wanted to know why I wasn't in class. I smiled, handed over my pass for inspection, and answered her accusatory questions without rancor. This took her by surprise. Apparently she expected me to try to stare her down, curse her out, or employ some other tactic used by black kids to keep the easily intimidated in check.

Her curiosity increased. With that mix of nasality and European accent that once defined ethnic Brooklyn, she peppered me with questions. "No," my father wasn't at home. "Yes," I was from the projects. "No," we weren't on welfare. "Yes," I was from Brownsville. This last response always generated first melancholy and then disdain from the middle-aged Jews I encountered in East Flatbush. She too had grown up in Brownsville ("when it was a fine place to live") and had shopped over on Pitkin Avenue, which she pronounced "Pit-kin" and everybody I knew in the 'Ville called "Pick-in." To the hall lady, my Brownsville was a distant planet inhabited by strange, dangerous people.

But being of liberal heart, she was willing to make an exception, because I was articulate and polite and told her my business. And as she sent me on my way she offered her blessing: "You aren't like those other kids from Brownsville, so keep it up." I've never forgotten this, and have pondered its subtext ever since. She was declaring me "assimilated," which in some ways I was. I already knew the right things to say and how to conduct myself in a way whites would accept if not respect. Yet despite my good manners and her stamp of approval, I wasn't any whiter in my eyes or hers than my comrades from the projects. Wrestling with the implications of her judgment has been a big part of my life.

As I've discovered over the years, many other spawn of the post–civil rights years have dealt with similar feelings. Separated by speech, style, outlook, opportunity, and, ultimately, money from the boys in the hood, these folks—some reared in traditional bourgeois families, some acquisitive buppies, some just plain bright—are now articulating their sagas between covers. These are not the nationalist, Afrocentric, and neo-Islamic works that fill the shelves of black bookstores and the tables of sidewalk vendors with tales of ancient glory and anti-European interpretations of history. They come from mainstream publishers and are intended for readers, white and black, who want evidence not of rage and separation but of individual pluck, racism overcome or perhaps ignored. White liberals tell readers what

poor folks already know about this nation's Third World despair—
Nicholas Lemann's *The Promised Land*, Alex Kotlowitz's *There Are No Children Here*, Jonathan Kozol's *Savage Inequalities*, Leon Bing's *Do or Die*. In comparison, these are introspective chronicles of the pursuit of life, liberty, and happiness in prep schools, Ivy League colleges, major corporations, the law, and that tight space where cultural mulattoes reside.

Shelby Steele's *The Content of Our Character* is the seminal text, the *Up From Slavery* of the Reagan decade. It's been followed by Lorene Cary's tale of a black prep-school girl, *Black Ice*; Stephen L. Carter's *Reflections of an Affirmative Action Baby*, a front-page feature in the *Times Book Review*; and Patricia J. Williams's *The Alchemy of Race and Rights: Diary of a Law Professor*, a deft blend of autobiography, pop-culture observation, and legalism from Harvard University Press. Jake Lamar's *Bourgeois Blues*, whose title is self-explanatory, will be published this month, and two upcoming autobiographical novels also fit the mold—Trey Ellis's second novel, *Home Repairs*, about sexual escapades among the young, elite, and tan, and Dennis Williams's *Crossover*, another revealing title. *Blacks in the White Establishment?*, Richard L. Zweigenhaft and G. William Domhoff's scholarly study of the ABC program that once placed ghetto kids in tony prep schools, is stuffed with minibios of current black corporate executives reflecting on 20-plus years of oft-thwarted upward mobility. *Kaffir Boy* author Mark Mathabane's *Love in Black and White*, cowritten with his wife about their interracial marriage, continues his journey from oppressed South African to Westernized sophisticate. And the hottest black book of all is *Makes You Wanna Holler* by Nathan McCall, a memoir of his evolution from robber to *Washington Post* staffer, which garnered a $500,000 advance from Random House and $200,000 from Columbia studios and John Singleton. McCall's book sounds like a throwback to *Manchild in the Promised Land*, but according to book biz sources, his postcriminal journey is what hooked publishing houses.

The purchase of McCall's work is one of the rare links between the mass market and these assimilationist texts. In this period of high African American media visibility, they represent an alternative. Even the most benign hip hop artists engage in dick-grabbing, air-humping, and other semitough postures, and the three top-grossing black films of the year (*Boyz N the Hood*, *New Jack City*, *Jungle Fever*) are rife with crack, obscenity, and violence—ghettocentricity packaged for multiculti mall consumption. The "Cosby," "Oprah," and "Arsenio" shows, on the other hand, are inoffensive, viewer-friendly products whose stars have reached the "not really black" stage. But these authors are neither homies nor MOR. They are self-conscious, smart, constantly measuring themselves vis-à-vis white competitors and black peers, concerned with history but suspicious of political and racial dogma. They are fixated on the ebb and flow of their everyday race relations, not with the police or the landlord, but with college professors, white-collar executives, white lovers. These are tales told not from the belly of the beast, but from the barely integrated mountaintops of academia, law, and mainstream journalism.

So while some publishing pros see these books as part of the over-all black culture boom, they obviously aren't intended for the same audiences that admire Furious Styles or Cliff Huxtable. Like Wynton Marsalis's New Orleans trilogy or the Urban Bush Women's diaspora dance experiments, they're for a select, demographically slender elite. To label them buppie books is too pejorative and too narrow, though they are products of an era that made black urban professionals possible. I doubt they will have much philosophical impact outside their intended market. But as the generational and political distinctions within the African American community sharpen, Steele, Carter, and the rest loom as lovely targets for separatists. If you're into conspiracy theories—and they're proliferating in black America today—their assimilationist slant and overt or implicit antinationalism are certain to incite the fiery.

# FORTY ACRES
# AND AN EMPIRE

## Spike Lee Plants the New Motown in Brooklyn

The week before the recent opening of Spike's Joint at 1 South Elliot Place in Fort Greene, Dennis Rupert and his carpenters hammered and sanded well past 2:00 A.M., transforming the corner storefront from a bland real estate office into the Spikeabilia Emporium. At noon on Sunday, July 22, a long line of people stood in the rain outside the freshly painted red, black, and green exterior, awaiting an opportunity to be among the first consumers to purchase souvenirs from Leeland and, unknowingly, walk through the handiwork of Rupert's Brooklyn-based construction company. The next evening, at the premiere party for *Mo' Better Blues*, folks craned their necks to get a better view of Magic Johnson, Ossie Davis, Denzel Washington, Eddie Murphy and, of course, Spike himself. But Dennis Rupert was in the house too. The tall, bearded thirty-ish construction boss had discarded his paint-splattered overalls for an African crown and multicolored Afrocentric garb.

If you're looking to understand why Spike Lee has become one of America's cutting-edge cultural icons, the best place to start is not his latest film, but the store bearing his name. Spike's Joint was built by Rupert's black company, the space was obtained from black real estate broker Earl Drummond, and it's located in Spike's predominantly black neighborhood. The store employs new jacks from the 'hood and is supervised by ex-Citibanker Pedro Barry, who left his corporate gig to be down with Spike. The space inside is packed with nearly as wide a range of T-shirts and other paraphernalia as Nike sells. Sure, there are the obligatory Michael Jordan T-shirts, but the rest of the gear, from posters to postcards to key rings, is Spike specific. Homeboy's even selling T-shirts already for his not-yet-shot fifth feature, *Jungle Fever.*

The merchandising, the store, who Spike got the space from, who built it, who runs it, and who works the registers all show that, to a degree unique among African American entertainers, Spike keeps his money "in the family." Since the civil rights era opened doors for black entertainers, most have opted—often begging and screaming—to be part of the establishment. In practical terms, that means having European Americans run your business, moving into expensive, white majority neighborhoods, proclaiming that your artistry is "universal" as a code word for "not just black," and being suspended in the plush twilight zone of crossover stardom. It's a lifestyle embraced by several generations of post–civil-rights-era stars from Sidney Poitier to Berry Gordy, from Diana Ross to Michael Jackson, from Lionel Richie to Arsenio Hall. Spike ain't living like that.

Save attorney Arthur Klein and line producer Jon Kilik, all of the 33-year-old director's key business and creative collaborators are African American: cinematographer Ernest Dickerson, coproducer Monty Ross, casting director Robi Reed, scenic designer Wynn Thomas, costumer Ruth E. Carter, poster designer Art Sims, Fireside Books editor Maliaka Adero, his family (composer Bill, actress Joie, photographer David), musician-actor Branford Marsalis, production manager Preston Holmes, and coauthor Lisa Jones.

This record of black-by-black employment makes Spike not only a symbol of African American achievement—we have plenty of totally worthless symbols already, many of whom hold elective office—but an active, aggressive brother true to his word. He talks like a guy who bleeds red, black, & green, and, time and again, he spreads the green around the black. J. Hoberman was dead on when he labeled his review of *She's Gotta Have It* "Birth of a Salesman." When I first came in regular contact with Spike in 1985, he had already shot *Joe's Bed-Stuy Barbershop* and *She's,* had the 40 Acres & a Mule logo, had designed his own rather primitive T-shirts for *She's,* and had laid plans to market books about his films that would be loosely modeled on one chronicling Wim Wender's *Paris, Texas.* A full year before *She's* was sold to Island, we sat in my basement and I interviewed him for a book that I, even as an investor in the film, thought was a quixotic venture. A film book? Homie better concentrate on just selling the film.

The interview and my introductory essay on Spike ended up in the first of four books tied into his features. In a creative, unprecedented manner, Spike has used these film journals to create an ongoing artistic autobiography that, like his merchandising, TV commercials, print ads, and music videos, are another source of promotion and cash.

Philosophically, Spike is a New Age cultural nationalist who manufactures entertainments informed by black music (*Mo' Better Blues*), institutions (*School Daze*), sexuality (*She's Gotta Have It*), and community life (*Do the Right Thing*). His dedication to the deification of black figures, while sometimes tiresome (e.g., the listing of black musical heroes in *Do*), gives his material its pungency. Mars Blackmon's fixation on Michael Jordan and disdain for Larry Bird in *She's*, the fraternity step shows and rich legacy of black college life in *School*, the humorous street-corner storytelling and the rage articulated by rap in *Do*, the improvisational and sartorial elegance of jazz in *Mo'*—all these are sweet bits of Aframericana that, in a sense, exist outside the narrative frames of his films. They pop up in each film almost as miniessays on his beloved black culture.

But Spike does not fall into PIM (positive image mentality) dogma. His features are rife with unfulfilled dreamers and dashed expectations. Jamie, Greer, and Mars all got "it" from Nola Darling but couldn't hold her. Jane Toussaint's loyalty to frat leader Big Brother Almighty is rewarded by her forced sexual submission to Half-Pint. Trumpeter Bleek Gilliam's musical career is destroyed in one mad moment of black-on-black violence. And, of course, Mookie is a narrow-minded fool sure to be rationalizing his crack selling after Sal's last payment runs out. Most of Spike's memorable characters are not stick-figure action heroes or comedians in star vehicles, but men and women whose psyches are warped by the demons bedeviling so many African Americans.

There is a nationalist underpinning to his financial and creative activities, yet Spike has no problem doing business with corporate America. His entrepreneurial integration has led him into ongoing business relationships with Nike, Universal, Barneys, the Gap, Levi Strauss, and Simon & Schuster. *She's* was very much a guerrilla enterprise that was distributed by Island, then a maverick studio. Ever since, Spike has worked with major studios and national advertisers. Is there a contradiction in this? Only if your head is still stuck in the '60s. In the face of modern corporate infotainment monoliths, the most realpolitik counterstrategy is to be in business with as many as possible. Diversifying protects you against cooptation by any single corporate entity or industry. With revenue flowing in from commercials, books, music videos, and merchandising, Spike has some major cushion should Hollywood get tired of his methods or his mouth.

In fact, as a model of post-Motown black media entrepreneurship,

40 Acres & a Mule is the premier example of what a viable '90s African American enterprise should be: community-based, diversified, black-staffed, and aligned-with-but-autonomous-from major information distributors. Spike's red, black, & green statements over the years—from blasting Quincy Jones's participation in *The Color Purple* to Arsenio Hall's tube tomming—can sound sanctimonious and self-serving ("See how black I am?" he seems to boast). Yet his very willingness to disrespect his star peers, while backing his words up via his subject matter and hiring practices, shines a highly uncomplimentary light on Eddie, Arsenio, et al.

Instead of the usual Hollywood paranoia ("I built the wall because I felt that there was supposed to be a wall there," Murphy recently told *Playboy* about his Elvis-like isolation from the world), Spike has substituted a vision that blends Booker T. Washington's sweat equity with Martin Scorsese's New York loyalty. Whatever you think about his filmmaking ability, Spike's subversion of entertainment industry orthodoxy in favor of economic nationalism may prove to be his most enduring legacy.

VILLAGE VOICE, 1990

# TRACY CHAPMAN

## Today's Black Woman

Records rarely change my life anymore. Not because music has gotten worse (though sometimes it's easy to think so) but because over the past 10 years, I've learned a little too much about the industry's talent, selection, and promotional policies. The companies call performers *recording artists,* though my expe-rience is that genuine artistry or self-expression distributed as popular music is largely accidental. In the realm of black music the available styles are further narrowed by a depressing pack mentality. Labels and radio stations deem it more important to be behind trends, not ahead of them, so the few innovative ideas out there can be refined and for-matted. Give or take (mostly take) a Jam & Lewis or Public Enemy, pop has failed to respond to the complexity of contemporary black life. Too many brothers and sisters are slaves to the same old rhythms.

One group shamefully underrepresented in record bins are college-educated, upwardly mobile, politicized black women—neither buppies nor B-girls, but with street sense and tempered careerism. They read *Essence,* glance at *Elle* and the *Wall Street Journal;* find *Cry Freedom*'s Denzel Washington sexier than *Sonny Spoon*'s Mario Van Peebles; con-tribute to Jesse's run; know the difference between the ANC and SWAPO; love Hiroshima; are amused by Salt-n-Pepa; and revere the voices of Anita Baker and Luther Vandross. Currently Gloria Naylor is their author of choice, B. Smith's their spot, Patrick Kelly their designer, and Fuzzy Navel their drink. Meanwhile, the music biz sees women as sexual mannequins defined by their fishnets.

Which is why Tracy Chapman is so damn exciting. Born 24 years ago in Cleveland, Chapman grew up in a home dominated by the singing and guitar playing of her mother, a part-time church and club singer. By 12, Chapman was writing and strumming her own songs, a pastime she continued while majoring in anthropology at Tufts. By her junior year she'd gone from busking to building a following in Boston's folk circuit. In 1986 Charles Koppelman, head of the high-powered SBK Productions, became her manager at the urging of his son Brian, then a Tufts undergrad himself. With SBK's backing, Chapman was signed to Elektra by honcho Bob Krasnow, the man who, grudgingly, allowed Anita Baker to oversee the production of *Rapture.* Knowledge of Koppelman's bucks and Krasnow's enthusiasm is the kind of insider info that primes my hype detector, but her music overcame this cyni-cal instinct. *Tracy Chapman* has not changed my life, but the LP has certainly enriched it.

Chapman is a romantic. She is not starry-eyed about love, but optimistic about social change and personal liberation. "Poor people gonna rise up and take what's theirs," she sings on "Talkin' 'Bout a Revolution," a spirited battle cry that argues naively yet vibrantly that a change is not just coming but under way. Chapman's achievement here is that during the song you figure she must know something you don't, a feeling effective agitprop inspires. In "Fast Car," she blends Springsteenesque images of freedom with a faith—that the female protagonist may yet escape her economic prison. When Chapman sings, "And I work in a market as a check-out-girl/I know things will get better/You'll find work, and I'll get promoted," I hear the yearning of so many young women I know, a refusal to accept the barriers of class and color, a refusal that defines their generation and their character. "She's Got a Ticket," almost a sequel to "Fast Car," has the heroine, fed up with life, exercising the male prerogative by fleeing her home in search of more control of her destiny. Again the message of female self-definition ("Some folks call her a runaway/A failure in the race/But she knows where her ticket takes her") is firm and vivid.

"Fast Car" is written in the first person, "Ticket" in the third, but, like the best of Chapman, they share a novelistic specificity. In "Behind the Wall" the narrator listens night after night as a husband beats his wife, then watches as the police repeatedly fail to intervene. What starts out as a depiction of the helplessness of the observer has by song's end become something more powerful. With the wife in an ambulance, Chapman portrays the twin evils of male power and indifference. Sometimes her writing seems too earnest. On "Across the Line," the tale of a small-town race riot, she falls victim to liberal preachiness ("On back streets of America/They kill the dream of America"). When she describes events and people, Chapman pierces; when she speechifies, she sounds like Hubert Humphrey.

Her music's passion is heated by a husky, plaintive voice that, depending on the song, recalls Joni Mitchell and Phoebe Snow. While lacking their jazzy flexibility, Chapman makes up for it with a unique mix of authority and melancholy, qualities that infuse her love songs. Producer David Kershenbaum backs Chapman with a bright, contentious rhythm section and arrangements that sympathetically surround her acoustic guitar. "For My Lover" cleverly borrows Neil Young's "Heart of Gold" riff, while "Revolution" has the anthemic intensity reminiscent of Kershenbaum's work with Joe Jackson and Graham Parker. "Mountain o' Things," a tongue-in-cheek celebration of materialism, fuses a Third World pulse (provided by percussionist Paulinho Da Costa) with slick r&b. Maybe that will help it crack black radio's conservatism.

Because of her humanism and the sparkling, unstereotypical production, *Tracy Chapman* has a mesmerizing freshness. Unlike, say, Suzanne Vega, a natural comparison, this sister comes across as neither too soft nor unnaturally sensitive. With one album out, Chapman's already focused on who she is and who she's singing for. Her music has a compassion that captures the fiery life force I associate with, as *Essence* might say, today's black woman.

VILLAGE VOICE, 1988

# THE EBONY AGENDA

Every month since 1945, the slick pages and photo-heavy profiles of *Ebony* magazine have chronicled its readers' upwardly mobile obsessions. Singers' homes are saluted (the June cover story is "Luther Vandross's $8.5 Million Hideaway"); athletes' salaries celebrated; mayors, judges, and congresspeople coddled. Filling the rest of its pages are testimony to black "firsts" (see May's story on National League president Bill White) and formula pieces like "Famous Daughters and Their Fathers" or "Bachelors of 1989." Overall *Ebony*, the flagship of the black-owned Johnson Publishing empire, provides regular indoctrination in the Positive Image Mentality that dominates the public utterances of black leaders.

*Positive* is a word I'd ban from the black vocabulary. It means blacks rarely attack other black public figures, no matter how destructive or stupid. It means a corrupt or incompetent mayor (anyone say Marion Barry?) can serve for years, certain that if *Ebony* or *Jet* profiled him he'd be called "embattled yet determined," rather than a hypocritical fool. It means never pointing out that a black mayor, a jewel in our community's crown, may not make a difference in the lives of a city's black citizens (anyone say Tom Bradley?). PIM is tunnel vision that sees all success stories as benefiting the race—role models for the young, proof we can compete on white terms. It is an elitist worldview that serves establishment blacks—the middle class Dr. King's efforts helped expand—but doesn't help the black masses. PIM loves achievement and ignores accountability. PIM creates a conspiracy of silence that muffles self-criticism, be it of Alton Maddox, David Dinkins, or Jesse Jackson.

By virtue of its allegiance to PIM, the most famous black publication in the world has become anachronistic and maybe even obsolete. *Ebony* vigorously promoted the civil rights agenda and helped produce my generation of college-educated, white-collar guys and gals with no memories of Jim Crow. We were reared not to demand but to expect to see ourselves in *People*, *Time*, the *Village Voice*, and even the *National Enquirer*—seeing Mike Tyson, Robin Givens, and Eddie Murphy all on one tabloid cover, I knew the March on Washington had worked. We don't always like how we're portrayed in white-controlled rags, this one included. Yet in the world it's helped create, *Ebony*'s stance (and writing) is painfully one-dimensional. Among younger readers *Jet* is more popular. Its postage-stamp stories and photo-filled pages make it perfect subway fodder—between Chambers and 96th streets you can survey the latest in sex, social trends, and showbiz and not feel cheated. A syndicated TV offshoot, *Ebony-Jet Showcase*, is simply Lifestyles of the Tan & Famous.

*Ebony*'s annual listing of the 100 "most influential" blacks is a perfect reflection of the magazine's bias. Every member of the congressional black caucus, no matter how weak, is included. So are the mayors of major cities and significant state officials (California's shrewd assembly speaker, Willie Brown; Virginia's lieutenant governor, Douglas Wilder). The heads of fraternities, sororities, and social organizations (such as Jack & Jill, which turns unsuspecting kids into teenage buppies) hold 16 slots. The youngest person in the 100 is 30-year-old "Singer-Dancer, Recording Artist, Philanthropist" Michael Jackson. Judging by their faces, almost everybody on the *Ebony* list is 35-plus, with the majority 40-to-55. Clearly youth isn't represented. Nor are very many businessmen not in leadership positions at black organizations, non-musical artists (in a shocker, Sammy Davis Jr. makes it and Stevie Wonder doesn't), or non-mainstream leaders.

Instead of *Ebony* listmakers Reverend T. J. Jemison of the National Baptist Convention, U.S.A., Inc., and James Henderson, president of the National Dental Association, my top 100 would have found room for Minister Louis Farrakhan, Eddie Murphy, Arthur Ashe, Toni Morrison, Angela Davis, *Essence* editor-in-chief Susan Taylor, multinational businessmen Reginald Lewis and Bruce Llewelyn, *Oakland Tribune* owner Robert Maynard, black ad agency president Thomas Burrell, superman Michael Jordan and B-boy Mike Tyson (though it's refreshing to see no athletes on the *Ebony* list, it seems extreme), Georgetown coach John Thompson, designer Patrick Kelly, August Wilson, Spike Lee, and Percy Sutton. As *New York* magazine did in a profile of powerful New Yorkers, I would have reserved a space for that most "influential" of grassroots capitalists, the crack dealer. The *Ebony* list automatically equates elective office with clout and race organizations with community impact. They meant that once, but those propositions seem naive in 1989.

Strangely, one of the most successful black businessmen ever, a man whose personal wealth is estimated at over $150 million by *Forbes* and whose ideas have impacted American minds for nearly 50 years, isn't included either. A personal hero of mine, he owns *Ebony* magazine and his name is John H. Johnson. A contradiction? Maybe, but it can't be helped. Any publisher who survives 10 minutes in this business deserves some respect. Working in an industry that claims blacks don't read, bucking newsstands resistant to black faces and advertisers who avoid black-owned media, Johnson is an epic survivor. Black magazines come and go (*Encore, Elan*) and others struggle to begin (the oft-delayed *Emerge*), but Johnson's mags cookie-cut their way to profitability. So I have to honor him, in my heart if not my head. Which is why I bought *Succeeding Against the Odds*, Johnson's autobiography, written with veteran *Ebony* editor Lerone Bennett Jr. As in any rags-to-riches tale there's a bunch of boasting—talk of his mountaintop Palm Springs home and White House visits grows tiresome. But the man who sold the concept of the black consumer market to corporate America understands persuasion. "Successful selling is a matter of finding common ground, no matter how narrow it might be, on which you and your client can stand together," he writes. "That's true in selling and life, especially in the area of race relations, where both Blacks and Whites must make a special effort to emphasize the things that unite them.

"Does that mean that you sacrifice your integrity? Certainly not. I've been selling on the edge for forty-seven years, and I don't think I've had to compromise my integrity. I've stooped in some cases to conquer, but I don't apologize for that—the conquering, I mean."

I like this guy. He's cocky, gung ho, shrewd, and relentless. But his boot-straps philosophy (he loved Nixon's "black capitalism") isn't a system for mass black advancement. Holding himself up as a symbol of "what could be," Johnson ignores the all-but-insurmountable barriers of education, capitalization, and systemic racism that make duplicating his journey so difficult today. In thinking positively he thinks incompletely. And that's putting it kindly.

VILLAGE VOICE, 1989

# SUPERFLY

Another Saturday night at Dapper Dan's. It's near midnight on 125th Street and the hip-hop boutique, made internationally famous when Mike Tyson rocked Mitch "Blood" Green outside its doors, is amped. Dap, a slim, serious man dressed in khaki shirt and pants and trademark red loafers, is showing off a table full of pants and pullover tops plastered with Bally logos. Three brothers in full gear—space-boot sneakers, gold-capped teeth, knuckle rings—fondle the merchandise. One pulls on a lime-green top. The other tries on Halloween-orange shorts with Bally printed across the groin. Dap and two of his team of African seamsters watch. Finally Dap tells them, "Whatever you want can be hemmed in 30 minutes. Just tell me what you want." The brothers continue to survey the goods. Just-Ice, notorious rap gangster and otherwise sweet guy, cruises in from his show at the Apollo. He needs a new outfit for the midnight gig, doesn't have time to run up to the Bronx, and wants to know can he put something on his bill.

Late into the Harlem night Dap sells to and negotiates with night-owl shoppers on the fly tip. For much of this decade, Dap, as well as a few competitors around the city, has been refining a hard-core urban style that celebrates aggression, brand-name materialism, and the larger-than-life aspirations of L.L. Cool J, Eric B. & Rakim, and the like. But while there's still plenty of juice in Dap's business, there has been an important musical shift that is profoundly affecting streetwear. Rap still rules, but its new jack swing offshoot, together with new wave disco, a/k/a house, is now the cutting edge of black street aesthetics. The fusion of British, gay, and new jack swing attitudes is catching so rapidly that the now standard B-boy look—sideways baseball cap, rope chains, sweat suit, and laceless name-brand sneakers—already symbolizes a cruder, more casual era. The hippest rap fashion statement of the mid-'80s was Run-D.M.C.; the hippest rap look of 1989 is De La Soul. Therein lies the tale.

Let's take it from the top. Baseball caps, except those bearing the Batman logo, are being displaced by an explosion of proudly nappy hair. Braids, dreads, and skinheads are all acceptable, but the fade is the current common denominator. Once it just meant keeping hair short on the sides, but in the image of Grace Jones and especially Cameo's Larry Blackmon the cut rose high. At Kinapes and other Afro-centric barbershops the fade flattop became a sculpture: cuts became lines, lines formed words, words turned into elaborate etchings. Mixed and matched with dreads, braids, and in Atlanta and on the West Coast even curls, the fade (the "Cameo," the "high-low") is the most culturally conscious and comfortably unisex hairstyle since the Afro. Not surprisingly, the Kente-cloth crown—popularized by Salt-n-Pepa—is the only headgear that competes with it. (A note about coloring: red, auburn, or straight-up yellow strands are flowing so flamboyantly through young ladies' hair that they look like autumn leaves. I'm not totally knocking it—some of my best friends are hazel—only because it beats wigs and extensions.)

To discuss bodies I'll call in Rosie Perez, Bushwick native, ex-"Soul Train" dancer, choreographer for the Boys, Heavy D., Bobby Brown ("My Prerogative"), and Diana Ross ("Workin' Overtime"), and currently an ultrahot urban tastemaker. "There are two main styles out there now: a hip-hop house blend and a Bobby Brown style, which is progressive r&b or more a new jack swing look owing to the group Guy." Hip hop is, to Perez, Heavy D. and his dancers switching from Coca-Cola shirts to bulky oversized suit jackets, polka-dot ties, and loose pleated trousers. Or wearing a Kente crown, shirt, and shorts in his "We Got Our Own Thing" video. Or Slick Rick, mixing stoopid gold and Kangol, with a suit jacket and overcoat slung over his shoulders like Frank Sinatra. It's a look that melts aspects of house's gay roots (handkerchiefs on heads is house) and English club style (buy your round black shades yet?) with B-boy attitude, just as much current dance music moves toward a unification of black and gay audiences not seen since early disco. De La Soul's "daisy age" mesh of bugged hair and multitextured snatches of fabrics and prints is as influential now, particularly with college kids, as L.L.'s Kangol ever was with B-boys. Moreover, the De La Soul hip hop/house blend is much more comfortably unisex than mid-'80s macho wear.

Just as new jack swing music has drawn from r&b and rap, Perez feels the clothes that accompany it juice old-school slickness with youngblood freshness. The big diamond rings, gold watches, and tinted shades that adorn Guy guru Teddy Riley could as easily rest on the Reverend Al Green. But the flowing white-on-white shirts and pants Guy and their followers sport is on point for '89 (see Keith Sweat and M.C. Hammer for further refinements in new jack swing gear). For women this look manifests itself in jewelry similar to that of their male counterparts, though the big, looping earrings are a holdover from the B-girl epoch.

On the dance floor black shoes, be they patent leather, spiced with metal doodads, or tied with ribbons, are the official fly footwear. Nike, Fila, and Adidas continue to click, but dressing up, not dressing down, is the hype move and these shoes are leading the way. "To me the shoes are the epitome of house," Perez argues. In her eyes, and mine too, the popularity of the big, black, bootlike shoes—which I first saw in England two years ago—is key. On B-boys, new jacks, or house servants, they're a sign of just how far we've traveled since "My Adidas."

VILLAGE VOICE, 1990

# BEIGE IS FINE

One Sunday afternoon I walk along Pennsylvania Avenue from Linden Boulevard to Livonia Avenue. On these four blocks of East New York's main drag I spy 14 advertising billboards and posters. One, on the side of a bus shelter, carrying an ad for *The Accidental Tourist,* is an anomaly as much for its subject as its tardiness. The others are more typical: Colt 45 ("It works every time"), Salem ("Fresh on the scene"), Budweiser ("This Bud's for you"), as well as Olde English 800 beer, Kool cigarettes, and other legal addictives. Down a similar stretch of Cascade Road in Atlanta's poor Southside neighborhood, according to a recent Atlanta *Constitution* survey, 16 of 22 billboards displayed beer and cigarette ads. Walk through any poor to working-class African American community and you'll see these products shoved at its residents via "blackface" marketing. Not just the cheap stuff, either. Blacks purchase at least half the cognac consumed in the U.S. each year, which is why you see that elegant Ed Bradley–looking dude assuming we drink Martel.

The unifying message of these ads is not simply the product's sex appeal—though Colt 45 and Olde English do suggest their product magically generates irresistibility for its drinkers—but the beauty of those who consume them. Whether a buppie couple laughingly frolics in a park with Newports or a long-haired Lena Horne type with a Salem cruises a handsome, wavy-haired man, these ads constitute a series of mature, sophisticated parties packed with fine, decidedly whitewashed revelers. The models are overwhelmingly yellow to light brown in complexion, and superbly conditioned. Despite Michael Jordan's and Spike Lee's popular TV spots, the ballplayer's color and the filmmaker's physique have had zip impact on advertising's projections of black beauty. In a year of superstar blacks, it's still pretty billboard faces that inject product lust, consumer desire, and the primacy of non-Negroid beauty into the African American psyche.

These faces, as ubiquitous as McDonald's arches and always gorgeously anonymous, influence black economic and sexual aspirations as much as anything in media. How conscious are the models of the way they're used? After hanging out with a number of them, I'd say they think about it—for example, Terry Alexander, best known to fanzine readers as Stephanie Mills's ex-beau, refuses liquor and cigarette ads. Some others turn them down too. But most are inhibited—or corrupted—by economics. Except for top faces like Gail O'Neill, Louise Vyent, Karen Alexander, and Naomi Campbell, who regularly peer at us from the covers of *Elle* or *Glamour*, jobs are too fleeting or poorly paid for black models to boycott "sin" products.

"At the beginning I used to avoid cigarette and liquor ads," Ivelka Reyes told me the other evening on the IRT's No. 3 train. Slender and petite, her exotic blend of Dominican, Egyptian, and Hawaiian blood has won her gigs dancing behind Billy Dee Williams in a Colt 45 commercial and with Al B. Sure! in his "Off on Your Own Girl" video. She's a "hyphen girl" (model-actress-dancer, etc.), one of the beautiful ones who ride the wash of seductive ad imagery. Hanging onto a pole in an all-black outfit highlighted by a big floppy hat and horn-rimmed glasses, Ivelka says, "I audition for young age roles—high school, college—and I didn't want to ruin that by appearing with a cigarette in my hand. But I had to change my mind. I realized that if they didn't use me, they're going to use someone else." Like her peers, she makes a distinction between "degrading work" (girlie mags) and promoting products that are unsavory, but hardly illegal. "It's an image that you're selling, not yourself. My body is just a vehicle. It's my transportation and I use it to do what I'm asked to do. That's how I see it," she says, before hopping off at Times Square for scuba lessons.

"Once they enter the studio, they have to leave their reservations at the door, and give their best effort to the product," says Bethann, a woman who knows well this balance of conscience and commerce. In the 1970s, Bethann, along with legendary black models like Pat Cleveland, Naomi Sims, and Billie Blair, were part of a black-is-beautiful movement in modeling. Marked by either dark brown skin or overflowing flair, and often both, Bethann and company broke through wearing Halston and Perry Ellis clothes and rode high until the day black wasn't so beautiful.

Bethann landed on her feet. Her son, Kadeem Hardison, is the nerdy Duane Wayne of "A Different World"; her multicultural modeling business, Bethann Management, just turned five; and she's founded the first socially conscious black model organization, the

Black Girls Group, which threw a jam-packed M.K.'s fundraiser for the homeless last winter. Bethann, a registered Republican who handles white, Asian, and African models as well as African Americans, asserts that black models are often limited by "liberal prejudice." For example, "Four years ago Perry Ellis calls me and says, 'You gotta find me a black girl.' Well, that's racism in itself. He wanted one black girl, while he's got 28 white girls working."

Pay for the happy guys and gals of Pennsylvania Avenue, including the photo session and use fees, is around $2400 for a significant billboard campaign. A white model may earn $4000 for the same work and equivalent exposure. And while cigarette and beer billboards will continue to proliferate, the images may change again, from black-is-beautiful to beige-is-fine to what? "I got a call the other day from someone looking for 'the global beauty,'" Bethann says sardonically. "That means less obvious ethnicity and more jobs going to the faces at the top. I tell you everybody's under pressure these days." Even the beautiful ones.

VILLAGE VOICE, 1989

# GANGSTA ATTITUDE

**B**ill Underwood was wearing a white suit of soft linen that shone radiantly under the lights of the Atlanta Airport Marriott ballroom. His eyes—small, piercing orbs that cut deep whenever he peered your way—were shaded by large, blue Kool Moe Dee–style glasses. Jack "The Rapper" Gibson, the genial host of the 1988 Family Affair, an annual gathering of black radio and record folks, presented Underwood, who also managed New Edition's Johnny Gill and ex-Slave lead singer Steve Arrington, with the Dave

Clark Award for his work in promotion. Before several thousand coworkers and friends, Underwood held center stage. I wish I could recall his exact words, but their essence was: "We make black music, a commodity sold worldwide that generates dollars that are turned into deutschmarks, francs, Krugerands, yen and don't flow back to us in the U.S. Until we control those revenues through our own network of distribution we will always be economic slaves."

Many words were uttered that night in praise of black music—as African Americans always wax eloquent at industry affairs. But Underwood cut through the bull and spoke, not about making deals with major corporations, but about taking power. His cool, laconic delivery and authoritative tone were as reminiscent of Michael Douglas's "greed is good" speech in *Wall Street* as anything I'd ever heard. Within the year Underwood was affiliated with a black-owned record distribution network that never got off the ground. The set up was that Underwood would insure payment for small black record companies from independent distributors, but apparently Underwood's warrior vibe intimidated the labels before he ever got to the distributors.

A couple of weeks ago Underwood, 36, was convicted in U.S. district court for using his music-related activities to camouflage drug dealing and a violent criminal organization, the Vigilantes, through which he ordered six murders. Under the Drug Kingpin Law, he could get life without parole and be liable for up to $1 million in fines. I'd heard rumors that Underwood was criminal-minded, but not even the street-savvy hustlers I know ever let on that he was that large. Within the business he was liked. Former Knick and current label-owner Earl Monroe once shared office space with him, and many of the nicest folks in the black music subculture provided character references. Managers have to be hard guys; promotion men are best described as musical traveling salesmen. So Underwood's uptown vibe was hardly unusual.

On at least one occasion, in fact, Underwood's streetwise rep made him an effective mediator. A new jack manager and an old school gangster-type manager were at odds over a gifted young performer/songwriter who, either out of ignorance or juvenile greed, had signed contracts with both. Though the new jack manager had made the kid a better deal, the older man wasn't about to yield. At a meeting between them the older man slapped his young competitor and threatened him with an extensive ass-kicking. Somehow Underwood got involved and, at a music conference in Atlantic City, helped forge a truce between the two that still holds.

Obviously Underwood had to be a man of respect to chill that situation. And even if it had been common knowledge that he was as deeply nefarious as the conviction asserts, he wouldn't have been excluded from the music game. Criminals have used and been embraced by undercapitalized showbiz types—musicians, club owners, agents—since Prohibition. During my nine years as a trade magazine columnist I came into contact with gangsters of all kinds. Virtually without exception, they were all more ostentatious than Underwood. He was always, in my presence, reserved, cordial, sometimes even playful—once he walked up behind me on Sixth Avenue and stepped on the back of my shoe.

While obviously not the nicest guy in the world, Underwood, a real-life gangster, didn't conform to the caricatures of black bad men now resurgent in the white media and among brothers too. From the West Coast, N.W.A, Ice-T, and Too Short are prime perpetrators, putting contemporary blaxploitation flicks on CD. On the retro-nuevo tip, *Harlem Nights* tried unsuccessfully to tap that same mentality. Harlem-born vocalist Oran "Juice" Jones, seeking to promote a new album, held a "Players Ball" at the Ritz, complete with blaxploitation on video monitors, a low-budget reenactment of the "Player of the Year" scene from *The Mack*, and new jacks sporting '70s pimp hats and '50s old school gangster stingy-brims. Even today's real street scramblers, though certainly more dangerous than rappers, often seem to live their lives as if *Scarface's* Tony Montana were their guru.

While these entertainers fool with gangsterism to titillate consumers, who also grew up on movie gang fetishism, Bill Underwood, with his business suit and chilly smile, was by day a cog in the entertainment machine that services these overblown images. That's why, for all the fear and fascination a band like N.W.A generates, they are unreliable chroniclers of the underworld. There is a subtle insidiousness to real evil that, with the exception of *The Godfather*, few pop-culture vehicles capture. Underwood was a bridge between real and cartoon machismo because he existed in the gap that divides them. So don't be surprised if someone doesn't take his story and make it into a movie—or, maybe better, a video.

VILLAGE VOICE, 1990

# SHADY DEALIN'

**W**e'd come in on the red-eye the night before and that bright California sun, flowing through the studio executive's big plate-glass windows like blood through a runner's heart, was messing with me. So I wore my bitchin', purchased-in-Westwood shades. Me and my posse of would-be cineastes—cowriter, director, and wannabe producer—sat on one side of the room. On the other side were young brat-pack execs with the cash to make our dreams come true. As bright as L.A.'s morning sun can be after the smog lifts, that's how intense the meeting got. And my shades didn't help. In a city ruled by visuals, I'd set a hostile tone—one exec cracked on them as we made our entrance. My posse rolled in from The Apple with a "These-Hollywood-dudes-aren't-gonna-house-us!" attitude, and subliminally the shades embodied some textbook passive-aggression. We exited unsure whether our script would be produced but with dignity intact. When you're an African American working in LaLa-land, that can be as important as making the deal.

Back in the '70s, when blaxploitation was in vogue and George Jefferson was America's reigning icon of black upward mobility, any deal was a victory. But post-Lee's *She's* and Townsend's credit cards, the telegenic, video-active tribe of the '90s is challenged to balance its desire for cash and control with the brutal fact that the system is still structured around Eurocentric sensibilities and dollars. The pressure is more extreme, because the opportunities are larger.

Nineteen-ninety will see the release of more features by and/or about African Americans, independent and studio-financed, than any year since the early '70s. Still in release from Christmas are *Harlem Nights*, *Driving Miss Daisy*, and *Glory*, while the indie films *The Game* and *The White Girl* are at local theaters alongside blaxploitation fare like *Crackhouse* with Jim Brown and *Heart Condition* with Denzel Washington. Three black indie productions stole the show at the Sundance Festival in Park City, Utah—top prizewinner *Chameleon Street* by Wendell Harris, Charles Burnett's Danny Glover vehicle *To Sleep with Anger*, and Reggie Hudlin's *House Party*. There's a lot more coming, including Robert Townsend's *Five Heartbeats*, the Barry Michael Cooper–scripted *New Jack City*, and our annual Spike statement, *Variations on the Mo' Better Blues*. And I guarantee you that on each of these projects, the African American artistic personnel, especially any gifted or persistent enough to supervise the direction, production, or writing, at some point went through the same attraction/repulsion rituals my posse did.

Reggie Hudlin, viewed as an up-and-coming black indie filmmaker for several years, had two features fall apart before New Line greenlighted *House Party*. The *L.A. Weekly*'s Anne Thompson, after viewing the film at Park City, wrote: "It's probably the most accessible and commercial black film since the reigning champ, *Purple Rain*." But that doesn't mean making *House Party* was anxiety-free. Reggie remembers one script meeting that centered on its aggressively black humor: "I got so mad I just sat there and said nothing because if I'd opened my mouth at that moment I would have just exploded and bumrushed the entire room. It was one of those times when they weren't just ignorant of the culture, but arrogantly so." Happily, Reggie and producer-brother Warrington Hudlin prevailed. The script stayed funky and the shooting went smoothly—in fact, his budget was increased after the film was underway. But during the editing, New Line fretted about *House Party*'s pacing. The Hudlins concluded studio reps didn't understand why references to Rudy Ray Moore's Dolemite rap, Dick Gregory's Bahamian diet, or the wack break-dance flick *Breakin'* would amuse African Americans. Again the Hudlins, with the help of their agent and attorney, got the cut they wanted.

As this story suggests, blacks working in Hollywood have more to overcome than overt racism—sometimes white people just don't understand. I had a conversation with a top producer who claimed to love "The Cosby Show" and "A Different World," yet was startled and then charmed by the novel idea that there were class distinctions among African Americans. Post-Lee, a few savvy Hollywood types have been acknowledging the cultural gap and empowering folks: Charles Lane, director-star of *Sidewalk Stories*, and Keenen Ivory Wayans, auteur of *I'm Gonna Git You Sucka*, have signed deals with Disney and Universal respectively.

Once hired, African American writers, young or with only one or two films in the can, are often drawn into conflicts over craft versus content. Say a sepia screenwriter proposes a poignant tale of a single mother's struggle to raise a son in Compton. Cool, says the studio. A vehicle for Whoopi Goldberg, right? But the deeper he gets into the story, the more the studio complains about "structure" and "beats." The writer worries that by turning the troubled kid into the head of a junior high school drug cartel he may be selling out. The studio says it's just a way to "heighten dramatic tension" and "enhance the conflict." They also tell him, "We make movies, you don't. Listen to us and take this check." Caught between ambition, race consciousness, and insecurity, the writer passes up lunch with his agent at Le Dome.

So why doesn't the writer just go out and get African American investors? After all, Spike did it. Well, some of Lee's investors were black, but some of the most crucial weren't. And *She's Gotta Have It* hasn't changed the reluctance of the *Black Enterprise* crowd to finance films. As a group they'll always take a cool condo over a hot script. The only dark entrepreneurs who've truly been inspired by Spike are in the music business (Russell Simmons, Freddie Jackson's manager Charles Huggins). That all Spike's post-*She's* films have been with studios is no accident—all roads still lead to Burbank.

A recurring daymare: premiere of my first film. Everybody's dressed in tuxedos and dresses embroidered with kinte. There are cheers when my name hits the screen. Two hours later I sip champagne. Alone. Someone says, just loud enough for me to hear, "I hope homie was well-paid." It's a paranoid vision, but when dealing with Hollywood, what else is appropriate?

Later for that, though. A couple of weeks ago in the same Los Angeles suite, though a darker room, sit a brat-pack executive, my cowriter, and myself. We have a truly in-depth discussion of how to make our script. Tuxedo time? Not yet. But you've got to make friends sometime. So despite their assumptions and my paranoia we're trying to work things out. Late that day we hop the fence of a public park in Beverly Hills. The exec lets me beat him in a one-on-one. That's gotta be a good sign.

VILLAGE VOICE, 1990

# BOY TALK

**C**ynthia was a butterscotch-brown 13-year-old cutie known around the Tilden Projects for her shiny black bangs and neon-blue coat. To the amazement of many she picked herself to be my first girlfriend. One day Frankie, a Puerto Rican buddy of mine who lived on the third floor, arranged a meeting at a nearby schoolyard. By the time we'd walked the three blocks home we were holding hands. Because she lived in 305 and I across the parking lot in 315, we could sit in our kitchens looking at each other as we talked for long hours on the phone. Unfortunately, those were to be the high points of our love affair.

You see, my boys greeted my first romance with snickers. After a touch football game, a couple of bloods said they'd been walking with her the other night and got caught in the rain. "So," said one kid I never did like, "I had to pull out my rubbers." To the delight of everybody but me, he pulled out a pack of Trojans. In retrospect, I can see he probably did it as much to show he had some as to humiliate me, but either way it worked. This incident, plus my boys' constant barrage of cherry-popping tales, led me to blow it with Cynthia. Yes, it must be told—my first romance died of peer pressure. One day when by some miracle I had the apartment to myself for an afternoon, I got Cynthia to come over. I pulled the curtains shut in the living room, screwed in the red light bulb my mom used for parties, and put on some Al Green albums. Twenty minutes later Cynthia quit me. Her exit line was classic: "I thought you were different."

Only then did I realize she'd approached me precisely because I was a four-eyed bookworm and not some fly boy or would-be gigolo. I was probably really what Cynthia wanted me to be and if I'd embraced that identity I would have kept her. Yet in Brownsville circa 1973 that was not a socially acceptable option. It was easier to attempt to fit in, grab your dick a little, and learn the homeboys' language of love, hoping that, if our teachers were right, we'd all grow out of it.

Our teachers were wrong. I thought of Cynthia and my boys while watching Eddie Murphy's *Harlem Nights*, a film purporting to recapture the glamour and grace of old Harlem, but whose greatest value is depicting the debasement of language among our New Jack stars. While Redd Foxx and Richard Pryor are hardly new to the words *pussy*, *motherfucker*, or *bitch*, the flow of obscenity from the screen and its particular application to the film's females is symptomatic, not simply of Murphy's attitude toward women, but of so many young men's. That director/writer Murphy defines *Harlem Nights*'s three most prominent actresses as a dykey madam with nasty feet, a high-yellow gangster's mistress who's a mercenary fantasy out of Kool Moe Dee's "They Want Money," and a hooker with a vagina like sunshine reflects a general objectification of women that saturates Murphy's art, too many rap records, and America's current manchild media masters. On the white side, bands like Guns N' Roses, comics like Andrew Dice Clay, and flicks like *Friday the 13th* are linked at the scrotum with unsavory records by 2 Live Crew and Too Short. Despite his natural gifts of mimicry and wit, Murphy may just be this nation's biggest movie star because he gives humor's voice to a vicious anger at women.

Misogyny is obviously nothing new. What is new is that a juvenile fascination-fear with women has made *bitch*, *slut*, *cunt*, and *ho* all too generally accepted parts of the male vocabulary. Even before they're old enough to have experienced adult heartbreak, youngbloods believe women can control them through desire, and that this control makes them vulnerable economically, as defined by the myth of Robin Givens (or if you prefer, Brigitte Nielsen). I'm not trying to be a born-again feminist, but talk to men, of all ages but particularly teens, and you pick up a crazy pleasure in the debasement of women that scares me more and more. The day after *Harlem Nights* opened, I listened to three kids in a local grocery store throwing cusswords to the wind, laughing at how Eddie served and then shot "Whitley"—giving actress Jasmine Guy the name she goes by on TV's "A Different World"— before she "did" him. Not even 13, they already knew the deal.

# OLD GLORY

**D**enzel Washington is about to get whipped. It seems Trip, Denzel's character in *Glory*, the Civil War drama about the U.S. Army's first black soldiers, has gone AWOL. Actually, homeboy skipped camp to get the much-needed shoes that racism had denied the company, which is certainly a legitimate reason, but regiment commander Matthew Broderick isn't having any—not even after Denzel is tied up and his shirt ripped off, revealing a back crisscrossed with slashes from slave days. Broderick, torn between Northern liberalism and military by-the-book, finally decides the army code applies to all. Behind a twitchy, glued-on mustache his tortured look shouts, "It's for their own good! Now these boys will know the rules are applied equally to everyone!"

As the whipping commences, Washington cuts Broderick one of the withering, contemptuous looks that brothers aim daily at racist or insensitive whites. And despite the lash and his tears, Denzel's stare doesn't waver. When I sit and discuss *Glory*'s pros and cons with brothers, it's Denzel's look we keep coming back to. It's as if Denzel's visage communicated some transcendental aspect of our rage. Yet Washington's character later dies, like any good wartime martyr, with Old Glory clutched in his hand. And this isn't a contradiction—it's a true cinematic depiction of conflicted souls. Despite slavery and unjust military discipline, Trip wants to be a man, which in the behavior box blacks are forced into means seeking white male approval. To die valiantly for the red-white-and-blue, to be allowed to wear Union blue, ultimately blows the mind of Denzel's hard-edged homie.

Denzel's acting is so resonant because, just as he died charging up a hill for an elusive manhood, his great-great-grandchildren battle for the same respect today. And the moments of heroism in this effort are still grounded in the belief that individual blacks can save themselves by serving another culture's goals. *Glory* made me flash on the image of General Colin Powell, the highest-ranking African American in the nation's history, leading the Pentagon press conference the morning U.S. troops tore up a black country in search of a Hispanic CIA snitch turned coke dealer. His chest dripping with medals, Powell, surely a man of incredible competence and guts to be assigned to head the Joint Chiefs of Staff, confidently led the nation through the logistics of our latest Third World adventure. Watching him made me realize the talk of his running for vice-president in 1992 was no joke. After the briefing, Bryant Gumbel and Tom Brokaw kicked the ballistics on an extended "Today" show, as Gumbel, with his usual telegenic charm, cosigned Stealth bomber diplomacy.

It's been several weeks since we collared Noriega. No one yet knows how many Panamanian civilians were wasted and the legality of the invasion under the War Powers Act is currently being debated. The crisp, polished performances of Powell and Gumbel have to make you wonder whether African Americans died in the Civil War and the civil rights movement just to allow a few of their descendants to be anointed spokesmen for the aims of empire. The answer most certainly is yes. Powell and Gumbel's affable explanations of imperialist aggression demonstrated that my race's quest for a piece of the pie has produced the best-paid house niggers in history.

I honestly admire Powell and Gumbel, as well as the self-sacrificing Civil War soldiers, for their ability to leap racial roadblocks. But there's no denying that our postslavery progress has created a crew of well-oiled cogs in the machinery of white world domination. Among our local sepia-toned public officials, only Charles Rangel has sounded the right note of skepticism. Though I disagree with his anti-drug-legalization stance (what about chiba, Charlie?), he showed heart in confronting a hostile media. It's disturbing that he's such an exception.

Now the soldiers are slowly coming home, a good percentage of them African American and hispanic, and I wonder how they felt walking through a predominantly African country with a machine gun. No question some were 100 percent down. Yo, bloods liked Rambo too! But how many fluctuated between racial anger and U.S.-sanctioned heroism? An important question for the '90s, since, with Grenada and Panama as warm-up exercises, it appears our next few miniwars will feature Yankee soldiers versus hispanic blacks. The pretext will be drugs and/or endangered American lives (with that justification, how about sending the National Guard to East New York or Compton?), but the subtext will be race. And leading us into the latest era of American macho will be a commanding brown man with Caribbean American roots and a smooth style on the mike. All of it, the upward mobility and the bloodshed, for the sake of Old Glory.

VILLAGE VOICE, 1990

# NATIVE DAUGHTERS

**A**lice Walker enters Jezebel's followed by friends, family, flacks, and every eye in the room. This party is for the just released *The Temple of My Familiar*, a novel that's taking some jabs to the chin from critics. We all know it's hard following up a cultural artifact. Just ask Alex Haley.

As two video crews follow, Walker moves past the Mary Jane candies jar by the door, the dazzling vintage dresses dangling from the ceiling, and strategically placed potted plants to chat with friends old and acquaintances new. Her soft, airy voice bares no traces of her struggling New York years or the mind-numbing stress of the promotional tour. At least book parties, compared to the glitz of Hollywood and the funk of the record biz, are polite affairs. And Jezebel's, a black-run restaurant specializing in spirited Creole-style soul food, is an appropriately low-key yet classy spot. *Essence* editor-in-chief Susan Taylor, New York black literary godmother-agent Marie Dutton-Brown, author-historian Paul Giddings, Amistad Press editor Charles Harris, actress Ruby Dee, 100 Black Women president Jewel McCabe-Jackson, "MacNeil/Lehrer" correspondent Charlayne Hunter-Gault, and filmmaker St. Clair Bourne are among the establishment blacks paying respects.

Gloria Steinem, a longtime supporter and old friend, is there too:

At one point she and Walker, arm in arm, stroll over to speak with Walker's daughter Rebecca, a talkative Yalie with sparkling eyes. Walker seems like a nice lady, very much the earth mother in her loose-fitting Third World garb and tightly woven braids. In fact, while many at the party sport Jezebel's usual immaculate buppie-yuppie look, maybe half the women there mirror Walker in style. The clothes, the braids, the ornate earrings, and the clear, "we-don't-eat-meat" complexions suggest a collective consciousness, a shared worldview—just like B-boys, punks, barristers. The evening's highlight is a performance by Sweet Honey in the Rock, a black feminist quartet who were political before Tracy Chapman and a cappella before Take 6, singing the antiapartheid "Somewhere There's a Child A-Cryin'," with Walker chipping in background vocals. The crowd soul-claps, Sweet Honey soars, and Walker, somewhat sheepishly, sways to the music in a perfectly realized moment of sisterly community.

I flash back to all the symposiums, op-ed pieces, book reviews, television programs, and passionate conversations instigated in particular by Walker's *The Color Purple* and in general by the rise of African American women's prose. Were *The Color Purple, For Colored Girls, The Women of Brewster Place*, etc., part of the publishing industry's conspiracy to denigrate the black man, as many male writers charged? It strikes me now, as a black male who had problems with the big black feminist works, that our literary landscape wasn't just altered by racism, but by the fresh, shared perspective these writers championed. These books eloquently reflected the fragmentation of black America in the post–civil rights years. In many cases, they simply wrote better than, for example, John Edgar Wideman or David Bradley.

When I was growing up, the black literary canon was as butch as boot camp (or at least it looked that way to me then): Richard Wright, Malcolm X with biographer Alex Haley, James Baldwin, Langston Hughes, Ralph Ellison, LeRoi Jones, and two bitter urban memoirs: Piri Thomas's *Down These Mean Streets* and Claude Brown's *Manchild in the Promised Land*. Yeah, I saw *Raisin in the Sun* 50 million times. But black lit as we were weaned on it in the late '60s/early '70s was hardcore urban, full of brothers persecuted by "the man." Women were metaphors rather than characters in the black man's unending struggle for power and identity. Spurred by the growth of black female college enrollment, a sales factor that will continue into the '90s, Walker and company have joined if not annexed that canon.

Encountering Walker, with her daughter and friends, helped me separate the woman from the hype. *The Color Purple* was a story she felt compelled to tell and she did it well. But its acceptance seemed more like sociology to me then and probably always will. At Coliseum Books on 57th Street a few Christmases ago, a white woman on line ahead of me was buying six copies of *The Color Purple* as stocking stuffers. Or I remember attending the first showing of Spielberg's film on 45th and Broadway at noon. I witnessed it with about 20 people, half of them interracial couples, white men with black women. Both memories testify to the book's popularity—and to my sharp sense of black male paranoia.

The IRT number 2 rolls across Brooklyn into Manhattan. In the conductor's car, sitting with crossed legs and a stern look, is a 16-year-old girl. She's wearing a bulky black leather jacket, lime stone-washed jeans, enormous shrimp earrings, and black hightop Reeboks. Her hair is piled high on top and cut low, fade style on the sides. She is doing two noteworthy things: furiously chewing gum and reading *The Color Purple*.

VILLAGE VOICE, 1989

# AUGUST

I once submitted a book proposal to a white woman editor on the feminist tip. It was one of those autobiographical coming-of-love manuscripts that all first novelists write. The editor, after perusing the proposal and sample chapter, inquired, "What are you trying to say about the problems between black men and women, and how does that relate to the destruction of the black family?" "Well . . . ," I started, and then, after some incoherent bumbling, came up with some knee-jerk rationale for the story's importance vis-à-vis those great looming sociological issues. Yet my reply was empty. Sure the book would have had some relationship to those subjects. But, like a lot of first-time novelists, I wasn't writing out of the need to create a political document, but to cleanse my soul of a beautifully painful past. My blackness is essential to my world view (and my self view), so, in ways obvious and oblique, race impacted on the tale not because I wanted it to but because it had to.

I definitely embrace cultural nationalism—I mean I'm red, black, & green on fighting the powers that be. However, the tendency of white gatekeepers and Afrocentric critics to judge black expressions from a cultural view often serves to denigrate the vibrancy of personal visions. All of which is a lead-in to a discussion of my favorite living writer, August Wilson. With the possible exception of Spike Lee and Public Enemy, there is perhaps no other African-American artist so burdened by critics with the weight of sociological baggage, yet he has remained a shining example of individual virtuosity.

With his two Pulitzer prizes and mainstream acclaim, Wilson stands at a strange angle to contemporary black culture. In the '90s, being a black Broadway playwright is very close to being a quaint museum piece: You receive annual back-pats from the *Times* and are destined to be embalmed in an "American Masters" profile on PBS. Kids who know of Toni Morrison, Alice Walker, and James Baldwin have most likely never heard of or certainly never seen his work. The possible exception may be *Fences*, and that's only because Eddie Murphy bought the film rights. Within the black theater world there is some justifiable suspicion about "the anointed one." That journal of the black male proletariat, the skin mag *Players*, wondered in a recent issue why his plays are always set in the past, as if Wilson's distance from current controversies was cowardly. Much like Sidney Poitier in his late '60s heyday, Wilson is dogged by the question, "Why do white folks love him so?"

It would be hip and real Afrocentric to buy into that view, but I can't touch this. After seeing *Ma Rainey's Black Bottom* and listening to a cast recording of the play, I became an August Wilson groupie. Since then I've followed Wilson's work around: saw *Fences* three times on Broadway; Metrolined to D.C. to catch *Joe Turner's Come and Gone* before it hit New York; took in *The Piano Lesson* at its Yale debut, then in Boston and finally twice on Broadway; and attended the premiere of *Two Trains Running* at Yale, and expect to see it again before it hits the Great White Way.

For me, Wilson is a spellbinding poet for whom drama is more vehicle than craft. Large sections of his plays lack the conflict you expect from such a celebrated dramatist. Yet as lyrical soliloquies strung together by threads of narrative his plays evoke a subtext of African American struggle, including the battle of spiritual versus secular religion, African versus European philosophies. There are no rapid-fire Mametesque exchanges in Wilson's world. Scenes evolve into operatic monologues in which a speaker—Slow Drag in *Ma Rainey*, Troy Maxim in *Fences*, Bynum the conjure man in *Joe Turner*, or Holloway in *Piano Lesson*—riffs in enchanted phrases Lester Young would love. Most other action stops as a single character steps up and solos. Although many black writers attempt it, few can capture the essence of colloquial African American language and infuse it with multilayered lyricism—without seeming hokey or contrived. I refer to Wilson, only half in jest, as "the black Shakespeare" because they share the ability to make characters large and small wax eloquent without distorting the overall work.

*Joe Turner*, his least successful Broadway production, is my favorite Wilson play simply because of its rhetorical richness. Bynum meets a stranger in the road, a mystical "shiny man," who changes his life: "We get near this bend in the road and he told me to hold out my hands. Then he rubbed them together with his and I look down and see they had blood on them. Told me to take and rub it all over me, say that was a way of cleaning myself. Then we went around a bend in that road. Got around that bend and it seem like it was twice as big as it was. The trees and everything bigger than life. Sparrows big as eagles. I turned around to look at this fellow and he had this light coming out of him. I had to cover up my eyes to keep from being blinded. He shined until all the light seemed like it seeped out of him and then he was gone and I was by myself in this strange place where everything was bigger than life."

On a muggy August Sunday afternoon I sit in the orchestra of the Walter Kerr Theater watching Charles Dutton's Boy Willie and Rocky Carroll's Lymon try to budge a haunted piano. The scene is comical and touching too, for Boy Willie is not simply wrestling with stubborn furniture, but a sad object of the past that he hopes will enrich his future. As he does, Wilson has Boy Willie tell jokes, spew insults, and recite little pearls of poetry from the stage. In a world of quick cuts and blandness, a time when the vaunted African American oral tradition has been debased by brothers mistaking obscenity for eloquence, Wilson's old-timey arias suit me fine.

VILLAGE VOICE, 1990

# GET ON UP

**N**ew Yorkers think Harlem is the spiritual home of black America. Between the Renaissance writers, the eminence of the Powell clan and Abyssinian Baptist, the legacy of Malcolm X, and influential trends good (bebop, rap) and bad (heroin, crack), locals have a great argument for that Manhattan neighborhood's central role in our evolution. But if Harlem is our spiritual home, then Chicago, particularly its South Side, is our dark, chocolate soul. New York has housed sundry intellectuals and attracted "Negroes" out of the aristocratic tobacco states of Virginia and North Carolina, but the South Side has its own rich heritage. Up from the black belt of the Mississippi Delta and the cotton fields of Alabama, ex-sharecroppers carried with them the blues, which they electrified, and a belief in sweat equity that has spawned many of America's biggest black-owned businesses, including Johnson Publishing (*Ebony, Jet*), our number one advertising agency (Burrell), and our most powerful female media mogul (Oprah Winfrey). Harold Washington, the one black big-city mayor to successfully negotiate the never-ending philosophical struggle between outside agitation and mainstream power, was very much a product of this tough, beautiful midwestern metropolis.

The creation and evolution of black Chicago, so central to the triumphs and failures of the race nationally, receives varied yet complementary discussions in three recently published books that combine to tell this story from the end of the Second World War to the dawn of Desert Storm. Most comprehensive is Nicholas Lemann's *The Promised Land: The Great Black Migration and How It Changed America* (Knopf), an ambitious chronicle of a movement of people that reshaped America. "In 1940, 77 per cent of black Americans still lived in the South— 49 per cent in the rural South," he writes. "The invention of the cotton picker was crucial to the great migration by blacks from the Southern countryside to the cities of the South, the West and the North. Between 1910 and 1970, six and a half million black Americans moved from the South to the North; five million of them moved after 1940, during the time of the mechanization of cotton farming. In 1970, when the migration ended, black America was only half Southern, and less than a quarter rural; 'urban' had become a euphemism for 'black.' The black migration was one of the largest and most rapid internal movements of people in history—perhaps the greatest not caused by the immediate threat of execution or starvation."

Lemann illustrates this journey by tracing the biography of one-time cotton-picker Ruby Lee Daniels, a peer of Muddy Waters who in 1946 traveled from the vicious overt apartheid of Clarksdale, Mississippi, to the nasty hypocritical apartheid of the icy North. As Lemann's role models of black pain and pathology, neither Daniels nor any of the other folks used as subjects come alive as personalities. The author is clearly more interested in them as types than as people. But that criticism aside, Daniels is well chosen—her failed marriages, wayward children, and decision to return South decades later are a neat summation of the urban experience that's shaped, or twisted, millions of lives.

If the South Side sagas of Richard Wright's *Native Son* and Lorraine Hansberry's *Raisin in the Sun* offer more insight into the human part of the early migrants' story, Lemann raises the level of discussion every time he cuts to the White House or Chicago City Hall. Inside these seats of power, Kennedy, Johnson, and Nixon (as well as the ubiquitous Daniel Patrick Moynihan) wrestle with their prejudices as they lose the war on poverty, while off Lake Michigan mayor Richard Daley uses his two decades in office to turn the New Deal idealism of huge public complexes into Sowetos with elevators. Now-notorious projects such as Cabrini-Green and the mammoth Robert Taylor Homes were begun within four years of Daley's first full term in office. Taylor, the largest public housing project in the world, home to Daniels's family for many troubled years, was a by-product of classic postwar big city Democratic policies. As Lemann writes, these buildings demonstrated "faith in tangible accomplishment; the bountiful creation of jobs for loyal Democratic contractors and construction unions; the provision by the machine of a substantial benefit to blacks, namely cheap decent housing; and, no need to be subtle or concealing about it, segregation."

What Lemann doesn't get about Chicago, especially in the '60s, is the vitality that coexisted with the tragedy of Chicago's black life. How did its embattled residents ever find time to go to the Regal Theatre or listen to pioneering soul-blues station WVON? There are scattered references to Muddy Waters, Howlin' Wolf, and Chess Records. Yet Lemann totally ignores the world Chicagoan Robert Pruter has written an entire book about. *Chicago Soul* (University of Illinois Press) is a meticulously detailed study of a music scene that in its variety and depth (Curtis Mayfield and the Impressions, Sam Cooke, the Dells, Jerry Butler, Etta James, the Staple Singers, Gene Chandler, Billy Stewart, and many others) rivaled the more celebrated movements in Detroit and Memphis.

Virtually all the Chicago blues and soul artists were either Southern migrants or their offspring, including the scene's most dominating presence, Curtis Mayfield. A product of the Cabrini-Green project who was born in the city in 1942, Mayfield created an optimistic, romantic, socially conscious body of work that skillfully blended his Southern blues and gospel roots with sophisticated big-city arrangements. Pruter honors Mayfield, as well as literally hundreds of lesser figures, with the intense love of obscure fact you'd expect from a *Goldmine* editor, but lacks the kind of sweeping overview and evocative description the material deserves.

Where Pruter's tunnel vision limits his scope, the tight focus of Alex Kotlowitz's *There Are No Children Here* (Nan A. Talese/Doubleday) ignites his story-telling. The *Wall Street Journal* staffer reports on two years in the lives of two black adolescents, Lafayette and Pharaoh Rivers, residents of Chicago's Horner Homes, a 34-year-old project on the near West Side, where the boys grow up listening to rap records, avoiding gang battle zones, and hustling for quarters outside Chicago Stadium. Lafayette, a tough-minded, unusually mature man-child, is the book's glue. Whether comforting his mother when welfare caseworkers have cut the family's benefits or loving his alcoholic father when everyone else in the family has stopped, Lafayette exhibits a grace under pressure that helps him survive his booby-trapped environment.

In lean, evocative prose, Kotlowitz achieves what Lemann doesn't—a multidimensional portrait of black project-dwellers. His committed intimacy is liberal reportage of a type increasingly rare in a time when white journalists look at black Americans through "underclass" stereotypes instead of their own eyes. It's easy to be depressed when you recall the dashed dreams of black migrants, to feel nostalgic for the great forgotten music of Chicago's soul. But reading about Lafayette's willful dignity on the road to manhood makes me hopeful that native sons are not yet an endangered species.

# SWEET FUNNY ROBIN

On Saturday night, March 17, Chris Rock walked offstage at Los Angeles's Comedy Store wanting to see the nation's funniest African American at work. Hopping in his rented blue convertible, he headed east down Sunset Boulevard. Rock, a slender 23-year-old Bedford-Stuyvesant native best known as the "rib man" in *I'm Gonna Git You Sucka*, fought the traffic down Sunset to Highland and then made a right. Past Olympic Boulevard the low buildings become increasingly nondescript, the faces at the bus stops get browner, and the accents on the street recall Mexico and the South. Once Rock's convertible hit Crenshaw Boulevard he was in the heart of working-class African American Los Angeles, where cop-turned-mayor Tom Bradley got his start, though this part of town now grabs the city's attention mainly for the odd drive-by incident. Turning left on Crenshaw at 43rd Street, Rock drove in front of the supermarket that black businessman Michael Williams has converted into a nightclub called the Comedy Act Theater.

Through the Comedy Act's open front door, Robin Harris bellowed, "Small world!" The audience roared, "Small world!" Harris was near the close of his semilegendary "Bey Bey's Kids" routine, a hilarious chronicle of the horrific afternoon he escorted a family of Compton youngsters to Disneyland and then watched them rob Goofy and get busy with Minnie. Rock cursed and steered the car into the parking lot, hoping he hadn't missed the whole set. Inside, past a feisty toy cop who made the youthful comic show his ID, Rock stood at the mouth of a long, wide, low-ceilinged room packed with the jheri curls, tight short dresses, long hairweaves, and Texas-Oklahoma-Louisiana accents that mark L.A.'s non-Hollywood black culture. Like most nightspots in town, the Comedy Act was dotted with semifamiliar faces from commercials, movies, and sitcom TV. May May Ali, the champ's comedian daughter, greeted Rock, talked shop a moment, and then delivered the bad news: Robin's last set was over.

Rock's face fell, then lit up as Harris—36, portly, round-eyed—walked up and inquired, "What you doin' pinhead?" After that warm greeting, the comics chatted briefly; Robin said he'd be in Chicago the next night for a gig at the New Regal Theater. Before they parted, Rock mentioned a summer tour they'd planned. Rock recalls, "He just looked at me with that we-gonna-make-money-together look." But Sunday, after rocking 2,400 patrons on the South Side, Harris went to sleep downtown at the Four Seasons Hotel and never woke up, victim of an apparent heart attack.

Harris earned his national rep as *Do The Right Thing*'s Sweet Dick Willie, whose bitter quips conveyed the convictions and confusions of one unemployed brother in Bed-Sty. He got larger playing an Eddie Murphy flunky in *Harlem Nights* and Kid's cantankerous father in *House Party*, taping a recently aired HBO comedy showcase, recording a soon-to-be-released album for Polygram, and preparing a sitcom pilot. Like Pryor in the '70s and Murphy in the '80s, the man was primed for a media explosion.

Yet there was nothing like seeing Harris at the Comedy Act, where as MC he took verbal potshots at anything that moved. The club's restrooms are near the stage and up a narrow staircase. To get there you moved past a gaggle of tables and chairs, which provided Harris with ample time to comment on your clothes, hair, or walk—all with the Comedy Act's spotlight bearing down on your inadequacies. One night rapper Heavy D.'s entrance caused a murmur. Harris had the spotlight aimed at D. and then fired: "Shit, so Heavy D.'s here. He's only Al B. Sure! Blown up!" That jibe worked on several levels: Sure! and D. (a) were the same complexion, (b) had similar haircuts, (c) wore similar New York-meets-London gear, and (d) were managed by the same company. The rapper tried gamely to snap back. Relishing the challenge, Harris gleefully asked the audience, "You wanna see how Heavy D. gets across a street?" Throwing the mike down, he got on his stomach and rolled to the other side of the stage. So much for Heavy D.

Harris's quips ("Like that suit, brother. It might come back in style"), his blend of midwestern and Cali accents (his family moved West when he was eight), and unglamorous looks (the sepia Jackie Gleason) made him an African American everyman who reminded folks of the father, uncle, or neighbor willing to snap on anything or anyone. His four directors, all black males—Spike Lee twice, Murphy, Reggie Hudlin, Keenen Wayans—all recognized a crucial bit of their past in Harris at the Comedy Act. Some compared Harris's urban folk style to Richard Pryor's, but he had neither the politics nor the conceptual daring of that troubled master (also a recent heart attack victim). Redd Foxx and the many Los Angeles–based blue comics of the '70s (Wildman Steve, Rudy Ray Moore) are really his forebears—all shared a certain old-school jive that, like the Comedy Act, recalled the chitlin circuit's glory days. It's not surprising that an institution as retro as the Comedy Act thrives in black Los Angeles: Tinseltown is one of America's most segregated cities. And Harris's comic persona of the put-upon working-class man spoke for the home-owning brothers who live off Crenshaw—guys who spend their lives trying to avoid gang-bangers, who pay taxes so they can watch "Sanford & Son" reruns or Rudy Ray Moore's *Dolemite* in peace. One popular Harris joke was about being stopped by one of Los Angeles's notoriously nasty cops. "You got a gun in the car?" the cop asks. Harris replied, "No, it's home with the dope."

"Robin Harris was the best," Rock said the Monday after Harris's death. "Eddie Murphy is the largest. Richard Pryor is the greatest ever. Damon Wayans is the most versatile. Robin didn't write the best, but his delivery . . ." Rock paused. "Robin made saying 'Fuck you' an art form."

Amen. God bless his sweet funky soul.

VILLAGE VOICE, 1990

# WOMEN OF COLOR

**B**ack when I began hanging out in the Village and other hotbeds of wanton sexuality, my mom and sis told me what time it was vis-à-vis white girls. I paraphrase: "Don't bring any blonds back here. After all those years of seeing Sidney Poitier, Wilt Chamberlain, and Sammy Davis, Jr., etc., posing with their white women in *Jet*'s 'The Week's Best Photos,' we don't want our shining black prince bringing a white girl home for Thanksgiving." They were not joking. For them the bonding of white females with black male celebrities insulted African American womanhood, and proved that America's fixation on Caucasian standards of beauty had messed up brothers' heads. This advisory was preventive medicine, and it worked. Save two sweet friendships with European Americans, my taste in miscegenation has leaned toward hispanics, and mostly I've gone out with African American women. When I was fortunate, they were black women as well.

The term "African American" speaks specifically to bloodlines. If you have African ancestry, you can legitimately be designated African American. But once African Americans start hyphenating, it can go on forever—most could claim Native American or European American ancestry as well. And possessing some African blood doesn't make you culturally black. From my mother's Virginia-bred, church-reared, working-class, '60s-dashiki-wearing perspective, the B word suggests certain cultural traits, some tangible, some not. A black mate for her son would have certain religious beliefs (Christian if not Baptist), looks (brown skin with Negroid features, please), and career goals (one with a future that doesn't preclude grandchildren). The intangibles might include: "Does she love Al Green?" "Is she race conscious?" "Is she regular?" (not bourgie or country). And finally: "How 'black' is she?"

Now, you may think some of these standards are wack. In a few cases I might agree with you. But I respect my mother's point of view on the matter, and I'm proud that she has a point of view. In the years since the civil rights movement forced official integration, cultural assimilation and nationalism have confused all discussions of women, sex, and race. Never before have so many African Americans been reared in predominantly white environments. Never before have so many African Americans challenged the hegemony of Christianity as the definer of our spiritual life. Never before have so many African Americans prospered in our capitalist system. And never have so many been imprisoned.

In this era, "Black is beautiful" doesn't mean what it used to. According to the definitions passed on by my mother, many prominent African American personalities aren't really black. Janet Jackson, Oprah Winfrey, ex-Miss America Vanessa Williams, and "Different World"'s Dawnn Lewis would fit nicely, but I'm not sure about Vanity, Lisa Bonet, Jennifer Beals, Vogue model Veronica Webb, ex–Miss America Suzette Charles, or "Different World"'s Cree Summers. All have African blood, but their look and sensibilities are drawn from traditions—bohemia (Bonet, Webb, Summers), preppie (Beals), and freaky (Vanity)—that fit none of the established (or is that stereotypical?) standards of blackness.

"Black is beautiful" has given way to multiculti flygirlism. Today's African American beauty may be mulatto or, increasingly, brought up in environments where Warrant is as culturally significant as GUY. By established standards, Idaho's Renee Tenison, *Playboy*'s Playmate of the Year 1990, is definitely not black, though at five foot six, 112 pounds, and, according to her Playmate data sheet, 36-23-32, she is very pretty indeed. As she sat across from me in the China Club a couple of weeks ago, amid equipment from Fox Network News and the curious stares of white men in business suits, a bright pink jacket covered her equally bright yellow, low-cut dress. Extra long enhanced hair (a weave, y'all) enveloped her face in a large ebony halo, and her clear reddish-brown skin suggested she could be Caribbean. Tenison isn't as poised or glib as beauty pageant winners Williams and Debbie Turner, nor is she as cutting-edge as downtown divas Webb and Bonet. But after 35 years of nudity she is the first African American woman picked as Playmate of the Year for the magazine's overwhelmingly white male readership.

Not too surprisingly, she's new to being black. "Growing up, I thought of myself as mixed," she says matter-of-factly. "But I've found that the general public perceives me as black, so I say I'm black." She'd never been to a city bigger than Boise before her Playmate photo session in Chicago. She's lived most of her 21 years in Melba, where she and her black father, white mother, twin sister, and three brothers constituted the town's minority citizens. When she was a teen, dates weren't plentiful, which she says was "70 percent" due to her skin color. She credits the turnaround in her social life "to my discovery of makeup," and not to any change in local racial attitudes. Her weight-lifter boyfriend, Mr. Idaho 1983, is white ("with a great bod"), and so is her musical taste. Her data sheet makes Cameo the token r&b act on a list dominated by such bands as .38 Special, ELO, Boston, Supertramp, and Van Halen circa 5150—all bland pop-rockers well past their commercial heyday. Either Idaho radio is way behind the times, Tenison is fatally unfunky, or—probably—both.

Though in general Tenison seemed nervous about all the attention, she wasn't at all fazed by questions about race—she just didn't have much of substance to say about it. My impression was that only winning the poll had induced her to give the issue much thought. She struck me not as color-blind but as race-neutral. Growing up in so overwhelmingly white a community, she responded, like so many reared in similar circumstances, by learning to minimize pigmentation. Ten or 20 years ago, Tenison's victory might have been hailed as some statement about civil rights. But neither she nor the white men in attendance made an issue of her color.

As she read a short speech, I noticed I was one of about eight African Americans, four of them men, at a club filled with several hundred attendees. Most were male yuppies—ad agency reps, corporate executives, publicity flacks—who did business with *Playboy*. I listened closely for white-boy lechery or subtly racist-sexist jokes. But to my journalistic disappointment, the young guns in effect were more interested in trading business cards than ogling Tenison. Even at *Playboy*, money has replaced sex. The only overt lust I observed came from a bespectacled Asian clutching a copy of *Playboy* to his bosom. As she told the audience about her Idaho background, he said, to no one in particular, "I know the story. I read the magazine. I read it." Black or African American? Didn't matter to my man. He had the Playmate of the Year's picture in his hand, and that's all he needed to know.

VILLAGE VOICE, 1990

# OWNER'S MANUAL

**O**n the D train, in Union Square Park, inside the offices of a major record company, brothers of all kinds come up to you if you're leafing through a copy of Shahrazad Ali's *The Blackman's Guide to Understanding the Blackwoman*. A messenger with a cameo cut says, "Yo, my man, that book is slammin'." A midthirties brother in a kufi, the faint scent of incense wafting from his body, implores me, "Study it, brother." "That's the bible," a record producer wearing a Malcolm X T-shirt tells me sternly. Published by black-owned Civilized Publications in Philadelphia, the book is a Nubian bestseller, and its visibility reflects not just the specific appeal of the text, but the intellectual hunger of a large African American book-buying and -selling community with little use for the *New York Times Book Review* or *Publishers Weekly*. The producers and retailers thrive by feeding the Afrocentric, fiercely nationalistic, Islam-influenced militance that mainstream media associate only with the activism of Sharpton-Mason-Maddox and the recordings of Public Enemy, Boogie Down Productions, Queen Latifah, etc. This material can be peeped at in black-owned bookstores—Liberation on Lenox Avenue, Nikuru in Park Slope—or in the displays of the sidewalk book hustlers who are now as ubiquitous around town as musk-oil salesmen, and good for them.

Another platform for this literature is *Your Black Books Guide*, a supplement to the fiery Afrocentric weekly, the *National Newport News Commentator*, which contains national listings and ads for bookstores, publishers, and distributors. The titles on the supplement's bestseller chart will never be found at Rizzoli's. The classics list is headed by Elijah Muhammad's *Message to the Blackman*, followed by Carter G. Woodson's *Mis-Education of the Negro* and Lerone Bennett's *Before the Mayflower*, a history of Africans in America. The fiction list includes mainstream perennials James Baldwin and Maya Angelou. But in first place is Sam Greenlee's *The Spook Who Sat by the Door*, a 1970s potboiler about a black CIA agent who uses his training to turn a street gang into a team of revolutionary terrorists—an apt metaphor for the reversal of cultural cooptation these works attempt. The non-fiction top 10 surveys the interests of the growing Afrocentric community. Two titles by Elijah Muhammad, *Message* and *How to Eat to Live*; a biography of the Black Muslim patriarch, *The Legacy of Elijah Muhammad*; and Malcolm X's Alex Haley–penned autobiography are all in the house. So are *Afrikan Holistic Health* by Llaila O. Afrika; two republished texts that recast world history through their dark vision, George G. M. James's *Stolen Legacy* and Woodson's *Mis-Education*; and poet Haki Madhutbuti's essay collection *Black Men: Obsolete, Single & Dangerous*.

For us victims of the Western cultural machine, any substantial sampling of these books' vigorous rejection of values that have enslaved non-Caucasian peoples can be enough to awaken the most complacent mind. The flip side of this militance is that, read with more enthusiasm than discernment, these books can replace one set of mental shackles with another. The number one title on *Your Black Books Guide*'s nonfiction list, Ali's *The Blackman's Guide to Understanding the Blackwoman* has risen to prominence by exploiting brothers' worst misogynistic instincts, and also sisters' readiness to submit. Ali's tome, which enjoys its own full-page ad in *YBBG* and carries the cover line "Read it before she does," opens with the following introduction: "The Blackman and the Blackwoman in America have a problem. They do not get along. Before the Blackman can devise a solution he must know the components of the problem. The first factor is that the Blackwoman is out of control. She does not submit to guidance by her God-given mate the Blackman. Her intention to overpower and subdue the Blackman is motivated by several factors, the most prevalent being her self-inflicted nearly psychotic insecurity." A representative Ali observation: "The Blackman is the only one who knows what it takes to make the Blackwoman happy because she has no idea what real happiness is." Of sisters who wear dreads Ali writes: "Her values may even be considered more uncivilized because she is living on a very low level of existence by choice."

Guide to what? An alternate title springs to mind: *Soul Sisters: An Owner's Manual.* This text is shrill and didactic, packed with absolutes and stereotypes, with no nuance and not a shred of doubt, and its sales testify to the widespread yearning for a simple, male-dominant solution to the challenges of male-female relations. A lot of it reads like a parody of '60s nationalism or a sepia-toned Andrew Dice Clay routine. When I read passages to women friends, they first burst out laughing and then, quickly, grow angry, with Ali for writing it and with men for believing it. As idiotic as much of Ali's book is, it's a significant document. In a world where Thomas Sowell and Alice Walker get large contracts from corporate book publishers for validating white right-wing and left-wing positions, it's essential that the Afrocentric view be successfully articulated in book form. That Ali's book is the first hot underground text of the '90s suggests how little Afrocentrism respects the advances of African American women—and how unsuccessful black feminists have been in forging alliances with this ideologically potent community.

# VIDEO BLACULINITY

It is the Sunday night of *The Return of Super Fly*'s opening weekend. At the 23rd Street West Triplex's 7:30 show, 15 people are scattered about theater two. My three-deep posse sits stretched over six seats. Behind us are two couples adorned in sweatsuits, jingling baby earrings, and beepers. The brother behind me regularly critiques the onscreen drug paraphernalia and weapons and is genuinely pissed when one thug fails to shoot another in the mouth. "Put a gun in a nigger's mouth, you damn well better squeeze off," he notes sagely.

The emptiness of the theater, the crappiness of the flick, and the audience's ongoing commentary create an acute blaxploitation flashback. I spent many happy adolescent Saturdays in Times Square or downtown Brooklyn watching black-oriented action films that seem quite vital in light of this un-fly return. That *The Return of Super Fly* shares the marquee with a "black" musical (*Graffiti Bridge*) and a neo-martial-arts movie (Steve Seagal's overwhelmingly black and hispanic *Marked for Death*) intensifies the déjà vu. The evening's most amusing moment occurs about 15 minutes into *Return* when a fortyish man walks down the aisle past us. Can't see his face, but don't need to. Outlined against the silhouette of the screen, he is sporting a big brimmed, old school, mack daddy hat. When someone says, "*The Mack* must be back too!" we roar. The irony being that if *The Mack* was updated to, say, *Marked for Death* quality, not just hardcore action fans like me would be in the house.

Vilified by black cultural gatekeepers, ghettoized by the film industry, and remembered nostalgically by many who grew up on them, blaxploitation movies are crucial to the current '70s retro-nuevo phase we appear to be entering. When rappers emerged as a national force in the early '80s they became real world replacements for the sepia tough guys of Hollywood. But the spread of crack-inspired new jack gangsterism, coinciding with an increase in VCR purchases by

African Americans and the release of vintage blaxploitation on video, has magnified their impact on the music and its self-image.

N.W.A's recent EP, *100 Miles and Runnin'*, is a sonic montage of blaxploitation (and exploitation) iconography: the venal, drug-dealing cops of *Super Fly* and *The Mack* populate several rhymes; the title cut's prison break is as bullet-ridden as convict Jim Brown's escape in *Riot* and as violent as the gang's journey back to Coney Island in *The Warriors*; sample after sample harks back to blaxploitation's dense, funky soundtracks. Listening to N.W.A, Ice Cube, or Ice-T, you realize that current gangsta rap has its strongest antecedents, outside simple reality, in the trash movies stockpiled by ghetto video stores. In both hip hop and urban youth culture the gang concept, the drive-by, the fetish for automatic weaponry, and the proliferation of dolled-up pubescent gun molls are fantasies of macho potency many African American males first bugged out to via video.

Any album by N.W.A or their hardcore pissing cousins is a surreal experience that compresses violence against police, scatological sex, and the thick reasoning of the half-smart into a compact disc vision of Southern California hell. The hardcore rappers of today talk like the spawn of the stud protagonist of the pioneering blaxploitation epic *Sweet Sweetback's Baadasssss Song*.

A less threatening, though highly bizarre blaxploitation echo is the sudden ubiquity of Rudy Ray Moore. The blues comedian became a funky cult figure in the '70s with a funny series of foul-mouthed albums and low-rent movies, including my personal favorites, *Dolemite* and *Petey Wheatstraw, the Devil's Son-in-Law*, both updated blues rhymes stretched out into screenplays. Moore appears throughout Eric B. & Rakim's "The Ghetto" video and engages in a new-school-versus-old-school rap-off on the new Big Daddy Kane album.

Kane is increasingly fascinated by displays of retro blaculinity. Not only is Moore on his album *Taste of Chocolate*, but Kane steals the woman of blaxploitation idol Jim Brown in his "I Can Do It Right" video—the football hero turned actor now hangs tough with the rapper in a potent linkage of blaxploitation and hip hop icons. Kane's most recent publicity photo displays him wearing an expensive, big-lapelled suit that, with all due respect, looks like it was copped out of either the A. J. Lester or Eleganza pimpwear catalogue.

While the most stereotypical and best remembered blaxploitation flicks dealt with detectives and street hustlers, others dramatized black self-empowerment and vigilantism. *Gordon's War*, a tale of black Vietnam vets attacking heroin dealers in Harlem, was brought to mind by recent news from Dallas. In that Sunbelt city, Al Sharpton's role as aggravating agitator is performed by John Wiley Price, a Dallas county commissioner as well known locally for his weight-lifting and Lotus sports car as our reverend is for his hair.

In September Price said of Dallas's search for a new police chief: "If you try to bring in a good old boy in this system, we're going to be in the streets. Physically, literally, shooting folks." But what elevated Price from apocalyptic orator to blaxploitation avenger was a November 5 incident when off-duty police officer Robert Bernal went jogging past Price's home. Price came outside. Everyone agrees on that. It's what happened next that's in dispute. According to Price, Bernal yelled obscenities and a racial epithet at him. Price then chased the cop. Bernal claims Price had an Uzi; Price says it was only a pellet gun. Blows were exchanged, but only Price was arrested on assault charges. In the aftermath, 1,000 African Americans marched on Dallas city hall for the next city council meeting. A grand jury decided there was no case against Price and the two men later issued apologetic joint statements.

"Hey, that was my home. I take a lot," he told the *Los Angeles Times*. "Next time I might get a scope or something and not run after him." In an age when the videography of manhood is often defined by brazen, cocksure boasters—drum-machine Panthers—and influenced by the cartoon heroism of bad old movies, John Wiley Price has made the perfect political statement with his movie-styled macho. Some blacks around Dallas feel he might be the city's next congressman—using an electoral strategy no doubt concocted after repeated viewings of *Sweetback*.

# BOX OFFICE RIOT

**F**riday, March 8, approximately 9:00 P.M. at the traditional old Hollywood hangout Le Dome on Sunset Boulevard, the producers, director, and one of the stars of New Jack City crowd two front tables. The East Coast returns on the Warner Bros.–distributed black gangster melodrama flow in. "Sold out the evening shows all over Manhattan," says producer George Jackson, a rotund Harlemite by way of Harvard in a black porkpie hat. "Washington. Philly. Detroit. They're all selling out. We have a hit!" His partner Doug McHenry, a Stanford grad raised in Oakland, sporting a Def Jam jacket and his trademark glasses, lets a toothy smile cross his face as he savors his shrimp cocktail. Director Mario Van Peebles, actor/comic Chris Rock, chat with girlfriends, agents, and managers. Members of the WEA record staff stop by to report that the soundtrack, filled with cutting-edge rap by New Jack star/rapper Ice-T and state-of-the-art r&b by Keith Sweat and Johnny Gill, is already on reorder due to overwhelming demand. Two white-haired, nicely tanned, elegantly attired old Hollywood couples stroll by and cut a curious look as an exuberant Jackson is told New Jack City is projected to gross $2.5 million its first day in release.

For Jackson and McHenry, black producers who've struggled to work inside Hollywood with modest commercial success (Krush Groove, Disorderlies) but no artistic respect, New Jack City's extensive press coverage and clear profit potential make this a triumphant moment. Still, a couple of times during the evening Jackson and McHenry express a worry particular to purveyors of black-oriented youth entertainment in America: "Do you think there'll be any trouble tonight?" The history of black youth entertainment during the hip hop era is rife with incidents of broken glass, fights, even shootings. Just as crack-emboldened criminals have dogged rap concerts, they have in the past ruined showings of macho movies like Tougher Than Leather and Raw as well as wholesome entertainments such as House Party and Mo' Better Blues.

What *should* be obvious sadly isn't: that these outbreaks are not caused by rappers or movies, but by the same crushing sociological forces that incubate all forms of black-on-black violence. The wanton disregard for the dignity, and very lives of others, that Wesley Snipes's Nino Brown embodies in *New Jack City* is precisely the attitude that concerns Jackson and McHenry.

Because large-scale social events for black youth are so infrequent, anything, from a concert or movie to an Afrocentric lecture, tends to attract more patrons than it can accommodate. *New Jack City* opened in 862 theaters, more than recent box-office successes like *Do the Right Thing* and *House Party*, but only half of the 1,586 screens Universal reserved for Michael J. Fox's *The Hard Way* (with a cameo by L.L. Cool J). As the first black youth feature since last winter's *House Party*, and the subject of extensive print, radio, and television advertising, *New Jack City* was sure to have a large opening weekend. Some theaters wouldn't book it. Sunrise Cinema, the Valley Stream multiplex that attracts kids from Brooklyn, Queens, and Long Island and has a history of violence (a black teen was shot there during *Godfather III*), passed on *New Jack City*. But Warner Bros., according to Jackson and McHenry, have been aggressive in booking it and last Friday were committed to opening in another 20 to 30 screens.

Unfortunately for the film's black creative team and its mammoth studio financier, *New Jack City* could not have come out at a more racially tense time for Los Angeles. Black truckers are suing a large white trucking company for masquerading as a minority firm to win a $10 million contract. Hall of Fame second baseman Joe Morgan recently won $540,000 in a suit against the security force at Los Angeles International Airport who roughed up the retired athlete after assuming he was a drug dealer. Former Laker star Jamal Wilkes, now heavily involved with real estate, was stopped by cops in December, handcuffed, and told there was a felony warrant out for his arrest— either profound ignorance or malicious harassment. Wilkes has decided not to sue, but, as a member of the Los Angeles Urban League, he and the organization are still waiting on a formal apology from the police.

But it was the videotaped beating of black construction worker Rodney G. King by three Los Angeles police officers March 3 that really traumatized the city. The tape, which not only captured the clubbing of King but the presence of 12 other officers as onlookers, leaped from local news to CNN to the networks. Even Mayor Tom Bradley, an ex-cop comatose to police brutality during his 18 years in office, called for the cops' indictment, though the area's city charter doesn't give him direct control of quasi-fascist Chief Daryl Gates or his overanxious charges. Los Angeles hasn't, to date, spawned its own Al Sharpton or Alton Maddox to articulate black anger, but even without a catalytic spokesman, L.A.'s black community is clearly on edge.

*New Jack City's* producers make their first stop at the Hollywood Mann (once Grauman's Chinese Theater), a well-kept, spacious, ornate old theater where Jackson, McHenry, Rock, and Van Peebles hook up with Warner Bros. film executives. In the back of the theater heads swell and chests puff out as the film works as intended—they laugh at Bill Nunn's Duh Duh Duh Man, laugh and cry with Rock's crack-crazed Pookie, and marvel at Snipes's Cagneyesque performance.

Jackson, McHenry, and Rock split for the Mann Westwood Fourplex. Westwood, long a trendy West Village–like hangout for Cali's white youth, is also a place where black teens have long claimed police harassment. Local businesses trace their fears back to fights at the premiere for *Mo' Better Blues* and, three years ago, during the opening weekend of Eddie Murphy's *Raw.*

The driver, a white man with a European accent, seems unsure of his directions, which irritates the anxious McHenry. That anxiousness turns to melancholy when, after passing the UCLA campus that abuts Westwood, the limo stops near a police barricade. Through tinted windows the glare of helmeted policemen in riot gear can be seen in the street lights. The avenue in front of the Westwood Fourplex is cordoned off: in the distance scattered bits of glass glisten on the empty street. An Erik Estrada–looking cop eyes the producers and says grimly, "Do not walk on that sidewalk." They oblige.

Later Jackson and McHenry will find out that 1,500 converged on the sidewalk in front of the theater for a sold-out 10 o'clock showing, that for some reason many frustrated moviegoers looted 17 stores, that the police were remarkably restrained in dealing with the wayward kids, that many would later cite the King beating as a spark for the riot, and, finally, that some of the teens reportedly shouted "Fight the Power!" and "Black Power!" as they broke windows.

But the police weren't saying much, and the producers knew little of this as their driver rolled unsteadily toward Marina Del Rey. Conversation in the car revolved around the fallout of what went down in Westwood. Was it an isolated incident? What role had the police played in inciting the riot? Would the theater refuse to show the film again, perhaps sparking a larger boycott? Jackson was confident Warner Bros. would back them in both holding onto theaters and, crucially, helping open it wider. "We tried to take a step forward and make a film that was *Lost Weekend* meets *Public Enemy,* not just *Public Enemy,*" said McHenry with resignation. "Unlike white filmmakers, who just show the gangster hero, and not the by-product of their criminality—that's the difference between us and the Italian gangster films or blaxploitation films." Spirits were bolstered by the sold-out late show at Marina Del Rey and positive comments about the flick from kids hanging at the outdoor mall that housed the theater.

From Marina Del Rey to the Universal City multiplex the conversation shifted back to grosses, *New Jack City*'s potential commercial impact on black film, and reviews that praised Snipes, Ice-T, Rock, and the film's hyper-hip dialogue. With over a score of screens, the Universal City complex is one of the nation's busiest movie houses. Yet *New Jack City* was only in one room. As the limo pulled up, several police cars were parked in front and officers could be seen speaking with theater personnel. Three Jackson/McHenry staffers stood in front of the theater. Yes, there had been trouble. A chain-snatching in line had led to a fight. Precisely the kind of everyday urban crime that, when transferred inside a movie theater, is blamed on the film as much as the perpetrator. Inside Theater 5 the midnight show progressed calmly, but not quietly. Brothers in full L.A. gear—Raider cap, jheri curls, white T-shirt, jeans, blue jacket—marched in and out, while one homegirl in a white sweat suit entertained the back of the theater with her commentary.

Rock leaned against a wall in the back impassively, watching himself smoke crack, get rehabbed, and then murdered, all in 35 millimeter. The producers spent their time talking to the young, mostly hispanic ushers, who said that patrons shut out of *New Jack City* ended up going to see *The Hard Way.* "They're making money off our audience," McHenry said with irritation, "simply because we're not in enough theaters."

By Monday, March 11, when reports of gang-related violence came in from Brooklyn, Chicago, and Las Vegas, Friday's travelers were dealing with, and in fact to some degree profiting from, the media heat. A *People* profile on Chris Rock was held, the comedian re-interviewed, and a larger piece scheduled for this week with quotes on *New Jack City* inserted. "The Today Show" and "CBS This Morning," who had previously declined to book anyone from the film, came calling for Mario Van Peebles. Jackson and McHenry, barraged with phone calls at the production office of *House Party II,* on which they are making their directorial debut, issued a statement that, in part, said, "We are making films because we have a very clear sense of our roots as African

Americans. We are dedicated to making movies that will accurately and responsibly depict our experiences and unique insights. *New Jack City* speaks for itself."

On the Monday after its opening, in the wake of the movie reviews, news stories, and a Warner Bros. offer to pay theaters for additional security, *New Jack City* earned $805,000, which made it the number one grossing film in America. A week later, *New Jack City* had made $16 million, number two to *Silence of the Lambs* and more than *The Hard Way*.

VILLAGE VOICE, 1991

# NIGGAS WITH ATTITUDE

LOS ANGELES—On TNT the night the four cops walked, the Lakers and the Portland Trailblazers were in game three of their play-off series. Forum fans were alerted in the fourth quarter to the state of emergency imposed on the area. The Forum, like the airport and several important thoroughfares, is located in a working-class African American city, a city that was starting to ignite even as A. C. Green boxed out Buck Williams in overtime. You could bet your life that even as the white fans cheered black toughness inside the arena they were fearing it outside.

On CNN, meanwhile, stores were being torched. A gun shop was broken into and its deadly contents carried into homes around South Central. A helicopter captured the bloody beating of a white trucker by angry new jacks—only later did it come to light that four blacks had saved him, two leaving the safety of their homes to do so. At the First A.M.E. church, Mayor Tom Bradley tried to put a pacifier in the mouths of the disgruntled, while the departing Daryl Gates talked of containing the fury that his repressive philosophy had unleashed.

At Kennedy Airport the next morning the 10:30 MGM Grand

flight was delayed two hours "because of the riots." One white woman with two blond cherubs and a West Indian nanny got very upset when informed of this delay, but most of the flight's upscale types didn't mention it—at least not loud enough for a black writer and his comedian buddy to overhear. Instead, they used their calling cards and gazed at the "Home" show on ABC.

"There'll be an additional fifteen minutes or so on our flight time today," the pilot announced as the plane passed Philadelphia. "We have to go around the back way into L.A. today—because of all the ruckus going on there all flights were delayed." Midway across America I'm wearing shades and happily listening to Arrested Development when one of the cherubs asks, "Are you high?" Instead of getting up and smacking her mother—my first impulse—I reply, "No, I'm asleep," and think about L.A.

Things got pretty loud this time, but the unstable melting pot has been having quiet riots for years. In the most segregated West Coast metropolis, life has always been cheap for people of color. The habitual nihilism, simmering anger, and casual violence of both the L.A.P.D. and the multiracial gang scene has been escalating ever since my first trip here in 1981. In the African American community, xenophobia toward hispanics and Asians, alienation from a city government run by a prototypical Negro pol, and a genocidal yet fertile youth culture primed black L.A.'s everyday people for the uprising. The naked racism of the acquittal uncorked a big one, but next week, next month, next century, all the small beeps of rioting that make the *Los Angeles Times* Metro section so entertaining will still be there—unless, by some unforeseen miracle, fundamental change occurs between the residents of this brown metropolis and those who presume to control it.

The early '80s choke-hold controversy, the backlash vote against Tom Bradley's run for governor, the Long Beach rap riot, the acceptance of drive-bys in the popular vernacular, *Boyz N the Hood*, the unpunished shooting of a black girl by a Korean grocer—all helped create this boil on the smog-shrouded soil. It's why N.W.A, a/k/a Niggas With Attitude, were to the '80s what the Beach Boys were to the '60s and the Eagles to the '70s—the definitive Southern California band. "Fuck Tha Police" spoke to the fantasies of this city's majority no less than "California Girls" and "Life in the Fast Lane."

As the plane came over the city at about 2:30 L.A. time, smoke billowed up from two, three, four, seven spots out the left side windows. On the right side I saw four others. As the plane passed over the Coliseum, a huge plume of ashy black air floated up under our right wing. We got a beautiful view of the coastline when the plane curved out over the Pacific

Ocean—a route determined, I later found out, by South Central residents taking potshots at arriving flights. As we sat on the ground for 25 minutes, an attendant told me the Beverly Center had been closed by looting. I took note for two reasons: This L.A. landmark was in the red-hot center of West Hollywood, an overwhelmingly white liberal (and gay) part of town, and La Cienega Boulevard, which borders this giant mall, was the usual route to my hotel. We were also told that curfews were in effect in Los Angeles, Culver City, and Long Beach—and to hold on to our plane tickets to prove we had pressing business on the street.

An Arab cab driver approached us and asked cautiously, "Where are you going?" When we told him, he wasn't hostile, just concerned. "You sure you have to stay there?" he queried, explaining that on La Cienega south of the Beverly Center motorists were getting pulled from their cars. He wasn't taking that route, and I certainly had no problem with that. I was insistent on my destination only because my hotel, the Mondrian, provided a panoramic view of the city.

From a news station on the cab radio, the voices of authority filled our ears. "We're on full tactical alert," said a Beverly Hills officer. "Fires near MacArthur Park are erupting faster than the Fire Department can respond." "At 98th and Vernon a fireman has been shot." "Avoid all side streets. Use only freeways or main thoroughfares." "All RTD bus service and the Blue Line train service will be canceled." "The Utah-Clippers playoff game is being moved to Saturday afternoon and the Dodgers-Phillies game, scheduled for tonight, will be moved to later in the season." From City Hall the mayor droned on but one line caught my ear: "The police are under orders to take back the streets." And then I looked east and saw a rainbow. Except this rainbow was thick and gray and stretched from midway in the sky down to the ground, with spirals of smoke rising inside like miniature tornadoes.

From the Mondrian's restaurant terrace one can see west from the power towers of Century City across Beverly Hills, the Wilshire District, Mid-City, Koreatown, and the cluster of skyscrapers that defines Downtown. Beyond these areas are places like Inglewood, Ladera Heights, South Central, East L.A., and sundry other hoods. For two hours I sat on that terrace watching fires rage and then smolder. Dowdy white couples, flaxen-haired models, and hip dudes in snakeskin boots stood and pointed at them. As soon as one stream of smoke expired, another puffed up. Fire engines screamed below us. Western Boulevard, a poor man's furniture and appliance strip run by mostly hispanic and Asian merchants that's a major artery into South Central, was lit up. The vibe from the other guests was chilly. Adversity breeds fellowship and I saw people, particularly white women, making new acquaintances among themselves. No such familiarity came my way.

As the evening fell and the curfew came into effect I started working the phones. Melissa Maxwell, a young filmmaker living off Wilshire, was very upset. On the way home she'd witnessed two cars of black youths shooting at each other. A local computer store had been cleaned out, a window smashed at a nearby bank. Across the street a business was aflame. Her neighbors in her apartment complex were gathering up their garden hoses. "There's a Persian carpet outlet on our block," she said nervously, "and we hear they're going to hit it tonight. If there's a fire in that store it could set off the whole block."

Cheryl Hill and her man live in West Hollywood two blocks west of Melrose, a fashionable white area. As thick clouds of smoke filled the air there, residents came outside seeking its source. "We looked around and we were the only blacks on the block, and we could feel the stares. No one said anything, but white folks were looking at us a little funny."

Sam Kitt, a white movie executive, was one of the last to leave his Burbank office building. The studio security guards advised him, "Don't stop for any red lights. If anybody gets in your way, make them a hood ornament." Out in the valley where Sam lives, the only sign of trouble is a fire "maybe twenty blocks away."

Denise Weeks, a television producer's assistant who lives off Pico in Mid-City, couldn't talk long. "Everybody on the block's getting their water hoses out," she said quickly. "There's a fire three blocks away in one direction and another in the other direction four blocks down. Talk to you later."

Dolores Forteno and her video camera had just returned to her home off Western. "I don't think there's a Korean nail shop left in town. I saw no violence—just fires. Lots of family-owned businesses burning. The good Chinese food restaurant, the Ethiopian cleaners, the place we shop for groceries—all gone. It's not a black-Korean thing here 'cause the population is 80 per cent Mexican and Salvadoran, so it's mostly hispanic on hispanic. They didn't mind me taping. Got them going in and coming out the swap meet. You got to come over and see it."

Eddie G., an actor from Crenshaw who was staying at the hotel instead of journeying home, took a biblical view. "God's a violent motherfucker," he said. "Forty days and forty nights of rain is violent. This is his retribution. God's with the niggas on this one." More profound than his religious interpretation was his news that the Bloods and Crips had declared a truce and gotten together "to burn this whole motherfucker down."

This was an observation/rumor that a number of people with gang and rap contacts repeated. The injury of several babies in recent drive-bys had apparently led to a temporary cessation of hostilities. This truce was then extended because of the King verdict and, according to street talk, channeled into taking black and hispanic fury outside South Central. For hardcore gang-bangers, it was a golden opportunity for the big payback.

At around nine I walked out into the hotel driveway in a blue jean shirt and pants, and gazed at Sunset Boulevard. On a normal Thursday the Comedy Store would have been jumping, cars zooming by, and the hotel's lights on to welcome guests. Tonight there was nothing to see but stale smoke clouds saturating the air. A hotel employee told me the Pink Dot down the block had a handwritten sign in the window that read, "Black Owned," and we both laughed. Three security guards in suits looked me over between their yawns. Then a van rolled by and the brother behind the wheel flashed a gang sign my way. It was time to go inside.

Nine a.m. Friday morning the numbers are coming in: 27 dead, 1,235 injured, 2,000 structural fires, 30 active fires, 3,000 arrested and $200 million in damages—all sure to go much higher. My buddy Chris Rock and I hit the road for Burbank and a celebrities-against-racism event called Wall of Justice. Along Sunset toward Highland, many windows are smashed, Asian store owners are sweeping the sidewalk in front of a diner, and British singer/songwriter Seal drives by in a black convertible. The police have blocked off Hollywood Boulevard going east, now a deteriorating neighborhood that's an L.A. cross between 14th Street and Times Square. There's been massive looting there. Somebody snatched Madonna's old bra from Frederick's of Hollywood.

The Wall of Justice media event draws an eclectic crew—Richard Grieco, Justine Bateman, Debbie Allen, Wesley Snipes, Jimmy Smits, Sean Penn, Anjelica Huston, Joie Lee, Bill Duke, Robert Culp, David Cassidy. A gauze wall has been set up on a Warner soundstage right next to a giant unfinished poster of Mel Gibson and Danny Glover for *Lethal Weapon* 3. The celebs are to sign this wall and then have their names collected on a petition protesting the King verdict. An instant anthem by the unlikely Tom Petty, "Peace in L.A.," is debuted. Wesley Snipes, wearing robes X-Clan would envy, drops a little Afrocentric science on this old-fashioned liberalism when he says from the podium, "The problem is universal racism in this country," but most of the talk is feel-good bromides.

In a corner of the sound stage, Propaganda Films is taping PSAs for the mayor's office, and they've managed to corner N.W.A's Eazy-E and Ren. I'm surprised by their presence but not their attitude. When the nice white-haired woman in the pink dress from the mayor's office asks them to say "Stop the violence" for the camera, Ren just looks through her. Eazy's got on wraparound shades and an adorable smirk. "I can't say that," Ren finally replies. "No," the pink-dress lady asserts, "you must say it." Ren just raises his hands as if to say "Fuck you," and walks away. Eazy, a savvier media manipulator, kicks a few lines about "It don't make sense for people to tear up their own neighborhood" and steps off.

As actors and directors talk of finding common ground, Ren, one of the FBI-censored voices on "Fuck tha Police," looks around and comments, "Half the mother-fuckers in here are fronting. I wasn't gonna say that stop the violence shit so they could feel good." He takes a call on his mobile phone and then continues: "This Bloods and Crips truce gonna end in just a couple of days. After all the looting's over, it's gonna go back how it was. The good thing about all this is that black people see the police for what he is. Can't trust him. Ain't no justice for a young black man."

On the way back from Burbank we decide to hit Western, not sure we can make it out to South Central and back before curfew. Western Furniture is boarded up. Selected Furniture is being nailed shut. Wilshire TV is burned and gone. These are just a few names of the stores I wrote down—could have been any one of a score of others. Anywhere selling consumer durables, that is—most of the fast-food joints seem untouched.

We cut down a side street onto Virginia Avenue, where two police cars and seven cops guard a mini-mall. As we drive across Mid-City toward the Beverly Center it's clear that the Rodney King uprising was primarily an economic event. Beautiful residential sections just blocks from ransacked mini-malls are untouched and peaceful. Sure blacks robbed blacks. But hispanics robbed hispanics, and blacks robbed hispanics, and everybody robbed Asians, and whites too got their share when the opportunity presented itself.

In 1992 economic outrage isn't bound by geography or race, but by class—no news there except maybe to the mainstream media and government officials. As King himself suggested on Friday, the first two hours of the uprising were probably about the verdict. The night and day that followed around L.A. and the nation were about every bit of hopelessness that's been festering since the '70s. Working and poor Americans have been in a depression since Reagan's first term and all these TV-news–designated "criminals" are going for theirs because they feel so damned deprived.

In 1965 African Americans in urban centers like Watts were seeking their bit of the civil rights miracle that was transforming the South. Their needs were as much economic as social, and those needs were never addressed. Twenty-seven years later a generation has grown up that knows zip about those past hopes and views this world with precious little optimism. Crucially, the folks who wear X hats, view Chuck D and KRS-One as cultural heroes, and know the sound of Tech-9's better than the 10 commandments are not going to respond to racist provocation the way liberals and their African American elders want them to.

Like George Jackson embracing the metaphor of the mythic black stud Stagger Lee, young people—women and men—celebrate the hardest parts of their imaginations and invent themselves as niggas-for-life with no apologies and incredible pride. Shooting AK-47s at cops and attacking Korean grocers who they've always viewed as economic imperialists is not an aberration. The same bold disdain has been there for years—just aimed mostly at each other, so no one gave a damn. But the nation does now and, like the jury in Simi Valley, it will interpret that attitude to fit its misconceived notions at its own risk.

Friday night on Sunset. No fires can be seen from the terrace, though copters still haunt the sky. Chris and I hit the hotel gym and then stand in our shorts in the driveway, marveling at the quiet of a street we've hung out on so many Fridays after dark. A taxi driver sleeps in his cab. Two parking attendants chill and talk. A black hotel manager in a blue blazer walks out, looks around and says hello. About five minutes later four county sheriffs walk up the driveway and two blue-blazered hotel staffers greet them. The group glances our way and one sheriff, a tall brother with a glistening dome, says, "I know him. That's Chris, the actor." Five minutes later the sheriffs are gone. Celebrity still means something in L.A. But L.A. will never again just mean celebrity.

VILLAGE VOICE, 1992

**3**

# SOUL CULTURE: TRAD AND RETRO-NUEVO

# STANDING IN THE
# SHADOWS OF MOTOWN

## The Unsung Session Men
## of Hitsville's Golden Era

**T**hey are simply some of the greatest records ever made. "Standing in the Shadows of Love." "Stop, in the Name of Love." "Signed, Sealed, Delivered." "The Way You Do the Things You Do." "Ain't Too Proud to Beg." "I Heard It Through the Grapevine." "Twenty-Five Miles." These songs and so many more were written, arranged, and recorded at 2648 West Grand Boulevard, a modest row house in central Detroit that housed Motown Records' Hitsville recording studio from 1959 to the early '70s.

We all know the names . . . child prodigy "Little" Stevie Wonder . . . the sepia Barbra Streisand, Diana Ross . . . the mercurial Marvin Gaye . . . pop's finest wordsmith and supplest architect of "the Motown sound," Eddie Holland, Lamont Dozier and Brian Holland . . . the designer of the '70s soul epics Norman ("Papa Was A Rolling Stone") Whitfield. And, of course, Berry Gordy, Jr., the aggressive, reclusive capitalist from Detroit who made it happen.

But what of the musicians? The key roles played by the Motown session men have only been sketchily documented, seminal contributions by drummer Benny Benjamin and Uriel Jones, guitarist Robert White, band leader/keyboardist Earl Van Dyke, keyboardist Johnny Griffith and bassist James Jamerson. The gala Motown twenty-fifth anniversary television version of Hitsville in May saw fit to include appearances by Linda Ronstadt and Adam Ant, but neglected to even mention these quintessential members of what was once the best band in America. Even in their heyday, they rarely received songwriting or arranging credits on their records. While their Memphis counterparts Booker T. & the M.G.'s became darlings of the music world, the men of Motown toiled in anonymity. Although it is hard to imagine contemporary bass playing without James Jamerson, I was only the second person in 20 years to interview him at length.

"You could compare our rhythm section to anything else happening at that time and we were just better," claims Johnny Griffith, who during the '60s often played sessions in New York and Chicago. "The Motown thing was so much tighter. When we locked into a groove it was hellacious. The key thing was that we all grew up together and had this Detroit way of approaching music."

From the '20s through the early '60s, Detroit was one of America's boom towns. Its growth was fueled by the assembly lines of the auto industry, as the city's residents worked around the clock to satisfy our thirst for the mobility and affluence that cars represented. Detroit attracted poor and working-class families from around the country, a large percentage of them Southern blacks. In the days before the landmark 1954 Brown vs. Board of Education Supreme Court decision and the dawn of the civil rights movement, the assembly line certainly beat sharecropping. Berry Gordy's family came from Mississippi, James Jamerson's from South Carolina, and Earl Van Dyke's from Kentucky.

With the discretionary capital that the Detroit gas-fueled economy provided, the parents of musically inclined youngsters were able to buy instruments, often pianos, and get professional training as well. The large, segregated high schools of Detroit also offered musical training for black youths. Jamerson was introduced to the bass by a teacher at Northwestern High in 1954 "because I had long fingers and big hands . . . I went through the books, learned how to read and was helping students in class after three months." Northwestern, one of Detroit's biggest black high schools, produced a number of other key Motown personnel, including Smokey Robinson.

Bebop was challenging and enchanting the city's young musicians in the '50s and the future Motown session players were caught up in its spirit. Jamerson recalls, "When I was in my teens I used to play jazz at this place where the musicians hung out. Barry Harris, the piano player, was the leader of us guys. As we got older we started playing in clubs like the Minor Key and at all the college dances. At this time I started playing with the heavyweights like Dizzy Gillespie. Different musicians from New York would come in and jam."

For Griffith and Van Dyke, bebop and Harris were also important.

"Musically he was the man," says Griffith. "The young players would all hang out at Barry's house, because he was the only guy who knew all the hit bebop changes. We'd all be learning together, just exchanging ideas."

"Detroit musicians back in that time weren't in competition, but just out to help one another," adds Van Dyke. "I remember the hardest tunes for me to get were 'Cherokee' and 'Lush Life.' Hank Jones taught it to Barry Harris. Barry Harris taught it to me. I taught it to somebody else. That was the Detroit way."

Despite all the inspiration of bebop, many found the best way to eat and still play was through r&b. Van Dyke played with obscure r&b guitarist Emmett Sheigh ("I was one of the Sheigh Riders") before graduating first to Lloyd Price and then to Aretha Franklin in the early '60s. Jamerson was gigging around Detroit, doing session work for local Detroit labels such as Golden World. Griffith also did sessions in Detroit and Chicago. All of this activity proved a prelude to the most important musical experience of their lives: Motown.

From 1959 to 1963 William "Mickey" Stevenson, Motown A&R director and producer, and Berry Gordy recruited musicians, mostly Detroit natives, for the house band. Jamerson joined in 1959 after playing on a session at the studio of Raymona Gordy, Berry's first wife. Van Dyke was lured back to Detroit after tiring of life on the road. Griffith cut an album on Motown's jazz label workshop before playing on Motown sessions in 1963.

Business at Motown began early, at least for the record business, with sessions starting often at nine or ten A.M. They also started late at night. Producer Clarence Paul, the man in charge of "Little" Stevie Wonder's recordings, enjoyed cutting late, feeling that recording at three or four in the morning brought out the best in musicians. Often after Earl Van Dyke & his Funk Brothers (basically the Motown band) ended their nightly sets at the Chit Chat Lounge, Motown staffers, including Berry himself, would stop by and get the musicians to accompany them back to Hitsville to record. Levi Stubbs recorded the vocals to "Baby, I Need Your Loving" between two and eight A.M. one summer morning after Brian Holland told him about the song at the Twenty Grand Nightclub.

Griffith remembers those days quite vividly. "We'd get lead sheets from the producer and they'd hum lines out to us. After a while it got more sophisticated and much more detailed. By 1965, the producers were getting much better and started to use strings heavily. It forced them to get more specific about what they wanted because you had to write for the string players they'd recruited from the Detroit Symphony. Later the producers would draw the outline and we'd work out the harmonies among ourselves."

Despite the almost constant recording going on at Hitsville, the number of Motown releases was always kept to a relative trickle, reflecting Gordy's philosophy of quality over quantity. Many now claim that the Motown vaults are overflowing with material that Motown's quality control committee felt was either uncommercial or too experimental. Van Dyke says his favorite Motown album, a William Stevenson/Ivy Hunter production featuring Marvin Gaye singing over Latin-influenced tracks "never hit the streets. There was a lot of stuff like that they rejected." Unreleased Motown music from the '60s still turns up on current albums, including Smokey Robinson's 1979 hit, "Cruising" and Stevie Wonder's "All I Do" from 1980's *Hotter Than July* LP.

Van Dyke also feels the genesis of several songs on Wonder's epic *Songs in the Key of Life* was in old Motown sessions. "Motown would always change the titles and sometimes words after the tracks had been cut. If you read the liner notes on *Songs* you see the names of all the Motown musicians right in there." For years musicologists have been trying to get Motown to release some of this unreleased material, but so far Motown has resisted the idea.

*Billboard*'s Adam White best described the Motown sound: "The elements: a bedrock bass line; an emphatic beat accentuated by tambourines; pounding percussion and piano tracks; saxophone-driven brass charts; shrill *femme* backup vocals in the classic call-and-response mode of gospel performances; and those swirling, riff-reinforcing strings of the Detroit Symphony."

These were built into almost all the classic Motown hits of the '60s. The mechanistic, most stereotypically Motown records were products of the Brian Holland-Lamont Dozier-Eddie Holland team. During the same period two other producer/writers, Smokey Robinson and Norman Whitfield, developed personal approaches that differed markedly from Holland-Dozier-Holland. Robinson's production, based on the graceful gamesmanship of his lyrics, made for a varied, eclectic output. Norman Whitfield made Motown's funkiest records, first in answer to Stax's Southern sound and later in response to Sly Stone's bodacious psychedelic soul.

Holland-Dozier-Holland, all former singers, were united by Gordy as a production and writing team in 1963. Their early records, such as Martha & the Vandellas's "Heat Wave" and Marvin Gaye's "How Sweet It Is to Be Loved by You," were above average, but still musically

standard r&b pop of the period. In 1964 their music grew more sophisticated as they arrived at a very efficient division of labor; Eddie Holland was the chief lyricist; Lamont Dozier wrote music and supervised
the horns, string, and background vocals; and Brian Holland wrote
music, worked directly with the session musicians, and ran the actual
recording sessions.

With the Supremes's "Baby Love" (1964), they hit upon one of
the most successful formulas in musical history. The leanness of these
melodies and heartfelt banality of the words was balanced by arrangements that grew increasingly dense and dramatic. "By 1967 and 1968
you could really hear the influence of classical music on their work,"
remembers Griffith. "Brian had sat down and studied classical music
to some degree. This really changed their style. You hear it on 'Standing in the Shadows of Love,' 'Bernadette' and 'Reach Out I'll Be
There.'

"H-D-H had everybody come on in to the studio at the same time,
like it was one big party. They'd give us four or five chords on a piece of
paper and we'd start studying and get the feel of the tune. Brian Holland would walk around and whisper little patterns in your ear. With
each player he'd give them one or two patterns to try."

H-D-H had to have the cooperation of Motown's musicians to
make their formula work, but once established ("I Can't Help Myself,"
"It's the Same Old Song," and "Sugar Pie, Honey Bunch"), it only
required fine tuning from record to record. In contrast, Robinson's
more free-form style demanded more creative input from the musicians. "Smokey always would start with a rhythm section of four
pieces," says Griffith. Robinson developed arranging and rhythmic
ideas with these small groups by adding additional instruments as the
song came together.

With the aid of the studio musicians, Miracles guitarist Marv
Tarplin, members of his group the Miracles, and the Motown staff
writers, Smokey shaped his wonderful lyrics into compelling music:
The Miracles's "Ooo Baby Baby," "I Second That Emotion," and "The
Tears of a Clown"; the Temptations's "The Way You Do the Things
You Do"; and the Four Tops's "Still Water (Love)" reflect the range of
Robinson's productions and his ability to maintain a consistent musical personality while drawing upon a variety of collaborators.

Norman Whitfield's records lack the aural textures of H-D-H, nor
do they have the variety and charm of Robinson. Instead, Whitfield's
records have something people don't normally associate with Motown:
funk. In fact, bassist Jamerson says, "Norman didn't just want funk, he

wanted monstrous funk." After starting as a paper pusher in the A&R department, Whitfield graduated to production in 1964, introducing a raw soulful edge to Motown music with the Marvelettes's "Too Many Fish in the Sea," the Temptations's "Ain't Too Proud to Beg," and both Gladys Knight & the Pips's and Marvin Gaye's version of "I Heard It Through the Grapevine."

. However, Whitfield didn't become an innovator until 1968. "He came into the studio one day and said, 'I wanna do something different, I wanna do something fresh,'" says Uriel Jones. With the Temptations providing the voices and longtime collaborator Barrett Strong ("Money") the words, Whitfield revolutionized Motown with three kinetic, uptempo hits ("Cloud Nine," "Psychedelic Shack," "Ball of Confusion") and the haunting "Papa Was a Rolling Stone." All these songs were based on riffs improvised to a large degree by Whitfield and the musicians in the studio.

But for all the production magic, the core of the Motown sound was its distinctive rhythm. Berry Gordy believed in a hard, emphatic beat, one often accentuated by either handclaps, or, his favorite, tambourines. Often guitarist Robert White's metallic down strokes would also land on the beat as on "Dancing in the Street."

Underpinning all these extras was Benny Benjamin, known around Hitsville, U.S.A., as "Papa Zita" because he resembled a dark Cuban and enjoyed peppering his speech occasionally with obscene Spanish phrases. Like his co-workers, Benjamin's background was in jazz, reflected on the Miracles's "Shop Around," Motown's first national hit in 1960, when he used brushes instead of sticks. In fact some other early Motown hits ("My Girl") have the feel of brush drumming even if Benjamin actually didn't use them.

Stevie Wonder fondly recalled, "Benny would be late for sessions, Benny'd be drunk sometimes. I mean, he was a beautiful cat, but . . . Benny would come up with stories, like, 'Man, you'd never believe it but like a goddamn elephant, man, in the middle of the road, stopped me from comin' to the sessions, so that's why I'm late, baby, so (clap of hands) it's cool!' But he was ready. He could play drums . . . you wouldn't even need a bass, that's how bad he was. Just listen to all that Motown stuff; the drums would just pop!"

"Oh, man, (Benjamin) was my favorite," adds James Jamerson joyfully. "When he died I couldn't eat for two weeks, it hurt me so bad. He and I were really the ones who tightened up the sound, the drum and the bass. We didn't need sheet music."

Along with providing the beat, Benjamin was the spirit of the

Motown band musicians as well. Whenever singers got out of line, feeling too big for the music or musicians, it was Benny Benjamin who cut them down to size. "They always used to fall out with Benny, probably because he used to lip a lot," says Van Dyke, chuckling. "When someone would give him some lip, he'd say, 'Look, I been down in this snake pit many a day and many a month and many a year. I seen them come and seen them go. And I'm still here.' That was the way it was with him and it was the truth. We did see many of them come and many of them go. That was all the way from Tony Martin to Billy Eckstine to Sammy Davis, Jr., and we were still there getting our little money."

In contrast to his studio precision, Benjamin was undisciplined in his private life, including ever-growing alcohol and drug addictions. "As Benny started deteriorating in the studio, which everybody noticed, they brought in two drummers," Van Dyke recalls, "Uriel Jones and Richard 'Pistol' Allen, to fill that one man's shoes. Yes sir, two drummers. Gladys Knight & the Pips's 'Heard It Through the Grapevine' in 1967 was about the first time they used two. Uriel Jones was playing the time and Benny was playing the pickups. Benny had gotten so he couldn't keep time."

Uriel Jones, however, has a different memory. He claims that young Stevie Wonder suggested using two drummers sometime in 1966. "Stevie could play drums and one day came in with a drum part he wanted us to play. He tried me and I couldn't play it. He tried Benny and he couldn't play it. So then he split it up between us. He sat us both down and said, 'Well, you do the foot in this part. You do the cymbal in this part.'"

Benjamin's death by a stroke in 1969 marked the beginning of the end for the Motown sound. Wonder sang long and passionately at his funeral. Little Steveland Morris had long idolized Benjamin, regarding the personable drummer as a second father. Appropriately, Stevie's drumming on many of his best records is pure Benny Benjamin.

Bassist James Jamerson was one of the first Motown staff musicians, working for Gordy and company from 1959 to 1973 following a gig in the band of another gifted Detroit native Jackie Wilson. Jamerson remembers the early Motown years clearly from twenty years' distance: "Holland-Dozier-Holland would give me the chord sheet, but they couldn't write for me. When they did, it didn't sound right. They'd let me go on and ad lib. I created, man. When they gave me that chord sheet, I'd look at it, but then start doing what I felt and what I thought would fit. All the musicians did. All of them made hits.

"I'd hear the melody line from the lyrics and I'd build the bass line around that. I always tried to support the melody. I had to. I'd make it repetitious, but also add things to it. Sometimes that was a problem because the bassist who worked the acts on the road couldn't play it. It was repetitious, but had to be funky and have emotion.

"My feel was always an Eastern feel. A spiritual thing. Take 'Standing in the Shadows of Love.' The bass line has an Arabic feel. I've been around a whole lot of people from the East, from China and Japan. Then I studied the African, Cuban and Indian scales. I brought all that with me to Motown.

"I picked things up from listening to people speak. From the intonation of their voices, I could capture a line. I look at people walking and get a beat from their movement. I'm telling you all my secrets now."

And on what tune was Jamerson's bass line formed by the sight of someone walking? "There was one of them heavy, funky tunes the Temptations did . . . I can't remember the name, but there was this big, fat woman walking around. She couldn't keep still. I wrote it by watching her move."

Jamerson now says his favorite bass parts are on the Four Tops's "Reach Out," "Bernadette," "Standing in the Shadows of Love," Marvin Gaye's "What's Goin' On" and Stevie Wonder's "Signed, Sealed, Delivered." "There was also this semi-jazz album Marvin Gaye did that had a version of 'Witch Craft' that I liked," Jamerson adds.

The pleasure of his Motown memories is diminished by his feelings that "in certain ways" he and his fellow musicians were exploited: "There is also sometimes a tear because I see now how I was treated and cheated. I didn't see that until I got a little older. Everybody, as time went on, got sort of strange. Especially after Motown moved out to California. If they see you, they're glad to see you. They just change their phone numbers so much. I don't believe in changing mine. I don't believe some of them know I'm still alive."

Health problems have frustrated Jamerson's efforts as a player and producer in recent years. When we talked he was resting in a suburban Los Angeles hospital from a recent illness. Still, he wants everyone to know, "I'm ready, willing, and able. Just give me a call."

Despite Jamerson's feeling of being exploited, though, Earl Van Dyke insists the pay was pretty good. "If you didn't come out of Motown with some money or some property, it wasn't Berry's fault. In 1965 I made $60,000. In 1966 I made close to $100,000, which included some outside work. In that time it was rare that a musician could own his own house, but I did. Everybody there was buying Cadillacs. Everybody had some money." In 1962 Van Dyke was offered $135 a week to join Motown's staff; by the mid-'60s studio musicians were taking home as much as $3,000 a week. Musicians were paid $52.50 for the first three hours, $52.50 for the next hour and a half, and $52.50 for every additional half hour. They were often awarded bonuses by the producers for performing on a particularly successful date. Defying the threat of a fine if caught, many Motown staffers also did outside work.

"I hold no grudges against Motown," asserts Van Dyke. "I hold grudges against myself because the opportunities were there to do more and I didn't take advantage of them. I just got locked into the fact that I was playing music and making a living. It was not what I wanted to play, but it was good. My children went to private school. It was grand."

Jamerson, however, feels some bitterness: "We were doing more of the job than we thought we were doing and we didn't get any songwriting credit. They didn't start giving any musicians credits on the records until the '70s." Did he complain about it? "I always asked. No one ever said anything. It did make me sort of mad, but what could I do?" Did he ever speak to Gordy about it? "Yes, but they felt that as long as you got paid your name didn't have to be on the record . . . I wrote some tunes, and they cut some of them, but they just put them on the shelf. They never got out."

## Epilogue: Gone Hollywood

Berry Gordy had always admired the movie moguls. In fact he saw himself an heir to the legacy of people like Samuel Goldwyn, who had pulled himself out of the ghetto through grit, determination, and vision. The famed Motown charm school approach to artist development was also based directly on the Hollywood star system, so it wasn't surprising that he was inexorably drawn to it. Since the mid-'60s Motown had a Los Angeles office and by 1970 Gordy was spending considerable time there, laying the groundwork for a shift of all Motown operations to the West Coast and negotiating with Paramount Pictures to distribute *Lady Sings the Blues*, the critically acclaimed Diana Ross vehicle. By the time Gordy had realized his lifelong ambition of directing (the dopey *Mahogany* in 1973), Motown had settled into a skyscraper on Sunset Boulevard and purchased a studio in Los Angeles.

Back in Detroit the musicians who worked for Motown knew that the good old days were ending, H-D-H had left in a flurry of lawsuits. One by one the stable of Motown acts grew smaller as the Isley Brothers, Gladys Knight & the Pips, the Spinners, and the Four Tops jumped ship. During the transitional years the Detroit musicians were flown out to Los Angeles for key sessions such as the early Jackson Five singles ("I Want You Back," "ABC") and Marvin Gaye's "What's Goin' On." Other tracks, cut by musicians in Los Angeles, were sent back for overdubbing. But it soon became apparent that if they were to continue their relationship with Motown, a move to Los Angeles was in order.

"Yeah, he [Gordy] said we'd have a job if we came out there," recalls Van Dyke, "but at the same rate of pay that it was here [in Detroit]. I didn't think I could survive in Tinseltown on that kind of money the way I could in Detroit. We negotiated, but there was no agreement over increased wages, and soon after they moved out there the contract with all the Detroit musicians ended. But even after that I did work for Motown on a premium wage scale."

Motown's relocation to Los Angeles had a profound effect on black music. Following Motown's lead, top r&b musicians from Chicago, New York, Memphis, New Orleans, Atlanta, and later Philadelphia, migrated to L.A., since that appeared to be where the action in black music was now centered. In the process, much of the regionalism in black music was lost. The "Detroit sound," the "Chicago sound" the "Memphis sound," all became part of the current state-of-the-art studio perfectionism of Los Angeles–based black pop.

Jamerson and other Motown musicians remained in Los Angeles. Van Dyke, Griffith and Jones disliked California living and returned to Detroit. Much to their dismay, the Motor City just wasn't the same. With Motown's departure fewer outside record companies traveled there to record. A coterie of musicians working at United Sound and led by George Clinton were formulating a new Detroit sound, one that made Norman Whitfield's "psychedelic" experiments positively old hat.

Detroit was no longer a city of hope, but an angry, disillusioned landscape of crumbling buildings and racial unrest still simmering from 1967's violent riot. By 1973 the Motown sound wasn't Diana Ross, but the sound of gunfire as Detroit was saddled with America's highest murder rate. As a result, the once vital nightclub scene that had nurtured a generation of Detroit musicians was dead.

Still the musicians survived. Van Dyke worked as a sideman and conductor for numerous performers, including a ten-year stint as musical director for another Detroit native, Freda Payne. Griffith had an instrumental hit on RCA Records, "Grand Central Shuttle," in 1973. Later he served as music director at Detroit's WGPR for four years. Griffith now produces radio commercials via his own production company.

Jones had put a lot of time into developing his interior decorating business, though he has never given up drumming. In fact, last summer Jones and Van Dyke did a series of free concerts, sponsored by Detroit's Parks & Recreations Authority, performing instrumental versions of Motown hits.

Despite Detroit's sad state, Griffith thinks there is still musical life in the old city. "The musicians, the singers, the producers are still here, but there isn't a support system anymore. Even if Motown didn't sign you, they were a sign that it could happen for you, even in Detroit. Now after you reach a certain point you have to leave. You can only go so far here now. It's a shame, but it's real. It is like what they say around Detroit now, 'We used to make cars here.' And great records."

MUSICIAN, 1983

# WHOSE TIME WAS IT?

PRINCE
THE TIME

Early in 1981 I interviewed Prince Rogers Nelson and Morris Day within weeks of each other. No one knew Prince would, after doing interviews in New York that winter, turn into pop's Howard Hughes, so I didn't tape our talk, which looks pretty dumb now, but, hey, I was young. (For Prince's take on meeting the press, refer to "All the Critics Love You in New York" on 1999.)

Looking back I'm struck by the degree of artifice these black cousins from the Minnesota tundra exhibited. Prince sat in an unlit

Madison Avenue hotel room illuminated only by the gray day peeping in a window. Enveloped in his now legendary gray raincoat—a Hendrix button on one lapel—he aimed his chin down and forehead forward across the table, a look documented in a zillion photos, and proceeded to tell a slew of lies. His mother is white, there's no r&b scene in Minneapolis/St. Paul, and he wasn't the mysterious producer-engineer Jamie Starr, the first in a long list of Princely pseudonyms (including Alexander Nevermind, Joey Coco, Camile).

When queried about the then shocking lyrics of *Dirty Mind*'s "Sister" and "Head," he replied, "I make music for my generation, and they'll understand the real reality of my songs." A day or two later I spotted him having lunch with his publicist, and he gave me a ticket to see him on "Saturday Night Live." Nice guy, I thought, a little eccentric, but hey, he's young.

Morris Day sat in my office at the long-gone biz mag *Record World* wearing two-tone Stacy Adams dress shoes, baggy pants, and an embroidered jacket with a creamy topcoat draped over his shoulders. No, he said, Prince is not Jamie Starr. No, Prince didn't play on the Time's first album. (Prince not only played most of the instruments on *The Time*, he wrote most of it, too!) And, no, the Time wasn't a funk band. "Funk is dead," he declared. "Cool is in." Mr. Nelson and Mr. Day fabricated from whole cloth in those interviews, and now we know why.

These midwestern slicksters had schemed together to concoct a mystique. To wit, Prince was supposed to be a blood-drinking, demon-loving dude who fucked his older sister, scheduled regular orgies, and, when up for air, was the greatest one-man band since Stevie Wonder. Day was the zoot-suited lady-killer who combined Jackie Wilson's onstage charisma with a comic arrogance worthy of George Jefferson. Together Day and Prince were twin peaks of a new wave of interracial musicians with roots in funk, rock, and their hometown's isolation. To themselves, and to the many who played along with the con, the turn-of-the-decade music of *Dirty Mind* and *The Time* truly confirmed them, as "Sexuality" put it, the "new breed leaders."

Ten years later, after *Purple Rain* and *Under a Cherry Moon*, after *Thriller* and Eddie Murphy's Delirious tour, after MTV, house, and New Jack Swing, after *Raising Hell* and *It Takes a Nation of Millions* and *Straight Outta Compton*, after *She's Gotta Have It* and Tracy Chapman and Living Colour and CDs and Janet Jackson's *Control*, it's amusing to listen to Prince singing and Day playing drums on a song called "New Power Generation." New? These brothers are both over 30. Day is married and on the wack ABC sitcom "New Attitude." And baby-faced Nelson recently gave up shaving, surely a sign of encroaching old age.

Yet here they come gaming again. There's nothing new about the anthem's sentiments—usually a tune like it pops up on every Prince project—nor about the groove, which (I do believe, Mr. Day) is funk. Or at least very funky. It's also one of several kickin' jams on Prince's *Graffiti Bridge* (Paisley Park) and the Time's *Pandemonium* (Paisley Park). These collections make it clear that, stripped of much of their self-created mystery, they're old-fashioned, small-town boys who perform and play their asses off. In 1991, that's still a winning concept.

Touring together 10 years ago, Prince and band (bassist Andre Cymone, guitarist Dez Dickerson, drummer David Z, and others), and the Time (Day, percussionist/valet Jerome Benton, bassist Terry Lewis, keyboardists Jimmy "Jam" Harris and Monte Moir, guitarist Jesse Johnson), formed a one-two punch that made Earth, Wind & Fire seem overblown, P-Funk indulgent, and everybody else just pros. The Time slammed with lean, streamlined songs full of naughty humor ("Cool," "777-9311"), while Prince's early band blended Wonder's melodic funk into anthemic rock 'n' roll. For both bands, Prince designed synthesizer lines that replaced horns, and he tortured lyrics that put a nice spin on lust and race.

Some of the best moments on the Time's *Pandemonium* and Prince's *Graffiti Bridge* (which includes four performances by the Time as well as guest appearances by Mavis Staples, Tevin Campbell, George Clinton, and Elisa) recall the early house-rockin' gigs at the Bottom Line, the Ritz, and the Palladium. Choice cuts for funkaholics on *Bridge* are Staples's solo turn on "Melody Cool," and the Time's "Release It," "Shake!" and "Love Machine" (the Day duet with Prince's latest E-girl, Minneapolis actress Elisa). In contrast, the best up-tempo moments on *Pandemonium* are not funk, but funk-rockers like "Blondie" and "Skillet," while the title cut is the closest they come to their sleek origins. *Bridge* is the sound track to Prince's fourth flick, due out in November, which explains the plethora of performers. He had conceived of this all-singing, all-dancing battle of bands before the Time reunion deal was sealed. (*Pandemonium* was once planned as a Day and Benton project.) You can hear the difference between Prince's mannered writing—the tailored for Day "Donald Trump (Black Version)"—and the true Time piece "Blondie," a fun big band workout. Like most of *Pandemonium*, unfortunately, it's burdened with dumb lyrics.

Appropriately Prince kept the more ambitiously convoluted songs on *Bridge* for himself. Since *Purple Rain*, Prince has been on a self-denial trip of epic proportions. If there's a radio-friendly tune on an album (be it "Adore" and "Housequake" on *Sign 'O' the Times* or "Anna Stesia" on *Lovesexy*), Prince has consistently overlooked it. He craves success on his terms, but in the latter half of the '80s, radio and even many old fans refused to follow him on his artistic leaps. The good news is that even the most melodically complicated Prince songs on *Bridge* are not as opaque as he's been. "The Question of U" snags a bit of melody from "Under the Cherry Moon," augmented by blues chords and a harpsichord. "Elephants & Flowers" meshes funky drums and keyboards that, compared to the lean Time tracks, are thick and bushy. "Joy in Repetition," "Still Would Stand All Time," and "Thieves in the Temple" all elaborate on familiar motifs from *Around the World in a Day* and *Parade*—the sensitive soul seeking the multiorgasmic soul mate, aided in his search by flowing countermelodies, swirling unison and harmonized backing voices, and unexpected bits of instrumentation. It's a big improvement over *Lovesexy* and the Bat Guano soundtrack.

The guest vocalists on *Graffiti Bridge* incite Prince to look up from his navel and write the straight-ahead pop-soul he recently has rejected. "Round and Round," featuring Quincy Jones's teen discovery Tevin Campbell, is bright, lively, and simple—the kind of precocious song Prince cut on his first two solo albums. It's as if Prince's lighter side was liberated by Campbell's squeaky cleaness.

I saw a trailer for *Graffiti Bridge* at a theater this summer before *Another 48 Hrs.* and enjoyed it more than the feature, though the word out of Cali is that it's a dog. No matter. The film has got Prince, Day, and the rest of the Minneapolis mob working together to create, between the two albums, 32 new pieces of music, full of the redemption-through-sex spirit and powerful dance hooks that turned us on in the first place. No word yet on a Prince-Time tour, but I'm hopeful. Hip hop has outlasted the Minneapolis sound as a recorded and cultural force, but who'd you rather see on stage, the Sugar Hill Gang or the Time?

VILLAGE VOICE, 1990

# TWO DETROIT SISTERS

**T**he posters for Diana Ross and Aretha Franklin's recent Radio City appearances were plastered around town. Ross posed with long, windswept hair, looking unselfconsciously glamorous, while Franklin gazed out guilelessly from under a straw hat. Both are more than 25 years removed from their artistic and cultural peak, when they defined two schools of music and womanhood: Motown versus Atlantic soul, unobtainable diva versus the folksy sister-next-door.

Ex-Supreme Ross spends much of her year living with her wealthy Norwegian shipbuilder husband in Europe; Franklin resides in her home town, leaving only for short annual tours. That Ross is viewed as the ultimate glamourpuss and Franklin the quintessential homegirl is, considering their backgrounds, quite an irony because these two women started life very differently.

Ross, born March 26, 1944, and Franklin, born March 25, 1942, were both reared in Detroit during the postwar boom years, a time when blacks saw the Motor City as a promised land with work in the metal vineyards of Ford, Chrysler, and General Motors. Ross, then known to family and friends as Dianne, grew up in the Brewster-Douglass public housing project, reading fashion magazines and working as a teen at the Hudson's department store that anchored the city's once teeming downtown. Aretha was the favorite daughter of Reverend C. L. Franklin, a preacher nationally recognized because of his widely heard radio broadcast and recordings. As Ross lived the life of the working poor, Franklin grew up in a home that enjoyed regular visits from Dr. Martin Luther King, Jr., Sam Cooke, a young Reverend James Cleveland, and other members of the gospel elite.

In the late '50s, Ross, possessor of a voice small, breathy, tart, and saccharine, hung with a bunch of neighborhood kids and began singing with the Primettes (who Berry Gordy later renamed the Supremes; their male counterparts the Primes later became the Temptations). A few miles away at the New Bethel Baptist Church, young Aretha's singing was already a known marvel, showcased at her father's sermons and barnstorming gospel caravans. Before she'd made one secular recording, Franklin was viewed by many, including the prescient talent scout John Hammond, as an inheritor and extension of Sister Rosetta Tharpe, Mahalia Jackson, and Dinah Washington.

Ross, in contrast, could have been just another early '60s girl-group vocalist if Gordy—her teacher, lover, and artistic father—hadn't been smitten by her round eyes and that siren blend of yearning and assurance. With Eddie and Brian Holland, along with Lamont Dozier, who designed some of Top 40's most enduring musical structures, Ross was constructed into everything the term "crossover" then meant: headlining Las Vegas, hosting hokey prime-time specials, having a bread named in her honor. She became an American pop-cultural icon only Madonna has matched since.

While Ross's skills and Gordy's ambitions made the Supremes's lead voice a projection of black capitalism's fondest dreams, Franklin's gifts equally reflected the '60s egalitarian vibe. During the height of soul music, young blacks and white Negrophiles expressed fidelity to their definition of real African American music as raw, undiluted, funky stuff (a time much like now). Franklin's vibrato, earthiness, and soaring shouts crystallized the aesthetics of that epoch just like protest marches and Afros. This pampered Daddy's girl was the natural woman's natural woman, though because of her father's station and her talent she in truth lived the life of a princess that Ross aspired to.

Watching them work the Radio City Music Hall stage within a week of each other (Franklin, September 14; Ross, September 20), it was fascinating how, in so many ways, they've become more similar with time. Both their bands were merely fair to lousy. (I'm being charitable.) Aretha was "supported" by H. B. Barnum's Vegas soul orchestra, though pianist Rudy Stanfield and solo background singer Stanley Banks had real chops. Anything up-tempo ("Rock Steady," "I Can't Turn You Loose," "Respect") was D.O.A. Ross eschewed live strings and horns for three synthesizers, which conveyed the melodies but faltered on the rhythmic nuances, especially on "Upside Down" and "Love Hangover." On the fashion front, less separated them than Ross fans would like you to believe; both women shimmied through plenty of purchased hair and several sequined costumes (final score: Ross 7, Franklin 4).

Sadly, each singer shared another similarity, long stretches of onstage sleepwalking. From Franklin, a notoriously reluctant performer, one doesn't expect consistency. However, Ross, at one point in her career, mounted over-the-top extravaganzas that were campy fun. This last performance was so tepid that a Ross impersonator with long black hair flowing past his shoulders almost upstaged the singer by sashaying in the aisles during the show. The Supremes medley wasn't even milked for its nostalgia value, the disco standards weren't even perfunctory, and her delivery of the Lionel Richie-penned "Missing You" was ghastly. Only on "God Bless the Child" and a new song, "When You Tell Me That You Love Me," did Ross project vocal authority.

Even so, Ross still has a shot at a hit with "The Force Behind the Power," her current album's title track. Written by Stevie Wonder, the song's a less ponderous take on the same theme as Michael Bolton's "Time, Love and Tenderness." Still, as star and singer, Ross has fallen so far that the peers she once overshadowed—Patti LaBelle, Gladys Knight, or Dionne Warwick—would slice her in a cutting contest. (Check out that trio's collaboration on Knight's single "Superwoman" for confirmation.)

Thankfully, Franklin's voice, though its upper range has been diminished, can still thrill when she wills it into action. Two lackluster songs into the gig, Aretha unleashed a spirited "I Never Loved a Man (The Way I Love You)," while her seventh song, the MOR chestnut "It's My Turn," was redeemed by Franklin's intelligent phrasing and the night's only surprising orchestral arrangement. But what separates Franklin from Ross and most other female singers is that she's also a fine instrumentalist; her piano playing is distinctively soulful. The evening took off with Franklin on piano as she sang Brenda Russell's "Get Here," keeping its lyric but inventing a new bluesy melody. Then she played a straight-up lusty "Dr. Feelgood" that said, "Oh, by the way, I'm still the Queen of Soul." The evening, like her current album, *What You See Is What You Sweat*, had its moments. Every Aretha recording since 1972's *Amazing Grace* has had dead spots, but when she extends herself, as on the new album's self-produced "You Can't Take Me for Granted," the lady still reigns.

Since both these Detroiters are just entering middle age and not showing any signs of retiring, it's intriguing to speculate on what their futures hold. Ross has been artistically barren for a decade. The Josphine Baker film she long coveted has been shot without her, while her performance mystique is going, going, gone. Yet with two children birthed after 40 and partial ownership of Motown, the family that nurtured her, Ross could well become a businesswoman-as-mother symbol, just another stage in her public saga of self-improvement.

Franklin, who lives the life of a happy hermit in a city many have written off, still has a chance to add to her artistic canon. That probably won't happen, however, until she stops competing with her acolytes on the dance floor (e.g., her atrocious remake of "Everyday People") and, like Natalie Cole and Anita Baker, again decides to interpret songs that showcase her voice. That's because sister 'Ree, like Ray Charles and a few other elders, remains a majestic connection to the royal roots of African American culture, history, and soul now being obscured by technology and time.

VILLAGE VOICE, 1991

# BERRY'S ASS

When I was a kid, Motown was a myth, a role model, a stack of records on the Motorola hi-fi in the living room. To white folks Motown may have been symbolized by Diana Ross, but in my house Motown was Eddie Kendricks and David Ruffin and Gladys Knight and, my personal favorites, Edwin Starr and Shorty "Function at the Junction" Long. Like so many '60s happenings, Motown seemed more socially significant than it was intended to be. Along with Sidney Poitier and Bill Cosby, Berry Gordy's record label was viewed as the cutting edge of integration in the entertainment industry. Every Copacabana date by Marvin Gaye, NBC "T.C.B." special starring the Temptations and the Supremes, and *Look* magazine feature on Gordy's family empire in Detroit was another step forward for first Negroes, then blacks. While white critics bashed the company for its Las Vegasization of rhythm & blues, Gordy's desire to be accepted by American mainstream institutions, even tacky ones like Vegas, seemed natural to the civil-rights generation, though not to their black-power kids. Growing up, I was fascinated by Motown's saga—so much so that years later I wrote a book about the company, not to muckrake, but to examine successful African American capitalism.

Unfortunately, Motown never took it to the next level, and for the last 20 years it's pimped off its '60s glory while self-destructive cheapness, poor planning, and changes in the recording industry fueled its decline. The tragedy of the biggest African American–founded business in American history being gobbled up by MCA was obscured by the company's sometimes tasteful (*Motown 25 Special, The Big Chill*), usually graceless (innumerable car and raisin commercials, countless bad '60s flicks) exploitation of its catalogue. Motown chic got so out of hand that many non-Motown soul records, even classics by Aretha Franklin and Otis Redding, are now mislabeled "Motown Sound."

But according to several yuppies of my acquaintance, Motown nostalgia is over. At thirtysomething parties "I Heard It Through the Grapevine" is giving way to '70s funk and disco. Judging by Deee-Lite, Black Box, Isaac Hayes's well-attended recent gigs at the Blue Note, and a slew of fashion and style indicators (e.g., *Paper*'s November issue), '70s retro-nuevo is the new move. And there are a new bunch of Motown books, which in this illiterate nation is the surest sign that any cultural wave has crested. Mary Wilson's *Dreamgirls: My Life as a Supreme*, published in 1986, was the right book to capitalize on the wave of Motown-powered commercials and the 20th anniversary of so many '60s events. Didn't hurt one bit, of course, that Wilson's breathy backstage bitching offered all viewers an intimate look at Motown's most celebrated soap opera—the Pygmalionlike relationship of Gordy and his grand creation, diva Diana Ross.

Since Wilson's bestseller, Motown books have appeared annually. Temptation Otis Williams did one. So did Smokey Robinson. Supremes valet Tony Turner purported to give Flo Ballard's side of the Supremes. Now, at the dawn of Day-Glo nostalgia, three new titles have hit the stores. The first, *The Motown Album*, is a coffee-table book ($50 a pop) whose mix of song lyrics and intimate pix, particularly of life at Motown's original Hitsville home, will thrill the hardcore. *Supreme Faith*, Mary Wilson's post-Ross book, is the predictable anticlimax. Since Wilson's never made great music on her own, her marital misadventures and struggle to keep her career afloat are melodrama, not cultural history. But Raynoma Gordy Singleton's *Berry, Me & Motown* is unprecedented.

Singleton, the first nonperforming Motowner to talk, isn't worried how dirt dishing will affect her career. She helped found Motown, and has been around the label on and off for its entire existence, which grants her a rare perspective. Most importantly, she was Berry's second wife. No previous Motown book has had Berry as its focus and certainly none has had as its author somebody who slept with him. Raynoma says it was love at first sight: "He was short, he had a pug nose. But it was the cutest nose on the planet, I thought. And those round light brown eyes seemed to bore holes in mine. He had that endearing, funny 'do. I'd liked his smell, too—a vague, musty aroma. That walk, almost a skip, with that cute behind of his. I even thought his teeth were beautiful."

I've never seen Gordy's ass described before, and it's moments like these that make up for Singleton's often florid prose. She depicts her ex-husband as a shrewd, selfish manipulator with the ability to create a "we're-all-in-this-together" atmosphere, all the while going for his. Nothing new there, but what Singleton does quite effectively is detail how a dude in mismatched socks and a greasy process evolved, year by year, into a sepia-tone blend of J. R. Ewing and Howard Hughes. A chapter on Raynoma's time as the solo Ross's road manager is the most concise, insightful view of the Berry Gordy-Diana Ross chemistry to date.

With her perfect pitch and eye for detail, Raynoma helped train musicians, Smokey Robinson and Brian Holland among them, and inaugurated the legendary Motown company meetings. Alas, she was also one of the first of many Berry betrayed. In 1959, just after a miscarriage, he talked her out of her 50 percent share in Tamla Records and Jobete Music Publishing, saying, "It's just a formality. You know whatever happens, I'm always going to take care of you." It was all downhill for Raynoma at Motown after that. As the company grew, she was pushed farther from power. Berry left her and, like so many other Motowners, she has spent the rest of her life in a dance of attraction-repulsion with the man. No matter how badly he's treated them, Motown personnel from the Detroit years, be they singers, musicians, or staff, are still obsessed with that magic time when they helped make the sound of young America, and with the MLK surrogate who led them to the mountaintop. Twenty years later, after abandoning Detroit and pioneering some of the worst aspects of whitewashed black culture, Gordy remains a hero. That's how immense his story and musical testament are. His soon-to-be-completed memoirs are sure to be full of half-truths, rewritten history, and paeans to the American dream. I'll be the first in line.

# BABYFACE

## LaFacing the Future

**E**arlier this year it was easy to dislike the work of producer-writers L.A. Reid and Kenny "Babyface" Edmonds. Paula Abdul's "Knocked Out," Pebbles's "Girlfriend," the Boys's "Dial My Heart," and Karyn White's "Love the Way You Love Me" are pop-r&b state of the art. Not coincidentally, each is uniformly nauseous. Funneling the teeny, tinny vocals of these "singers" through perky if lockstep rhythms, a battery of keyboards, and hooks as mechanized as a McDonald's french fry slicer, L.A. and Babyface concoct franchised hits for the disenfranchised. Lacking the humor and humanity of Jimmy "Jam" Harris and Terry Lewis, L.A. and Babyface make great music (as opposed to hits) only when the artist's personality is paramount. The Whispers's "Rock Steady" and Bobby Brown's "Don't Be Cruel" achieve pop perfection, for examples because their vocal dexterity and street-honed attitude infuse the hooks with life. While Harris/Lewis elevate mediocre talents (Janet Jackson, Cherrelle, Human League) to unexpected peaks, LaFace haven't yet done any heavy lifting.

The LaFace team's most sensitive work is on a pair of ballads cut with their now defunct band, the Deele: "Two Occasions," a love song so tender Curtis Mayfield could have written it for the Impressions, and its companion, "Shoot 'Em Up Movies," a novelty that recalls the Drifters' "Saturday Night at the Movies." Both are warm-hearted, sunny soul songs, sentimental without being corny. Maybe the most emotionally satisfying of all, however, is Babyface's hard-to-find first solo album, *Babyface* (Solar), a little gem that never found its audience. Soon after its uneventful mid-'80s release, L.A. and Babyface went into their manic production push-button hit period.

But now, with two recent releases, they've superseded their previous work, boxing out the skinny melodies of fellow new jack swingers and rejuvenating (or retro-nuevoing) black pop songwriting. First, in praise of a famous man, let me say Bobby Brown's "Off on Your Own" from the *Ghostbusters II* (MCA) soundtrack is simply brilliant. Unlike earlier LaFace productions, including most of Brown's *Don't Be Cruel*, where tracks lock into a groove and stay put, "Off on Your Own" has highs, lows, and *drama*. Brown's petulance and pride bounces off the richly arranged backing tracks that match the edge of Brown's Teddy Riley–produced "My Prerogative."

No single song in Babyface's second solo album, *Tender Lover* (Solar), is better than "Off on Your Own," but overall this 11-cut collection juxtaposes the best elements of that uptempo masterpiece with the suppleness of the Deele's ballads. In photos Babyface's extensively cosmeticized look and greased-up hair are pure West Coast gigolo. Yet the man is not merely a student of women, but an adoring worshipper. On "Soon as I Get Home From Work," already a Quiet Storm radio staple, Babyface tells his lady, "I give good love/I'll buy your clothes/I'll cook your dinner too/Soon as I get home from work" and "You're the kind of woman who needs a man with lots of cash/With a stack of major credit cards/And you won't have to ask." Not surprisingly, a lot of women like this song and more than a few men hate it. "Whip Appeal" has a kinky title and words that more than hint at s&m ("It's a strange kind of relationship") snaking seductively over the music until, in its final third, Babyface turns up the vocal heat and, via slick backing harmonies and clever counter melodies, slaps the song home. Not as inspired but above average slow jams are "Where Will You Go" and "Given a Chance." Unifying the ballads are the inventive lead- and backing-vocal arrangements. Though his tenor is no match for the elite love men (Luther Vandross, Al Green), Babyface has superb phrasing. His witty tempo changes and slurs give his heart-struck musings an emotional kick reminiscent of another shrewd young balladeer, Keith Sweat.

The party tracks are, again, distinguished by Babyface's singing and a series of intricate melodies that make "Knocked Out," "Dial My Heart," and the other fast-food hits sound juvenile. On the hectic "It's No Crime," the tricky "Tender Lover" (a killer melody!), and percolating "Let's Be Romantic," Babyface and L.A. turn out shiny and sharp pop in the noble tradition of Leon Sylvers, Quincy Jones, and Holland-Dozier-Holland's late '60s Four Top recordings. The beats don't pound you like Riley's, but then none of the current New York hip hop influenced producer-auteurs (Riley, Kyle West, Sweat) have compiled as many exquisitely hummable dance songs on one album. New Jack Swing began uptown, but *Tender Lover* says out-of-towners (LaFace just moved from Los Angeles to Atlanta) have shifted the balance of power.

In fact since the mid-'80s (sometime after the release of Lionel Richie's *Can't Slow Down*) New York, first with hip hop and now with New Jack Swing, has been directing black pop. That epoch may be over. Additional evidence is provided by Chuckii Booker's debut, *Chuckii* (Atlantic), which, while not as assured as *Tender Lover*, is damn promising. *Chuckii's* centerpiece, "Turned Away," is a dazzling song that rolls a clunky drum program under several layers of glowing, gorgeous synth lines, soaring backing harmonies, and Booker's own earnest implorings of love. "Turned Away" has a sensual, crystalline quality not matched by the rest of the album. Still, the up-tempo "(Don't You Know) I Love U" and "Hotel Happiness," and the slow "Heavenly Father," all based on righteous gospel piano riffs, tell you this former L.A. session man has chops and a future.

Moreover *Chuckii*, and Babyface's *Tender Lover*, testify, just maybe, that the latest period of street song dominance in black music is giving way to sing-along, upscale tales of urban romance. Like Ray Parker Jr., Richie, and Sylvers, Babyface brings together sweat and silk.

VILLAGE VOICE, 1989

# LISA STANSFIELD

## Britain in Effect

The early '70s were a magical time in African American pop, as Lisa Stansfield clearly understands. This promising British soul girl's debut, *Affection* (Arista), is primo retro-nuevo because it recalls, quite shrewdly, brilliant black music of the past without being slavish or condescending. The source material for Stansfield and writing-production collaborators Ian Devany and Andy Morris is the broad sonic canvases of passion and pain of Marvin Gaye, Barry White, and Gamble & Huff. Back in the day when 'BLS was the Total Black Experience in sound, these experimental soul men blended the science of large string and horn ensembles with funky, often Latin-influenced rhythm sections, pushing the limits of '60s gospel-based soul. Judging from the slinky, sweet, deeply emotive sound of *Affection*, Stansfield, Devany, and Morris have done their homework.

Like the work of Sade's guitarist, saxophonist, and arranger Stewart Mathewman, *Affection* has an expansive dynamic range, mixing real and synthetic sweeteners (horns and strings) for drama and contrast. And like Soul II Soul's Jazzie B. and Nellie Hooper, Stansfield, Devany, and Morris surveyed hip hop for beat magic and then molded intricate, sophisticated bass and keyboard grooves around the street beats. Comparisons with other crucial Brit-soul are not coincidental. Stansfield and posse, along with Sade, Soul II Soul, Loose Ends, George Michael, Swing Out Sister, Ruby Turner, Simply Red, Neneh Cherry, Culture Club, and the best of Stock, Aitken and Waterman, confirm that the Anglo fascination with r&b, nurtured during the Motown era, has fully evolved from fandom to facility, from scholarship to mastery.

While the melodic ideas of America's contemporary black pop have been beat down by hip hop and narrowly defined by trendy a&r personnel, the miscegenated music of England, spurred on by a mid-'80s renaissance of "rare grooves" (a/k/a '70s r&b and funk), has produced its own historically hip, contemporary hopping sound. *Affection*'s least satisfying moments are two straight-up house tracks, "The Love in Me" and "This Is the Right Time" (the only track handled by executive producers Cold Cut—Jazz Summers and Tim Parry). But the majority of this CD's 13 cuts (10 on album) sustain their retro-nuevo intentions. *Affection*'s production team succeeds by putting '70s instrumentation and arrangements over stoopid '90s beats. "What Did I Do to You?" has a high hat driven rhythm buttressed by a bass line and recurring string and flute parts that recall Jerry Hey's arrangements for Michael Jackson's *Off the Wall*, while the hyperactive bass, brassy horns, and big string sound of "Live Together," all wrapped around a tinny drum machine and pro-brotherhood lyric, suggest Gamble & Huff meeting Marley Marl. "Sincerity," as well as the title cut, are beat-box ballads with intelligently minimalist r&b backing—

thick bass, cutesy keyboard motifs, Latin percussion, tambourine, flute. "Mighty Love," "When Are You Coming Back?," "You Can't Deny It," and the ubiquitous single "All Around the World" all sport sturdy r&b melodies and lyrics, enhanced by full, vibrant arrangements that evoke the work of master soul orchestrators—Motown's Paul Riser, Curtis Mayfield's Johnn Pate, and the late Earth, Wind & Fire guru Charles Stephany.

But *Affection* isn't beautiful just because it's clever. Fact is, Stansfield is the best white soul singer since Teena Marie (step back you Michaelses, George and Bolton). Husky, strident, moody, percussive all describe this winsome white girl's chops. Rarely girlish and never coy. Stansfield sings knowingly of love and lust, both hers and his. Her backing vocals on "Live Together"—stacked in an alto choir with a solo voice sailing over them—are a pretty thing. More emotionally affecting is her work on "When Are You Coming Back?" when she leans into the rhythm of each word, communicating the anxiety of losing her lover. Two different choral sections serve as hooks ("tell me when are you coming back" and "don't stray for too long"), each sung in a different register, but with similar melancholy flavor over a deeply sexy groove.

As an r&b formalist, the subtlety of *Affection* just rocks my world. The British invasion of the '90s, adorned in funky dreads, pale white-faced makeup, and the latest Brixton street gear, is here and has taken musical form. Folks talk a lot these days about world beat, but I'd put my money on the U.K.'s mulatto soul as a key direction for multinational, multiracial fun. And I say that quite affectionately.

# RICK JAMES'S
# GHETTO LIFE

One thing 'bout the ghetto
You don't have to worry
It'll be there tomorrow

—RICK JAMES

**R**ick James's *Street Songs*
reminds me of my favorite period in black pop music, the early '70s,
when, as Greil Marcus noted in *Mystery Train,* "social comment" was
unusually prominent in black lyrics. Sly's *There's a Riot Going On,*
Curtis Mayfield's *Super Fly,* Marvin Gaye's *What's Going On,* Willie
Hutch's "Brothers Gonna Work it Out," the Temptations's "Papa Was
a Rolling Stone," several Gamble and Huff productions, and a number
of other records featured brash, inventive music and lyrics that were
streetwise and either overtly or obliquely political. It seemed natural to
me—an idealistic adolescent—that pop music wasn't just about love
and sex and dancing, that it could (and should) reflect the realities of
the world in a critical and perhaps even affectionate way. Or even simply chronicle as honestly as possible an individual's private struggles
and triumphs.

The rest of the decade revealed how innocent my vision and
remarkable that epoch was. With the exception of Gil Scott-Heron
and Stevie Wonder, few Afro-American music makers have since
shown much interest in addressing, even for a song or two, the myriad
problems and stories to be found in our black neighborhoods. In 10
years people will understand more about how blacks lived in 1981 by
listening to "The Adventures of Grandmaster Flash on the Wheels of
Steel" than grooving to Quincy Jones's *The Dude* or Chaka Kahn's

*Whatcha Gonna Do for Me,* despite their spectacular aural beauty. It is in this context that *Street Songs* strikes me as special. On three of its eight cuts—two descriptions of his life growing up in Buffalo, one straightforward political protest—James digs into the real world of his songs, balancing out the fun and games of the rest of the album and revealing aspects of his personality not apparent on *Come Get It, Bustin' Out of L Seven, Fire It Up,* and *Garden of Love.*

In "Ghetto Life," the teenage James runs the streets, aimlessly chasing pussy and searching for direction. He feels that strange restlessness that overcomes young black men when they realize that their entire life might be spent inside invisible ghetto walls "playing tag with winos" or perhaps becoming one. James offers no profound plan for altering life in the slums, but he does suggest optimistically we "got to build it from the ground, people got to come together" as if it might even happen, a stance I'll have over acceptance any day. The song is driven by an adequate funk track, noteworthy for its understated use of Larry Hansen's violin and voices of Temptations Melvin Franklin, Otis Williams, and Richard Street.

"Pass the joint, I think I want to talk/'Bout the place I was born/I was torn," says James during "Below the Funk (Pass the J)" a marijuana induced stream-of-consciousness song. The tempo is fast, too fast for dancing, and at 2:36, it's unusually short by current black-music standards, but perfect for James's rapid-fire delivery and the song's scatter-shot imagery. Images of Mama ("With eight kids and no father/Said she couldn't hack it"), racism in Buffalo ("Now the love I find in the city/Is such a crying pity/Ain't no love for brothers"), and questions of sexual preference ("The gossip is so tragic/They call me a faggot/Me and all my women laugh at it") flow through the song.

James's most political song is "Mr. Policeman," an uncompromising attack on police violence against blacks. This is the kind of song typical of the late Bob Marley or Stevie Wonder in one of his more inspired moments, and the presence of both men is felt, as the rhythm is reggae in the style of "Master Blaster" and Wonder contributes an energetic, rambling harmonica solo. Like Smokey Robinson on "Food for Thought" (the second track on *Being With You*), James views reggae as a vehicle for attacking social ills, an obvious reflection of Marley's impact. When James says "I've seen you in my neighborhood/You look to me up to no good," he speaks for many blacks.

The rest of *Street Songs* is chucky dance music punctuated by punchy horn lines, such as Los Angeles's favorite cruising record, "Give It to Me," as well as slightly inferior models like "Call Me Up" and "Make Love to Me," "Super Freak," a new wave–influenced celebration of an outstanding groupie, and "Fire and Desire," a ballad with James protégé Teena Marie slipping and sliding through a sultry vocal embrace. Good stuff, all this. Yet *Street Songs* would be just another good piece of product without the other three songs to give it depth. That it just became the nation's number one black album makes me hope (with fingers crossed) that a new golden age is coming. We shall see.

VILLAGE VOICE, 1981

# FRANKIE BEVERLY STAYS HOME

A man confessing his love for his family and his woman at the dinner table resulting in blushes and hugs all around; the warm and easy intimacy of close friends laughing over a bottle of wine very late on a Saturday night; the optimism of a black father telling his son how much things have changed; the eerie quality of evening in Los Angeles as the sun sets softly over the Pacific and the lights of the Hollywood Hills begin their seductive twinkle; these are some of the engaging images I find floating through Frankie Beverly's music; he is a songwriter of quiet force who is yet to receive the respect due him in jaded dance-mad New York City.

Beverly and his band Maze (official title: Maze Featuring Frankie Beverly) are champions of black stay-at-homes nationwide. As a unit they make simple easy-listening funk, similar in aural texture to the

Crusaders, perfect for contemplating your life, relaxing with a drug of choice, or savoring the tender tension of foreplay. From the self-titled debut album, through *Golden Time of Day*, *Inspiration*, *Joy and Pain*, and the current double album *Live in New Orleans* (three sides cut at that city's Saenger Theatre, one in the San Francisco studio), Maze has singlemindedly forged a trademark sound, thereby avoiding the trendiness that pollutes so much black pop.

All but one of *Live*'s 12 songs feature slow to medium tempos (the exception is "Running Away," an attempted dance hit that failed to impress New York's club jocks) with arrangements rich in glowing electric pianos, humming organs, and tasteful synthesizer figures. The rhythm section of drummer Billy Johnson, bassist Robin Duhe, and percussionists McKinnley William and Roame Lowry interlocks as smoothly as the keyboards. They never push the beat, even on the live tracks, a discipline vital to the aura of Beverly's soothing compositions.

With these sultry grooves as the frame, Beverly paints his wholesome pictures on top with voice and pen. In his phrasing I hear echoes of his benefactor Marvin Gaye (he booked Maze on a mid-'70s tour, providing exposure that led to their Capitol contract) and his idol Sam Cooke. But Beverly's voice has a rougher, more working-class quality that differentiates him from those love men. Instead, he sounds like a dedicated husband still madly in love with his wife after all these years. "Reasons," my favorite song on the *Live* studio side, is a typically sincere testimony to the power of love ("you've given me a reason to try one more time") and unending fidelity. There is a wonderful maturity in Beverly's voice and words. His love songs exist in a world where one-night stands are spurned and real affection is sought, appreciated, returned.

Beverly also shows a real gift for nonspecific protest songs in the tradition of the Isley Brothers's "Fight the Power" and Earth, Wind & Fire's "Let Me Talk"—songs that refer to the troubles of black Americans minus the nuts-and-bolts rhetoric of a Gil Scott-Heron. In addition to "We Need Love to Live," a tribute to Atlanta's murdered children, *Live* includes two inspirational numbers with the upbeat '60s flavor of Curtis Mayfield's "People Get Ready" and "We're a Winner" and Sam Cooke's eloquent "A Change Is Gonna Come," "Changing Times" ("We'll get through these changing times") and "Running Away" (which, like Booker T. Washington, preaches that "the things you want are the things you have to earn"). While Beverly hasn't yet matched the greatness of Cooke, Mayfield, or Gaye as a singer or writer, his mellow but substantial catalogue suggests he may one day join their hallowed ranks. Whatever reservations you may have about live recordings, I think *Live in New Orleans* provides an excellent point of entry into Beverly's soulful maze.

VILLAGE VOICE, 1981

# TOO MUCH LUTHER VANDROSS

**S**ome say the record industry is crumbling, but it depends on where you stand. If you're the CBS executive by the bar in Studio 54's Rubber Room last Wednesday night, you're definitely feeling the tremors. Profits have slid 50 percent from over $100 million this fiscal year and personnel have already been cut to the bone. Between sips of Scotch and soda you wonder why your glass is shaking and the nights seem so damn long.

If you're honored guest Luther Vandross, you say hello to the tired middle-aged man in the gray suit and keep on stepping. Your mind is easy. When CBS signed Vandross last year the conglomerate committed itself to making him a major star and praise the Lord, did so. Soon Clive Davis, Arista's aristocratic honcho, gave him big bucks to revive Aretha Franklin and, again, for a hefty sum, CBS enticed Vandross to mold big-voiced Cheryl Lynn into an album seller. Mr. V. succeeded at both assignments, and now Davis has assigned him to work with Dionne Warwick while other companies deluge him with offers to rescue the lame, the blind, and the baffled—fallen funk warriors the Brothers Johnson, for instance. No way is Vandross the right producer for Louis and George Johnson, but the man is "hot," and that's all the managers need to know. When the hot producer fever strikes industryites lose all perspective and often a lot of money. And now executives like our friend at the bar are lined up, checkbooks in hand, to give Vandross anything he wants. All have forgotten that it is precisely this undisciplined lust for hot commodities that helped unbalance their bottom line in the first place. By tossing dollars at producer-writers to refurbish old or damaged goods the record industry encourages them to bastardize their talent and squeeze fresh ideas into formulas.

Given this avaricious tradition, I'm disturbed by signs of creative stagnation on Vandross's *Forever, for Always, for Love.* Listening to it I wonder whether Vandross's ascendance from background singer to jingle singer to featured vocalist in Change to solo act to producer-writer in the space of three years doesn't contain the seeds, not of disaster, but of a missed opportunity for Vandross to establish himself as the foremost singer of his generation.

If Vandross had emerged in the late '50s or early '60s, where his musical roots are, it would have been difficult for him to move as swiftly up the ladder. Like his idols Diana Ross and Dionne Warwick, he'd have had to fit his vision into that of Holland-Dozier-Holland or Burt Bacharach and Hal David. His musical personality would have been shaped not by his crystal line enunciation, impeccable phrasing and relaxed delivery—the smoothest voice since Sam Cooke or even Nat King Cole. Instead he would have been forced to synthesize his own idiosyncrasies with the quirks of genuine musical auteurs, and in the process create a greater whole. Emerging in the '80s, Vandross is free of constraints. His ambitions run free, as his self-produced albums and work with Franklin and Lynn attest.

But freedom exacts its own price. For Vandross, it means the freedom to compose, and unfortunately he's hardly his own best screenwriter. As if in compensation for "Never Too Much" or "Jump to It," each written with bassist Marcus Miller, both *Never Too Much* and *Forever, for Always, for Love* feature several meandering, mediocre songs unworthy of his instrument. The title cut isn't 6:24 worth of song, but an overlong mishmash that cops lyrics from "The Way We Were" and melodic ideas from "A House Is Not a Home," and that isn't even a decent vehicle for Vandross's precision phrasing or heartfelt emotionalism. Vandross's spoken intro ("I sing this song, to remind myself that there was a time when I didn't have no one, didn't have no love") links it with prestardom days and clearly comes straight from the heart. But instead of the sentimental tribute to love Vandross intends, "Forever" sounds flaccid and dull, like ersatz Johnny Mathis. "Once You Know How," another waltz-time ballad, while slightly better is still too delicate for its own good. Awash in strings, tinkly piano, and French horns, both songs cry out "we're classy," but are really bombast without body. These aren't songs for a great singer, but songs a great singer thinks he should sing—attempted standards that are barely tolerable filler.

A great singer needs strong material and when he's got it Vandross is just that. His most spirited performances, on record and last Friday night at his two sold-out shows at Radio City Music Hall, include "Since I Lost My Baby," "If This World Were Mine," and "A House Is Not a Home," written by four of pop's most sensitive songwriters: Smokey Robinson, Marvin Gaye, and Bacharach & David. When Vandross sings "The sun is shining, there's plenty of light/A new day is dawning, sunny and bright" at the beginning of "Baby," you are transported to a place, a day, a time. This specificity of Robinson's lyric and the easy escalating drama of its melody, augmented superbly by Vandross's arrangement for an all-star team of background vocalists, makes it the most soulful song on the new album. His duet with Lynn on "World" at Radio City was warm and wonderfully light-hearted, with Lynn's vivaciousness the perfect foil for Vandross's cuddly charm. On "House," a journey through dramatic twist and stagey tricks (stopping at the same point in the song in both shows for a drink of water), Vandross was as crowd-pleasingly masterful as Sinatra, Betty Carter, Aretha, Al Green, Mabel Mercer, you name it.

For Vandross on record to be as exceptional as Vandross in concert would be simple. Instead of relying so heavily on his own songs (and sacrificing some songwriting royalties), Vandross should record just his best songs, continue using vintage oldies, and cut originals by today's better songwriters (e.g., Ashford & Simpson, Randy Newman, Sam Dees). He has a classic album in him, maybe more than one, and as a critic and a fan I'd like to see him get it.

VILLAGE VOICE, 1982

# TILL THE DAY THEY DIE

Last week in the *New York Times* Mick Jagger talked about life as a 39-year-old rock 'n' roll millionaire. In the interview old Mick compared himself to bluesmen who played, quite literally, until the day they died. Mick implied that, given the time off for bad behavior, he might do the same. That's nice (I mean what else does he know how to do?), but if he wanted to hang up his rock 'n' roll jockstrap he'd still be drinking Dom Perignon. In most cases all those elderly black musicians he compares himself to kept on working not simply because they loved it, but because that house note did have to be paid. They knew that outside the entertainment industry's protective cocoon, life can be very unkind to a 40-year-old black man with no skills other than singing, dancing, and guitar picking. For them there are only taxi cabs, dishwashing, assembly lines, and the simple joys of government assistance.

So if I'm more sympathetic to the recent records of Tyrone Davis and Johnny Taylor, both 45, and Z.Z. Hill, who is 43, than I am to watching Mick prance across the screen at the Loew's Astor Plaza, it's because I know that at this point in the lives of Davis, Taylor, and Hill these records aren't just pieces of product, but attempts to sustain a lifestyle that, while not as pampered as Jagger's, still beats working for a living. Today each sings with the conviction, precision, and ribald charm learned through over 20 up-and-down years of recording and performing, and I respect them for their ability to keep on going.

But don't let my tone give you the wrong idea. This is not a eulogy, nor am I bucking for reissue liner notes. Though you couldn't tell by New York's terrible trio of urban contemporary stations, all three are selling records at a steady clip to black audiences in the South, Midwest, and even out in Los Angeles (which, quiet as it's kept, is closer in temperament to Newport News, Virginia, than to any major urban metropolis I've ever visited). The musical taste of New York seems to be solidifying into such an arid, self-satisfied introspection that the music on Davis's self-titled album, Taylor's *Just Ain't Good Enough*, and the Hill's *The Rhythm and the Blues* would probably sound like some goddamn soul revival to many of our natives, reflecting how dreadfully ignorant we often are about the rest of America. These men represent a dedication to the tradition of secular salvation (soul singing to you) that has never lost its core audience outside the Northeast.

For example, Davis's "Are You Serious," the killer track on his current *Hi-Rise* album, went to number three on the black album chart without (to my knowledge) getting one iota of Big Apple airplay. A shame, since we're missing a commanding vocal performance, one that starts slowly, building power, and then slides authoritatively over a laidback midtempo groove. Producer Leo Graham demonstrates, as he has in the past with the Manhattans and Champaign, that there is still room for black pop that isn't trendy, synthesized-dependent, or juvenile, and that in an era when Jennifer Holiday is considered a "soul" singer in some quarters, it doesn't take bombast to make soulful music.

If you haven't heard "Serious," you can be sure nothing from Johnnie Taylor's album was even considered by radio here. Where Davis's southern lust is at least tempered by years of South Side cool, Taylor's voice has always dripped the kind of downhome agony and ecstasy that can burn a hole right through your speakers. Even on "Disco Lady"—that trashy thing—my man was bringing it on home. Alas, that platinum record proved a trap for Taylor, since it led him to believe that future crossover success was assured. After fleeing the crumbling Stax empire in the early '70s with "Who's Making Love" and "(I Just Wanna) Testify" behind him, Taylor, like contemporaries Davis, Bobby Womack, and Gladys Knight, sought financial security in the crossover paradise Columbia Records promised.

At least Taylor had "Disco Lady." The others went straight down in the Black Rock, and Taylor's subsequent attempts to recapture the "Disco Lady" audience failed miserably, while his more rootsy records (check your local cutout bin for Taylor's Columbia *Greatest Hits* album) were wasted on a company demanding crossover or exile. That he now records for Otis Smith's Beverly Glen Records is so appropriate. Last year Smith's only act was Womack, another Columbia reject, whose "If You Think You're Lonely Now" was a heartening and miraculous number-one black single. Taylor's revival hasn't been as emphatic, simply because the music on *Enough* isn't as vibrant as on Womack's *The Poet*. But on decent songs like "I'm So Proud" (produced by Bobby

Womack's brother Cecil) and the title track, Taylor's aggressive gospelly approach is right on time. He never did have much range (and hasn't improved with age), but his attack is still as fiery as it was in 1969. When he shouts I keep looking for the collection plate.

Z.Z. Hill has never confused his listeners with such spiritual considerations. His raspy, insinuating delivery, dirty asides, and uncompromisingly soap opera-ish material mark him as a man of solely earthy concerns. Strangely, where Davis and Taylor failed to dent New York radio, Hill's "Cheating in the Next Room," from his *Down Home* album on Malaco, did sneak onto BLS for a hot minute. "Cheating" and *Down Home* were underground soul phenomena of 1982, intentionally old-fashioned music that has sold steadily for well over a year. The album has been on *Billboard*'s black chart for 55 weeks, longer than anything other than Luther Vandross's *Never Too Much*. *The Rhythm and the Blues* isn't as successful as *Down Home* (it's more like 'Search for Tomorrow" than "General Hospital"), but on songs such as "Outside Thang," "Open House at My House," and "Someone Else Is Steppin' In" Hill is right in his element, sliding in and out of suggestive lyrics with the dexterity of a poor man's Bobby Bland.

All three of these albums are on the indie labels based outside of New York; Beverly Glenn is in Los Angeles, Hi-Rise has just moved from California to Dallas, and good old Malaco has been in Jackson, Mississippi, since the King Floyd days. In contrast there is not one old-styled soul man on any of the major labels today, probably because they don't think there is a market for them. Maybe there isn't in New York (though I'm not totally convinced of that), but this country has a big heart. And as the strength, both commercial and stylistic, of these albums attests, it still craves good brown-eyed soul.

VILLAGE VOICE, 1984

# LIONEL RICHIE
## Truly Still Easy

**T**o truly appreciate the rise of Lionel Richie and the bittersweet taste it has for some of his early fans, you have to go back to 1976, the year of the Commodores's first platinum album, when they were one of the best party bands in pop. Without the spiritual verbiage of Earth, Wind & Fire's Maurice White and the cosmic jive of P-Funk's George Clinton as media hooks, the Commodores were the black equivalent of Journey or REO Speedwagon—dedicated professionals whose group identity obscured their individuality, making them seem decidedly bland.

Throughout that era the Commodores maintained a delicate balance between thumping funk-rock tracks written collectively and Richie's growing sophistication as a ballad composer. Funk jams such as "Slippery When Wet," "Fancy Dancer," and the instrumental "Machine Gun," made Commodores concerts big fun, with Richie and drummer Walter Orange exchanging lead vocals, and bassist Ronald LaPread, guitarist Thomas McClary, keyboardist Milan Williams, and trumpeter William King leading about with the raunch & roll vigor you expect from six Southern boys on a Saturday night. Despite Richie's ballads, the group was very much a musical democracy. Richie never dominated the group the way White or Clinton did. When the Commodores were interviewed, Richie often had to squeeze comments between Orange and the loquacious King. The Commodores's real leader was the late Benny Ashburn, the Harlem-based manager who was father, brother, and boss man to them. Ashburn made the Commodores maintain their balance by preaching community, keeping egos in line, and fighting off the wolves who tear into the soul of every successful band. Equally significant was that Ashburn was one of the few truly independent black capitalists prospering in the music industry. For all the propaganda spewed forth about Earth, Wind & Fire and P-Funk as exponents of black culture, both groups have been controlled by white managers, unlike the more superficially conservative Commodores.

But by 1977 Richie's slow tempo love songs were superseding the funk, attracting older, more integrated audiences. With its slow modulation from quiet piano and vocal passages rising to crescendos of strings, horns, and choral harmonies, "This Is Your Life," from 1975's *Caught in the Act*, set the standard for subsequent Richie ballads like "Zoom," "Sweet Love," and "Just to Be Close to You," all still exciting fusions of country, soul, and MOR. Richie's voice, oozing with country melancholy, projected lyrics as sentimental and courtly as roses on the first date. The key to Richie's ballads isn't their undistinctive parts, but the gosh-darn wholesomeness of the whole. A Richie ballad is never sexy, occasionally romantic, and almost always incredibly nice. Richie has been the archetype for a new breed of black pop vocalist—singers who owe as much in vocal attack and material to MOR and adult contemporary as to soul. Listen to James Ingram, Stacy Lattisaw, Jeffrey Osborne, or the Peabo Bryson-Roberta Flack duet on "Tonight I Celebrate My Love" and you hear voices that aren't based on cliched reinterpretations of gospel music. This is a vision that encompasses Billy Eckstine, Sam Cooke, Jerry Butler, and Otis Redding's "Sitting on the Dock of the Bay"—not to mention Perry Como.

By the time of "Easy," a wonderfully realized southern landscape in sound, and "Three Times a Lady," the ultimate testimony to the sweet and the sappy (and the start of a dull, dull period in Richie's writing), it was clear that Richie's early funk voice was just a facade. He wanted to be Kenny Rogers and didn't care how hokey that sounded. The Commodores's equilibrium was snapping. The break became irreparable on *Midnight Magic* with "Still" and "Sail On," two number-one ballads that made Richie's solo career inevitable. Soundwise they are completely different; "Still" has the ponderous strings and flowing French horns of MOR, while "Sail On" somehow fused corny chord changes, Latin percussion, and country into an inventive little "I'm hitting the road" song. Richie was hot now, but it wasn't until Orange injured his leg in an accident, postponing the national tour, that he had time to write "Lady" for Kenny Rogers. "Lady," an awesomely redundant song (see "Three Times a Lady"), got Richie the kind of establishment respect Motown acts have craved since the Supremes first played the Copacabana. In rapid succession Richie produced a lukewarm Kenny Rogers album; Rogers's high-powered manager Ken Kragen started seducing Richie; Ashburn's health began to deteriorate; and the rumors of dissension within the Commodores family grew. Even after the terrible "Endless Love" Richie might have stayed closer to the Commodores if a heart attack hadn't felled Ashburn in 1982. The glue that had held the Commodores together was gone. So was a genuine black success story.

The Commodores hired another black manager, ex-television executive Chuck Smiley, and then spent a great deal of time in Europe, polishing a new stage show, writing new material, and seeking a voice. The logical choice is Orange, the lead singer on the single "Only You" and four other cuts on 13, the Commodores's first full post-Richie album. He sounds good on the churning funk tune "Touchdown," but doesn't have the flexibility to front a band with the musical range of the Commodores. My choice is Harold Hudson, member of the Commodores's backing band, Mean Machine, co-writer with Richie of "Lady (You Bring Me Up)," and possessor of a cool, smart pop tenor. On "Painted Picture," a studio single released on a post-Richie greatest hits package, he impressed with control and tone. On 13's "I'm in Love," an excellent midtempo pop song with a sensitive, elaborate arrangement, "Turn Off the Lights," and "Welcome Home," Hudson gives the Commodores the freshness needed to mold a new personality.

Richie didn't need a new one. We all know his "gosh, golly gee" persona from People, Jet, the Grammy Awards, etc. What Richie did need after leaving the Commodores was some uptempo material with a pop sheen. "All Night Long (All Night)" from Can't Slow Down and "Serves You Right" and "You Are" from his self-titled debut greatly enlivened his performance at Radio City Music Hall two weeks ago. During Richie's last performance with the Commodores at Radio City, the ballads turned a once fiery funk band into Barry Manilow.

But Richie's bottom line is still ballads and Can't Slow Down showcases his best batch since Midnight Magic. While "Truly" was in the maudlin style of "Endless Love," here "Hello" takes that overblown approach in a more subtle direction. The arrangement is understated, highlighted by a tasty acoustic guitar bridge and a Carmichael string chart that supports one of Richie's best melodies. "Penny Lover," like "You Are" written with wife Brenda, is sung with Richie's customary commitment. The album's closer, and my personal favorite, "Stuck On You," sways with the Southern flavor of "Sweet Love" and "Easy." Richie, in an era when cynicism is fashionable, leads with his heart, I just wish it was still beating for the Commodores.

# THE BEST OF
# GIL SCOTT-HERON

**T**elling the truth is a damn hard thing to do in the '80s.

It is easier to lie and say, for example, that America will once again be the dominant force it was 20 years ago. Then, a lot of your fellow Americans will pat you on the back, shake your hand, and maybe even pull the lever for you on election day. Even better, you could give a speech about "winnable" nuclear war, mention the joys of deterrence, and how Europeans really do like having all those foreign bombs in their kitchen. Say that enough and, hey, you're guaranteed a place in any number of prestigious think tanks or maybe just cold cash to build a Jacuzzi in your bomb shelter. Ah, the fruits of deceit are sweet.

But telling the truth . . . well that could get you in trouble. If you analyze the world scene and realize that the needs, desires, and agenda of the third world are the most urgent issues of the globe; if you figure out that "nuclear nightmare diplomacy" is a joke; that maybe . . . just maybe, South Africa is a racist (did someone say fascistic?) republic that no "moral" government should support, and you just might have a problem with some folks. This is especially true when you make records for a living, because everybody else making records for a living is lying. Not big lies about politics, but little lies that suggest all that is happening on this globe is kissing and dancing. These are lies of omission that make pop music the playground of jive and the banal.

All of which brings us to Gil Scott-Heron, keyboardist, poet, singer, rapper, and teller of uncomfortable truths. For over a decade, even before the company releasing this album existed, Scott-Heron has been cutting through the crap. He was in fact the first person signed to Arista Records and it is a tribute to the label's integrity he is still on it. In general men like Scott-Heron, one who goes against the flow and looks squarely at the future, are not welcome at the corporate record companies of America.

You see, Scott-Heron is not just a musician. He is a leader. Back in 1975, before Andrew Young was United Nations Ambassador for the United States, before names like Zimbabwe, Namibia, and SWAPO were important to the American media, he cut *From South Africa to South Carolina* and made the connection between black oppression on both sides of the Atlantic explicit on "Johannesburg." In 1977, two years before the MUSE anti-nuke benefit at Madison Square Garden and six years before Meryl Streep starred in "Silkwood," Scott-Heron wrote the chilling "We Almost Lost Detroit" and then followed it with the uncompromising "Shut 'Em Down" as Three Mile Island glowed in the Pennsylvania sky. Be it "The Bottle" or "Angel Dust" he has attacked the debilitating effects of drug abuse, a stance no other pop musician has had the guts to take. As the quality of life and the desire for morality has ebbed in his homeland Scott-Heron has chronicled our decline with a savage eye ("The Revolution Will Not Be Televised"), a defiant tongue ("Superman"), and a mind that probes the icy soul of our troubled confused country ("Winter in America").

Our spiritual failures have created a longing across the land for "celluloid heroes" that has been met by "Hollywierd," a creation of nostalgia who has turned foreign policy into a " 'B' Movie" full of brimstone and breast beating. The sequel is "Re-Ron," a new age synth-funk masterpiece with music by Material's Bill Laswell and rage from Scott-Heron. "He's terrorized jeopardized and sent our spies to plant them mines and he promoted lies all for the bottom line," Scott-Heron intones over electro-drums and staccato keyboard riffs. This is not the stuff said by musicians in the age of MTV, pretty boy musicians, and George Lucas's epics of the white man's revenge. "The Temple of Doom"? It is in our hearts and minds. Gil Scott-Heron knows it. He says it. And scares all the right people. But they shouldn't be you. In " 'B' Movie" he writes, "This ain't really your life," and I think he means it doesn't have to be.

LINER NOTES, ARISTA RECORDS, 1984

# NOT THE AVERAGE KIND

Love me now 'cause I'm special
Not the average kind

—"IN A SPECIAL WAY"

I'm in love with DeBarge. Why? They are quite simply the most exquisite exponents of the love ballad to emerge in the '80s, a quartet whose best work is in the sensitive falsetto tradition of Smokey Robinson, the Moments, and the Stylistics, while tipping their musical hats to Stevie Wonder, Earth, Wind & Fire, and that quiet genius of romance Curtis Mayfield. For a young black group to consciously buck the groove allegiance of most post-disco black popsters makes them anachronistic radicals, classicist when everybody else is putting on their boogie shoes. I'm hoping DeBarge's success will bring back the healthy balance of beat and emotion that I was weaned on and that was part of black music's charm for white America.

At first DeBarge seemed like unlikely creators of remarkable love songs. Judging by the super cutesy color pictures and lame stories that filled black teen magazines the last couple of years, I was sure this family quintet from Grand Rapids (Mark, Eldra, James, Randy and sister Bunny) had to be the worst thing this side of Donny and Marie. Their self-titled 1981 debut album did nothing to alter that perception. The only inkling of DeBarge's potential came indirectly. Brothers Tommy and Bobby were key members of Switch, a promising self-contained band that languished on Motown for six albums, building a substantial Southern following, but never getting over the hump. (Their first album on Total Experience is due next month.)

Then I heard "I Like It" and "All This Love," the best singles of 1983 this side of Michael Jackson, and swooned. The comfortable tempo and simple changes of "I Like It," written and sung by Randy and Eldra, recalls the sweet, easy charm of, say, "How Sweet It Is (To Be Loved by You)." Randy provides a healthy midrange lead that plays off El's Eddie Kendricks (rather than Philip Bailey) falsetto. Where "I Like It" had an innocent r&b sound, "All This Love" has the delicate sophistication of Bacharach & David's collaborations for Dionne Warwick. Over Spanish-flavored acoustic guitar accompaniment by Jose Feliciano and Charles Fearing and exquisite string and horn arrangements by Benjamin Wright, El sings with surprising subtlety and conviction about how love has cleansed his soul. It is a great performance, one as brilliant in its way as Michael Jackson's on "Human Nature," with which it shares a soothing tempo and natural adolescent romanticism. Unfortunately for El, clearly DeBarge's budding musical leader, he has been compared to Michael ever since they performed on Motown 25. Folks snickered at El's stage movements in comparison to the sublime Mr. Michael J., but comparing Jackson to anybody this side of Tommy Tune is a joke.

Moreover, El and his kin, despite the hype, are not Jackson imitators, a fact made clear by the often magical *In a Special Way*. The first single, "Time Will Reveal," is as fine in its way as "I Like It" and "All This Love," showing that unlike Lionel Richie, DeBarge aren't falling into formula to cross their ballads over. Maurice White almost produced this album and his influence is evident in "Time"'s use of electric piano, its unhurried midtempo groove, and the cool interplay between El's voice and his family's backing vocals. The effect of the devotional love songs of White and Mayfield are also felt in El's "Queen of My Heart," which has a similar tempo and sound to "Time," but a slightly weaker hook.

El's most surprising composition is the title cut, which opens with a jagged acoustic piano and maintains its churchy feeling even when overlaid with clever pop production flourishes (shimmering cymbals, a synthesizer masquerading as a harmonica). It is a song and sound that has the audacity of a Stevie Wonder, but, as with all El's obvious antecedents, is a far from slavish imitation as Dr. J's skybound leaps are from the airborne leaps of Elgin Baylor. El's gone back and learned from the midtempo masters of black music and managed to refine their ideas while developing his own identity. And El isn't even the whole story. Mark shows signs of being a fine writer himself with the understated "Stay with Me," on which El and Bunny duet. Bunny shines on her own song, "A Dream," built around a playful piano figure, her carefully modulated vocal, and husky support from her brothers on the chorus.

With so many ballads doesn't the album drag a bit? No and yes. All the ballads I've cited are strong and varied enough to be hypnotic, not monotonous. But there is a monotony on the album and it comes from the uptempo stuff. "I Give Up on You" and "Be My Lady," written by family boogie man Mark, and "Baby, Won't Ya Come Quick," by El, are all at least okay, but wouldn't turn out any parties I know of. Still, there is more than enough good boogie around. DeBarge has something else, something special to offer. Whether they, and El in particular, continue to develop or even stay at this level, is a big question mark. What I can say is that there is no one making better love music right now than DeBarge. And I'm not even blushing.

VILLAGE VOICE, 1984

# CHOCOLATE CHIPS AT THE ICE CAPADES

Three years before the Jacksons's current magical mystery tour (the magic is Michael, the mystery where you can buy tickets), they rolled into Madison Square Garden with one of the best pop concerts since Earth, Wind & Fire at its mid-'70s peak. The boys rose out of the floor, backlit by blinding white lights that themselves rose up to hover above the stage; clips from the messianic *The Triumph* video and the Ed Sullivan show heightened excitement; and a Doug Henning now-you-see-Michael-now-you-don't illusion during "Don't Stop ('Til You Get Enough)" boogied that dance classic right through the Garden roof.

The Jacksons, in the midst of what was then their most lucrative national tour, were in peak form. Randy's rumbling piano intro to "Shake Your Body," Tito's (yes, Tito's) re-creation of the jagged "Heartbreak Hotel" guitar solo, and Marlon and Jackie's capable if static harmonies were more than adequate. Michael was in exquisite voice; thrilling on "Can You Feel It," soap-opera sentimental on "She's Out of My Life" and "Ben," and just as smooth and gritty as he needed to be on "Heartbreak Hotel" and "Rock with Me." The Jackson boys did their usual pointing they-went-thataway steps. Even occasional hit-and-run mugging attacks couldn't undercut the positive feeling. The predominantly black teen and young adult crowd had grown up with Michael, and watching him stride so confidently across the stage, a young man no longer a boy, was an affirmation of our maturity. The Jacksons had been introduced by Motown as a great black family and despite some rough spots—Jermaine remained behind when the family skipped to Epic for big money—they had survived 10 years in the entertainment business, dignity intact. They were black royalty, sort of like the Kennedy kids except not fucked up.

Though from the beginning they had white fans (you don't get four number-one singles in a row without penetrating the allowances of suburban America), there was never any question in the minds of my black contemporaries that they were, in a very special way, ours. Admittedly this was probably not a view shared by Michael, a staunch integrationist in the Roy Wilkins mold, but America being America I thought he'd never fully escape the constraints of his color. It was his heritage, his tradition, blah-blah-blah. But on *Off the Wall*, aided and abetted by Hollywood's favorite producer Quincy Jones, Michael succeeded in creating colorblind cinemascope hits. On *Triumph*'s "Heartbreak Hotel," he found a voice that integrated soul, rock, funk, and classical pretensions into his peculiar paranoia. In "Beat It," "Billie Jean," and "Wanna Be Startin' Somethin'" he turned the gloss of *Off the Wall* and the passion of "Heartbreak Hotel" into a fascinating combination of fury and ear candy that took him as far as he wanted to go. His brothers? Despite improved musicianship and some good songs on *Destiny* and *Triumph*, they were basically just going along on a very strange ride. Strange because of that paranoid trilogy on *Thriller*, the dazzle of his videos and sales of his vanity documentary; the stunning star turn on *Motown 25*; the adulation of Brooke Shields, Emmanuel Lewis, and Yul Brynner; his ascendance into tabloid heaven up there with Elvis, "Dynasty" stars, and weight loss programs had all led to supernatural sales of *Thriller*, which in turn led to the amazingly white-bread crowds that have attended every show of the Victory Tour since the first one in Kansas City July 6.

As that concert testified, Michael is the first black star of his generation to follow Bill Cosby and Mr. T. into the kindergartens and bridge tournaments of our vast country. For those Americans Victory is like going to the Ice Capades. No dangerous adolescent lust or unbridled urban anger rippled through the crowd that beautiful still evening in the heartland. Instead we had kids spending much of the time looking at a huge TV screen to ascertain whether the doll-like stick figure wiggling in the distance was indeed Michael. Parents like the ones sitting behind me getting loudly drunk and spilling beer on my shoes enjoyed the spectacle of it, though the only non-*Thriller* material they seemed to know came during the Jackson Five medley. They were looking for family entertainment: a little sentiment, a little fantasy, a little dancing, a little nostalgia, a lot of glitter. And they got it, though not as much as they should have. For this was just the first show of a long tour, and the first show of any tour is always, to some degree, a glorified rehearsal. In basic content, what we got in Kansas City was pretty much what we got in the Meadowlands Sunday night, but a few technical differences made the earlier show problematic and the one we're seeing now a triumph of arena-rock. Drummer Phillip Moffitt often rushed the tempo, messing up the delicately modulated rhythms of "Off the Wall" and "Billie Jean." Minus the sidelined Jackie and plus the reclaimed Jermaine, the harmonics weren't up to the multilayered majesty of Michael's solo material. The band started slowly, though by "Beat It" and the show-closing "Shake Your Body" they were falling into some sweet grooves. And disappointingly, the staging had changed little since 1981, and what was new wasn't necessarily fresh. Michael had picked up some new breakdance glides, but the choreography was basically right out of *Motown 25*, and the corny battle-of-good-and-evil opening was distressingly reminiscent of Earth, Wind & Fire's 1982 tour.

All of which wouldn't have mattered so much if the Jacksons had played music from *Victory*, putting these familiar items in updated context. But the only new song was from Jermaine's Arista album. The Jacksons explained later that they wanted the audience to be more familiar with the material before doing it live, but this reasoning undermines the avowed purpose of both album and tour, which at least according to Marlon, Tito, and Randy is intended to showcase the "other" brothers.

Taken in that context *Victory* is a mixed bag. As the youngest, best-looking, and most musically gifted Jackson, Randy is in the perfect position to fill the teen idol shoes Jermaine once wore. His past songs, including a collaboration with Michael on "Shake," suggested a writer of promise, and that promise is realized by the track on "One More Chance," on which he plays almost all the instruments. It is coolly supple, filled with intricate guitar and keyboard parts that support a cute melody. But here as in "The Hurt," Randy's voice betrays him; he sounds studied and dull, not up to his own music. Marlon's "Body," written with veteran West Coast session keyboardist-arranger John Barnes, is a melodic dance track reminiscent of "Wanna Be Startin' Somethin'," but without the polish or passion. Things pick up considerably with Tito's (yes Tito's) "We Can Change the World," an overtly reggae, densely arranged, lyrically vague "social commentary" with a quietly cooking groove. Though synthesizer-laden, as are most of *Victory*'s tunes, Tito's arrangement has a warmth complemented by singing that is surprisingly relaxed compared to Randy's. In fact (heresy) I'd compare it favorably to Michael's "Be Not Always," on which Michael is so "sensitive" he becomes a parody of his own image. Both songs are pleas to, well, save the world blah-blah-blah. Michael just tries to be so damn heavy it's funny.

No, this isn't *Thriller*. But for Jackie it is a real victory. His two songs, "Torture" and "Wait," are easily the album's best. Under Jackie's guidance, "Torture"'s touching Jermaine-Michael duet accentuates the troubled feel of the synth-bass and strings and the tense melody. The song's air of tragedy suggests a range of emotion the rest of *Victory* lacks. Though the Jacksons's backing vocals sound slightly off-key, that disjointed quality enhances the melancholy mood. And where "Torture" is a grim gem, "Wait" is a buoyant, fun romp, reminiscent of "Lovely One" and "Things I Do for You" only better. Written and produced by Jackie with Toto's Paich and Porcaro, it's slicked up neo-Motown with more than a touch of the Thom Bell Spinners—the bass and bits of the horn charts are lifted whole from "Rubberband Man." With Toto sprightly and immaculate and the Jacksons cutting loose vocally in a bright, trebly mix, "Wait" jumps. Jackie's speaking voice is higher than bro Michael's, but here (in the studio) he has more bottom and turns in a remarkably swinging lead vocal. A brief spirited solo turn by Michael doesn't hurt, but it is Jackie who carries "Wait."

Unfortunately, Jackie's only appearance at the Meadowlands Sunday night was on crutches before the show. And, no, the Jacksons still didn't do any songs from *Victory* (but, like wow, man, Jagger may come on for "State of Schlock" at the Garden). Despite this frustrating conservatism, the Jacksons gave the decidedly chocolate-chip crowd in Jersey a hard, lean, mean show. Drummer Moffitt and rhythm guitarist David Williams anchored the supertight rhythm section, with the laser lights and smoke providing an effective backdrop for the music and some fresh bits of choreography.

Michael? Well Peter Pan was nowhere to be seen, but James Brown and Jackie Wilson were, for Michael was as aggressive, fiery, and *macho* as any '60s soul man. With a sneering intense scowl on his face, Michael shook his pelvis, moonwalked, and sang with heart and a whole lot of deep-fried soul. The contrast with Kansas City was stark. There he seemed a fairy prince off in the distance, far removed and detached from his subjects and even the show itself. In Jersey he walked the waterfront with a chip on his shoulder, moving and singing with real blood in his eye. This was particularly true of the show's first half, when even during "She's Out of My Life" he threw in some break-dance movements signifying that on this night all sweetness must be cut with funk. It might have been that Jersey swampland air, but more likely it was that Michael, like his band, was now in midtour form and fully ready to justify to the skeptical just how much he was worth. I wondered, looking at the family of four in front of me, whether Mom and Pop were quite ready for this Michael, a cat who would just as soon have kicked the ass of those gang leaders in "Beat It" as started a chorus line. Springsteen may be the boss and Prince the royal contender, but guess who still wears the crown.

# MARVIN GAYE OBITUARY

MARCH 1983—In the motel's living room two women in their late thirties, wearing too much makeup, and clothes too tight covering too much flesh, hovered over a hot plate, concerned that everything would taste right "for him." In the bedroom, behind closed doors, dressed in a robe and stocking cap, his face covered with a facial mask, Marvin Gaye, accompanied by three biceped roadies (bodyguards?), watched a fight on "Wide World of Sports." Marvin and I sat next to each other in tacky motel chairs, his attention wandering from our conversation to the fight.

I anticipated an upbeat conversation full of the self-righteous I-told-you-so fervor so many performers, back from commercial death, inflict upon interviewers and the public. After all, Gaye was in the midst of one of the most thrilling comebacks in pop music history. "Sexual Healing," some freedom from the IRS, CBS's mammoth music machine in high gear for him, and adoration from two generations of fans, were all part of a wave of prosperity. Even his stage act, in the past marked by a palpable diffidence, had been spellbinding. The night before, at San Mateo's Circle Star Theatre, he had been brilliant, performing all the good stuff, and even reviving Mary Wells's "Two Lovers," one of Smokey's best early songs about a total schizophrenic, a man who was both lovingly faithful and totally amoral.

Gaye's voice was soft, relaxed, and strangely monotonous (he spoke with almost no inflection). His precise elocution was reminiscent of your stereotypical English gentleman, but he spoke of a world far removed from delicacy and style. These were words of isolation, alienation, and downright confusion. His reviewer acclaim had in no way silenced the demons that made his last Motown album *In Our Lifetime* (despite its premature release by Motown) an explicit battle between the devil and the Lord for his heart, soul, and future.

I said to him, "The times seem to call for the kind of social commentary you provided on 'What's Going On.'

"It seems to me I have to do some soul searching to see what I want to say," he said. "You can say something. Or you can say something profound. It calls for fasting, feeling, praying, lots of prayer, and maybe we can come up with a more spiritual social statement, to give people more food for thought."

"I take it this process hasn't been going on within you in quite some time."

"I have been apathetic, because I know the end is near. Sometimes, I feel like going off and taking a vacation and enjoying the last 10 or 15 years and forgetting about my message, which I feel is in a form of being a true messenger of God."

"What about doing like Al Green and turning your back on the whole thing?"

"That's his role. My role is not necessarily his. That doesn't make me a devil. It's just that my role is different, you see. If he wants to turn to God and become without sin and have his reputation become that, then that is what it should be. I am not concerned with what my role should be. I am only concerned with completing my mission here on Earth. My mission is what it is and I think I'm presenting it in a proper way. What people think about me is their business."

"What is your mission?"

Without a moment's hesitation he responded, "My mission is to tell the world and people about the upcoming holocaust and to find all those of higher consciousness who can be saved. Those who can't can be left alone."

A year later I reflected on those words while reading the comments of Rev. Marvin Gaye, Sr., Marvin's father, from his Los Angeles jail cell. It had all gone wrong for Marvin since our talk. The physical assaults on others, including his 70-year-old father, Marvin's self-inflicted psychological degradation of himself with his "sniffing," and the lack of creative energy it all suggested, meant Marvin's unrest was real. Still, to me, the most frightening comment was Rev. Gaye's response to whether he loved his son or not: "Let's say that I didn't dislike him."

**Summer 1958**—Stardom was taking its toll on the Moonglows, one of the '50s top vocal groups. One member had been hospitalized for drug abuse. Another was tripping on the glamour and friendly little girls. Harvey Fuqua, the Moonglows's founder and most level-headed member, was disturbed to see how the Moonglows were not profiting from their fame. It was during this period of growing disillusionment that four Washington, D.C., teens, the Marquees, finally talked Fuqua into listening to them in his hotel room. Well Fuqua was "freaked out" by them, particularly the lanky kid in the back named Marvin Gaye. By the winter of 1959 two editions of the Moonglows had come and gone when Fuqua accepted an offer to move to Detroit as a partner in Gwen Gordy and Billy Davis's Anna records.

That Fuqua kept Marvin with him is testimony to his eye for talent and the growth of a friendship that in many ways would parallel that of future Motown co-workers Smokey Robinson and Berry Gordy. On the surface Marvin was this seemingly calm, tall, smooth-skinned charmer whom the ladies found most seductive. Marvin was cool. Yet there was an insecurity and a spirituality in his soul that overwhelmed his worldly desire, causing great inner turmoil. This conflict could be traced to his often strained relationship with his father, a well-known minister in Washington, D.C. Rev. Gaye was flamboyant, persuasive, and yet disquieting as well. There was a strange, repressed sexuality about him that caused whispers in the nation's capital. His son, so sensitive and so clearly possessed of his father's spiritual determination and his own special musical gifts (he sang, played piano and drums), sought to establish his own identity.

So he pursued a career in singing "the devil's music" and in Fuqua found a strong, masculine figure who respected his talent. Together they'd sit for hours at the piano, Fuqua showing Marvin chord progressions. Marvin took instruction well, but his rebel's edge would flash when something conflicted with his views. His combination of sex and spirituality, malleability and conviction, made Fuqua feel Marvin was something special. Marvin, not crazy about returning to D.C., accepted Fuqua's invitation.

Marvin never recorded for Anna records. But he sure met the label's namesake, Gwen's sister Anna. "Right away Anna snatched him," Fuqua told Aaron Fuchs, "just snatched him immediately." Anna was something. She was 17 years older than Marvin, but folks in Detroit thought she was more than a match for most men. Ambitious, shrewd, and quite "fine," she introduced Marvin to brother Berry, leading to session work as a pianist and drummer. Later, after Berry had established Motown as an independent label, Marvin cut *The Soulful Moods of Marvin Gaye*, a collection of MOR standards done with a bit of jazz flavor. It was an effort, the first of several by Motown, to reach the supper club audience that supported black crooners Nat King Cole, Johnny Mathis, and Sam Cooke. It flopped and some were doubtful he'd get another chance. Yeah, he was Berry's brother-in-law (that's the reason some figured he got the shot in the first place), but Berry was cold-blooded about business.

Then in July Stevenson and Berry's brother George had an idea for a dance record. Marvin wasn't crazy about singing hardcore r&b. But Anna was used to being pampered and Marvin's pretty face didn't pay bills. Neither did a drummer's salary. With Marvin's songwriting a "Stubborn Kind of Fellow" was recorded late in the month. "You could hear the man screaming on that tune, you could tell he was hungry," says Dave Hamilton, who played guitar on it. "If you listen to that song you'll say, 'Hey, man, he was trying to make it because he was on his last leg.'" Despite "Stubborn" cracking the r&b top ten Marvin's future at Motown was in no way assured. He was already getting a reputation for being "moody" and "difficult." It wasn't until December that he cut anything else with hit potential. "Hitch Hike," a thumping boogie turn that again called for a rougher style than Gaye enjoyed, was produced by Stevenson and his bright young assistant Clarence Paul. "Stubborn"'s groove wears better than "Hitch Hike"'s twenty years later, yet his second hit was probably more important to his career. Gaye proved he wasn't a one-hit wonder. He proved too that the intangible "thing" some heard in Gaye's performance of "Stubborn" was not a fluke. The man had sex appeal. "I never wanted to sing the hot stuff," he would later tell David Ritz in *Essence*. "With a great deal of bucking, I did it because . . . well I wanted the money and the glory. So I worked with all the producers. But I wanted to be a pop singer—like Nat Cole or Sinatra or Tony Bennett. I wanted to be a pop singer like Sam Cooke, proving that our kind of music and our kind of feeling could work in the context of pop ballads. Motown never gave me the push I needed."

Cholly Atkins, Motown's choreographer during the glory years, remembers things differently. "Marvin had the greatest opportunity in the world and we were grooming him for it," Atkins says. "He almost had first choice to replace Sam Cooke when Sam passed away. He had his foot in the door. He was playing smart supper clubs and doing excellent, but it wasn't his bag. He wanted to go on not shaving with a skull cap on and old dungarees, you know what I mean, instead of the tuxedo and stuff. That's what he felt comfortable doing . . . But he has his own thoughts about where he wants to go or what he wants to do with his life. And he doesn't like anybody influencing him otherwise."

Beans Bowles, a road manager and Motown executive in the mid-'60s, remembers Marvin as a "very disturbed young man . . . because of what he wanted to do and the frustrations he had trying to do them. He wanted to play football. He tried to join the Detroit Lions."

In 1970, at 31, Marvin tried to get Detroit's local NFL franchise to let him attend rookie camp. This was the period after Tammi Terrell's death when he was, against Motown's wishes, working on *What's*

*Going On.* Yet he was willing to stop all that for the opportunity to play pro football. Why?

"My father was a minister and he wanted me in church most of the time," he told the *Detroit Free Press*. "I played very little sandlot football and I got me a few whippins for staying after school watching the team practice." This parental discipline only ignited Marvin's contrary nature and his fantasies. "I don't want to be known as the black George Plimpton," he said, somewhat insulted by the comparison. "I have no ulterior motive . . . I'm not writing a book. I just love football. I love the glory of it . . . there's an ego thing involved . . . and the glory is with the pros."

The Lions, not surprisingly, turned him down flat. Marvin's attempt didn't surprise those who knew him then either. At Motown picnics he always played all out, trying to outshine his contemporaries at every opportunity. One time he severely strained an ankle running a pass pattern. In Los Angeles in the early '70s he developed quite a reputation as a treacherous half-court basketball player. He even tried to buy a piece of a WFL franchise in the mid-'70s.

There were two levels to Marvin's often fanatical attachment to sports. One was a deep seated desire to prove his manhood, his strength, his macho, in a world where brute power met delicate grace in physical celebration. For all his sex appeal and interest in sexuality ("you make a person think you're going to do something, but never do until you're ready"), Gaye wanted to assert his physical superiority over other men.

Linked to this was a need for teamwork, a need to enjoy the fruits of collaboration. All his best work, be it some early hits with Micky Stevenson, "Let's Get It On" with Ed Townsend, "What's Going On" with Alfred Cleveland, or "Midnight Love" with Harvey Fuqua, was done in tandem with others. For all his self-conscious artistic arrogance, he was a team player. In the '60s Marvin bent his voice to the wishes of Motown, but he did so his way, vocally if not musically. He claimed he had three different voices, a falsetto, a gritty gospel shout, and a smooth midrange close to his speaking voice. Depending on the tune's key, tone, and intention he was able to accommodate it, becoming a creative slave to the music's will. On the early hits ("Ain't That Peculiar," "Hitch-Hike") Gaye is rough, ready, and willing. His glide through the opening verse of "Ain't No Mountain High Enough" is the riff Nick Ashford, the song's co-writer and producer, has been reaching for all these years. On Berry Gordy's "Try It Baby" Marvin's coolly slick delivery reminds us of the Harlem bars I visited with my father as a child. His version of "Grapevine" is so intense, so pretty, so goddamn black in spirit, it seems to catalogue that world of black male emotions Charles Fuller evokes in his insightful *Soldier's Play*. Listening to Marvin's three-record *Anthology* LP will confirm that no Motown artist gave as much to the music as he did. If he had never made another record after December 31, 1969, his contributions to the company would have given a lasting fame even greater than that reserved for Levi Stubbs and Martha Reeves. But, as Marvin often tried to tell them, he had even more to offer.

In 1971, Motown released *What's Going On*, a landmark that, forgive the heresy, is as important and as successfully ambitious as *Sgt. Pepper*. What?! I said this before Gaye's demise and I still say it. Stanley Crouch, in a well-reasoned analysis of *What's Going On*, explains it better than anyone ever has.

"His is a talent for which the studio must have been invented. Through over dubbing, Gaye imparted lyric, rhythmic, and emotional counterpoint to his material. The result was a swirling stream-of-consciousness that enabled him to protest, show allegiance, love, hate, dismiss, and desire in one proverbial fell swoop. In his way, what Gaye did was reiterate electronically the polyrhythmic African underpinnings of black American music and reassess the domestic polyphony which is its linear extension."

Furthermore, Crouch asserted, "The upshot of his genius was the ease and power with which he could pivot from a superficially simple but virtuosic use of rests and accents to a multilinear layered density. In fact, if one were to say that James Brown could be the Fletcher Henderson and Count Basie of rhythm and blues, then Marvin Gaye is obviously its Ellington and Miles Davis."

Though lyrically Marvin never again reached as far outside his personal experience for material, the musical ambience of *What's Going On* was refined with varying degrees of effectiveness for the rest of his career.

Part of the reason for Gaye's introspection was a series of personal dramas—a costly divorce from Anna, a tempestuous marriage to a woman 17 years his junior, constant creative hassles with Motown, and antagonism with his father over religion, money, and his mother. Drugs became his escape hatch and his prison. As his *In Our Lifetime* so brazenly articulates, the devil was after his soul and damned if he wasn't determined to win.

April 1983—Any purchaser of other Rupert Murdoch newsstock publications knows the details of Marvin Gaye's death. I expect the trial, if his father isn't declared insane, to be an evil spectacle, full of drugs, sex, and interfamily conflicts. It won't be fun. What was, and will always be my favorite memory of Marvin, was his performance of the National Anthem at the 1983 NBA Allstar game. Dressed as dapperly as any nightclub star, standing before an audience of die-hard sports fans, and some of the world's greatest athletes, Gaye turned out our nation's most confusing melody, asserting an aesthetic and intellectual power that rocked the house. I play it over and over now. CBS was going to release it as a single. Don't you think they should now?

VILLAGE VOICE, 1984

# FAMILY TIES
## Bobby Womack, Linda Womack,
## & Cecil Womack

I suppose we should blame James Brown. Ever since 1965, when he stifled the melody and filled every crevice of "Papa's Got a Brand New Bag" with rhythm, black pop music has never been the same. As hip hop legions and new wavy trendoids like Cameo and Ready for the World attest, carefully crafted pop soul has been and continues to be an endangered species, protected only by a few, like Luther Vandross and Whitney Houston. Hey, I'll always have a soft spot in my hard head for the pounding master-mixes of DJ Red Alert and company, but as time passes I find myself gravitating toward soul-era values, when songs were vehicles for fabulous vocal flights and tales of love—lost, stolen, and passionately reclaimed all in less than three minutes. I'm drawn back to the old music because, quite simply, secular salvation in love has rarely been better expressed than in this music's sweet passion. The key is to fuse it all together—heart and stomp, soul and sequencers.

Bobby Womack's "I Wish He Didn't Trust Me So Much," the hit

single from *So Many Rivers* (MCA), conjures up less admirable memories. Bobby wants his best friend's wife and is torn between loyalty and lust. The song gains an eerie resonance when you know that Bobby married Sam Cooke's widow just months after his mentor died in a 1964 shooting. The arrangement utilizes many current gizmos—electro this, synth that—but the sound is old-fashioned soul. Likewise, "Strange & Funny," the commercially unsuccessful single from Linda Womack and Cecil Womack's *Radio M.U.S.C. Man* (Elektra), is filled with descending keyboard blips, French horn–like synthesizers, and other techno touches. Yet this tale of love and decay, written by Cecil, Linda, and Bobby, throbs with the same emotional truth of "I Wish He Didn't Trust Me So Much." When Linda sings "Fork in the road/He's south, I'm east," she captures the feeling of late-night telephone conversations we all know too well.

Both *So Many Rivers* and *Radio M.U.S.C. Man* have an earthy spirituality they inherited from Cooke. Bobby was a rising gospel star when Cooke "turned him out" along with Lou Rawls and Johnnie Taylor. After divorcing Barbara Cooke, Bobby went on to build a singer-songwriter soul career. Like Bobby, Cecil was a member of the Valentinos, the Womack family vocal group, and a behind the scenes songwriter, including a stint at Gamble & Huff's Philadelphia International Records, where he wrote the classic "Love TKO" for Teddy Pendergrass. That song was inspired by Linda Womack, Sam Cooke's daughter (at different points Bobby was her stepfather, now her brother-in-law, and Cecil was her stepuncle, now her husband), and her voice still echoes Sam's silky phrasing. Linked by love, blood, and history with Cooke, this trio has stayed true to soul, though as related by "Only Survivor," Cecil's song for Bobby on *So Many Rivers*, it hasn't been easy.

Womack's best records were made in the early to mid-'70s (seek out his 1977 *Safety Zone*) when he was in the black music mainstream. His "I Can Understand It" from that period was a pioneering disco groove. Ever since, Bobby has had two left feet when it comes to dance music. Even his spectacular 1982 comeback, *The Poet*, contained no crowd rocking grooves. The up-tempo "So Baby, Don't Leave Home Without It" on *So Many Rivers* has an electro shuffle beat and synthesized horn line that sounds as corny as its title. "So Many Rivers" has a snappy beat and aspires to the crossover sound of Lionel Richie's "Running with the Night," but simply isn't as much fun as it wants to be. "Gypsy Woman," never one of Curtis Mayfield's better copyrights, isn't saved by Bobby's sped-up interpretation.

But if you skip the boogie, *So Many Rivers* is damn near a masterpiece. "I Wish He Didn't Trust Me So Much" is magic. "Got to Be with You Tonight" is almost as brilliant, with Womack wailing over a flowing gospel chorus, Wilton Felder's sinewy sax, and some tasty acoustic piano licks. On "Let Me Kiss It Where It Hurts," Womack consoles a woman ("You were young/Fancy free/A virgin to life") who has been messed over by some heartless dude. Womack's conversational vocal is suspiciously self-serving; as the title suggests, Womack's interest in this exploited sister is not what you'd call platonic. Finally, covering Sam Cooke's swaying "That's Where It's At," Bobby's right at home. This is the kind of slow drag folks don't write anymore. Bobby, the veteran of more basement parties than he cares to remember, sings it gritty and warm.

Mid-tempo is the rhythm of Linda & Cecil Womack's *Radio M.U.S.C. Man*, a sign of equilibrium between this working-class Ashford & Simpson. Cecil doesn't have his brother's vocal range, but does have his tenderness, a quality complemented by the cool, supple charm of Linda's voice. As on their previous album, *Love Wars*, Linda and Cecil's performances are a dialogue of love. Linda bemoans her man's loss of integrity, as in "Romeo and Juliet (Where Are You?)" and threatens to leave if his infidelities continue ("Eyes"), while Cecil claims the good days are coming (in a revitalization of George Harrison's "Here Comes the Sun") and that their bonds can be rebuilt ("No Mercy"). Using a song fragment from an otherwise lost Cooke tape, Linda and Cecil composed their most characteristic song, "Love's Calling," a story of frustrated romance where Cecil's voice carries the verse while Linda sings haunting counterpoint. In contrast to Bobby's ballad/boogie dichotomy, his brother and sister-in-law can mesh sophisticated dance tempos with their sensually obsessed lyrics. The music swells and falls deftly to underscore the lyrics and heighten the tension of the sexual battlefield. This consistency of tone makes *Radio M.U.S.C. Man* one of the year's best.

Nevertheless, this is the last Womack & Womack album on Elektra. (Cecil and Elektra president Bob Krasnow had a disagreement.) A tough break, but the quality of their music is so undeniable they'll resurface (as they already have with three songs on the new Pendergrass LP), and, with Bro Bobby, carry on as black music's longest established family-owned firm.

# THE TIME HAS COME
## Jimmy "Jam" Harris/Terry Lewis

**P**roducers of black pop often work best in pairs. We can start with the "dark" ages (we refer of course to the '50s) when Jerry Leiber and Mike Stoller set the tone with Tin Pan Alley rhythm & bluesism. The '60s spawned the Holland-Dozier-Holland machine (actually a duo, since Eddie Holland primarily wrote lyrics; Brian Holland and Lamont Dozier directed sessions), the elegant Nick Ashford and Valerie Simpson, Isaac Hayes and David Porter's corn pone soul, and the judgmental romanticism of Kenny Gamble and Leon Huff. Since the mid-'70s Reggie Lucas and Mtume's sweet funk, Bernard Edwards and Nile Rodgers's (what else?) chic dance jams, Kashif and Paul Laurence's synthesizer blips, and Russell Simmons and Larry Smith's B-boy minimalism have all shaped the contours of black pop.

Why this duo-ism? Maybe because good black pop demands two very different elements: strong, chromatic melodies keyed to street-corner vernacular (slang, y'all) and distinctive rhythmic innovations (fresh beats, home folks). Four ears can really define the balance between the 'R' and the 'B.'

Jimmy "Jam" Harris and Terry Lewis, original members of the Time, now Minneapolis-based free-lance producers, are the latest entries into the funky pantheon listed above. Their career started by accident. After sneaking away to produce Klymaxx in 1984, they missed the airplane that was to rush them to a Time gig. Their employer, Prince, delivered an ultimatum: Stay home and work under my supervision or scram. Asserting their manhood (and, alas, emasculating the best groove band of the decade), Harris and Lewis declined and went on to create for the SOS Band a series of seductive mid-tempo jams, including the landmark "Just Be Good to Me." The crackling assurance of the rhythm matched with the arrangement's dramatic support of the title's pleading hook signaled the arrival of Harris and Lewis. Freed from the purple one's reign, Harris and Lewis cold-crushed 1985, reviving Thelma Houston ("You Used to Hold Me So Tight"), introducing Cherrelle ("I Didn't Mean to Turn You On") and Alexander O'Neal ("Innocent"), understanding Cheryl Lynn's booming voice ("Encore"), and, in general, married Minneapolis aggression to LaLa-land slickness.

Still, it wasn't until this winter that Harris and Lewis proved they were more than the latest flavor of the month by displaying unexpected versatility. "Tender Love," written and produced for the Force M.D.'s and the film *Krush Groove*, highlights the prettiest piano melody on black radio since Lionel Richie was a Commodore. The tune projects an open-hearted sensitivity that has slipped the Force M.D.'s, hip hop doo-woppers from Staten Island once seen as curiosities, into the ear of the black music mainstream. "Saturday Love" by Cherrelle and Alexander O'Neal, a vibrant melody (sharp instrumental bridge, too!), is the latest contribution to that enduring genre: the day song. The "Sunday, Monday, Tuesday, Wednesday, Thursday, Friday, Saturday" chorus supports Cherrelle's knowing yet girlish pipes and O'Neal's primo tenor. If pop radio is as receptive to quality black pop as some now claim, "Saturday Love" will be this spring's "How Sweet It Is to Be Loved by You."

Finally, and most impressively, there is Janet Jackson's "What Have You Done for Me Lately," which has the lean meanness of the original Time's live performances. But instead of Morris Day's self-satisfied whine cruising over the track's brazen energy, we're treated to the artistic and sexual liberation of Janet Jackson. Over a tough computer beat she lays out her old man with the angry assertiveness of a full-grown woman. In fact, throughout *Control* (A&M), on which Harris and Lewis give her coproduction credit, Janet is a stylish vamp who destroys her little-sister image. She has, after all, been married and divorced (to James DeBarge of DeBarge) and taken an apartment outside the Jacksons' Encino enclave. Collaborating with Harris and Lewis—and playing keyboards—Janet has made the most satisfying album of Harris and Lewis's career and the best Jackson album since *Thriller*. Side one is packed with rocking funk and impertinent imagery. On the title track Janet sings, "When I was 17 I did what my Daddy told me/I let my mother mold me/But that was long ago/Now I'm in control." This sexy groove melts into the stomping "Nasty," where "Miss Jackson to you" is as sassy as Vanity and Apollonia wish to be.

Side two's opener, "The Pleasure Principle," makes Janet sound too much like New Edition's Ralph Tresvant, and we don't need another lyric about riding in a limo. But "When I Think of You" is deservedly already a disco favorite because of its neo-Motown bass line, Fairlight computer ejaculations, and exquisitely timed instrumental breaks. "Let's Wait Awhile" and "Funny How Time Flies (When You're Having Fun)," both ballads, are the only songs that make Janet sound like Michael, except that it's hard to imagine her bro singing as explicitly about sex as Janet does. During "Let's," she tells her boyfriend the first time wasn't so hot, so why don't we chill. But by "Funny" she's moaning in French over an obvious rip-off of Michael's "The Lady in My Life." Even if these ballads don't completely succeed as music, they work as statements of Janet's womanhood, clearly one of *Control*'s purposes. Jackson aside, the album claims another triumph. The Harris/Lewis production duo has legs, and they know how to use them.

VILLAGE VOICE, 1986

# ANITA BAKER

## A Quiet Storm

The age of retro-nuevo has arrived in black music and I couldn't be happier, though I didn't think I would be. After all, white music makers have been knee-deep in it throughout the decade with revived rockabilly, Farfisas, Ray-Ban shades, and '80s records with that crummy four-track sound, like Springsteen's *The River*, which made me laugh. No matter how many critics hailed this stuff, I wondered why working stiffs would buy a state-of-the-art stereo to

listen to records that sounded like oatmeal. And all that talk from neocon-
servative rockers about "purist" sounds struck me as nostalgic babbling.

So I listened to black pop and chilled. Then, sometime after the vic-
tories of *Thriller* and *Purple Rain*, which sent black mediocrities to the
studio to Xerox them, I realized my favorite music was growing smug.
With the exception of go-go, rap, and the occasional mainstream singer
(Luther Vandross, Maze's Frankie Beverly), clearly black pop was dilut-
ing itself with synthesizer-induced crossover dreams.

Too much black pop was (often still is) as enticing as a ripped
diaphragm and not nearly as dangerous—awash in futurism, manipulated by the whims of corporate marketers, and betrayed by artists yearning to be the musical equivalent of Cosby's Dr. Huxtable. Call it soul,
rhythm & blues, funk or black pop, the music that had inspired me when
my mother made me polish the living room furniture (I "Simonized" to
Gladys Knight's "The Nitty Gritty") was now juvenile, middle class, slow
witted (lot of lousy lyricists out there), and so dependent on instrumentation that the beauty of the Afro-American vocal chord no longer mattered. In reaction I dove into Stax, Motown, Al Green, and Miles Davis
(circa '50s) to luxuriate in the soul satisfaction of heartfelt music.

But in the last year or so several developments have made me realize that retro-nuevo is on the rise: Sade's two albums, Freddie Jack-
son's "Rock Me Tonight," Aretha Franklin's "Who's Zoomin' Who,"
anything slow by Bobby Womack, the writing of his brother and sister-
in-law Cecil Womack and Linda Womack, the stage shows of New
Edition and the Force M.D.'s, Luther Vandross's *The Night I Fell in
Love*, amateur night (every Wednesday) at the Apollo, plans to revive
Philadelphia's Uptown and Chicago's Regal, the proliferation of
"Quiet Storm" formats (ballads from Sarah Vaughan to Whitney
Houston), Morris Day's videos, the funk on Prince's *Parade*, the Fat
Boys's "Sex Machine," L.L. Cool J's *Radio*, and most recently Anita
Baker's *Rapture* (Elektra).

What all this suggests is that black pop, its audience and
entrepreneurs, is more conscious of the best of its tradition than at any
time in memory. To varying degrees all of them re-create—vocally (Jackson, Womack, Franklin), visually (Day, New Edition, Force M.D.'s),
rhythmically (Fat Boys, Prince, L.L. Cool J), atmospherically (Sade,
Baker), or historically (reviving chitlin' circuit palaces and the ballad on
black radio)—some elemental part of black experience in contemporary
terms. Post–World War II black pop has never before emphasized looking back, one reason for its ongoing creativity. On the dark side, it can be
shortsighted in its judgments. Blacks helped the white usurpation of rock

'n' roll by spurning Chuck Berry and Little Richard in the early '60s, as if soul were the only valid black pop. The hostility both men feel toward the black community today is an outgrowth of that rejection.

To me retro-nuevo can be summed up as an embrace of the past to create passionate, fresh music. I cite as my chief example Anita Baker's *Rapture*, an album of contemporary intelligence and old-fashioned pipes. The intelligence is primarily Baker's. As executive producer, Baker has made an eight-cut album with no uptempo songs, a complete reversal of the norm for black female vocalists, underlining her understanding of her instrument and the reason why more women should demand control of their recordings. The pipes are Baker's too. Wrapping her voice in arrangements that support her and using *human* bass players and drummers, Baker shines with the maturity of a Dinah Washington and the mellow caress of Patti Austin's CTI recordings (e.g., *End of the Rainbows*). It is unashamedly adult music that, like Baker's 1982 Beverly Glen hit "Angel," sounds progressive despite its anachronistic value.

Baker, a petite Detroit native, has a voice that belies her body. Emanating deep in her throat, it has a firm, husky, dipped-in-brandy texture that on Rod Temperton's "Mystery" and David Lasley's "You Bring Me Joy"—revivals of previously recorded songs—showcases her interpretive skill. On "Joy" there are some gospel vocal breaks and touches of Patti Labelleish shouting. But jazz is Baker's deepest influence. On "Caught Up in the Rapture" she sings the hook like an alto saxophonist blowing softly through his mouthpiece, in sweet contrast to the acoustic guitar of producer Michael Powell. "Sweet Love" is a pretty El Lay r&b love song that Baker uses as a vehicle to sustain phrases and slide through verses with the gentle style of Wes Montgomery's guitar. Her own "Been So Long" would have been in heavy rotation at WRVR back in the days when Austin, Angela Bofill, Dee Dee Bridgewater, and Phyllis Hyman were updating Nina Simone. Two-thirds of the way through, Baker begins scatting with a teasing confidence that suggests in another era the lady might have been playing the Village Gate. But this is the '80s, so it's not surprising that Baker's other composition, "Watch Your Step," is glossy pop-soul in the Michael McDonald mold. *Rapture* isn't a total triumph; "No One in the World" and "Same Ole Love" are simply listenable. Still, six hits out of eight at-bats would make even Don Mattingly envious. Retro-nuevo? Maybe there is a touch of wishful thinking in this proposition. But listening to Baker's voice, and its sympathetic setting, I have to hope this is the future.

VILLAGE VOICE, 1986

# BOBBY "BLUE" BLAND
## Storm Warnings

It's hard to understand the blues if you're not black and over 40 (maybe 45), and didn't grow up in an area where the blues was a staple of radio programming and the local clubs. So if that means most of the people at blues concerts in white venues since the mid-'60s don't really appreciate the blues as it was intended to be savored—myself included—so be it. I say this not to promote some black purist agenda but because of an experience I had last summer at the Apollo Theater. Bobby "Blue" Bland was there and the old theater was about two-thirds full, mostly with folks 30-plus and a good many in their forties. It struck me that this was the first time I'd be seeing the music with a predominantly black audience, an audience for whom the blues wasn't a pleasing historic document—as it was for my contemporaries, white and black—but at one time was as essential to their lives as funk and rap have been to mine.

And it *was* different. When Bland's raspy voice ground out "Stormy Monday," "Lead Me On," or any of his melancholy, tragicomic blues standards, the audience's reaction was enthusiastically cool. Heads rocked. Feet patted. Friends nudged each other at key lines. And, as if at church, black men in leisure suits and Kangol caps and women with thick round glasses and newly minted jheri curls just like Bland's grunted and responded with "Yeah" at all the right moments. Nowhere were the shrill shouts and rock 'n' roll yelps that white audiences have used at every blues show I've ever attended.

But while for white audiences the blues is often an excuse for a pep rally, to the Apollo crowd Bland's secular sermons on love inspired a religious feeling. Bland is a master of "sleeping around" songs and at the Apollo I realized that I'd always underestimated their meaning. Bland didn't simply celebrate or even just meditate on infidelity, though those elements are always there; he presented morality plays where lust, no matter how joyfully consummated, was paid off in heartbreak and frustration. Bland's blues are the gospel of bad news, the tales of choices made and the consequences of these decisions. Where most contemporary black pop concerns itself with receiving sex and/or love, the blues dealt with the next morning and the day after that, often with great humor—though Bland's voice and arrangements make one feel a deep blue cloud is always hovering about, even when he's laughing.

At that Apollo show Bland did only one recent song, "Members Only," the title cut from his 1985 Malaco debut after years of corporate neglect at MCA. Not a bad track (or album), but Bland was right in feeling it paled next to the depressing majesty of his Duke recordings. His latest on Malaco, *After All*, is better than *Members Only*, but no one will mistake it for *Two Steps from the Blues*, and I expect to hear little of it when I next see this ever touring bluesman. On it Bland's trademark rasp, now very worn around the edges, is cushioned by Wolf Stephenson and Tommy Crouch's sympathetic production: This is the dude who made the late Z.Z. Hill the most important bluesman of the '80s until Robert Cray's ascension. Bland's voice is surrounded by Muscle Shoals stomps, slow shuffles, and tasty blues guitar solos, so that songs like "Second Hand Heart" and "I Hear You Thinkin'" sound either nostalgically perfect or like sadly anachronistic testaments to southern soul, depending on the listener's mood. My favorites are "I Hear You Thinkin'," a horn-driven rocking tune about a lady engaged in extramarital horizontal enrichment, and "Walkin' & Talkin' & Singin' the Blues," a song purporting to be about wooing a lover but actually about the singer's dedication to his music. "Walkin'" has a bunch of great lines like "solitude is made for the lonely/darkness for the blind," but the clincher is "happiness is for everyone/the blues is for me." Which for me sums up Bland's music, the bittersweet reality of the blues, and its often forgotten power to purge the listener of personal demons. No other current style of popular music—with the exception of country—has the earthy grounding to do that. Which says a lot about what music isn't in the '80s.

**4**

# TO BE A BLACK MAN

# WHY DID
# EDMUND PERRY DIE?

**E**arly in the morning of Thursday, June 13—little more than 12 hours after Edmund Perry had been fatally shot by police officer Lee Van Houten—family and friends sat stunned in the Perry living room, victims of the world they'd kept barred outside the door for so long. Nichole Perry, a bright, usually vivacious 19-year-old engineering major at Cornell University, said little.

In the center of the room sat Veronica Perry, a portly 37-year-old woman with thin legs, round, thoughtful eyes, and a stern, resolute mouth that so many times had expressed passion for her children and their dreams. "Dear Jesus," she said, "make me understand. I've always been faithful to God. Tell me why you have done this to me?"

The 1985 Phillips Exeter Academy yearbook lay on a table near Mrs. Perry and, after resting her Bible, she opened it, flipping to a photograph of Edmund. In the photo he is leaning against a brick wall, one sneaker anchoring his body as the other casually touches the brick. Relaxed in a two-tone Nike track suit, hands coolly placed in the pants pockets, Edmund looks "chilly." His eyes peer past the camera into the distance, a hint of a smile sneaks across his wide brown face.

Speaking to everyone in the room, yet to no one in particular, Mrs. Perry said, "This is what my baby wrote," and read from the yearbook. "'Goodbye Exeter you taught and showed me many things . . . God bless you for that. Some things I saw I did not like, and some things I learned I'd rather not know. Nevertheless, it had to be done because I could never learn not to learn. It's a pity we part on a less than friendly basis, but we do . . . Work to adjust yourself in a changing world, as will I.'"

Mrs. Perry smiled as she clasped the yearbook. The outside world may have killed her son, but she could still feel his spirit.

According to the police account, Edmund Perry and an unidenti-
fied accomplice attacked Lee Van Houten at 9:30 P.M., June 12. In
plainclothes, Van Houten was patrolling Morningside Drive across
from St. Luke's Hospital. Backup police in a car were supposed to keep
him in view, but had lost sight of him. Grabbed from behind, Van
Houten says he was forced to the ground, where in order to protect
himself he shot three times, striking Perry in the abdomen once. If the
story of this 24-year-old policeman with two years on the job is to be
believed—and the police say they have witnesses to corroborate his
account—his use of deadly force was justified. It was in the line of
duty.

If Edmund Perry had a criminal record or a history of violence, one
might not question the police story or even notice the gray areas that
dot the official account of the shooting and its aftermath. However,
mugging and assault had never been part of Edmund Perry's biography. Not hardly. This isn't to say that bright young people sometimes
don't go wrong. But Edmund Perry had come so far in his 17 years,
against such long odds—and there's so much confusion about how his
life ended—that it's hard not to think something doesn't stink in the
26th Precinct.

Was Edmund, like so many other victims in this city, just too black
for his own good?

The Perry family's connection to Harlem, specifically the area
around 114th Street, dates back several generations. His great-grand-
mother, Paige Edwards, and grandmother, Eva Rutledge, have been
members of the 115th Street Memorial Baptist Church for some 40
years. Veronica Perry has told friends that one of her grandfathers
helped lay the cornerstone of P.S. 113, also on 115th Street.

These roots mean a lot to Veronica Perry. Though Edmund was
born at Brooklyn's Kings County Hospital, she and her husband,
Jonah, reared him in Harlem and, as a result, she grew active in moni-
toring the local schools her children attended. She became an important and often outspoken force on the P.S. 113 PTA. Four years ago,
she was a key member in the successful fight to keep P.S. 113's afterschool program open. So it wasn't surprising in 1982 that her name
surfaced as Bill Perkins and Pamela Green, local Democratic leaders
and chief officers of the Sojourner Truth Democratic Club, sought a
candidate for a spot on Community School Board 3. Between raising
kids, the PTA, and her job as an assistant teacher at the Lenox Hill
Neighborhood Head Start Program, it was hard to run Veronica down.
When Perkins and Green finally caught up with her, they found her a

touch naive about the technicalities of electioneering, but were impressed with her character. "A tough chick, able to deal with a lot of pressures" was Perkins's assessment. In 1983 she was elected to the community board with the largest plurality in Harlem.

The Perry home wasn't without its demons. Husband Jonah has suffered debilitating battles with alcohol. But unlike so many working-class families in which the bottle separates husband and wife, Jonah's problem didn't shatter the Perrys, and friends give the credit to Veronica's patience. It would be easy to paint her as just another stereotypical black matriarch, but clichés don't describe this woman or the values she instilled in Jonah, Jr., Edmund, and Nichole.

Values, in fact, that were necessary in the battle the Perry children have had to wage every day in resisting the drug culture that thrives half a block away. On Eighth Avenue, from about 112th Street up to 118th Street, and especially 116th Street, is a valley of the living dead, one of the vilest open drugstores in the city that has been in business at least since Edmund Perry took his first steps. Like the Temple of Doom, it lurks full of enticing trap doors and quick getaways from poverty, always ready to steal the life of any willing victim while the police ride on by, watching and knowing and failing to act.

"This drug trade makes it hard for a kid from 114th Street to amount to anything," says Charles Moses, a *Newsday* reporter who instructed Edmund as part of a sixth-grade class in newspaper production at P.S. 113. "The parents there are involved in a never-ending battle against the drug pushers. They're organized and use their money to seduce kids into it." Moses remembers an instance where local pushers sought to rent the P.S. 113 gym for Thursday night basketball games. When a school official refused, the pushers went to a school board meeting seeking to stop their antagonist from receiving tenure.

This was the world Edmund was reared in, but not swayed by. As he told a *New York Times* reporter in a piece on 114th Street last August: "It's Harlem. It's not the worst place to grow up and it's not the best place. My mother put ideas into my head that there was something else." That drive to achieve "something else" crystallized at Intermediate 88, also known as Wadleigh. Even though a teacher and three other employees of the school were arrested last May for selling marijuana, cocaine, and heroin to undercover cops, the neighborhood's faith in the institution hasn't been lost, and a large part of the reason was that Edmund—"Eddie" to his classmates—was groomed in its dingy halls.

"He was something special," says E.E. Plummer, Edmund's mentor at Wadleigh. In the seventh grade Edmund was reading and doing arithmetic at a 12th-grade level. When he was 12, Edmund and his brother participated in a poetry reading at the Metropolitan Museum of Art. His contribution read in part:

> *If I lived in Egypt*
> *I wouldn't want a lion's face*
> *Or anything else to replace my face.*

Edmund was not simply a bookworm, though. He made model airplanes—good training to steady his hands, he said, because he was going to be a doctor. In the family tradition, he was an active member of the Memorial Baptist Church's youth organization. He could dance all right, according to a girl who had the pleasure, and could speak Spanish well enough to startle friends with a flurry of words, some clean, some not. In addition, Edmund was one of the many city kids who view basketball as close to a spiritual experience.

So it was at Wadleigh that his mother's teachings began to bear fruit and it was at Wadleigh that five years ago John Herney, then the new head of admissions at Phillips Exeter Academy, interviewed him. "I liked him," Herney remembers. "He was pretty confident. Had a happy-go-lucky attitude and didn't take things too seriously. The people at Wadleigh thought very highly of him." In conjunction with A Better Chance (ABC), a program that since 1964 has sent inner city kids to the nation's finest prep schools, Herney invited the 14-year-old boy to enter a world so different from 114th Street.

"Exeter, New Hampshire, has a population of 12,000," according to the Exeter catalogue, and a "country courthouse, a public library, seven churches, and a coeducational public high school. Its winding, shaded streets and simple white houses, largely of colonial design, give it the characteristic aspect of the New Hampshire town remote from urban influence." Exeter is also the third oldest city in the state, cold as hell in the winter and 50 miles north of Boston. To be truthful, the town is basically an adjunct to Phillips Exeter Academy, founded in 1781 and one of the most prestigious prep schools in the country. Daniel Webster was the first of many famous alumni, and the Daughters of the American Revolution and the late, ultraconservative publisher William Loeb have scholarships named after them. The school has a library of 250,000 volumes, a special 14-seat round-table teaching system called the Harkness Plan that replaces traditional classrooms, and in the 1984–85 academic year only 40 blacks and hispanics among its 970 students. Tuition, plus room and board, is $9,500 a year.

In short, Edmund Perry spent nearly eight months a year, for four years, rubbing elbows and competing with rich white kids. This was something the Perrys already knew something about. Also through the ABC program Jonah was attending Westminster Academy in upstate New York, and he coached his brother on what to expect. Going to Exeter, though, made Edmund more than just another bright young man from his block. He was now—to his mother, his church fellows, and neighbors—a heroic symbol whose academic achievements would be held up to his contemporaries. Older blacks sat at the dinner table or on 114th Street stoops and talked about him in reverential tones. Though they may be unaware of Du Bois's idea of "the talented tenth," the concept comes naturally to many blacks to whom the word "leadership" takes on a spiritual connotation.

Whether they seek it or not, the Edmund Perrys of the world have to face up to these expectations. It is the Moses theory of black American salvation. Blacks look for a leader who will, through charisma, moral certitude, intelligence, and defiance, lead us out of America's proverbial wilderness. A young star like Edmund is a potential Moses until proven otherwise.

Yet there is irony in how a young man like Edmund Perry was being groomed. Away he and his contemporaries go to New England prep schools, where they're taught more than mathematics and science, but the values that have nothing to do with black leadership and everything to do with being a functioning member of the power elite. The question such training raises, of course, is how you can lead an oppressed people if you have been schooled—sometimes subtly, sometimes overtly—to identify with those who turn the screws?

Yet, according to teachers and students, Edmund overcame the cultural conflicts and the academic challenges that Exeter threw at him. Looking over Edmund's transcript, Exeter principal Stephen Kurtz remarked, "He had an outstanding academic record, especially for a kid from the inner city. But there is no padding in his record. What he got he earned here." An 11.0 index represents straight A's; Edmund's average hovered around 8.0. He spent his junior year in Barcelona, living with a local family and studying Spanish. He also lettered in football.

Just as important was his role as one of the leaders of Exeter's minority population. Last semester Lamont O'Neil, a tall, lanky sophomore from Brooklyn, often felt overwhelmed. "At the end of the semester he [Edmund] and another senior came over to my room and talked to me about how to survive at Exeter," O'Neil recalls. "It would be easy to forget who you were there, but he didn't." In O'Neil's yearbook Edmund wrote a message, one that says much about how he viewed the nonacademic lessons of Exeter. "Remember, man, to get ahead in this world you must control your own destiny. So don't allow someone to trick you into going against your will. Your feelings will guide you right, and even though you may not be able to explain your feelings to another person, you always understand after a little thinking to yourself. Always know what you feel and who you are . . ."

Edmund was instrumental in aiding another senior, Tamara Horne, a young woman from Cleveland, in reviving the Afro-Exonian society, a black campus organization founded in 1966 that had become moribund in recent years. Exeter principal Kurtz describes the Afro-Exonians "as a loose organization" and plays down any black-white tension at the school. Yet the group was criticized by many white students as a "segregated group" and even "communistic." Exeter held a two-month-long symposium on racism early this year featuring speakers such as Eleanor Holmes Norton. Representing the Afro-Exonians, Edmund spoke about the need for the organization before what O'Neil recalls as "hostile an audience as he'd probably speak before in his life." At another forum, students remember Edmund criticizing and impressing a government spokesman defending U.S. policy in South Africa.

But for all his racial pride, Edmund seems to have been comfortable with whites. He was, because of his intelligence and energy, a bit of a lady's man and, in fact, dated a blond student from Philadelphia; during one vacation he took her on a guided tour of New York and Harlem. One of his closest friends at Exeter was a white student named Kennett Marshal, who would later call Exeter students around the country, urging them to come to Edmund's funeral and offering to pay some of the expenses. At the rally on June 21 protesting Edmund's shooting, Marshal walked arm in arm with Veronica Perry.

A product of his mother's determination, the often vicious Harlem environment, and now four years of intellectual stimulation and culture shock, Edmund Perry had emerged as a strong and complicated man. To some he was funny and engaging, a person it was fun to sit near at the regular Sunday brunches held by the minority students. However, Edmund could easily rub you the wrong way. He could be too brash, too bold, too damn cocky. The bravado of the streets and the arrogance of intellect made him argumentative. He was the boy from Harlem and sometimes he wore that title like an obnoxious badge.

Yet behind all the extroverted posturing there was still often a homesick kid. On cold New Hampshire nights, when other students from New York gathered in his McConnell Hall room to rap about school, women, and sports, Edmund sometimes asked if, just for a little while, couldn't they make believe they were back home.

On Sunday, June 2, before his family and a few friends, Edmund Perry was graduated from Phillips Exeter Academy and then a week later was honored, along with several others from the neighborhood, at Memorial Baptist for his accomplishments. Despite his homesickness at Exeter, Edmund passed up Yale. Instead he had decided to go to Stanford, where he planned to major in business administration. After graduation he landed a summer job at the Wall Street brokerage house Kidder Peabody & Co., even though he had been told before coming down that all the openings for college students had been filled. Though he had begun work right away, he wasn't rolling in money—he still borrowed money from his mother to get to work some mornings, but he was used to getting around without much cash.

Early on the evening of June 12 he hung out and played basketball in the Wadleigh schoolyard until 9 P.M. A little later, he was seen playing cards with some friends on the stoop of 265 West 114th Street. Nichole, playing outside the house that evening, recalled Edmund saying he was going to walk with somebody up to 116th Street.

At some point between, say, 9:15 and 9:30, Edmund went through Morningside Park, a stretch of green that separates Harlem (or "the valley") and Morningside Heights and that runs from 124th Street to 110th Street. During the day Morningside Park is pleasant enough. Basketball teams battle on its courts. People read the paper on its benches. Men teach their sons baseball on its rocky diamond. But at night its dark trees and thick underbrush make it a forbidding place. More than one mugging crew has been seen sprinting out, triumphant, with a woman's handbag. Even some of the hard dudes on 114th Street express fear of the park after dark "unless I was packing." Yet there Edmund Perry went—late of 114th Street, Phillips Exeter, and a bright future in an unfair world.

Numerous questions surround the events of 9:30 P.M., June 12, but the grand jury convened to review the case is unlikely to answer them. Instead District Attorney Robert Morgenthau's office appears to be focusing on proving that a robbery did occur, that Edmund Perry (and by implication, brother Jonah) attacked Van Houten, and that "defendant" Perry was killed in the course of the robbery. Chances are that after hearing Van Houten and other police witnesses, the grand jury will let the officer walk. The case, though, will not end there. Attorney C. Vernon Mason, police brutality activist and Manhattan district attorney candidate, plans to file a civil suit on behalf of the family against Van Houten and the city of "wrongful death."

Central to the official version is not just Van Houten's testimony but the assumption that Edmund's background meant nothing—that when Edmund saw a chance to mug a white person he took it. Really, what other motivation would a young nigger need? Motivation is precisely what's missing from the police account, and they seem to be aware of this. According to Mason, since Edmund's shooting eight young people, all residents of 114th Street, have been picked up by the police and questioned not about the shooting, but about Edmund's character. (One of those detained, 16-year-old Alicia Arroyo, has filed a $5 million suit against the city, charging that the 26th Precinct violated juvenile offender laws by questioning her without a parent present.)

In the view of Edmund Perry's family, he was in the wrong place at the wrong time and he was the victim of either a mistake or a cold-blooded murder and cover-up. The questions they and Vernon Mason have raised don't establish Edmund's innocence, but they cast doubt on the police account.

One witness, identified as an off-duty security guard at St. Luke's, told *Newsday* (June 15) that Perry and Van Houten spoke briefly, perhaps exchanging a light for a cigarette, and then went in the opposite directions. The story went on: "As Perry walked away, he said, two blacks and a Hispanic youth slipped through a hole in a fence around Morningside Park and attacked the officer. The first shot was fired, the guard said. Perry then turned around and was hit by the second, he said. The guard said he had not told police his story." It's not known whether this person has been interviewed by the police or has appeared before the grand jury.

According to police, Van Houten was in plainclothes patrolling the area because a rash of car break-ins had occurred near St. Luke's. He was out of view of two officers in a back-up car when the shooting took place. Mason has a source at the hospital who claims Van Houten, like several other police officers, worked part-time as a security guard at St. Luke's and was doing so on June 12. (The director of public affairs at St. Luke's will not comment on the case.) Van Houten's use of deadly force might be understandable, though still unnecessary, if he felt he was all alone in a life-threatening situation. If Van Houten was moonlighting for St. Luke's at the time of the shooting, it might also explain why the first car on the scene was a regular patrol car.

In the police account, Van Houten pulled his revolver from an ankle holster after being tackled on the ground; he responded to what he considered a life-threatening situation. But Mason has a source who claims that Van Houten was standing when he shot Edmund, who was directly in front of him, unarmed, and not within reach. According to Mason, "Our medical examiner, Dr. Sidney Weinberg [just retired as Suffolk County coroner] has in his preliminary examination found no powder burns on Edmund's clothes as evidence of close contact between the gun and the wound, both of which suggest a distance between Van Houten and Perry." If this is the case, and even *if* Edmund had tried to jump Van Houten moments before, was the policeman justified in shooting someone who was unarmed?

The police do not deny that Edmund, handcuffed and bleeding, was left on the ground, while Van Houten was taken to the hospital first. He was less than a hundred feet from St. Luke's. The police could have carried him there. Was it just another instance of one white cop's life being more valuable than that of a black person? In Weinberg's estimation, the gunshot alone should not have killed Edmund. Which leads to another question: Would Edmund have died had he received swifter treatment?

According to the police, Van Houten was treated for cuts and bruises and was kept overnight for tests. He later showed up at the June 19 grand jury hearings in a neck brace. But according to Perry family friends, they saw Van Houten walk out of St. Luke's surrounded by eight plainclothes and uniformed police around 1 A.M. Van Houten, they claim, walked with a cane in his right hand and had no visible facial or physical injuries.

"Usually someone from the hospital keeps the family aware of a patient's condition," says Mason, who came to the hospital at the family's request. "They wouldn't let Mrs. Perry anywhere near the operating room, but kept her in the emergency room. At no time did we have any sense Edmund was dying." The hospital officially informed the family at 2:20 A.M. that Edmund had died. "Veronica Perry was hysterical," Mason remembers. "Just in terms of the humanity of it we were all left totally unprepared for his death."

The family was told by a hospital spokesman that the time of death was 12:55. But chief of detectives Richard Nicastro at the police press conference said he died at 1:55 A.M. If the original time of death is correct, a gap of an hour and a half existed between Edmund's death and when the family was informed. Why such a gap? While the Perrys lingered in this twilight zone, Van Houten left the hospital and the police knew a shooting had escalated into a homicide.

Right now if you're a young black person, each moment near a New York City policeman has to send a blast of anxiety into your heart. With frightening prescience, Edmund Perry had included in his Exeter yearbook these words from rapper Melle Mel:

> You search for justice and what do you find?
> You find just us on the unemployment line ...
> You find just us sweatin' from dawn to dusk.
> There's no Justice, there's Just Us ...

Eleanor Bumpers, Michael Stewart, and now Edmund Perry. Justice. Or Just Us?

VILLAGE VOICE, 1985

# BLACKLASH

**W**hen I was a child, Supreme Court justice Thurgood Marshall was one of those semimythological black saints of the civil rights movement, a role model whose story of struggle and achievement was hauled out every February on public TV and in the black-history supplement to *Our Weekly Reader.* Liberal teachers, determined to prove that "to get a good job, you need a good education" blah-blah-blah, hung headshots of Marshall, Marian Anderson, Jackie Robinson, George Washington Carver, and countless selfless others in our classroom. I recall no pictures of Elijah Muhammad or Nat Turner.

"See and you shall be" was the generally specious philosophy of the liberal educators who promoted this NAACP-approved pantheon. These were men and women of dignity who endured the tortures of racism without lashing back and without rancor. My generation was advised to follow their lead—turn the other cheek, read good books (particularly the Good Book), and otherwise emulate the civil rights role models—to attain mainstream success. In '60s terms it was perfect that Sidney Poitier, the epitome of upwardly mobile Negrohood, portrayed Marshall in a recent television flick. Bringing the landmark *Brown v. Board of Education* case before the Supreme Court, Poitier rendered Marshall as a living statue—stoic, deliberate, eloquent, patient, and, above all, dignified.

Needless to say, life has taught me that most of those well-intentioned '60s truisms simplified and thus distorted the textures of real life. Where Poitier was as proper as a starched white collar on ABC, in his farewell press conference Marshall sat with his top button open, his tie slightly off center, and his body slumped forward. With his pronounced Southern accent, impish humor (Q: "How do you feel?" A: "I feel with my hands"), and exasperated replies to reporters, Marshall came alive for the first time to many of my generation, no longer just a legend carved out of *Ebony*'s Mount Rushmore-like profiles of black leaders. This press conference presented him as a wise, tough, folksy old man, kind of like you'd want your grandfather to be. I got more sense of Marshall the man in the half hour I listened than I'd had in the rest of my life. Largely that's because he'd been isolated on the bench since I was 10. Instead of bringing Marshall closer to us, his role modeling distanced us from his humanity.

President Bush's always acute attention to image is why he has leaned so heavily on Clarence Thomas's bootstraps saga in introducing him to America. A poor, Georgia-born product of a broken home, Thomas cites as key influences his grandparents, who raised him to believe in hard work, and the white nuns at St. Benedict the Moor, his elementary school. At St. John Vianney Minor Seminary in Savannah, and elsewhere in the Catholic church, he encountered enough prejudice to decide against a career as a clergyman. Somewhere along the line he developed an antipathy toward civil rights leaders ("bitch, bitch, bitch, moan, and whine" is how he once described them) and a belief that the will of the individual African American to achieve had been weakened by government aid that, in fact, had turned into reverse racism.

Crucial to understanding Thomas's philosophy, and his future on the Supreme Court, is his posture on the 1954 desegregation ruling. The 43-year-old U.S. Circuit Court judge believes that ruling implied that all-black schools were inherently inferior, and that that was wrong. I agree with him on that—there are potentially great benefits in an all African American educational environment, as Howard, Spelman, and Morehouse have demonstrated. The problem is that Thomas proposes no practical remedies to upgrade all the black schools that racism has rendered educationally inferior. Like other fashionable black neocons, Thomas has problems with the implications of many government-funded programs to aid blacks and other minorities. But what is their substitute? If the government hadn't worked to integrate schools (and the nation), integration wouldn't have happened—and the Republicans wouldn't need to cultivate token blacks like Thomas. The future Supreme Court justice backs up his words only with misdeeds: As Ronald Reagan's chairman of the Equal Employment Opportunity Commission (1982–89), he was lax in enforcing laws against all forms of discrimination. And when he did go after offenders his rulings were narrow, so no more sweeping antidiscrimination precedents were set.

Thomas's presence on the Supreme Court will make him the best known (and most powerful) black Republican of this century. Given the black establishment's predilection for finding the silver lining in any prominent black (*Black Enterprise* even squeezed out a favorable cover on HUD's Sam Pierce), we may yet see Thomas receiving awards at the annual black-tie galas the major civil rights organizations now substitute for grassroots organizing. But the initial reaction to Thomas suggests that we've matured a little. In the wake of Marion Barry's arrogant ignorance and Thomas's devotion to conservative dogma, the champions of black role models have finally realized that skin color is no indicator of a black agenda.

It's clear now that the most insensitive aspects of Thomas Sowell's, Shelby Steele's, and Stanley Crouch's writings were harbingers of the rise of Thomas and black New Haven Republican congressman Gary Franks—folks disenchanted by the fallout from the civil rights movement who've found in neoconservatism a way to assuage old personal resentments, vent their dismay at liberal ineptitude, and befriend the monied right. The public discourse on African American life will be incredibly contentious in the '90s, as black George Willses—some motivated by principle, others by pure opportunism—begin to challenge the likes of Jesse Jackson and Benjamin Hooks as racial spokespersons.

A decade after the white conservative renaissance, Thomas augurs a blacklash against the fading icons of the civil rights generation, one already long in motion from the other direction via black youth's deification of Malcolm X. If Thomas and company can tap into the black business class, particularly middle-management buppies, as well as working-class blacks crying out for moral leadership (and tough law enforcement), the Republicans can neutralize the urban Democratic machines that spawn black mayors.

In predominantly black classrooms across America, teachers, trying to be sensitive to the psyches of their young black charges, cut pictures of Judge Thomas out of the paper and tape them to the wall. There he hangs next to Michael Jordan, Jesse Jackson, Oprah Winfrey, Spike Lee, and Arsenio Hall—the '90s in full effect.

VILLAGE VOICE, 1991

# THE MAGIC TOUCH

**B**y all the standards I've grown up with, Earvin "Magic" Johnson is a real man. A great athlete further endowed with the attributes of leadership, invention, and sex appeal, he has been one of America's few admirable public figures since the dawn of the cold-gettin'-paid '80s. Yeah, he's made crazy bank but, unlike Michael Jordan's commercial–tie-in–enhanced persona, Johnson's fortune was based on winning teamwork. Succeeding in an era obsessed with triumph and money, Johnson nevertheless embodied qualities of unselfishness our national culture was devaluing.

Never in the game's 100-year history had a player of his height performed with so many skills. At 6-9, he dribbled and threw no-look passes like Bob Cousy or Marques Haynes; he could spin at midcourt

like Earl Monroe and direct the fast break with more daring than anyone Naismith's game has ever seen; he could play the low post like
Adrian Dantley, snatch key rebounds like Bill Russell, and had a hook
shot only his legendary teammate Kareem Abdul-Jabbar could match
for accuracy. His synthesis of a forward's size, a center's power, and a
guard's dexterity has no precedent. To watch Johnson in motion was to
experience the workings of a jazzman's brain in the body of a graceful
giant, to see a game elevated to an art, and to witness a joyful excel-
lence even Celtic fans couldn't deny.

The legacy of Johnson the ballplayer is clear and complete; the
legacy of Johnson the practicing heterosexual male will take a lot
longer to discern. He is a tall, charismatic, handsome, rich, lusty
African American man, and in manifesting those qualities he contracted the HIV virus. In star-fixated L.A., his Showtime was Hollywood in Inglewood, and as that show's leading man, Johnson enjoyed
his pick of starlets. Like Eddie Murphy, Arsenio Hall, Michael Jordan,
and Mike Tyson, Johnson was co-chairman of what Run-D.M.C.
labeled N.F.L.—"that's Niggas Fuckin' Large"—a loose bicoastal posse
of black male stars who hung together, sharing adult fun and games. As
one of the most eligible African Americans in the country, traveling in
circles rife with beautiful, eminently available women (and men, if so
desired), Johnson was a target that, say folks in L.A., was not difficult
to hit.

In the private room at Roxbury's on Sunset Boulevard, at R&B
Live's Wednesday-night black pack gatherings, at private pool parties
and awards shows, Johnson was as large as Jack Nicholson or any other
entertainment-biz heavy. Ample sex was one of the many rewards for
his on-court greatness and, in sex-saturated Tinseltown, he savored it.
Even as AIDS ravaged poor blacks and gays in the '80s, in N.F.L. circles
fucking continued on unabated and unprotected. So did sharing
women. Now, phone lines between L.A. and condos all over the country are burning up as many of these moneyed, ego-driven men try to
figure out who gave Johnson the HIV virus, when it may have happened and, most important to the callers, did I do her too? Considering that Johnson had been single until this past September, and has
been crisscrossing the nation annually for a decade, we can only speculate as to how many thousands of women he slept with.

The exploration of Johnson's sex life, and that of his N.F.L. peers,
has just begun. Despite the initial wave of support and admiration for
Johnson and his exemplary courage, there surely will be an increasingly
public discussion of his sexuality, one motivated largely by voyeurism.

An old rumor about an involvement with another NBA player resurfaced the moment Johnson's press conference was announced and could be heard floating around the Garden at last Saturday's Knicks game. That discussion may well get ugly as ex-lovers rush to sell their stories to the press and TV.

On the everyday level, Johnson's announcement has shriveled the penises of lots of single guys, who, unless they are involved in a long-term, deeply emotional relationship, are for the moment resigning themselves to masturbation and lots of long, wet kisses. But in the longer term, I see young men, particularly young brothers, reacting to Johnson's revelation with fear and paranoia. It had already been a bad year for African American males, with Rick James's arrest on torture charges, Run of Run-D.M.C.'s alleged rape, Mike Tyson at the center of sundry sexual abuse cases, and the Clarence Thomas-Anita Hill sitcom. Like everyone else, I see the silver lining of increased AIDS awareness among straight men. But awareness is not acceptance. For those young men whose sexism expresses itself in rap's worst attitudes—people who already suspect females of all manner of manipulation—this event may fuel further hatred of women, just as society-in-general's growing awareness of AIDS in recent years has resulted in increased gay bashing.

Class, always a factor in sexual relations, is important here too. Poor black women residing in high-risk communities already burdened with the welfare stigma may now be viewed with increased suspicion as likely HIV carriers. Ice Cube's warning "Don't Fuck with a Bitch from the Projects" may take on a new, more sinister meaning for many men. While about .5 percent of all current AIDS cases are female to male, that still comes out to 7,500 heterosexual men by conservative estimate. The majority of them are brown-skinned and live in inner-city 'hoods like the South Bronx.

Johnson's admission has been a severe psychological blow to lots of men; you hear it in their voices and see it in the anguish in their eyes. "Woman as sexual demon" has been a theme of black music since the blues, but this adds just another layer of incomprehension to male-female relationships. Yet the fact remains that it is women, not men, who are in the most danger of HIV infection during heterosexual sex. With all the focus on Johnson's misfortune, the media have forgotten the incredible anxiety faced by women who've slept with him—and, of course, the special turmoil his pregnant wife must be experiencing.

The frustration and suspicion AIDS introduced into the nation's sex life a decade ago has now reached all heterosexual males. But if men begin toning down their activity, how will the frustration inherent in this new world order affect the daily dynamics of the discourse between men and women? Will some men, still drawn by macho's lingering allure, engage in sexual Russian roulette—casual sex without condoms—just to get a rep as a bedroom daredevil?

Magic Johnson has displayed remarkable grace under pressure, but I'm not sure his fans will handle this challenge to their notions of what constitutes real manhood so smoothly. The safety net for male promiscuity is gone, but not the desire for male domination of women. The magic man's on-court career has ended, but in the bedrooms and motels of horny masculine America, I don't think Showtime is over yet.

VILLAGE VOICE, 1991

# SEMICONSCIOUSNESS

The Five Percent School, a/k/a the Allah School in Mecca, is a long, one-story brick building that stands on an otherwise empty lot on 126th Street and Adam Clayton Powell Boulevard. A large number seven, which a guy told me represents "the Arab crescent," is painted on the front. On Father's Day, to help repair damage done to the school by a fire, a rap benefit starring Big Daddy Kane was held at the Apollo, just around the corner. The Five Percenters aren't numerologists or Farrakhanite Muslims, though the latter are close kin. They are a religious sect that views black men as gods on earth, particularly the Five Percent who are righteous in their knowledge. Eighty-five percent of us are deaf, dumb, and blind; the Nation of Islam make up 10 percent; and the Five Percent sit atop this pyramid.

Upon embrace of the Five Percent tenets one takes on a triumphant

new name. When I was a teen, three sons of the folks next door became
Five Percenters, renaming themselves Powerful, Knowledge, and True
God. Five Percenter women, the soil for their nation's growth, are
referred to as "earths." At the Apollo, the Five Percenter security guards,
the Fruit of Allah, lacked the spit and polish of the Fruit of Islam:
Instead of suits and ties, they wore black T-shirts and kufis. Onstage
young rappers like Lakim Shabbazz (known for his jam "Black Is Back")
and King Sun wore kufis and, like many in the audience, large Egyptian
heads with fade haircuts dangling from gold chains. The evening's rappers, with the exception of the sublime Kane, were fairly typical,
although the performers' commitment to the Five Percent's god-here-
on-earth philosophy gave their boasts of lyrical superiority added edge.

Decidedly Afrocentric, sexually chauvinistic, and, crucially,
young—the crowd was almost entirely 15-to-30—the Five Percent
nation rises out of a spiritual vacuum in the black community. The Five
Percenters fill this space by massaging egos and healing insecurities.
Years of indoctrination in Christianity and white superiority drove
these brothers and sisters to empower themselves by celebrating the
homeboy as godhead. Many leading rap stars (Big Daddy Kane, Rakim)
are down with the Five Percenters, which certainly dovetails with the
me-ism imbedded in the form. That the religion is quietly spreading
among youngbloods is another thread in the embryonic new African
American consciousness movement, aspects of which can be found in
rap (Public Enemy, Boogie Down Productions), Spike Lee's *Do the
Right Thing*, much current black street fashion (e.g., Black to the
Future T-shirts), and the rapid embrace of "African American" by folks.

These flickers are not a flame. No one at the Apollo was shouting,
"It's nation time!" or suggesting they be given several southern states
as reparations. The new mood isn't separatist, though the need for
"self-sufficiency," meaning more black business development and overall community control, is on a lot of people's minds. The roadblock to
the growth of this consciousness is ignorance. Kids wear African
medallions but don't know where Zambia is; young mothers give their
kids pseudo-African names but buy earrings made from South African
gold; all kinds of folks praise Louis Farrakhan and Al Sharpton's willingness to blast "the man" but never think of renouncing Big Macs or
picketing City Hall. Malcolm X's steely-eyed visage is now a fetish,
adorning T-shirts, buttons, and posters. Yet few of those who sport
flashy Malcolm X gear have read his Alex Haley–penned autobiography, or heard his many speeches. This makes the slain leader a stick figure; people read things into him without reading him.

Call it feel-good nationalism, racial pride for the video age. Revolutionary images are televised via videos, commercials, and newsbites. What's lacking is not interest or unrest but the philosophical underpinning that nationalism, Marxism, and integration gave these kids' parents. The crippling problem, of course, is that most of them don't read a great deal, except maybe rap lyrics. And as much as I admire many rap lyricists, most raps are evocatively cinematic but lack philosophical specificity. Public Enemy, for example, can be credited with stimulating a lot of this black consciousness. But as their chaotic recent statements attest, they were often as vague in their direction as they were lethal rhythmically.

It frustrates me. The potential is there for something powerful to happen, something that has nothing to do with fads and fashion, but that can mature into a real youth movement that truly addresses many grievances. Until a philosophy spreads or a new jack leader emerges, the Five Percent, the Nation of Islam, gangs, and even rap will divert this new black consciousness without effectively confronting the powers that be.

VILLAGE VOICE, 1990

# HANDS ON

Jesse Jackson has large hands and when he speaks they help shape his words. Often he gestures with palms open, turned toward the sky with his fingers extended wide as if to invite his listeners in. His hands also work as anchors when one or both rest on the podium, grounding his body while the rhetoric soars. Sitting five feet to his right as he addressed a Congressional Black Caucus youth session in Washington last month, I watched Jackson's hands while marveling at his verbal technique and detecting a message underneath his words. For nearly two hours Jackson gave a motivational speech reminiscent of his "I Am Somebody" era. He railed against drugs: "Now we've lost more lives to dope than we ever did to the rope"; "Drugs are the number one threat in the history of our existence." He predicted that Bush's drug war will fail "without a war on poverty, spiritual and material." He joked that blacks in New York were "drunk with doubt" about Dinkins's chance of beating Ed Koch. And he lashed out at black academic lassitude: "There is too much bullshitting going on in our classrooms"; "This thing all boils down to a mind contest and drunk minds don't win it." But Jackson's talk—an unannounced impromptu rap before some 700 spectators in a conference room—was really about dread, a dread that echoed through the session, and also through recent conferences of the National Urban League and Southern Christian Leadership Conference.

Quite simply, established blacks see a grave threat to their legacy of advancement in civil rights, social equality, and upward mobility. The culprits aren't simply Reaganism and crack—the generation gap between African American youth and their elders is also to blame. Armed with suits, ties, and business cards, the men and women of the NUL, SCLC, and Black Caucus have walked through doors the civil rights movement opened. Their individual triumphs began in a world of Christian devotion where college was a goal worthy of sacrifice, and the music of Motown and Aretha appealed to parents and kids both. Today, Jesse Jackson's campaign inspires all strata of African Americans. Yet otherwise the community is fragmented along class and cultural lines. In the chasm between buppies and B-boys there are Afrocentrists, Farrakhanites, womanists, the willfully whitewashed, and many other shades of black. Somehow, despite the thirst for education, the moral certitude so essential to the civil rights movement hasn't been inculcated into the young.

Recently I've found myself in the curious position of liaison between two crucial African American subsets, civil rights organizations and the B-boy nation. As executive director of the Stop the Violence Movement, a collective of rappers and record industry folk whose "Self Destruction" 12-inch has earned $150,000 for NUL black-on-black violence programs, I've been embraced by mainstreamers desperate for any bridge to younger blacks. This summer Public Enemy's Chuck D, Stetsasonic's Daddy-O and Delite, Boogie Down Productions's D-Nice, and M.C. Lyte all spoke before junior high and high schoolers at the NUL convention. Heavy D., representing Stop the

Violence, received an award from the SCLC in Atlanta. At the Black Caucus, Public Enemy executive producer and STV member Bill Stephney and I appeared on a panel that originally included only actor Lou Gossett and community activists involved in youth outreach programs. Yet Jackson and, in another pleasant surprise, my former congresswoman, Shirley Chisholm, asked to speak as well, pointing up the importance of the session to the caucus leadership.

The basic strategy seems to be to shout out our history from the top of the mountain. The NUL's black-on-black crime slogan is "Crime Is Not a Part of Our Black Heritage." At the Black Caucus students from black colleges were encouraged to celebrate the coming 30th anniversaries of several pivotal events in the civil rights movement. Ironies abound, of course. At the NUL convention Chuck D spoke eloquently on a favorite theme: the miseducation of black youth and rap's role as black "television" that provides a national dialogue among blacks without white middlemen. Then, at the Black Caucus, Stephney and I had a long talk with ex-Black Panther (and current Ron Dellums aide) Malik Edwards. He felt Public Enemy could have benefited from a better understanding of how radicals dealt with the media in the '60s in handling their recent battle with the press.

I agree with all of them—Jackson, Chuck D, Edwards, etc.—about this information gap. I share their fear. But I also know that while speeches and records like "Self Destruction" can't hurt, more is required, particularly from those who've made it. The idea I advocate is a self-help Peace Corps for African America. If a minivan of successful black professionals lectured regularly at Boys & Girls in Brooklyn, Clinton in the Bronx, or Jackson in Queens—about their careers, about being a black in the mainstream, about anything they know—it would make a difference in many lives. Mayor Dinkins could set the tone for such an effort by regularly visiting, say, Norman Thomas High to talk about the process of government. Jackson, NUL's John Jacobs, and SCLC's Joseph Lowery challenge kids to achieve, but the obligation is deeper than speeches and programs. We don't just need role models. We need firsthand information.

My life was enhanced by just such an experience. When I was 13 I attended summer classes at a school in Bed-Sty as part of one of those "wasteful" Great Society programs called Model Cities. In one class, taught by a very hip young brother, we learned to play chess, subjected our James Brown–bred ears to John Coltrane, and were forced to compare how the *Times*, *News*, and *Post* covered the same story. Sometimes it was boring. On several occasions I skipped his class. Yet, two decades later, that brother's interaction lingers with me, because I admired his style and the way he expanded my analytical powers. Exhortation is fine. But nothing beats a good, strong hand on a kid's shoulder.

VILLAGE VOICE, 1989

# RACE LOYALTY

Look on the bright side. The recent "he said–she said" soap opera on Capitol Hill tuned America in to a varied cast of educated, articulate African American men and women speaking eloquently about the integrity of their friends and colleagues. Most whites, and a whole lot of black folks, have never before had the chance to observe real-life buppies, as opposed to the ones on "The Cosby Show" or "L.A. Law." The force-fed black achievement lesson was an unexpected and welcome sidebar to the prime-time drama. That one of these clean-cut teams, while speaking from the heart with deep conviction and occasional wit, was there in support of a liar . . . well, that's what gave this public-affairs show entertainment value.

This wasn't just ambiguity in action or the complexity of human nature in effect. Whether you believed in the judge or the professor or just couldn't make up your mind, it was clear that perjury was transpiring before your eyes. Public lying, while often practiced, is rarely so well-advertised. And if there's anything more delicious than catching someone in a lie, it is catching someone in a lie about sex. Is Clarence Thomas a feel-copping boss or a porno pervert? Is Anita Hill a spurned

lover or a psycho bitch? We watched for clues in the first showcase for
our submerged national perversity since Laura Palmer turned up in
that plastic bag.

In short, this would have been great fun for me if the lead actors
hadn't been black. It would have been just another example of why
white people are so fucked up—something to furnish jokes on rap
records, provide punch-lines at Slave Theater rallies, and be invoked by
self-righteous callers to WLIB. But Clarence and Anita are blacks,
proud products of the post-desegregation era challenging each other in
a Senate chamber over pubic hair on Coke cans. It made me wanna
holler, throw up both my hands.

Their race makes this soap opera a mystery that, like Charles
Fuller's A *Soldier's Play*, a Pulitzer Prize–winner about the intraracial
struggle behind a black man's murder, is as much about the why of the
action as it is about the action itself. When we find out conclusively
who lied (as we will long about 2010, when one of Thomas's law clerks
leaks the story to *Ms.*), we'll still have to figure out whether Thomas's
alleged harassment was a matter of lust and power, or of lust, power,
and race. That all the women who've reported being approached
aggressively by Thomas to date have been black (a third joined the
nonappearing Angela Wright after the hearings were over on Monday)
suggests that he could have felt that underlying racial loyalty would
shield him from exposure. As Michele Wallace detailed to the discomfort of many in *Black Macho and the Myth of the Superwoman*, black
women have long taken crap from brothers that was supposed to uplift
the race—a "race" that always seems to start with one individual black
man of ambition. In the usual trickle-down theory of empowerment,
this is supposed to uplift them, too—eventually.

Let's not forget that Hill was an eager participant in the Reagan
administration as well as Thomas. Yet in this conservative environment, a version of the same man-woman power dynamic that culmi-
nated during the civil rights era (King and his women) and the black
power epoch (see Bobby Seale's A *Lonely Rage*) bonded the two. To
me it seems highly unlikely that she screwed him or anything like it.
But I believe she did have a philosophical and emotional stake in her
boss—that she saw a path opening for herself as Thomas advanced
through the Republican hierarchy, and that it was the opportunity
their relationship afforded her, even after their association had ended,
that kept her publicly silent for a decade. On the one hand, this professional woman was unable to escape her race consciousness. On the

other, she experienced the same conflict between her career and her personal life that bedevils so many professional men.

Among African Americans, racism still outweighs sexism as a lightning rod for anger and mobilization. Hill (and apparently others) repressed her charges for years as Thomas accumulated the perks of assimilation—the fellowship of powerful white males, status as a symbol of what other blacks could attain, a white wife—that have been taken as rewards by brothers for generations. That Hill spoke up now, for whatever reason, is a major leap over the barricades of racial solidarity.

Thomas's shrewd, impassioned cries of "high-tech lynching" were, in this context, predictable. The racial paranoia that neocon Shelby Steele so gleefully attacks, and that in fact defines so much black life, is precisely what Steele's judicial bedfellow played to the day after Hill's damning testimony. Some see this ploy as pure hypocrisy, and I think there's something to that view. Yet to totally discount Thomas's protestations on this point is to overlook the contours of the man's nature. The great irony is that he defended himself with the same reasoning that probably kept Hill from busting him—the knowledge that white racism is always poised to pull a black man down.

Looking for a silver lining in Thomas's 52-48 confirmation vote? Well, maybe his tortuous journey to America's most prestigious retirement home will grant him an insight into the vulnerability of the disenfranchised that hanging with Bush's crowd had dulled. It is a long shot, but a lifetime gives a man a lot of time to evolve. The flip side? If ever anyone can be expected to take an antipress position in First Amendment cases, Supreme Court Justice Clarence Thomas is the guy.

VILLAGE VOICE, 1991

# DINKINS'S WORLD, SHARPTON'S PEOPLE

**A** few weeks ago at Sylvia's Restaurant on Lenox Avenue, David Dinkins told a story. While attending Brooklyn Law School, he said, he lived in Riverton Houses and sold shopping bags at a liquor store on St. Nicholas Avenue. At two cents a bag, it was awfully hard keeping up with his bills. Sometimes things got so bad his car would "break down on 135th Street, right over by the Red Rooster," a premier Harlem watering hole that no longer exists, like so much of the city that molded Dinkins. At the end of each month Dinkins and his wife Joyce "threw all the bills in a hat and picked out which ones to pay." When some bill collectors irritated Dinkins with their persistence, he told Joyce, "If these creditors keep bothering me, I won't put them in the hat." In the crowd-created humidity of one of Sylvia's dining rooms there was laughter after this perhaps apocryphal tale, and murmurs of genuine appreciation when he added, "Y'all put me in the hat."

Decent, plodding, responsible career bureaucrat that he is, Dinkins always seems right but never righteous, fair but rarely familiar. Like many successful blacks of the Korean War generation, a group for whom anger was no option and guile a mechanism of incremental achievement, Dinkins always seems to be masking his deepest emotions, not because he's cold or detached, but because his public utterances are usually intended to reassure whites (and more blacks and latinos than whites suspect) that he's not inclined to restructure the system or alter the status quo. The man just wants a more humane, warmhearted, responsive, chocolate-chip version of your typical big city Democratic machine. His decorum and rhetoric sometimes recall Hubert Humphrey's 1968 presidential campaign speeches. I pray the results are less catastrophic.

Up close and personal in a small room, Dinkins is a much more

imposing presence: funnier, folksier, and more animated than via elec-
tronics, voice deeper and richer than I'd thought. He seemed very
comfortable, and he had every reason to be, since he was surrounded
by peers who shared his integrationist background and outlook. Some
were well-known (Charlie Rangel, Percy Sutton), but most were ordi-
nary middle-aged black folks, predominantly male—like the Woodses,
who own Sylvia's, Joe Holland of La Famil restaurant, Big Al Thompson of Consolidated Beverages, *Manchild in the Promised Land* author
Claude Brown, state senator Joe Galiber, and ex-basketball star Nate
Archibald. Systems analysts, financial planners, and health trainers
filled the room. Malcolmites Calvin Butts and Spike Lee, also present,
were notably younger and more militant than most of those in the
house.

Dinkins is a product of the bridge generation: those who lived
through the transition from domestic apartheid to legal equality. Their
stories testify to a systemic evolution in America's treatment of African
Americans. For many, of course, things have changed for the worse. Yet
most at Sylvia's were optimistic that Mayor Dinkins would improve
lives in black New York—some lives, not all lives. One black business
type noted that Dinkins in City Hall would immediately improve his
access to municipal contracts and, by virtue of the number of blacks
he employs, increase the incomes of many families. While not quite
trickle-down theory, this was certainly an old-boy-network attitude
toward empowerment, one inspired by three mayoral terms during
which black business access to city government was sporadic when not
yet another avenue for fraud.

To many of Dinkins's peers, this minority-business view of government's role—which is reflected in Dinkins's literature—is a very realistic and practical way the race will benefit from a Dinkins victory. But
what Dinkins doesn't address very well, in his persona or rhetoric (and
what distinguishes Butts and Spike, for example, from Dinkins's crew)
is black anger over white oppression. It's a feeling no serious black
mayoral candidate can risk articulating. Even Jesse Jackson has toned
down the intensity of his language since 1984. But that anger lives and,
with every racial incident and tabloid headline, it grows.

Which is why every Wednesday evening at Brooklyn's Slave I Theater, the Reverend Al Sharpton convenes a very loyal and angry congre-
gation. After Howard Beach-Tawana Brawley-Bensonhurst-etc., he's
perceived as the grassroots hero Dinkins's integrationist reserve will
never let him be. In a restored movie house decorated with murals of
black slaves escaping ghostly white plantation owners, and portraits of

historic figures such as Dr. King, Malcolm X, John Kennedy, Lyndon Johnson, Marcus Garvey, and Bruce Lee, another side of black New York filters in. Kente crowns, short bushy Afros speckled with gray, women with two or three kids adorned with African garb, folks survey-ing the *City Sun* and discussing 'LIB: These are just a few of the images I associate with Sharpton's Afrocentric, politically aware, actively suspicious aggregation.

The singing of the black nationalist anthem "Lift Every Voice and Sing" is followed by feisty chants of "No Justice! No Peace!" Speakers have included black historian Professor Phil Mackey, Tawana Brawley, Brooklyn's Bishop Anthony Monk, Public Enemy's Professor Griff, broadcaster Bob Law, and barrister Alton Maddox. Sharpton himself usually closes the show.

At the meeting following his tax-evasion indictment, Sharpton was compared—from the podium, in the audience, and by himself—to Marcus Garvey, whose Back-to-Africa Movement was waylaid by fraud and tax charges. This was part of an overall theme of "a conspiracy to destroy particular kinds of black leaders" such as Farrakhan, Maddox, C. Vernon Mason, Chuck D, and of course Sharpton. To the Dinkins crowd and, probably you reading this, this may all sound like racial paranoia. Can't imagine these words passing Dinkins's lips (though they may linger in his mind). Which is precisely why Sharpton, unless convicted and imprisoned or superseded by another neonationalist leader, will be part of New York's life for a very long time. Though many cringe when Sharpton appears, he's the city's most consistent and celebrated spokesman for the disenchanted, displaced, and dis-gusted African American. Sharpton's not on the scene of every major racial incident in this town just because he gets there first. Families of the afflicted invite and embrace him. He is not part of the system, and will express, in words outrageous and confrontational, their outrage. Media cartoon image and shady dealings aside, who ya gonna call when whites step on your neck?

No, Sharpton ain't Malcolm X or Adam Clayton Powell or even Al Vann (whose invisibility has given him license to grow in Brooklyn), but Dinkins isn't either. And if Dinkins doesn't win the primary, a big reason will be because his reasoned strategies for cross-cultural cooper-ation and responsible criticism didn't move Sharpton's people to the polls.

# DARE TO BE BLACK

I'm buggin' out and my companions on the bus to Atlantic City are not helping. Across the aisle, two pale white women in their midforties are talking about hopping on the 4:10 A.M. back to New York, showering, and then going to work. Gleefully they scheme a trip to Vegas two weeks later. In the back of the bus two foul-mouthed black women debate who's going to use the restroom first. I'm off to A.C. for a music biz convention, a weekend of flattery and flirtation, but my mind is back in New York.

A white woman was raped in Central Park by a group of black teenagers. Damn, I think as we roll past Asbury Park, you don't need a weatherman to know which way this shit is gonna blow. At the convention no one seems too concerned—there are deals to be made and the youth market to be exploited—so I put my thoughts away for a day or two. It's a relief, in a way. But Saturday morning I scoop up the tabs for my crash course in wilding (yo, fellas, it's wildin'). It makes me sad to be so right.

"Summer's coming. With no school at all and lots of warm weather. Will more wolves be making 'mischief' in Central Park? Or anywhere they damn well choose?" asks the *Daily News*. The paper asserts, "The only way to deter these marauding bands is to use the full force of the law against them. The kid gloves have to come off." Typical official reaction: no mention of root causes, nor talk of funding summer or afterschool programs. Throw them under the jail. Law enforcement as social policy. It's a joke, but the mayor, several presidents, and many media tycoons tell it well. And then there's the rap angle. So rap lyrics incite violence, huh? Well, if mild-ass "Wild Thing," a stupid pop record disdained by New York black kids, could cause the Central Park rape, Koch better hope no kids take Public Enemy to heart, or lots of authority figures will be walking around with their heads knocked off. In fact, it's a confirmation of how wack the alleged attackers were that of all the raps in the world they chose to sing that one in detention.

The following Thursday I'm at the Fort Greene office of 40 Acres and a Mule to ask Spike Lee about a rally he's staging for a video Saturday. Hadn't intended to query Lee on the attack, but it comes up. "I anticipated what was gonna happen when I first heard about it. Headlines for four days in a row. More at the *Post*. I know in my heart if these kids had raped a black woman it would have been on page fifteen. Editors would have thought it's another example of niggers killing niggers." These comments are fairly typical of the adult black response. It occurs to me that the shoot will be the perfect place to find out what black kids think.

Nine A.M. in a park across the street from Boys & Girls High. About 400 black youngsters, many similar in age and background to the accused, gathered in the chill to appear in a Public Enemy video. It's "Fight the Power" from the soundtrack of Spike's *Do the Right Thing*, a film about racial turmoil in Brooklyn. The concept is a miniversion of the 1963 March on Washington, except that Chuck D and Flavor Flav are at the head blasting the white media machine, capitalist culture, Elvis Presley, and the failure of integration. The ever-growing crowd, filled with personalized fade haircuts, African medallions, fresh sneakers, and newly acquired "Fight the Power" T-shirts, were drawn by the power of celebrity (being in a video, maybe meeting Spike or P.E.). Anxious and tired of standing around, many are more than happy to have something to do.

"Yo, that wasn't wildin'. Wildin' just going out and having fun," heavyset Joseph Handy, 18, tells me. "When you go wildin' you don't go rapin' somebody." Three of his homies overhear this and decide to get in it. "Wildin' ain't that shit in the park. It's going to B. Altman's or Lord & Taylor's and boosting some shit. That was some pervert Harlem shit. Brooklyn niggers take money," says Supreme, 18. Then Dog, 21, jumped in. "Them boys didn't show no remorse. No, I'm sorry. Nothing. Well, they going to jail and gonna learn a lesson. They gonna get served regardless." *Served* is street style for being dicked down, in this case sexually assaulted in prison. Michael, 16, joined in. "The media's boosting this up more. It's just about some crime. She's a white girl and got some bank. So they on it. . . . Yo, you should put in it that there are too many girls out here to talk to for brothers to be doin' what they did."

Another guy, more straitlaced and not part of this posse, comes over to volunteer that "two brothers were hung last year in Central Park and it wasn't publicized. Did you know that?" Joseph and his crew look at him funny and step off. As Spike's people move them around the park awaiting Public Enemy, I kick it with a bunch of other marchers, ranging from 11 to 24. Comments fall into three categories: disgust at the attackers (Erika Reis, 17: "One of them was wearing a 'Dare to Be Black' T-shirt. He really didn't know what it meant"); suspicion of media motives (Sonya Thompson, 16: "If it had been some white boys it wouldn't have been kept so big"); despair over the conditions that surround poor city kids of color. Generally they were more resigned than angry. As the crime confirms the paranoia of many whites in the city, the reaction has reinforced the cynicism of most blacks about how they're viewed. Brotherhood means little to most of the kids carrying signs reading Little Rock or Salem. It is a past—not just removed, but for many, naïve and silly.

When Flavor Flav arrived in all his clock-swinging glory and sprawled atop the roof of a car, the crowd screamed and, at that moment, the two young men standing next to me just got more determined. James, 15, is also KKC. His partner, named by his mother Kawane and himself Saran, are building a rap group in their bedrooms in nearby Lafayette Gardens. Like many people I met at the convention in Atlantic City, they don't read the paper "but once in a while," had no opinion on Central Park, and don't go out much since there isn't much organized legal activity for teenagers. KKC says, "We spend most of our time inside writin' rhymes and making beats."

**VILLAGE VOICE, 1989**

# B-BOY BOOJIE
# BACKCOURT MAN

## Mark "Action" Jackson Stirs the Knicks

**M**ark Jackson, Brooklyn born, Queens reared, St. John's educated, and Rookie of the Year bound, has already convinced some of New York's most desperate individuals—Knicks season-ticket holders—that he's capable of minor miracles. Though only 6-3, Jackson can jam with all the authoritative flash "black basketball" relishes; there hasn't been a player in the Knicks backcourt who could shake 'n' bake like number 13 since the breathtaking, schizophrenic all b-boy duo of Michael Ray Richardson and Ray Williams back in the 50-win 1980–81 season. To see Jackson get Isiah Thomas 15 feet from the hoop, freeze him with a between-the-legs dribble, then curl around the Chicago houserocker and slam the ball home the way Jackson did on Christmas Day, well, that's a highlight film I'll carry around in my head for years.

But thanks to teenage CYO ball experience and high school training in the well-coached Catholic league, Jackson also plays superb give-and-go, pick-and-roll, Bobby Knight–style "white basketball." There's no question, for example, that Patrick Ewing is enjoying an all-Star season because Jackson feeds him on the break and in the paint in sweet spots he hasn't seen since he thrived under John Thompson's calculated program at Georgetown. "Freaking" on an opponent in the open court or running Rick Pitino's set offense, Jackson always triggers a ripple of anticipation.

If Mark Jackson resembles anyone it's the young Dennis Johnson: guiding the break with sensitivity, controlling the game's tempo in half-court, streak-shooting when necessary, and rebounding ferociously for his size. (It's a comment on Jackson's fire—and on his teammates' inadequacies—that for most of the season, he's out-rebounded Pat Cummings and leaper Gerald Wilkins and is within 20 boards of forward Kenny Walker and seven-foot center Bill Cartwright.) At point guard, the ability to analyze situations while in motion, to see options, decide, and execute in a split second, is the difference between flash and flat, between Mark Jackson and Rory Sparrow, between winning and losing.

Mark is special for me because of our parallel backgrounds. When he was seven his parents, Harry and Marie, moved their family from East New York, a decaying working-class neighborhood in Brooklyn, out to St. Albans, Queens, arguably the most stable black middle-class community in the city. At approximately the same time, my mother moved our family from the piss-poor Tilden projects in Brownsville into neighboring East New York. East New York didn't get any better when we got there, but in a house about ten blocks from the Jacksons's old residence, we made a home. It was there, after admiring St. John's star (and NBA washout) Mel Davis on the tube, that I caught the J train to Jamaica Estates for four years of weekday mornings to study communications and cheer the Redmen.

In the school cafeteria at Marillac Hall, over in "the black corner" by the vending machines, I was introduced to black middle-class offspring of Hollis, Cambria Heights, and St. Albans. They had cars, basement rec rooms, and hard-working fathers with city jobs. Though Mark Jackson was still riding the E and GG way out to Bishop Loughlin in Fort Greene when I was an undergrad, his family fits the St. John's mold; his father, once an East New York truant officer, works for the transit authority; his mother, always active in community school boards, now works in a bank.

They're not exactly the Huxtables; the Jacksons have more in common with the tight-knit Irish and Italian Catholic families that send their kids to St. John's because it's relatively cheap, the kids can stay at home, and old-fashioned values are preached in the expectation they'll be absorbed unquestioningly. Of their four oldest kids, the Jacksons admit to being happy with the fate of three, a solid parental shooting percentage. (Their youngest, Troy, 14, spends his days at I.S. 192 and nights as a Knicks ball-boy.)

Of all things, Mark also majored in Communications Arts at St. John's. But his classroom lesson was learned in parochial school. "The best thing that happened to Mark was that during his first year at Loughlin he found he had to do more work in the classroom," remembers Mark's father, Harry Jackson. "That first year his marks were very low. His pride told him he didn't want to be at the bottom of his class. The school had a trophy for the most improved student. One night we went up to school for parent-teacher night and Mark showed us the trophy and said, 'I just want you to know that belongs to me.' And it did. He was fourteen years old." That's a nice anecdote, one his parents are happy to relate. It is the sincere story of a city boy whose inner drive overwhelms his limitations.

Jackson's on-court mix of b-boy and textbooks is also a blend of East New York and St. Albans, suggesting a physical equivalent of the mental balancing act so many of my black friends and I live everyday. In ways large and small, we shift unconsciously between a black street sense and the lessons of white structures. It reminds me of Mark's St. Albans homeboys, Joey "Run" Simmons of Run-D.M.C. and his manager-brother Russell, who, for all their dick-grabbing bravado, have intelligently exploited the cultural advantages of being middle-class.

In fact, it may be Mark's quiet ability to synthesize disparate influences that has led so many people to underestimate him. When he attended Loughlin, Pearl Washington at Boys and Girls and Kenny Smith at Archbishop Molloy were considered the top guards in town. Both were fly 'n' funky. Bloods would travel from all over to their school games and playground scrimmages in search of that magical moment for the memory bank. But nobody was hip hopping subway routes to catch Mark's game. Kenny Burford, point guard on the 1982–83 North Babylon team that won the State A division championship, remembers playing against Jackson: "He was a very mature player even when he was fifteen. But he was overshadowed by Pearl and Smith. We were all at the Five Star basketball camp at Bryn Mawr College in 1983; Pearl, Kenny Smith, Reggie Williams, Muggsy Bogues, Mark, and some other top players. Mark was always solid but when you looked at the other guys it didn't seem like Mark had what they had."

What he had only came out in bursts at St. John's where Jackson started out as another victim of Looie Carnesecca's upper-classmen-first philosophy. It was clear—at least to me—that during his sophomore year, Jackson had more ability than starting point guard Mark Moses, and I still think if Mark had been handed the ball, the Redmen's journey to the Final Four in 1985 would have dragged an NCAA championship back to Alumni Hall. When Jackson ran the show during his junior and senior years he set an NCAA record for assists as a junior (328) and for career games played at St. John's (131). As Chris Mullin and Walter Berry exited, Jackson grew in stature. But responsibility for running the team kept Jackson from exhibiting fresh style, and the doubts Burford expressed resurfaced. Too slow. No shot. Weak one-on-one moves. Not NBA caliber.

Like many college stars who played under dominating coaches (best example: Michael Jordan), Jackson has found his wildstyle side liberated by the pro game; Pearl and, to a lesser degree, Smith are still seeking their NBA equilibrium. During the Knicks recent blowout of the Nets at the Garden, Jackson and Washington found themselves head-to-head at midcourt after a Jackson steal. Instead of trying to drive past Pearl, Mark came down to medium tempo, casually turned his back on his friend once they reached the lane and, suddenly, threw out an Adrian Dantley left body-fake and spun right for two. Calm, calculated, cerebral ball. Pearl came back, wildly shoulder-faking like a thousand guys I've guarded on Brooklyn playgrounds, and then drove to his left. But in his haste for revenge, he lost his balance and landed on his butt under the Knicks basket. Later, Pearl, truly snake-bitten as a pro, suffered the latest in a series of leg injuries.

As a public figure Jackson is in the "local boy makes good" phase of his career, a part he plays obligingly. He and his family wanted the Knicks and unlike his more celebrated St. John's comrades Chris Mullin and Walter Berry, fate and the Knicks wanted him too. A knowledgeable sports scribe criticizes Mark for being "tense" with the local press. *Intense* might be closer to the truth. Like any good communications major, Jackson is acutely aware of what he says and how he says it. He's not going to embarrass black folk by stumbling over words; nor is he going to outrage whites with fits of ego like a previous local sportsman named Jackson. Not that Mark's a choir boy; he's often been spotted at black hangouts like Bentley's and the Red Parrot looking for new love. Still, there's a stability and serenity about Jackson that, in this city bereft of homegrown heroes, could eventually make him a leading citizen the way Julius Erving is in Philadelphia. Mark has a dignity we need a lot more of in New York.

"His off court personality fits with the way he plays," says a Jackson pal who works in the NBA. "He's nice, quiet, laidback; confident but not flashy. Unlike some guys he won't try to impress them people he meets with the fact he's on the Knicks. He's been around the good and bad element, and he knows the difference. I've always thought he could be a great lawyer or CEO because he just has this calmness about him."

Certainly those of us in the upper decks of the Garden are considerably calmer since Jackson's arrival. Sure, we still have to scream at Pat Cummings and Kenny Walker regularly. And things would be a lot better with Bernard popping 15-footers down the stretch of close games. But it's become hard to work up a venomous lather with the Knicks winning 15 of 23 at home. Now if they'd only run some plays for Johnny "Got-a-J-and-Know-How-To-Use-It" Newman, play on the road the way they do here and, please, find a real back-up guard for Mark before they bury him with a Lou Gehrig iron man award, we could have a playoff team before Jabbar retires.

Don't get me wrong; The Knicks still have a wonderful shot at the lottery this year—an injury to Jackson or Ewing would guarantee it. But it's been a long time since there's been something to root for in the Garden besides a win. The cardinal sin of the last seasons under Hubie "You Are in My System" Brown was not losing, but the stultifying way they lost. If an opposing star didn't destroy them in spectacular fashion—I'll never forget Michael Jordan soaring for 50, opening day 1986—not even the hard-backed Garden seats could keep your eyes open. Ever since Rick Pitino started Jackson in the second game of this season, he's been the master of ceremonies for a smooth, funky floor show. And no matter how long it takes Bianchi and Pitino to build a lasting playoff team, we know there'll be some stupid-fresh moments as long as the Knicks start a point guard who's middle name is "Action."

VILLAGE VOICE, 1988

# TO BE A BLACK MAN

Life is cool. I'm working on going pop—on accumulating plenty of paper. Women are treating me with undue respect. My nieces loved *Fantasia*. But the comforts of middle-class bachelorhood aren't what's on my mind. I've never been a Dinkins fan, but to see the man slammed for 20 years of urban neglect while Ed Koch bays like a jackal in the *Post* is wearing on me. So is the thought of black men and women in the Saudi Arabian desert, waiting to die protecting an overfed monarchy for Mobil Oil. Finally there are the little daily nuances of racial aggravation. Like dripping water on a rock, hate eventually takes its toll.

To be a black man is to be a shadow, a nightmare, a statistic. It's being brown in a society that loves pink and pale. It's being nappy in a country of blow-dryers. It's being Nat Turner and Willie Horton and Luther Campbell in the dreams of people you've never met. It's being painted in by numbers—the numbers of unemployed, drug-addicted, incarcerated, dropped-out, murdered.

A little black boy walks past me on a downtown Brooklyn street. He's wearing a backpack, boxer jeans, and a Pirates baseball cap. There's an embryonic sway to his walk. I wonder if crackheads haunt his hallway, if his teachers are really teaching, and if he knows anyone who explains why books are more potent than guns. Drugs, flowing here in cargo hulls, briefcases, and diplomatic pouches, are destroying this country one young soul at a time. They are so prevalent in black communities they seem aimed at turning the wiry little bodies of kids like this into excrement. He disappears out of eyesight and I worry where he'll end up.

To be a black man is to experience love burdened by sociology, old wives' tales, and the gargoyles of womanist literature. It's to hear "Black men ain't shit" said by women over pig's feet and to feel the phrase "He's just like his daddy" cut through you like a razor. It's to know that any accidental pregnancy ends up tabulated by the U.S. Department of Blame, part of our government's ongoing effort to highlight African American irresponsibility. An infidelity, a romantic misjudgment, a lover's quarrel is often judged not on an individual basis, but under a microscope of negative expectations.

To be a black man is to understand that Alice Walker's Mister is the best known African American male literary character of the era, and that John Edgar Wideman will have to write another 10 books about brothers as brilliant as *Philadelphia Fire* before getting his due. It's spending your childhood watching white boys from Wayne to Stallone squeeze off in big-screen phallic fantasies and then wonder why folks get uptight about blaxploitation flicks disguised as rap records.

To be a black man is to be pissed off by the treacherous, jheri-curled coon Benny in *Total Recall*, to read the reviews and realize no white critics noticed him. It's to see John Turturro in *Mo' Better Blues* and then in *Miller's Crossing* and say, "Yo, what's the diff?" It's to know brothers would have gone to see *Glory* if only Hollywood had the guts to plaster the streets with posters of Denzel Washington clutching a gun and ready to get dumb on a Confederate soldier.

It's spending a lifetime sucking back rage at taxi drivers, coworkers, and salespeople. It's wearing a suit to a business meeting a white dude can take in jeans. It's recognizing that if an answering machine's missing on the job your name will surely come up. It's standing in a police lineup knowing damn well how much one poor brother looks like another. It's hoping no one drops a pocketbook in your vicinity.

To be a black man is to enter an elevator and have a white woman shift her bags away from you. It's to see the white man next to her push out his chest and try to stare you down. It's watching them pirouette to avoid brushing against you. It's to laugh at their timidity and then want to pull out a nine-millimeter automatic and mow down every white mother-fucker in sight.

Being a black man can be wonderful. But I'm not living like that this week.

VILLAGE VOICE, 1991

# 5

# BIG CITY OF DREAMS

# MIDDLE-CLASS HEAVEN

In the summer of 1958 the late Robert Arthur Ford, Sr., a cook turned corrections officer who ran the kitchen at Rikers Island, went to the Municipal Credit Union and obtained a loan of approximately $3,000. Tired of life in a six-floor tenement walk-up on Amsterdam Avenue and 152nd Street, the elder Ford yearned to move his wife and three kids to a place that provided grass, better schools, and the opportunity to own something. In short, he dreamed of Queens.

So that September he moved to 205th Street and 115th Drive in a neighborhood called St. Albans. Mr. Ford was not alone. Starting in the early '50s, in a migration as significant in black New York social history as the shift of black Manhattanites from San Juan Hill to Harlem, families from Harlem, Brooklyn, and the Bronx sought middle-class haven in St. Albans. They also ventured out to neighboring Hollis, Cambria Heights, Jamaica, South Ozone Park, and, later, Laurelton and Queens Village.

Today, black Queens is famous (and infamous) for spawning Run-D.M.C., Mark Jackson, and a bunch of vicious drug kingpins. But rappers, Knickerbockers, and criminals don't truly reflect its history, nor what still counts most about its present. Life flows on: Homes depreciate, basements and streets flood due to inadequate sewers, kids take their synthesizer lessons, planes drone past bound for Kennedy. Your typical St. Albans abode is a modest two-story structure with a patch of grass, minor shrubbery, a barbecue pit, and, inside so many living rooms, big comfortable living-room chairs for men like Ford, Sr.

"Most of my father's friends and relatives, all equally middle-class, either had moved out there or were in the process of moving at that time," says my friend Robert Ford, Jr., a scuffling music businessman known to friends as Rocky, over a plate of potato salad, greens, and well-seasoned ribs. In the long white-and-green back room of Sylvia's he speaks quickly and humorously about a land he's left behind.

"There was a whole mentality that went with Queens," he says. "My father thought it was a big deal to read the Sunday *Times* on the patio in his bathrobe. He worked two jobs for the rest of his life to pay the mortgage. He and his friends all said they moved out there for the sake of their kids. Yet he didn't have time to teach me to throw a curve or to swim. In Harlem we used to take weekend outings, but that ended when we moved to St. Albans largely because he was always working. But, in his mind, his children were in a better environment."

Initially, St. Albans was very much an integrated community. The Fords were the third black family on the block. A few doors down from the Fords were the Johnsons, a white family quite open to their new neighbors. Yet within five years the Johnsons and all the other whites were gone. It's a spectacle so many black families, including my own, witnessed in our attempts at upward mobility. Work, save, move, integrate, and watch the moving vans drive up. "There is a certain inescapable lunacy in the behavior of my father and Mr. Johnson," Rocky suggests. "My father sought paradise in moving around white people who were like them, though he knew how prejudiced they could be. Mr. Johnson, and so many like him, disregarded the evidence of their experience—knowing us and other blacks on the block—and believed we would run the neighborhood down. And you know what happened? They moved out to Long Island, trying to run away from us, but blacks kept moving after them as if being around white folks guaranteed a good life." Through the '50s into the '70s St. Albans became home base for more and more city workers (as well as musicians like Count Basie and James Brown). Hollis was considered a touch more working-class. Ford Sr. thought Ozone Park and Jamaica were "Harlem with grass," a description that captures the uppity attitude associated with St. Albans residents.

It was while attending St. John's University in the late '70s that I first encountered St. Albans kids. They gave me a deep jolt of culture shock. Essentially the difference between me (working-class boy reared in Brooklyn projects by a single parent) and them (blessed with two parents, house, and car) was the material things they took for granted, basements, cars, and fathers among them. Parents traveled upstate to Peg Leg Bates's black Adirondack resort, or maybe to a place on Long Island. They manifested their hard-earned middle-class status in swimming pools, social club memberships, and latent conservatism. Queens's female offspring, at least when I was a schoolboy, had a certain bourgie cachet that drew J-train loads of Brooklyn boys scheming on their well-groomed charms.

"My father used to say problems would come when his group began to take in roomers, people who didn't have a stake in the property," says Rocky. Linden Boulevard, which runs through the heart of St. Albans, is pockmarked with drug spots. Yet overall the crack craze hasn't overwhelmed Rocky's home turf as it has the now notorious streets of Jamaica. The drug presence is felt in other ways, however. St. Albans's own Mark Jackson was recently subpoenaed as a character witness for reputed drug dealer Tommy Mickens. Don't fear, Knick fans: He knew Mickens as a sponsor of basketball tournaments in Queens, a reflection of how embedded the drug industry is in the body of our city—even in the best of neighborhoods.

Back 31 years ago, blacks with a little bank stepped off the 125th Streets of America first chance they had. The fact that St. Albans was a two-fare zone quite removed from the city's cultural core, and that their exit would undermine Harlem's tax base, churches, and social diversity, meant nothing to them. Uplifting the race with the fruits of your work ethic was a nice idea, but at the dawn of the civil rights era the Fords, like the Youngers in A Raisin in the Sun, believed that progress equaled a nice house next to Mr. Johnson.

As we walk into Sylvia's always crowded front room, Rocky says, "There are drug pockets in St. Albans, but it's still a homeowners neighborhood, a place where black people protect their property and mow the lawn. I think 205th Street is still as pretty as the day we moved in."

Outside Sylvia's the temperature pushes 85 and Lenox Avenue, full of hip-hopping new jacks and old men with languid southern eyes, spreads before us. Rocky resides on 120th Street in a brownstone his Aunt Hazel purchased around the same time Robert Sr. went to Queens. "You know, she bought her house for about the same amount of money as my father. Now it's worth twice what his house is. If my father and his friends had all stayed in Harlem, who knows how different things would be?" Rocky says he loves life uptown, though he definitely watches his back late at night. What would Robert Sr. think? "My father would have been horrified." He laughs deeply. "He would never have understood. Never understood."

VILLAGE VOICE, 1989

# FORT TO THE FUTURE

**N**ola Darling didn't live in Fort Greene—the loft that served as her residence in *She's Gotta Have It* was situated in the Heights, under the Brooklyn Bridge. But the bulk of that film's action occurred about a mile or so away on Spike Lee's home turf. Sitting in Fort Greene Park, the love-struck Jamie read newspapers, argued with Mars Blackmon about Larry Bird, and tried, unsuccessfully, to domesticate Nola. At the top of the park, on the base of Stanford White's monument to dead sailors, the film's color dance scene was photographed. *SGHI* was important not only because it put Spike Lee on the cultural map, but because it shed light on a neighborhood now so overflowing with African American movers and shakers that some speak of a renaissance or, more trendily, "the new black aesthetic." But aesthetically and economically Fort Greene isn't '20s Harlem or the East Village of the '60s: It's a community peculiar to its time, whose residents—despite their prominent roles in our popular culture, or perhaps because of them—may never fit comfortably under any cultural banner.

Through the '60s and '70s, jazz musicians were attracted to Fort Greene's beautiful and relatively inexpensive brownstones, the artistic ambience created by Pratt Institute, the short subway ride to work in the Village. Among these urban homesteaders were vocalist Betty Carter, trumpeter Lester Bowie, pianist Cecil Taylor, and bassist Bill Lee, Spike's father. But since the mid-'80s, a slew of sub-30 achievers has ventured into the Fort: Branford (and for a minute Wynton) Marsalis, Living Colour's Vernon Reid, actress/singer Alva Rogers, saxophonist/bandleader Steve Coleman and other members of the jazz collective M-Base, Public Enemy executive producer Bill Stephney, cinematographer Ernest Dickerson, actress Sandye Wilson of *Sidewalk Stories*, and Stetsasonic's Daddy-O are a few of the more visible Fort Greeners. Less celebrated but crucial to the community's mix is an ever-growing list of creative professionals—the publicists, video producers, entertainment attorneys, record promoters, literary agents, graphic artists, clothing designers, cartoonists, sound engineers, and jingle singers who daily parade up and down DeKalb Avenue, eating Italian food at Cino's, buying groceries at Perry's, or, to satisfy a late-night craving, venturing up to Junior's.

Contrary to the expectation of many, this accumulation of African American talent hasn't created an overly social atmosphere. There is no in hangout that attracts a cross section of these artistic pros. The Brooklyn Academy of Music, supposedly a progressive institution, has sponsored few events highlighting the nearby talent. Parties tend to be linked to business ventures, like the recent wrap party for *A Love Supreme* on Tillary Street. One reason, quite simply, is that folks be busy. Fort Greeners are always "in the studio," "on the road," or "on the Coast." And while the stars of the Harlem Renaissance were united by poetry and class, and the Black Arts folks by theater and avant-garde jazz, the Fort Greene tribe works in opera, fashion, graphic arts, and photography as well as the obvious disciplines of film, literature, and music. People don't gather around regularly to read poetry or rehearse plays. At a Fort Greene party you're more likely to see the latest videos, discuss the latest rap jam, or, more tellingly, compare law firms and devise marketing strategies. Recent coverage in *Newsday* and the *Times* has emphasized a respect for Malcolm X and a new black aesthetic as collective characteristics of Fort Greene's talented 10th. But as a resident and critic I find both conceptual packages lacking.

That many contemporary African American artists regard Malcolm X as an inspirational figure is undeniable. But they also look to Nelson and Winnie Mandela, James Brown, Muhammad Ali, and that old standby Martin Luther King. Sure Malcolm is central to the meaning of Thulani and Anthony Davis's *X* and Lee's *Do the Right Thing*, but that doesn't make him a unifying factor. Malcolmania has become a media hook that suggests more political commitment in Fort Greene than is readily apparent, exploiting his status as a pop icon rather than respecting him for the radical philosopher he was.

Similarly, the idea of a "new black aesthetic," first promulgated by Greg Tate in these pages and later exploited by novelist Trey Ellis, fits many of these artists as loosely as linen pants. *New* is always a dangerous word in art, since it suggests both a break with the past and the start of a different direction. If anything, Living Colour and Branford Marsalis reclaim past African American culture that's been lost or ignored by this generation, positing rockers (Chuck Berry, Little Richard, Jimi Hendrix) and jazzmen (Charlie Parker, John Coltrane, vintage Miles Davis) as keys to sustaining a strong collective self-image. I love this retro-nuevo attitude, but it ain't new.

As Thulani Davis pointed out at a symposium following Tate's black aesthetic article, what is new about Fort Greeners—what separates them from their (our) forefathers—is technology and marketing acumen. With the aid of samplers, computers, VCRs, and college educations at some prestigious institutions, these artists cross-reference their culture like crazy, in their art and their everyday conversation. But overriding it all is the idea of businessperson/artist. While Spike Lee is the obvious model of this impulse, there are others: Bill Stephney, who runs Weasel Promotions and the embryonic SOUL (Soul of Urban Listeners) Records out of his brownstone; writer/illustrator Barbara Brandon, who has sold a weekly cartoon feature, "Where I'm Coming From," to the *Detroit Free Press*; and designer Evette Marie and filmmaker Naima Fuller, who run a profitable fashion designer business while raising cash for an antidrug feature *Country Rock*. Fort Greeners aren't simply bottom-line-oriented buppies, though some fit that description—they're astute enough to know that art without finance is a nuisance. And while they're certainly not neoconservatives, their appreciation of market forces and image-building are not foreign to the philosophies of self-sufficiency advocates like Shelby Steele.

As businessman/marketeer/careerist, Spike Lee is still a walking advertisement for Steele's theories, and as such he's Fort Greene's central energy source. Not only did his success increase real estate values and stimulate entrepreneurship, but he employs or works with a significant percentage of his neighbors. His 40 Acres and a Mule Filmworks, located in an old fire station on DeKalb, is the shining symbol of this community's unexpected glamour and its significant opportunity. You see, I'm willing to admit I might be wrong—it's possible that the work of Fort Greene's residents will ultimately be seen as the product of a unified milieu. But right now the genius of the Fort Greene posse is more entrepreneurial than artistic. The key isn't sloganeering or hip hype. It is for this community to produce works that capture the flavors of African American diversity with the same intuitive accuracy as *She's Gotta Have It*.

VILLAGE VOICE, 1990

# GARBAGE TIME

**A**t first it was easy to ignore them. They were hungry. They were homeless. They were black. They tipped over garbage cans and ripped open plastic bags, usually between 1:30 and 3:30 the night before a sanitation pickup, in search of those precious urban commodities, refundable cans and bottles. Morning after, gobs of food, bits of paper, the odd personal item—a torn family photo, a party invitation, a microwave popcorn bag—lay in the sun in front of an otherwise well-kept brownstone.

In a city of starving people, who was I to begrudge the homeless useful items they discovered in the block's discards? Then, in true New York fashion, my liberalism was put to the test. It started with the unfortunate fact that I live in a building that's not only on the corner, but bordered by thick bushes. As a result, my residence is usually the last surveyed by the homeless, who then proceed around the corner to tally up. Anything unwanted is either chucked into the bushes or left leaning against them. That practice has generated many summonses for the landlord and intense irritation in the building's residents.

One morning I walked outside to find little blue snowflakes decorating the bushes and sidewalk. On closer inspection these flakes proved to be bits of some neighbor's canceled checks. I scooped up as many pieces as I could, dumped them into one of the building's garbage cans, and wondered, "How long will this stuff remain in there?" It was a bad omen.

A week later my phone rang at 7 A.M. I hadn't gone to bed until 3, so everything that happened subsequently had a dreamy, surreal quality. An angry female voice shouted, "I'm from the block association and I'm calling to say we got your number from your garbage and we'll be reporting you for illegal dumping!" I believe I said, "Thank you." Dazed and confused, I threw on some clothes. The front of the building was clear, but around the corner and next to the bushes was a horrendous sight.

Just before turning in four hours before, I'd put out two huge bags. In a year-end cleaning effort I'd rifled through my files for original drafts, copies, old letters, notes on scrap paper, as well as old financial documents and sundry other potentially revealing items. Because of its intimate nature, I'd decided to be smooth and wait until real late to take it outside.

Now all of it stretched out before me as if the insides of my mind had been scattered like beer cans at a softball game. With the frenzy of the deeply embarrassed, I scrambled around, pulling my papers together as well-dressed bups and yups strode by. On my hands and knees, digging a letter out from under a parked car, I knew I'd rarely felt more vulnerable.

Or angry. Years ago I'd stopped giving change to male beggars. I'd only reach into my pocket for a mother with a child. Then that became so common, I grew callous to them as well. A true urbanite, the more I was confronted with need, the more alienated I became from the needy. On the subway, the street, or outside McDonald's, beggars have become so irksome that only a saint doesn't wish at some point that they'd all disappear.

That the majority of those I see are black deeply complicates my reluctance to give. Homelessness, particularly in a community that's long been victimized by the depression overcoming working-class America, is a problem no city, state, or federal government has dealt with. But as I washed my hands that morning and contemplated my now refilled garbage can, there was only one thing on my mind: "What am I gonna do about protecting my garbage?"

Three days later, around 2 A.M., I heard someone jostling the cans. I jumped out of bed and slid into some sneakers and a jacket. Outside my bag was gone. From around the corner I heard the distinctive rustling of plastic. An adult black male, early twenties, wearing a wool cap, beat-up troop jacket, jeans, and old sneakers had just finished dumping the contents of my garbage at the base of a tree when I said, "Yo!"

I'd like to claim the ensuing conversation resulted in some communication breakthrough across the lines of class and economics that separated us on the Afrocentric tip. But this being the real world, we simply cut a deal. Stop rummaging through my garbage and I'd leave any refundable containers next to the can. That said, he hit up on me for some cash, but I stuck to my principles. We parted on as friendly terms as you can with a stranger who's just violated your privacy at two in the morning.

Of course that conversation didn't change a thing. Next week there was more of my trash on a New York City street. My man was probably righteous, but to really safeguard my stuff I'd have to cut deals with everyone at the nearest homeless shelter. Faced with that reality, I now treat my rubbish with more respect. With scissors or my hands I rip private papers to shreds; attempt to separate periodicals, bottles, cans, etc. By purchasing a computer I've cut down on my paper use. In short, I've cooled out and come back to terms with urban reality. I guess that's just life during wartime.

VILLAGE VOICE, 1991

# GUSTO

It's a little after midnight at the bar of the Apollo Theater. The old vaudeville house is jammed for the second of two Easter Sunday rap shows top-lining Eric B. and Rakim. But in a room full of 5 Percenter Gods and their Earths, that holiday is irrelevant. The audience is gathered tonight to celebrate certain venerable urban verities—athletic wear as finery, black pride sloganeering disguised as fighting the power, and hard-core rap. Ed O.G. & the Bull Dogs, Main Source, Gang Starr, and of course the headliners eschewed dancers, new jack beats, and slick onstage production. The artists on the bill, rookies and vets alike, are old school in attitude. The vibe in the Apollo is old school too. So many cock diesel brothers squeezed into one space arouses memories of criminal-minded madness at rap gigs dating back to the '70s.

Sipping a Coke, I'm looking at a kid's dungaree jacket with the phrase "Stick up kids are out to tax" in silver sequins on the back when Ben calls my name. Bodyguard and valet, protector and confidant to rappers since the Hollis Crew's heyday, Ben is a New York hip hop fixture whose slight build belies his fiery temper. Legend has it that Ben knocked out the obnoxious actor Anthony Michael Hall at a Run-D.M.C. party a few years back.

"What's up?"

"They got Gusto. Came into his spot, said they were police. Handcuffed him. Found him today with three in his head."

Ben paid for his drinks and stepped off. David "Gusto" Crumpler, lifelong resident of the Bronx, former boxer, partner in several uptown establishments including Arthur's Roundtable on 174th Street and Bronx River Avenue, and friend to the hip hop nation, had been found in a park on 166th Street. There were three bullets in his head.

In the weeks since Gusto's death more details of his execution-style murder have emerged. According to family friends, Gusto, his brother Reggie, and one or two others were in an office in the building next to the Roundtable at approximately 1:30 A.M. March 31 when three men (informants differ as to their race) arrived at the back door. How they got inside isn't clear, but once there they used badges to identify themselves as police officers, quickly handcuffed Gusto, and took him out to an unmarked car. His brother Reggie attempted to follow the car, but lost the trail.

About nine hours later, on Easter morning, Gusto's body was found in the park, handcuffed face down on a mattress. Six days later, there was a wake at the Bentas Funeral Home that attracted rappers, singers, and friends from up and downtown. Two days after that Gusto was interred in a North Carolina burial plot he now shares with his mother and grandmother.

I first encountered Gusto when he started hanging around the record business in the mid-'80s. A stocky five foot nine, he was built like a slightly smaller version of Mike Tyson. Yet what you noticed were his eyes, which were small, penetrating, and, when they surveyed you, quite intimidating. Meeting him you immediately sensed Gusto knew too much—he looked mean, but also sad. "You look up the word 'street' in the dictionary," recalled one acquaintance, "and Gusto was the definition." Yet though he never totally let his guard down with me (or, for that matter, I with him), he was also quite funny in a rough-hewn way, often telling jokes and amusing anecdotes.

In 1987 we came to spend a lot of time around each other, mostly because I was asked to write a black detective flick for a hip hop–influenced r&b singer and Gusto was asked to be a story consultant. At Knicks games, seafood restaurants, and various clubs, the singer would start telling stories and Gusto would finish them. For example, the scene where Nino Brown walks a man naked down a Harlem street at gunpoint in *New*

*Jack City* was a real one that Gusto had witnessed years before. I never asked how he knew these things—it was just understood that he did.

When friends say "he was a product of his environment," they're not just talking about our often brutal street life. "His father was the kind of man who literally would pull his own teeth with pliers. When you have a father like that there's only a certain way you can act to earn respect." Many of the music people he hung with got off on Gusto's tough-guy aura. In their eyes his presence at a press party or in a music video gave them a cutting edge of reality, feeding their own gangster fantasies. Together Gusto and these music makers would watch *The Mack* or *Superfly*, reviling these blaxploitation melodramas as cartoon reflections of their reality or fuel for their daydreams.

Then one day he turned up a four-man vocal group and named it after himself. Two years before the first stirrings of New Jack Swing, Gusto, who had very sharp musical taste, was mixing r&b with hip hop attitude just like Keith Sweat or Guy. He traveled to black music conventions and met with industry executives. Still, Gusto's one single on 4th & B'way records went nowhere and there was no album follow-up. Many of the same record biz brothers who'd profiled with him later fronted on Gusto when he needed their expertise. He was still pumping money into the group's demo tapes at the time of his murder.

Who killed Gusto and why is a matter of conjecture—no suspects means no information from the Bronx district attorney's office. Word uptown is that there are men claiming to be police arresting reputed drug figures and then extorting money from them. Sounds like the Larry Davis defense, doesn't it? Whether Gusto was a criminal kingpin or not, it's painful to know someone so cold-bloodedly executed. According to family friends, Gusto had been badly beaten, suggesting he had been tortured before he was shot.

Given the volume of crime in the Bronx and the circumstances of his life and death, his killers may never be caught. As I watched Rakim stalk the Apollo stage, I reflected on the mid-'80s, when rap was spreading crosscountry like a secret code and crack was spawning a new urban gangster. At many points the two businesses intersected, the dealers creating an evil mythology of Uzi-fed potency that rap mirrored, celebrated, and condemned. Somewhere in the blurred lines between the two, David "Gusto" Crumpler, who would have been 34 on April 28, lived and died.

# THIS CHRISTMAS

**E**bony and I were going through Fort Greene Park on our way to see *Township Fever* at BAM when I was overcome by a very childish emotion. I wanted to run through the leaves and I did, knowing that my 10-year-old niece would chase me. And, as often happens when the child in me overwhelms the adult, there was an accident. Not three steps into our chase, Ebony's foot struck a rock and she flopped, face first, into a clump of fallen Fort Greene foliage. Happily, she wasn't hurt. Unhappily, the sleeve of her new winter coat was now smeared with dog doo-doo. I was appalled. She was amused. She giggled on the way back to my place, and giggled as I vigorously wiped the mess away and sprayed it with Right Guard. "You got dog doo-doo on my new coat," she said, quite delighted by my lack of adult omnipotence.

I was supposed to take her to the *Sesame Street* show at the Garden, but when *Township Fever* opened in Brooklyn, I decided to substitute an Afrocentric cultural experience for what she really wanted to see. I'd taken her to see *The Piano Lesson*, which she'd both understood and enjoyed. But *Township Fever*, with its shifts from bright, elaborate musical numbers to long-winded sections of exposition, made her squirm. I spent much of the second act with my arm around her, trying to use fatherly affection to sustain her flagging interest. I was surprised. Unlike most young residents of planet Earth, Ebony has always preferred sedentary activities like reading books and watching television to, for example, jumping rope. Nor did speaking up in class or most other assertive pursuits interest her. It was as if there was a level of active behavior she wouldn't, or couldn't, engage in.

But that didn't mean she wasn't stubborn. That night, while dining at a local bistro, she chafed under my finicky instruction to eat her french fries with a fork. "This is not McDonald's," I said sternly. Her response was to use the fork awkwardly and roll her eyes. During the cab ride home she sat away from me, clearly pissed at bachelor uncle's unwanted discipline.

For a while I thought that would be her last memory of me. Five days later I received an anguished message from my mother. CAT scan. Brain tumor. Down State Medical Center. Surgery. Ebony had always been sickly. But since October she hadn't put in a full week of school, and a series of intense, inexplicable headaches led her pediatrician to send her to Kings County Hospital for tests. Within hours the tumor had been found and Ebony placed in Down State's children's ICU unit across from Kings County.

My mother, herself sidelined by a broken leg, was depressed by her inability to travel to her granddaughter's aid. Ebony's little sister Amber missed her so much that one night she slept in her bed. Ebony's mother, my sister, was relatively cool, though her calm seemed part of the same mask she often employed to distance unwanted advice—or in this case, pain. The day after the diagnosis Ebony's father stood in the hallway outside the ICU unit wiping away a tear. He explained that the tumor, on the left side of her head, had blocked the flow of fluid from brain to spine. Pressure from the tumor and the collected fluid was causing headaches and endangering her young life. He was teary because he'd just given permission for a tube to be inserted in her skull to siphon off the backed-up fluid. Inserted? That's the word we used instead of drilled.

Before this procedure I entered the ICU. A little Trinidadian boy was propped spread-eagle on a bed with a network of tubes and tape spread across his skinny chest. "Open-heart surgery," Ebony's father whispered. A left turn past a desk where two Caribbean nurses did paperwork. Then Ebony was in front of me, lying on her left side with tubes stuck in both arms. Her lips were dry. Her yellow skin was pale. Her voice, when it spoke my name, was small and weary. As I stood there I could feel blood rushing into my head. Then we were ushered out as the neurosurgeon entered.

In the hallway we riffed through Ebony's life—her introspection, melancholy, ailments, and lack of confidence. Had she known all along something was wrong? Had the tumor, near the part of the brain that controls balance, made her clumsy? Had the family misinterpreted these signs for years? Back inside the ICU, a large patch of hair on the right side of her head was gone. In its place was a bandage and from under it a tube snaked into a plastic bag and into that bag ran a trickle of brownish fluid. An injection of morphine had rendered her doll-like: arms limp, eyes empty of emotion, pulse rate a crawl. As nurses and doctors filled out forms, wired and unwired tubes, and discussed work hours, I stood with eyes open and prayed. The doctors decided to operate the next day.

The operation lasted from 9:30 A.M. till 4. Doctors say the tumor was the size of a plum and they got 99 percent of it. A bunch of questions, including the crucial "Is it benign or malignant?" can't be answered until samples are tested. But in the short run, we know Ebony's pain has lessened and she's still with us.

Three days later most of the tubes are gone. Her mother feeds her mashed potatoes and ground-up chicken. While she moves her right arm easily, Ebony seems reluctant to use her left. This tendency is troubling, but that's a worry for another time. Her teacher, who Ebony feels "looks like Janet Jackson," stops by. Ebony's bookish personality has led her teacher to nickname her "the suburban girl." But on this day, a week before Christmas, Ebony is not having it. In a strong voice she says, "The suburban girl is gone. Ebony George is back and here to stay." Can't get a better present than that.

VILLAGE VOICE, 1991

# DINING ON DAVE

**T**wo Steps Down is a dark, homey, black-owned restaurant in Fort Greene that serves a working-to middle-class clientele. Unlike Junior's, which is 12 blocks away, Two Steps doesn't cater to kids—its atmosphere is subdued, and its prices are Manhattan-style. Many who hang at its upstairs bar are lesbians, while its ground-floor dining area is usually filled with couples and families. If you happen to be nosy, then sitting in Two Steps Down is a good way to get a feel for the mood of adult, open-minded African Americans.

When the Community Activist, the Local Shopkeeper, and the Nosy Journalist sat around eating shrimp, lobster, and baked potato one recent Wednesday night, talk turned to the Mayor. Conversation was animated and remarkably one-sided. For this particular group of Brooklynites,

David Dinkins is no longer the mayor, but a historic figure whose time is over. For them his regime has been sliding downhill since Election Eve. The consensus at the table was not simply that the dapper tennis bum was inept in dealing with our cascading fiscal crisis or in articulating his vision of New York—it was that he hadn't stood up for the race.

"He hasn't fulfilled the key job of even the worst hack politician," said the Journalist. "He hasn't taken care of his own. The layoffs, the cuts in services, the weak-ass speeches, all have hit African Americans and latinos hard."

The feeling at the table was that Giuliani would have been a better mayor, not because he would have been sensitive to nonwhites, but because his insensitivity would have galvanized African Americans to protest just as Koch's nastiness did. "Giuliani would have scolded black people in Crown Heights like Dinkins did," the Shopkeeper said. "Giuliani would have crossed the picket line in East Flatbush. And you know what? If Giuliani crosses that line outside the Korean grocery store, the next day we have 200 more pickets."

"You could have started four new organizations off the anger alone," the Activist said.

"But," the Shopkeeper said, "with Dinkins as mayor, black people get caught in the discussion mode. 'Let's not let white folks know how we feel about his action.' Having Dinkins as mayor has worked like a giant pacifier. His presence diverts our anger at a time we have more right than ever before."

The Journalist chimed in. "He won by the skin of his teeth last time and that small margin of support has been eroded. Unless he turns into Harold Washington and starts challenging the status quo instead of being its flak jacket, he's outta here."

So, at least in the view of these seers, had Dinkins's future been decided. The future is what now captured their imagination. "The latinos are upset, man," the Journalist observed. "Dinkins has dissed them over and over. Carrillo is just the latest hit. I could see them going solo in the next election."

"Brother, they are still pissed about how the Committee for a Just New York jerked Badillo around in '85," the Shopkeeper said. "They outflanked him with Denny Farrell, just so David Dinkins could finally get the Manhattan borough president's gig. It's a deal that will haunt the city for years, 'cause I think it'll be hard to put that kind of coalition together again."

The Activist leaned forward. His voice got lower. "We haven't been asleep, my brothers. We've been talking."

"That's all you guys do," the Journalist interjected.

"No. We agitate. We attend community meetings. We mobilize people in ways no one else in this city does. Dinkins gets booed in Crown Heights. We didn't because our grassroots credibility is there."

"Come on," the Shopkeeper said. "You said you brothers have been planning something."

"Dinkins, Percy Sutton, Basil Paterson, Charles Rangel—the gang of four—have been running black politics in this town without challenge for years," the Activist asserted. "We can't allow them to retire without letting them know our dissatisfaction. I mean people say this or that about Rangel. Bitch and moan. But he runs unopposed. So he can say my constituency approves of my activities."

"Inaction speaks louder than words," said the Journalist.

"So what does this mean regarding the mayor?" asked the Shopkeeper.

"It means that we may run a slate of candidates to challenge him in the primaries. A black alternative that I believe could be enough to defeat him."

"Is Calvin Butts involved?" the Shopkeeper asked.

"The black Mario Cuomo," the Journalist interjected. "We know all the elders at Abyssinian kept a tight rein on him while he was assistant pastor. So he would step up to the plate on a lot of issues and talk about running, knowing full well that when the time came he couldn't make that move without the backing of the church, which they held back. He had to wait until Reverend Proctor retired."

"But now," said the Shopkeeper, "he's the head man. The elders could still give him a hard time. But now that he's got the carrot, the stick can't seem so heavy."

Ignoring the questions the Activist replied, "The age of skin-color politics is over. People talk about when you elect a politician you have to hold him accountable. How you gonna hold a man accountable once he's got the power? The accountability they respond to is on Election Day."

"I'm shocked and happy," the Journalist said.

"Why?" the Shopkeeper asked.

"For him to say this—well, it just means that Dinkins's election has finally proven, to people in the street, to color-struck people, that black mayors are often just bureaucrats with no vision, no sense of truly empowering other folks."

The Activist replied, "At least under Koch we had a target to rally the people against. Right now we are dying in this city. Feeling rage and frustration, but there is no target, no focus."

"This could be a great story if it happens," the Journalist said.

"If it happens," the Shopkeeper said. "I've been waiting a long time for the activist community to mount a real election campaign. I'm not gonna get too excited yet."

"Brother, you'll be one of the first ones we come to for a campaign contribution."

"Well, you better come correct."

It was a long time to '93, and the Journalist hoped this talk wasn't just bravado—that the strong-voiced men from the rallies and press conferences might finally test their rhetoric of resistance in the electoral battleground. After all these years and all those press conferences and all that rhetoric, Vernon Mason, though oft defeated, had been one of the few critics of the black establishment actually to run for office. Disabling Dinkins in the '93 Democratic primary would be the ultimate statement of contempt for integration. In the short run, maybe the result would be Andy Stein as mayor—but in the long run it could be a neonationalist Adam Clayton Powell for the whole city.

**VILLAGE VOICE, 1991**

# MOTHER'S DAY

**D**ee worries about the young. Every night, through the windows of her Ebbets Field apartment, she hears the "Pop! Pop! Pop!" of weapons, then the screams and shouts of people running and, finally, the wail of sirens. Dee peeps out onto the streets of Flatbush—she's afraid to stand directly in front of the window—and views young black and latino bodies stretched out on the asphalt, bits of their insides beside them.

"There have always been people out here in the street selling drugs," she says, sipping white wine in the backyard of a Brooklyn restaurant. Her eyes are resolute and melancholy behind thick, slightly tinted glasses. "But the killing of each other—kids not 15 or 16—that's what I don't understand. All these young people throwing away their lives, which is the most precious thing they have, and having no respect for anyone else or their life."

Dee came up from Norfolk to New York in the late '50s, one of many Virginians to travel by Greyhound to the Apple and settle here as part of the last African American generation to migrate North. She moved into the Ebbets Field housing project not long after it opened and, from high above Brooklyn, has watched her community devolve from promised land to killing field.

Now Dee counts the days and her money, hoping that she can move back home sometime fairly soon. New York has provided a comfortable bureaucratic city job for over 20 years, many great parties (Dee has been up on the latest dances since the days of the camel walk and watusi), and experiences she'd never have had back in Norfolk, a southern port city dominated since World War II by a shipyard. Yet for all its advantages, life in New York has surely taxed Dee. Though she still "has that old spark," Dee's not seeing anyone now and despairs of finding a decent, unmarried, middle-aged man in New York. The great love of her life ended in disappointment. They dated for over a decade and stayed married for a year—it was as if the wedding ceremony marked the end of their romance, not the start of a new life. But Dee's enduring sorrow is the death of her son, Ken.

Dee and my mother met at a Crown Heights church in 1959—two Virginia girls in Brooklyn with young sons and hopes for the future. Dee and Ken were like family to us. In fact they were much closer than our relatives down South. Dee worked hard to shelter her son from the guns, the gangs, and the intensifying cycle of street drugs (glue, marijuana, heroin, angel dust, cocaine, crack). And she succeeded, producing a sensitive, mild-mannered man with a passion for music I first noticed when he used to sing along to Gene Chandler's "Duke of Earl."

Ken was trying to network his way into doing background vocals for records and commercials when he was diagnosed as having AIDS. Looking back, I deeply regret how uptight that made me. No one I'd known as long or as intimately as Ken had contracted the illness before and it frightened me. In retrospect I can see that I didn't give Ken or his mother the support they deserved. Maybe in the back of my mind I thought I'd be contaminated. Who knows? It was an irrational response, so there's no real justification to be offered. For my emotional negligence no apologies will suffice.

Dee handled Ken's death in 1989 as bravely as any parent could. Still, he was her only child, her baby, her link to the future. On Mother's Day, my mother, Dee, and I saw A *Rage in Harlem* and then dined, talking over chicken and shrimp about wayward friends, financing retirement dreams, the sad state of the Brooklyn they'd reared children in, and Governor Doug Wilder—"Everybody down in Newport News says he shouldn't be messing with that rich white woman," Dee said. Dee mentioned her son in passing. Neither my mother nor I spoke his name.

A few years ago Ken and I took our moms out on Mother's Day. We saw a play—I believe August Wilson's *Joe Turner's Come and Gone*—and had dinner in the city. It was a relatively unmemorable event, the conversation and atmosphere were not very different from this Mother's Day. Yet in the most important way the bond between our two families is now unbalanced. I hope Ken knows that somewhere in Brooklyn, a place where the death of young black men too often resembles self-destruction, his extended family had Mother's Day dinner and felt his presence with us.

VILLAGE VOICE, 1991

*Dee and Ken's names have been changed.*

# MARILYN

Ebony's doll is slim and white with blue eyes and long, straight blond hair.

"Don't you want a black doll?" her bachelor uncle inquired.

"No," Ebony replied, "I like Marilyn."

Eight years in existence yet firm in her judgments, she agreed that her uncle could, indeed, buy her another doll. But Marilyn was No. 1

and that was the way it was going to stay. Her uncle's attempts to separate Ebony from Marilyn were sparked when she told her mother how beautiful Marilyn and her golden hair were. Neither mother, grandmother, nor bachelor uncle were thrilled by the comment, but, practically speaking, this could be a toughie to turn around.

In her tight little bedroom—which just a few moments before had housed bachelor uncle—were "thousands of dolls," according to her mother, of differing shades and brand names, split roughly 50-50 black and white. Of that number, five are regular play companions, and all of those are white. Ebony, like her mommy and daddy, is light-complexioned, closer in hue to Florence Joyner than, say, Jackie Joyner-Kersee. "She might like the white dolls because that's her skin color," observed Ebony's mother. "But she knows she's black. That's why her name's Ebony." For good measure Ebony's middle name is Alleaha, a Swahili handle meaning "honor" that her mother "got out of one of those name books."

Another factor in Ebony's attraction might be home video.

From age two Ebony has been a couch potato. As she learned her ABCs, Ebony was stuffing tapes in the VCR, pushing buttons, and buggin' out. Pollyanna, portrayed by the Aryan Hayley Mills, was a Sunday-night Walt Disney character, an orphaned English lass learning uplifting lessons about life in small-town America. Ebony loved her. She'd sit there for hours rewinding the tapes. Maybe Marilyn is an outgrowth of Pollyanna. Maybe not.

Bachelor uncles know little of such things. But they're painfully aware that upsetting eight-year-old girls, especially without Mommy in effect, is the road to ruination. Like her mother, Ebony is stubborn, obsessed by the things she likes (Papa Smurfs, reading, Marilyn) and quite disdainful of those she doesn't (sitting still in class, arithmetic). She was in her disdainful mode. Her "lesson" in racial imagery ended when her mouth poked out and she refused the hugs and kisses of bachelor uncle.

The question "Want to go play in the park?" rekindled communication. Out in a hilly Brooklyn park full of squirrels and loosely leashed dogs, Ebony ran with up-raised arms yelling happily in a high-pitched voice. She giggled as she scampered past the tennis courts and up and around a steep hill.

Then she almost tripped. Bachelor uncle grabbed her. She laughed louder. In that moment of sudden adult responsibility bachelor uncle recalled an afternoon when she just refused to sit up straight on the subway as the three West Indian ladies laughed at their struggle, and that horrid afternoon when the sight of Michael Jackson turning into a werewolf made her cry. She kept repeating "Michael Jackson is not a monster!"—an observation bachelor uncle always did his best to believe.

The thing about kids, he thought, is that they need so much of you and any failure—in judgment or communication—can be so profound. Suddenly he really felt scared. Not just about Ebony's almost accident but the inevitability of bachelor uncle becoming real-life Daddy. He needed a drink.

At the McDonald's on Fulton and Flatbush, Ebony wrestled french fries to the ground and nibbled off the edges of her cheeseburger. Around them women, men, and offspring, all black and hispanic, munched ferociously on Mickey Dee's fare. Bachelor uncle surveyed the room for black dolls. Nope. At least the dreaded Cabbage Patch craze had passed.

He looked over at Ebony, now doing serious damage to her hands with a ketchup package, and pondered her toothy beauty. Marilyn lay beside her tray, motionless, with bits of red stuck in her hair, plastic yet somehow very threatening.

By the time Ebony is 15 or 16, Marilyn will be a memory, he thought. She'll have been exorcised by heavy doses of book-learning and lectures from Mommy, Grandma, etc. Yet he feared the power of the doll and the culture that created her. To this day Ebony's grandmother, a teacher forged in the fire of Ocean Hill-Brownsville back in the dashiki-and-Afro era, still calls soft, straight hair "good hair." It's an involuntary echo of a past he hopes won't haunt Ebony's future.

VILLAGE VOICE, 1989

# BYRON

I know Byron real well, but I don't like him. He's a crack dealer from Jamaica—St. Ann's Parish, I believe. But as Byron's story illustrates, not every Jamaican dealer is part of a dangerous international posse. Byron lives smaller than that. Days and nights he can be found chillin' outside one of East New York's tight two-story row houses. His gear includes a blousey beige cotton shirt and matching shorts, size 13 white slip-ons, a beeper, two slim gold chains (one dangling a diamond-studded B), a stubbly beard over blotchy brown skin, and dark shades concealing red eyes perpetually in search of suckers.

Six years ago, Byron and his crew commandeered an abandoned residence on my mother's block. Fortunately, they didn't turn it into a crackhouse, if only because crack hadn't yet devolved from freebase into a widely marketed commodity. Instead, they acted as urban homesteaders, fixing windows and hooking up electricity (though it's said the people next door were paid off for helping them avoid Con Ed). If they'd opened a crackhouse, Byron's evil might have been easier to contain, since that would have quickly mobilized the block against him. With Byron selling out of a series of storefronts around East New York, however, opposition to his presence on the block was soft. His black and hispanic neighbors reasoned, "Let sleeping dogs lie," and Byron was certainly a dog. One otherwise solid father figure said, "We're too busy just surviving to be fighting drug dealers every day. As long as he keeps the block clear of his shit, then leave him alone." The father figure's one move was to build a high, pretty, white gate in front of his house. The problem was, containment didn't work. Inevitably, physical and moral corruption followed Byron's acceptance on the block. The father figure and the rest of us who failed to act became co-conspirators in Byron's endeavors and watched, in passive sorrow, as several of the block's offspring were destroyed, not by Byron directly, but by our failure of collective will.

The Moores feared Byron from day one and, sadly, members of this Jamaican family were the block's chief victims. One of their four sons, Leroi, started working with Byron when he was 15. A year later Mrs. Moore was sobbing in front of her house, surrounded by neighbors, after hearing Leroi had caught two in the chest in one of those "drug-related" deaths that add up to black self-genocide. "Unfortunate, my man. You know, what else can I say?" was Byron's response. The Moores blamed Byron, and there was some talk of Mr. Moore sneaking across the roofs with a hunting rifle to Byron's place, but that was nothing but a wish. The Moores's oldest son and family jewel David— lanky, handsome, bright—would a year later join his brother as a victim of crack mania. David just walked out of a Livonia Avenue grocery and into the crossfire of a drug turf war. His blood hit the street before his bags and he was DOA. Byron claims no knowledge of who "did" David. I think he's lying.

I was part of the problem, too. I didn't barrage the local precinct with calls about removing him from the block. Nor did I organize the neighbors. What I did was nothing as the stench of Byron's hustle fouled the air of the place I'd lived my teen years. In fact, I must admit that in an ironic way I was sort of rooting for Byron to become Nicky Barnes south, so that when he got sent upstate and/or shot—whichever came first—I'd have plenty to write about. (How does the book title *My Friendship with a Jamaican Drug King* strike you?) But two years later, after Byron had turned a once lovely little neighborhood girl into a drug moll and used her name to rent an apartment, it was clear the bum would never be more than another working-class dealer.

Like so many brothers, Byron is neither cruel nor smart enough to rise above his station as a low-level outlaw. Plenty of money has passed through his hands in the past six years, yet he has precious little to show for his risky efforts. A couple of his good buddies are dead. Across his abdomen runs a deep scar inflicted by a crazed basehead's steak knife. One dubious attempt at legitimacy—the purchase of a rig for trucking—ended in repossession. Some of his employees don't count so good, resulting in lost revenue. Byron's cars, all purchased in the name of some woman or other, are often stopped by police. One night on Linden Boulevard, a patrol car pulled him over. An officer, maybe as an inducement to get Byron to pay protection, told him the police were watching him. To prove the point the officer dropped Byron's keys down the sewer. Good for your funky ass, I thought, but obviously didn't say.

Saw him the other day while visiting my mother. Byron wasn't happy. With his crack-crazed girlie, a daughter teachers say needs a shrink, and those long, nervous nights watching his back for Dominicans, cops, and customers, my brother is feeling very tired. A vacation might help. He suggests the B-boy Martha's Vineyard, Virginia Beach. What about upstate? I ask. He laughs. He thinks I'm joking.

VILLAGE VOICE, 1989

*Some details have been changed to protect the anonymity of sources.*

# NEW LOTS AVENUE

One recent afternoon Cynthia Baily was walking down New Lots Avenue in East New York with her seven-year-old daughter Essence and an armful of groceries. A blue sedan pulled up beside her. The black man inside called out, "Act like you don't know me!" Being that this was the kind of car only a cop would be seen in and that she wasn't carrying anything more criminal than a McDonald's Happy Meal, she decided to stop.

When she looked at the driver, Cynthia asked, "What you doin' around here?" Cousin Johnny replied, "Workin'."

"In this car?"

"Nice, huh?"

Cynthia's cousin Johnny had been a cop. And he still was, only more so.

"Now I'm with DEA."

"Since when?"

"Since the last two years. How's your mother?"

They exchanged family updates—what this and that cousin or aunt was doing. Then Cynthia said, "You better be chill around here."

"Don't worry, all I'm doing is taking pictures. You know the Puerto Rican dude who lives there? They call him Victorious?"

"The Victorious that lives over there?" She pointed toward a brown two-story row house. Johnny nodded affirmatively. "Yeah, I know him well."

"Well," he said, holding up his camera, "this is for him."

Victorious was a hard-working guy. Had a job in the cafeteria of a municipal building, sold jewelry on the side, and, according to cousin Johnny of the Drug Enforcement Administration, was very friendly with some brothers from Colombia. Victorious had gone to junior high school with Cynthia, had hung out with her on the block many nights, and shared his dope chiba over the years. He was a homie. "So he's in trouble?" she inquired.

"No more than any of the other people I take pictures of. I'm all over the five boroughs. It pays good." Johnny was from a rock-solid middle-class family in St. Albans. Both his parents worked for the city, and he'd gone to a college in Jersey to major in criminal justice. Now he lives just above Yonkers in a cozy little suburban home, just like his white colleagues. He was even trying to make law enforcement a family affair: He'd talked a nephew into joining the cop world. Currently his nephew was working in a buy-and-bust operation in Harlem. Johnny was hoping in a couple of years he'd join DEA too.

As Johnny sat, camera in lap, he joked with his second cousin Essence. Cynthia said, "I know it's good money and all, but these niggers out here are crazy today." Cynthia then added she'd recently taken the civil service exam; maybe one day she'd be a cop. But join DEA? No way.

"Tell your mother I said hello," he said as they walked away. Then he pulled out his camera and took a snapshot of Essence waving at him.

That evening, when Johnny wasn't around, Cynthia stopped by Victorious's house. His parents lived downstairs and Victorious and his wife lived upstairs. Cynthia wondered if they could step outside.

Cynthia could see his breath as they talked in the cold. It surprised him that Cynthia had a DEA agent for a cousin. But nothing else she said did. Victorious told her the DEA had busted his apartment just the month before, confiscating "a lot of money," but didn't find any drugs. His wife had been there when it happened and the DEA had given her a receipt on the way out. She hadn't been sleeping too well since she received it—in fact, she'd moved back to her mother's house.

Victorious claimed the money came from his city job and his jewelry business. Cynthia didn't speak on it: It wasn't her business.

"Just be chill," Cynthia told him. "Maybe you better just try and get your money back, you know, and start a video store or a laundry. People always have to get their clothes washed."

As Cynthia walked away, Victorious stood in the doorway of the brown two-story building, his head turning left and right as he peered into the cars parked along New Lots Avenue.

Not long after that Victorious moved.

VILLAGE VOICE, 1990

*Names and some details have been changed to protect the anonymity of sources.*

# SISTERS WHO SING

I t is 1:30 a.m. on a Wednesday night and Trisha stands on the downtown IRT platform at 14th Street. She leans against a metal pole with a thick black garment bag over her shoulder. Trisha is cocoa brown with shiny auburn hair pulled back in a bun that contrasts nicely with her gold loop earrings. Her skin is smooth but her eyes are covered in makeup that would look extreme if you didn't know that 45 minutes ago she was singing background vocals at a jazz club. She would have liked to catch a cab. But the gig didn't pay much and the bassist who offered her a lift in his van was way too frisky to ride with.

So she chews gum, shifts her weight from side to side, and stoically awaits the No. 4. She's used to waiting. Trisha began piano lessons at eight. Sang in the church choir as a teen. Attended Music & Art. Tried to get into Juilliard. Ended up at Baruch taking some tired-ass accounting courses her moms talked her into. She split early. So now she temps by day, studies *Backstage* and *Billboard*, and listens to every CD ever made. Trisha watches her pennies, saving up money to cut demos. As soon as she feels ready she's going to take her songs—mostly lyrics, really—and lay down some tracks. Except for Anita and Regina Belle and maybe Whitney, none of those ladies already making records scares her. I've known girls like Trisha since I started writing about music. Befriended many, dated a few, and watched them all climb and stumble because they were all certain they could blow better than most folks already on the radio.

You see, Trisha is a sister who sings. Sisters who sing fill audition studios, take voice lessons, study modern dance, and profess to want a classy image even as they call for a hair-weave appointment. Sisters who sing idolize some great African-American songstress. Billie (Holiday), Sarah (Vaughan), Aretha (Franklin), or, if they're between 25 and 30, perhaps Chaka (Khan). Sisters who sing are ambitious, aggressive, insecure, curious, vain, flirtatious, starry-eyed, cynical, sexy, and spiritual, whenever they get the chance. Most sisters who sing never "make it," though that usually depends on how they define success. There are jingles singers you never heard of making more in residuals than most folks with hit records. Still, no Broadway show singing, McDonald's commercial, or national tour backing a black male love man or hip rock band satisfies the craving to outdiva Diana Ross.

Sisters who sing love music so much that at given moments they'll just burst into song, enraptured by the sound of their voices, singing so hard that standing next to them you feel the vibrations of their vocal cords wash over you. Sisters who sing are the great romantic icons of gay culture, the heart of the music business, and the inspiration for generation after generation of sisters who sing to keep on singing. Sisters who sing are beautiful and soulful. If you're not careful, they'll break your heart just like a real deep blues.

A few years back I got caught up in a complicated, self-serving, and exciting network of relationships with three sisters who sing. Hanna was an artist in the purest sense—she studied her craft simply for the pleasure of it. An always-optimistic BAP with an unbelievably sweet personality, Hanna felt she'd end up a star, though she didn't have a clue how. Where Hanna was highbrow and charmingly impractical, Ruth was smooth and always equipped with an agenda. She knew her range was limited, but believed her long auburn hair and bedroom eyes more than compensated. If she had to make awful dance records to get over, well, Ruth would always say, "A girl has to eat," even while she giggled at the sexist gibberish that passed for lyrics. Raphaela was the shrewdest of the three. A Broadway baby with major musical credits and visions of Diana, she acted at singing better than she sang, but Raphaela knew most folks couldn't tell the difference. In a little-girl voice she often asked naïve questions about the recording industry. Yet behind that facade Raphaela had a will of iron. She invested her money wisely and was determined never to be controlled by any force—be it a man, back-stabbing rivals, or the color of her skin. All three knew each other, though they weren't close. They often competed for jobs and on many occasions measured themselves against each other. For several years in the early '80s I hung around them as Hanna's lover, Ruth's occasional fuck, and Raphaela's blue-balls victim. In the process I was privy to the ways they dealt with the frustrations, false starts, lousy contracts, sexual advances, and personal shortcomings that combine to separate the average singer from Whitney, Anita, et al.

None managed to challenge for the crown, though each has achieved some of what she sought. Raphaela moved to Los Angeles and made a couple of respected if not celebrated recordings. She's got a good deal, a capable manager, and, who knows, may yet land that breakthrough hit. In the meantime, after dating several Left Coast celebrities—the kind of guys who show up in Arsenio Hall's audience but never get interviewed—she's marrying a middle-aged business-man. Ruth went out with a slew of record producers, as well as one Yankee and one major comic, in search of her own Berry Gordy. She finally caught one but, quite wisely, he said he'd marry her only if she'd stop trying to make records. When I last spoke to Ruth she was taking acting lessons.

Hanna, seeking artistic depth and her ethnic identity, has become an acolyte of South African culture, traveling to Johannesburg, net-working with musicians there, and proselytizing for their work here. Every now and then I run into her on the subway, carrying her shoulder bag and running her fingers through her designer dreads, and listen to her talk about all the sisters who sing in Soweto.

# LAST EXIT FROM BROOKLYN

**S**tarrett City dominates Brooklyn's Spring Creek section, a blip on the map bordered by East New York, Canarsie, the Belt Parkway, and a huge garbage dump that gives Starrett City its distinctive aroma. The sprawling complex, the Co-Op City of Brooklyn, is built on wasteland that once housed a batting range, a miniature golf course, one lonely Carvel, and the ass-end of Pennsylvania Avenue. That horrific stretch of road was so bumpy it used to serve as weekend entertainment for families who could afford a car but not Coney Island's Cyclone.

Today a repaved version of the same strip is Starrett City's spine, separating Delmar Loop from Elmar Loop and Twin Pines Loop from Freeport Loop. The names of Starrett's streets have amused residents and visitors since its doors opened in 1974. When Cynthia Bailey was a kid in the Fairfield Towers development just across Flatlands Avenue, she and her friends used to sit sipping beers and laughing at those corny names. Starrett City, with its large mall, long green patches of sod, and private health club, was quite an attraction for kids from Fairfield Towers, a private development, and the Linden Houses, a large city project. But those black and hispanic youths were hardly welcomed by Starrett's management—they were often kicked off the premises by security guards or even detained for trespassing. While basketball and touch football games between Fairfield and Linden happened all the time, Starrett's kids were discouraged from joining the competition. The whole idea of Starrett was to create a predominantly white ethnic enclave in the increasingly brown far end of the borough. It was racial engineering of the most discriminatory kind. The sales pitch was simple: "Brooklyn like it used to be."

"It was like they were trying to say everything outside Starrett City didn't exist," Cynthia recalls today from her Census Bureau office on

Pennsylvania Avenue. All these years later Cynthia walks freely through Starrett City trying to ascertain the ethnic, economic, and sociological patterns of its willfully self-contained neighborhood. Though Cynthia isn't big on irony, she sees the humor in this turn of events. But mostly she sees a good summertime job. Armed with an address register, pencils, pads, and the wholehearted support of the U.S. government, Cynthia hunts down unresponding Starrett City residents. Her findings? "People really don't want to be bothered. Not really." Cynthia, a smallish woman with a laid-back demeanor and a fondness for Kool cigarettes, hasn't been physically assaulted, but confronts verbal harassment daily.

"This big guy, big old black guy six-foot-something or another, cracked the door and said, 'I filed it already.' When I told him our records didn't show that he got all nasty. But, get this, he didn't close the door! He just kept it cracked to tell me off. As if I was gonna stand and listen. It was all right with me. I just went back and told my supervisor—she's supposed to make follow-up visits. Know what she said? 'No, not me honey. No one's slamming a door in my face.' Hey, I don't blame her."

Between typical New York responses to government inquiry and a less than committed work force, Cynthia has found it fascinating to walk through today's Starrett City, which remains predominantly white but is now probably about 40 percent "minority." "I can see where they try to keep the number of black kids down," she says. "So many of the black families are young couples with, maybe, one or two kids. A lot of them don't have any kids. I guess you gotta be just starting out with both parents working to pay the rent. But it's also like they figure they'll move out to a house in a year or two. It doesn't matter much to them that I'm black. Least I don't think so. Some of them cooperate, but they mostly act too busy. That suits me. I get paid for making ten contacts a day, good or bad."

"Now what the bug-out of the job is are the white families. You got Russian Jews and all kinds of people from Europe. Fresh off the boat. You got to sit with them and go step-by-step through the form. And they all got kids. Swear to God, I didn't know white people could have so many kids."

Standing on Pennsylvania Avenue looking south you see the Belt Parkway. Beyond that bit of road is Jamaica Bay, the home of undernourished sea gulls, garbage-ducking fish, and the odd ex-Gotti associate. Do a 180 and you face Spring Creek and East New York, the domain of Congressman Major Owens, low-level drug dealers of various nationalities, and thousands of working-poor folk. In that Brooklyn, Brooklyn like it is now, they hoped their garbage would be collected and the children would survive the daily gauntlet of crackheads and police to and from school. But in Brooklyn like it used to be, Cynthia and I stood and watched an express bus bringing residents home from Manhattan, back to the nostalgic illusion that was their bit of Pennsylvania Avenue.

VILLAGE VOICE, 1990

# OVERNIGHTMARES

Late at night, just before sleep, I turn on WCBS, News Radio 88. In the darkness I watch the dial's orange glow and listen to a concise 15-minute account of the world's latest nightmares before I slip into mine. Freed from the hurly-burly of traffic tie-ups, warmongering presidential press conferences, and tales of Wall Street rip-offs, radio news opens itself to the brutal rhythms of the New York night. In bedrooms across town people make love, read, take drugs, and worry about money, activities that often combust to create violence, a small percentage of which ends up on the nightly police blotter. In the calmly bureaucratic tones of official reports, the announcers talk of perpetrators, suspected arson, and confiscated AK-47s. It all sounds too sadly routine to be shocking. But listen close and you can hear the sound of weeping children. For every overnight robbery, fire, or murder on News Radio 88 there's a kid crying out in pain, bewilderment, and, very often in this age of nine-millimeter justice, thirst for immediate vengeance. Overnight, you hear reports about the streets that during daylight are mere filler, such as Queens's Jamaica

Avenue and Brooklyn's Pennsylvania Avenue. Judging by the station's commercials and relentless traffic updates, most of 88's listeners are suburbanites. For them, these streets are almost as foreign as Baghdad.

My old neighborhood's main drag, Pennsylvania Avenue, runs from Jamaica Avenue to the Belt Parkway (or vice versa) past the Liberty Avenue A train, Thomas Jefferson High School, the elevated New Lots IRT, Roberto Clemente Elementary School, the gas stations and fast food outlets clustered around Linden Boulevard, and a couple of low-budget malls before disappearing inside Starrett City. For most commuters, it's nothing more than a shortcut through East New York. Under Koch, whose call-in show appearances on WCBS set the stage for his meathead meanderings in the *Post*, some fool city agency painted flowerpots and shutters on the blocked-up windows of abandoned buildings on Pennsylvania to make the ride more congenial for commuting drivers. Koch literally tried to paint over East New York's neglect. But these days, under David Dinkins and black bureaucratic teammate Lee Brown, there's no way to whitewash the evil enveloping the 'hood's citizens. As in Detroit, Cleveland, Philadelphia, Newark, and the list grows on, mainstream African American empowerment in New York has come just as our metropolis has slid from bustling North American urban center into chaotic Third World country, its tax base of residents and businesses fleeing in fear of a brown city.

This summer in East New York, years of governmental racism and incompetence have conspired with the terror of crackology—the death-affirming mentality of crack's sellers and abusers—to fill the overnight news with the dying gasp of neighborhood babies. Four died within an eight-day period in July and more have been shot since. A one-year-old was snuffed by a bullet aimed at her father. A three-year-old was hit walking with her mother. A nine-year-old was murdered sleeping in the family car. All these young lives ended on streets within walking distance of Pennsylvania Avenue, all were documented and exploited by the over-heated rhetoric from the likes of William Bennett—he compared East New York to Beirut while demanding bigger jails.

This summer at P.S. 328 on Alabama Avenue between Sutter and Blake, about three blocks from where a stray bullet killed nine-year-old Veronica Corales, a state-funded summer program for 88 children aged six to eight ran through August. All of those attending were in danger of being held back; some were discipline problems, slow learners, offspring of immigrants from the Caribbean and South America. Before mathematics and English, right after roll call, the children would often talk about the shootings. Many had known Veronica. Some in the program had collected money for her family by selling pies. But for all the children Veronica's death, as well as all the others, wasn't a News 88 update, the front page of a newspaper, or a throwaway line in hip hop's latest critically acclaimed celebration of black-instigated violence. These murders were the stuff of nightmares.

Lying in bed semiconscious with the radio on, I hear the latest cry from East New York—a 10-year-old shot accidentally by a local teen. Sitting up, I grab the phone. Out in East New York near Pennsylvania Avenue my nieces, 10 and three, are sleeping. My alarm is unfounded, but how can I be happy? Lavell Robinson, visiting East New York from Utica, was shot in the stomach by a local teen showing off his .38. *Showing off his .38.* Shutting off my radio, I try my damnedest not to dream.

VILLAGE VOICE, 1990

# AFRO ED

In 1968, as part of Lyndon Johnson's "great society," the federal government's Model Cities Program earmarked millions of dollars to help disadvantaged youths such as yours truly. That summer, several hundred African American kids were paid a stipend to attend classes at Bed-Sty's Alexander Hamilton High, where we were under the direction of a staff that was predominantly black and, as I recall it, male. I'd never before been in an environment with that many brothers at the head of the class. In fact, up until then I'd only had one black male teacher, Mr. West, who was tall, played piano, and had the biggest Adam's apple in the world.

The Model Cities instructors taught me chess, distributed books on African history, and encouraged me to savor how the rhythm section interacted on "Sex Machine" as it boomed through the cafeteria.

But most important was the brother who showed me how to think ana-lytically. In a humid corner classroom, late in afternoons made for ice pops on the corner and ball in the park, a dark brown, moderately Afroed teacher would play Coltrane for Stax/Motown ears and then make us read the papers.

He'd pull out the *Post*, then a liberal journal; the *Daily News*, then renowned for its Sunday-morning page-five mug shot of Saturday night's most heinous black criminal; and the *Times*, which I'd never read before, partly because it wasn't readily available in my neighbor-hood. He'd select a news event covered by all three, read it aloud, and then force us to examine headlines, tone, structure, style, and fact selection in search of each publication's hidden agenda. We were being trained to analyze "objective information" and the bias behind its presentation. To this day I find myself drawing upon those lessons.

Since all the other counselors that summer were black as well, I chalk up my man's special impact to intelligence and ability, not race. Yet it's hard to separate the two in my mind: Was he just a sharp teacher, or was his teaching so sharp 'cause he was black? Two decades later that question haunts me as the city plans a predominantly black male high school. Last week the Board of Education spent 90 minutes at a public hearing letting Assemblyman Roger Green and the other architects of the Ujamaa Institute proposal outline their plans for an experimental high school on the Crown Heights campus of Medgar Evers College with a special emphasis on young black and hispanic men. New York is the second city to institute such a plan: Milwaukee had already projected an elementary and a middle school exclusively for black males as a way of moving them off the endangered species list.

Ujamaa, which means family in Swahili, wouldn't be all-black or all-male, but its 300 to 400 students would be largely black and largely male. Ujamaa's curriculum zeroes in on conditions affecting young brothers, which Green says will "promote positive mentoring and bonding" just as basketball or football teams do. The central idea is that the failure of black males in traditional schools demands innova-tive measures. Some might call them desperate.

There's merit to Ujamaa, but only if you believe the New York City school system could effectively run an Afrocentric school. Obviously, black male teachers and administrators would be expected to domi-nate its staff. Would the United Federation of Teachers agree to the shift in personnel that would entail? Since there's already a significant shortage of brothers in the system, where would the school's staff come from, especially with many younger teachers laid off in the ongoing budget crisis? It would be tempting to move to a teaching environment where your culture is crucial, even if that meant abandoning black kids in the compromised situation you come out of.

Anyway, whose culture will end up shaping the curriculum? There will be bitter battles over textbooks and supplementary reading lists. Sure Malcolm X's autobiography will be a standard text, but the writings (and recordings and videos) of the less iconic Elijah Muhammad and Louis Farrakhan need to be available as well—because students need to understand the context of Malcolm's career, and because both men command serious respect in the communities Ujamaa's students will come out of. To truly provide an Afrocentric worldview will require an in-depth analysis of colonialism, nationalism, West Africa, Islam, Santería, Rastafarianism, and other non-Western philosophies currently given short shrift in New York schools. And even if such material is covered, will it get respect?

A New York Civil Liberties Union press conference, called to threaten the board with a lawsuit if it established the school, made clear that such a curriculum would trouble liberal African American intellectuals as well as many whites. Dr. Kenneth B. Clark, a psychologist whose research informed the Supreme Court's 1954 school desegregation decision, said, "It's isolating these youngsters and telling them, 'You're different. We're having this school because black males have more social and crime problems.'" He even labeled the idea "a prep school for correctional institutions." NYCLU board member Michael Meyers charged straight up that the school would be a site for "Afrocentrism-based indoctrination" and that he opposed such teaching. Such strident criticism makes clear that even if Ujamaa opens its doors the classroom material may be sapped of all significant difference.

African American Board of Ed member and Merrill Lynch vice-president Dr. Westina L. Matthews inquired of Ujamaa's sponsors at the meeting, "I'm from the business community. Are these students going to be ready to work?" A profound question, and not just in the way Matthews intended. Clearly she wonders if the school will help increase the pool of potential white-collar workers in the city. But any true Afrocentric education would not only give them the tools to work at a big corporation, but insight into what it means to work for businesses that have always exploited Third World peoples.

Finally, while I'm totally for a school with an Afrocentric attitude, the maleness of its orientation disturbs me. Machismo and the "they-want-money" view of women is so widespread among young African

American males that I don't believe a healthy, nonconfrontational view
of women can be inculcated without incorporating a womanist view—
and the female students to defend and exemplify it—into the learning
environment. The same classes that survey the literature of the Nation
of Islam must also take the time to read Michele Wallace and Audre
Lorde, and somehow this seems unlikely to me. An emphasis on black
male victimization will serve to institutionalize the self-serving male
chauvinism already stifling the community.

I hope I'm dead wrong. The lessons will be varied, intelligently
non-Eurocentric; teachers will be versed in African American culture
and skilled in celebrating it; Green will mean it when he says as many
as 40 percent of the students can be female, and womanist materials
will be in the mix—perhaps reinforced by the sexual makeup of
Medgar Evers, which is two-thirds female. It can be done. But by the
New York City Board of Education?

VILLAGE VOICE, 1991

# THE BROWNSVILLE
# BOMBER

**S**ummer 1974.

Past the hopscotch question mark and to the left of the skelly
court was a pitching rubber drawn in white chalk. During the course of
your average Brownsville summer it moved around a bit, but basically
it stayed about 70 feet from the concrete barrel that served double
duty as funhouse and backstop. All the little kids had been chased
away and the stickball crew, the black guys from 305 and 315 Livonia

Avenue and the Puerto Ricans from 360 Dumont, were hanging around with sleek brown and orange broom handles and bats autographed by Thurman Munson, Danny Cater, and Horace Clarke, from Yankee Bat Day. Black tape was wrapped around the ends of bats and sticks for a solid grip. We'd spent so many summers on this asphalt stickball field, pounding Pinsy Pinky runner balls into gloves and playing from noon to dark while ring-a-levio games, baby carriages, little brothers and sisters swirled around. As we'd gotten older, the endless summer of our adolescence had given way to the distractions of teen life; loose joints, part-time jobs, blue-light parties and, on occasion, reading books.

On this day we were all out there again because Mickey was back home and, well, we all just wanted to be around. Bill Travers in the *Daily News* always called him Willie Randolph, which confused me because around the Tilden project he was always Mickey as in Mantle, since he was one of the best hitters on the block. Whatever you called him, Randolph was the only guy on our block, or for that matter in all of Brownsville, that we knew of with a big league baseball contract. It meant a lot to me since not only did I live in the same project but was three years behind him at the same high school, and, after a so-so year of JV ball, was trying out for the varsity. Since both our project and high school were named after Samuel J. Tilden, New York State governor and presidential candidate of yesteryear, I thought maybe I'd stumbled upon a good omen.

A stickball game started and somehow I managed to get to pitch to Mickey, er, Willie. It would have been glorious to strike him out, but my hero was the Yankees's underappreciated sinkerballer Mel Stottlemyre—in my mind as good as the Mets's Seaver and Koosman—so it would have been fine if he merely grounded into an imaginary double play. Oh, well. The Tilden projects were (still are) 16 stories high. Surrounding the roof is a metal railing, and right on top an incinerator. This is important information. In a moment of ill-timed machismo, I reared back and fired a high hard one. Armed with a brown stickball bat and batting instruction from a Pittsburgh Pirate system known for producing hitters, Randolph smacked the pink projectile way up in the air, over the asphalt infield, over the fence that was an automatic double, over the alley that was a triple, and—crash!—right up against the fence over the 16th floor of a building whose number time has mercifully obscured. I remember thinking, "I hope he makes it to the major leagues. At least then I'll have a good story to tell."

Summer 1986.

Brownsville is not one of the neighborhoods Borough President Howard Golden highlights in his rosy reports about Brooklyn's future. In *Brooklyn in the 21st Century*, prepared by the Fund for the Borough of Brooklyn with Golden's cooperation, my childhood home—high- and low-rise projects, the dying shopping strips of Belmont and Pitkin Avenues, Arab and Korean store owners, hard-working blacks and his- panics, and more crack salesmen than summer jobs (are crackhouses Reagan's real urban enterprise zones?)—is mentioned just twice. Brownsville is one of those places where "the underclass," the fashion- able term for distancing America from its poor, multiplies and survives.

For Randolph, his friends, and me, too, one of the keys to survival in the Brownsville of the '70s was the number 2 (now 3) elevated IRT subway that runs through Brownsville and past what used to be my window at 315 Livonia Avenue. It was a magic carpet to "the Deuce" (a/k/a 42nd Street) and the movies; to Coney Island (after you switched to the D); and to Shea and Yankee stadiums. Mickey Ran- dolph took the 2 to the Deuce to the 7—he was a Mets fan. I took the 2 to the 4—I thought Horace Clarke was a fine second baseman. Time sure does pass.

Earlier this season, I took that ride again, getting on at Rockaway Avenue in Brownsville and taking that long trip from Brooklyn to the Bronx, anxiously anticipating the moment when the 4 train explodes into sunlight and there, white as a little boy's birthday cake, is Yankee Stadium.

In my stickball days I'd come down the steps and head left to the bleachers. This evening I hang a right past Babe Ruth Park, the hand- ball courts, and suit-and-tie crowd entering the Stadium Club, right up to the press gate. While working for the *Amsterdam News* as a col- lege student in the late '70s, I'd often taken this journey, and Ran- dolph, traded to the Yankees in 1975, had been good to me, introduc- ing me to a couple of players and basically making an insecure college kid feel alright. Good thing, too, because the Yankee clubhouse was as taut as a newly strung tennis racket. Reggie Jackson was always nasty to me. Thurman Munson was mean. Graig Nettles was a redneck. Billy Martin's office was the hellhole of an unstable enemy. Except for Oscar Gamble, a funny motormouth who knew his on-base percentage and homer-to-at-bat ratio from day to day, even the other Yankees were wary of writers they didn't know and many they did. Later, when Geof- frey Stokes dissected Yankee psychology in his *Voice* piece "The Para- noid Style of Yankee Baseball," I knew exactly what he meant.

Now things seem different. Randolph was no longer just a sane soul in a room of gifted egotists, but co-captain of a team with pitchers too young to know what to do or too old to do it well, a rookie manager still to be tested under fire, and some of the greatest players in the game. Captain! Hard to imagine homeboy from Brooklyn—*a negro*—being captain of America's Team.

Walking into the clubhouse this time I didn't have to hold my breath for fear that someone would step on my toes. My first impression: Winfield is bigger than any of those aforementioned Yankee stars, yet when he sat watching Carol Jenkins on "Live at Five" or strutted past the Winfield Foundation letters stapled to the bulletin board, he didn't dominate the room the way those money players did. I don't know what the departed Don Baylor meant in the clubhouse, but in comparison to the "good old days," something was different; whether it meant there was a leadership vacuum or just non-Yankee normal baseball tranquillity, I don't know.

Randolph sat in the center of the room, watching "Live at Five," too, and lacing up his cleats. He recognized me immediately, smiled, and we started talking. Our talk that night and in subsequent conversations was defined and divided in two parts: the "Mickey" Randolph story of how a Brooklyn boy grew into a major league ballplayer; and the tale of number 30, Willie Randolph, a man obsessed with consistency, privacy, and pride. So the following is on the order of a double-sided single: "Homeboys on Parade" b/w "Yankee Attitude (Why Willie Randolph Has Outlasted Fred Stanley, Bucky Dent, Andre Robertson, Bobby Meacham, and 24 Other Double Play Partners)."

## SIDE ONE

Mickey Randolph didn't hang out, which was unusual for the neighborhood's top athletes, who enjoyed basking in the respect their ability generated. The difference was probably that most of the stars of the 'Ville played hoops; and like the notorious World B. Free (then Lloyd "All World" Free of Canarsie High) most Brownsville players chanted the mantra "Give up the pill." While these cats were holding court Randolph was upstairs. "I remember they would call me, 'Hey Mickey, come on down, man, we're playing ring-a-levio,' or, 'We're playin' man-hunt,' and I'd go, 'Naw, man, I got to get my rest,'" he says with a chuckle in the Yankee dugout. "But that's what I thought I needed to do to be prepared to win the next day. I didn't know that guys had a beer or two or got drunk or smoked a joint. I actually believed that athletes got their rest at night. I remember my homeboys hanging out on the corner partying, and I was upstairs watching the Mets at eight o'clock."

Part of Randolph's baseball orientation may have resulted from living in 360, which the black guys in 315 and 305 called "the Puerto Rican building." "Hispanic building?" he says with a smile. "Yeah, the majority of them were. They make them good rice and beans and are a good band of people. I remember even going to Puerto Rico, my first time being out of Brooklyn. I must have been 10 or 11 years old. We had an all-star team within this league and they won a trip to Puerto Rico for a week; we went on a little tour of three cities. I remember sleeping with a net over me. It was so weird. I just wanted to play ball. It could have been with the Russians; I didn't care who it was with."

Crucial to Randolph's development as a young player was his friendship with a gardener at the Tilden projects named Frank Tepedino. His namesake and nephew was a scrubby reserve outfielder with the Yankees from 1969 to 1972 and another nephew, Russell, played second base on the same Tilden JV baseball team I did. "Frank gave me my first break," Randolph says. "He got tired of chasing me off his grass and everything, so he said, 'Listen, you guys really want to play ball? Come on down to Five Diamonds [in Prospect Park] on Saturday and we'll play.'"

Tepedino introduced him to American Legion ball, where he competed against Italians and Jews from outside Brooklyn's dark neighborhoods, and also to a few tricks of the trade. Man on first. Ball hit up the middle. Randolph fields it and, instead of flipping underhand or turning his body to throw sideways, he flips it backhand. "Frank showed that to me when I was 11 or 12," he says, grabbing a ball and twisting his wrist to demonstrate. "I remember him very vividly saying, 'Get close to the base. Get that ball and flip your wrist around and shovel it.' I would sit in my room and put a pillow on the bed and just take a hardball and for hours just stand there throwing the ball into that pillow."

Gifted basketball players are scouted in junior high, but relatively little attention is paid to New York City baseball players. For every Randolph, or fellow Brooklynite Julio Cruz (White Sox), or Shawon Dunston (Cubs), a slew of basketball players emerges from the inner city every year. Part of the problem is the lack of fields and the poor quality of those that exist. Willie and I traded stories about the Tilden High School field in East Flatbush; I remember twice getting hit in the throat on bad hops, he got it once in the mouth. Randolph once took his spikes and dug up a rock "as big as a damn basketball" in the short-stop hole. Quality instruction is in short supply as well. Basically, "you just had to get what you could from this guy or that guy, and keep your eyes open for anything else," says Randolph, who in the off-season does clinics around the metropolitan area.

Fear keeps many baseball scouts out of Brownsville and neighbor-hoods like it. "Half of them are afraid they're gonna get mugged," he says. "Some scouts came out to see me and stayed in the car." Still, by his senior year at Tilden, Randolph was all-city at shortstop, and enough of a prospect that the Mets, Expos, and Royals all took a look, but the Pirates were the only ones that showed real interest.

In the '70s the Pirates were one of the most popular teams in black America because they were already ready and willing to sign and play black and hispanic players. In fact, they are the only major league team in history to put nine black/hispanic players in the game at one time. However, the open-door racial policies of the Pirates didn't mean they liked scouting in Brooklyn, either. Randolph signed his Pittsburgh Pirate contract in a car outside diamond seven at the Prospect Park Parade Grounds. "It's the seventh inning of a game and they call me off the field. They say, 'Listen we got to go back to Pittsburgh. We want you to sign. You got to sign, and gotta sign it now. We ain't gonna wait.' I got in the car. On this particular day they did not want to get out of the car. They just wanted to get it done and over with."

At one point during our dugout talk another reporter, whom I didn't see, sat down behind me with an open notebook. Randolph had me stop taping and told my fellow scribe quite firmly not to take notes. Willie considered this a private interview. Said reporter remarked that he was after his own "angle" and retreated a few feet. Willie had been comfortable talking about his pre-Yankee days, but his rebuff of the other reporter made me remember that Willie is a New York Yankee, not simply some homeboy I grew up with.

## Side Two

Sitting in front of Randolph's locker some weeks later, waiting for him to emerge from the weight room, it struck me that the second base-man is the Yankees's Invisible Man; through temperament and study he has kept his true character obscure on the most reported about sports franchise in America. If Randolph were a b-boy, I'd say he was "fronting." My man wouldn't lie to the *Daily News*, but he's much too wise to tell folks what he really thinks about his years with the pinstriped crew. Listen to how Randolph schooled the troubled and now departed Bobby Meacham on reporters: "He told me, 'Just answer what they ask you. Don't volunteer additional comments.'"

So I shouldn't have been surprised when, in contrast to my previous visit, he was initially quite guarded. He asked me very directly what I was trying to "get," as if he suspected I was out to do a hatchet job. That homeboy stuff had worn off. Randolph was just pursuing his policy of cautious engagement, quite aware that at Yankee Stadium, giving the wrong quote to the right reporter is like setting fire to our ass. And through 21 managerial changes, four World Series, four All-Star selections, more seasons in pinstripes than any black Yankee except Elston Howard (12) and Roy White (14), this is one Brownsville cat who has kept himself quite chilly.

Ask him about the media and he says, "I'm much more open these days because I'm more mature. I feel like I can converse without falling into traps that I might have fell into earlier," but he makes it clear scribes are not his closest friends. "I got burned sometimes early in my career which probably made me a little tougher. It's like when you grew up on the block and someone came out of their face wrong, you don't forget it. You don't make the same mistakes."

Privacy, you see, is a big issue with Randolph. You have rarely seen pictures of his wife Gretchen, his high school sweetheart who lived in 305 Livonia, or his three kids. Away from the ballpark with the exception of the baseball clinics and some charitable appearances, he keeps a low profile, attending Broadway shows (he was one of the few to like *Big Deal*) and catching some jazz in the Village. Randolph assiduously avoids the celebrity backstage hustle. "The PR guy is pushing, 'Come on, let's get the publicity picture.' I say 'That's for you. Does the man want to do that? Did he request me to come back here?' So I just go do my thing, sit back, check it out, slip out the side door, in my car, and I'm gone."

Aside from his don't-crowd me, I-won't-crowd-you attitude, another factor in his reticence may be that his current contract ends this season. That will make him a 32-year-old second baseman with three to four quality years ahead of him. From the Yankees' viewpoint, he may be nearing the end of his values as trade bait. Is the recently acquired (and younger) Wayne Tolleson next season's second sacker? I hope not. Despite making more errors in the first half of this season than he did all of last, Willie can still pick it, and because of his exceptional batting eye (he's been in the base-on-balls top five all season), he's still a good number two hitter even if Lou Piniella doesn't think so. Randolph would definitely be a valuable commodity in the open market, someone teams like the Orioles and the Padres would covet. Of course Randolph doesn't want to go. His roots are too deep in this city and his team.

So first we talked with the tape recorder off. I explained what I was looking for and Randolph listened, nodding at me and saying little. And, to my surprise, the Invisible Man began to open up about the Yankees. "People think, 'Oh, you're never involved in any controversy.' That's not necessarily true. That's not true at all. I've had my spats and squabbles with ownership. I don't run to the paper and publicize it like some guys might. I just let it roll off my back. I don't let it get to the point that it starts eating at me and affects my play."

In 1982 boss George fined and flogged Randolph for missing an off-day workout. "I had a prior commitment with the Mental Health Association and I felt I couldn't cancel. There were over 1,000 people there to see me. Kids. There was a little bickering about it in the papers. He was really pissed about it. This was during the strike year. We weren't even playing ball and he feels we're playing horseshit, I can't just disappoint the kids and tell them I can't come."

Billy Martin and Dick Howser turned out to be his favorite managers: Billy for his style, and the Kansas City manager (now recovering from brain surgery) for his temperament. "Billy Martin taught me a lot. He was my first manager. He believed in me at a very young age. Not too many rookies play under Billy. He gave me a chance to play and really didn't mess with my game. I like Billy's aggressive style. Now, the total contrast was Dick Howser. Dick Howser was a coach before he became a manager, so I had a chance to get to know him before he took the job. He was the kind of guy who wouldn't say a lot, but he was open for suggestions. If you had any problems you could go and talk to him. He just treated me with a lot of respect and, hey, we won 103 ball games that year (1980), so you can't argue with that. You don't win 103 games by sitting on your butt in the manager's seat."

Then he adds with an ironic smile and a laugh, "Managers can't do it for you, Nelson. You got to go out there yourself. No one's gonna help you at that plate facing that ninety-mph fastball. No one can turn that double play for you." For him, the difference between competitive ballclubs, like the current Yankees, and the championship squads of the late '70s is not found in the batting averages and the ERAs. "When you think about those years you remember we had a veteran team with a certain moxie, a certain attitude that I think got us over a lot," he says with obvious affection. "Today we have a tremendous amount of talent. Man for man, I think we have much more talent than many other teams. But that doesn't always win you championships. You have to have a certain makeup, a certain arrogance, a cockiness about yourself; just the way you played the game. Nettles, Reggie, Thurman, Chris [Chambliss], Mickey [Rivers], Goose [Gossage], all those guys—they knew how to win; that's all." Which suggests that some of the qualities I found so intimidating at the time were part of what made them so cold-blooded in all those memorable battles with the Red Sox, Royals, and Dodgers. "At times it got to the point that we felt we could turn it on when we had to. It seemed that way anyway. It's a bad habit to get into but we seemed to be able to do that. It was amazing."

It was ten years ago this summer that Randolph, the star of Yankee training camp, won the second base job opposite shortstop Fred "Chicken" Stanley. That same historic season the renovated Yankee Stadium reopened, Billy Martin and George Steinbrenner were the toast (not just the talk) of the town, Thurman Munson was the only straw in the drink, and behind the steady starting pitching of Catfish Hunter, Ed Figueros, and Don Gullett, the Yankees won the American League East by 10 1/2 over Boston, bringing the franchise its first pennant in 12 years. Randolph, Piniella, and Guidry (who that year appeared in only seven major league contests) are the only survivors from that campaign. Piniella, of course, is managing, and, as captains, Guidry and Randolph are following in the cleat marks of Babe Ruth, Lou Gehrig, Munson, and Nettles (also Roger Peckinpaugh and Everett Scott). No one made a big deal about Randolph being the Yankees' first black captain, and neither does he. What apparently is more significant to him is the time it took for management to acknowledge his leadership with the title. My impression is that Randolph wanted to be made captain when Nettles went to San Diego in spring 1984.

"Nothing. Nothing really," Randolph answers very softly when asked what difference being co-captain has made. "I feel that for the last five or six years I've been a leader in my own way on this club. You know in your own mind, you know from the response from your teammates. No writer or no one else has to tell you, 'He's a leader.'" He takes on a whining, mocking voice to say, "'Oh, I think I've arrived. I think I'm a leader.' I don't need that. My relationship with my teammates is what makes me captain, not statistics or longevity. When it happened, it was a highlight for me, but you have to understand it was talked about for awhile. So maybe a little bit of the oomph kinda went away a little bit. It wasn't like I just said, 'Oh, well.' But I was already comfortable with the way I perceived myself and what I meant to this team when they announced it. I don't want to play it down, but you have to know the history of the whole thing."

Roy White, the senior black Yankee when Randolph joined the club, currently hitting coach, backs him up. Standing by the batting cage watching Randolph work on his swing, White recalls that in '76, "he was a quiet kind of shy young man with a lot of talent you immediately noticed," but that today "Willie is a leader on the club and is a lot more verbal about it than people realize. In the clubhouse, in the dugout, on the bus, he talks to guys, gets on them. He's very good with the younger players." Meacham felt that way and, according to Stokes's book on the 1983 Yankee season, *Pinstripe Pandemonium*, that was true then with Meacham, Andre Robertson, and Brian Dayett. Stokes also remarked "it sometimes seemed as though there were two different Willie Randolphs wearing pinstripes."

Randolph's attitude is that of the classic other-borough New Yorker. Where out-of-towners like Reggie Jackson, Dave Winfield, George Steinbrenner, and Billy Martin came to the Apple to get drunk on the city's glamour and power, Randolph sips from the cup lightly. A camera ad. A Gillette spot with Steve Garvey and Steve Carlton. Some stuff on WPIX and SportsChannel. That's all this hometown hero has tasted. He says, "I haven't really pursued it. I've been open for it," yet Randolph must know that solid second basemen with barely over 30 lifetime homers don't get Madison Avenue calls unless they chase.

He hasn't. He won't. He's still got the baseball obsessiveness that kept him upstairs at night watching the Mets and perfecting his double play toss. The difference, over the long run, between some of the gifted Puerto Rican players in 360 Dumont and Willie "Mickey" Randolph wasn't raw talent. There were cats we played with who could put the ball on the roof of the Tilden projects, and field as sweet as Topps bubble gum. What separated Randolph from his local peers is what separates the 1976 Yankees and 1986 Yankees.

"When you walk out in the field you have to really feel like you can win; that you're the best at what you can do. That's how I approach my job," he says near the end of our talk, buttoning up the most famous jersey in professional sports. "It's all about attitude."

# SUMMERTIME BLUES

**S**ummer in the city and crime is everywhere. Shrouded in the haze of these superhumid days are various acts of commonplace larceny that, at best, may end up on the police blotter. The hot weather, combined with the mind-numbing encyclopedia of ills that make New York feel on the verge of anarchy, make every moment seem ripe for malfeasance.

"Nelson!"

I turn over in my bed, suspended in that netherworld of sleep and waking. "Nelson! I've been robbed!" The voice is familiar—a close friend who lives four blocks away. I awaken in that time between dawn and total darkness, a time conducive to both love and mayhem. I let my man in. It's not pretty. There's a gash on his forehead and a deep cut on one cheek; his left eye is filled with blood. Coming back from a late date, car in the shop, he walked home from the subway and was bum-rushed by a five-man posse of new jack knuckleheads.

One punk swung from the hip, knocking him down and sending my man's keys flying from his head into the Brooklyn night. As they circled their prey, one pulled out a small-caliber gun. After taunting him for sport, they seized his wallet and took off. He's quite matter-of-fact about it. No outrage. No tears. "Go out with me to try to find my keys," he asks. Which, after grabbing my flashlight, we do.

A hint of light blue barely illuminates the vacant streets. We walk to the spot where, just moments before, my man had been vicked, flashing light on the pavement and the nearby shrubbery. It seems fruitless, but my man, without the flashlight, finds his keys amongst the bushes.

He gets into his house that morning, but his credit cards, driver's license, and peace of mind are gone. He now talks of leaving the neighborhood, even Brooklyn, although he doesn't want to. There's that unease in his soul that all violent crime victims feel long after the fact.

That my man is young and black and male, just like his attackers, hasn't complicated the issue for him—to him the crime was as color-blind as the gun aimed at his face. But divorcing color from crime in New York is impossible.

A week later, two blocks from where my man was robbed, a long-limbed black teen scampers into a black-owned barber shop. He runs past one waiting customer and the earnest, stern-faced young barber, then out into the shop's sun-drenched backyard. As the teen goes by the barber turns slightly to watch before he returns to trimming my Caesar.

A brown-uniformed traffic officer—caucasian, maybe hispanic—peeks inside the shop suspiciously, then walks away. Within a minute a traffic department tow truck pulls up. Within five minutes there are three police cars at the curb outside. Cops white, black, and hispanic enter. One black cop walks over to the barber and asks, "Did somebody just run through here?" The barber replies, "I didn't see anyone." The cop doesn't seem to believe him, but he doesn't press the issue and he doesn't ask me.

A white cop walks into the yard while the other cops prance around, read a couple of fliers on the wall, and glance at the game show on the tube. The barber is doing a smooth job on my Caesar and, since the cops are already looking in the right place, I don't volunteer any info, particularly since I really don't know what happened. Clearly it involved the suspicious traffic officer and the long-limbed teen. Clearly because he was a city employee (and a fellow enforcer), the response was extra swift. When the cop who went into the backyard comes out empty-handed, I do feel a slight urge to say something, to transfer my nagging contempt for young criminals to this fool. But all I'd really be doing is implicating the barber in what may or may not have been a crime.

The cops and the traffic officers depart and now the barber is working on my beard. From out of the backyard comes the teen, feeling cocky for having avoided arrest. The barber tells him, "Yo man, you better stop messing with people." The teen isn't sweating it. "I told him not to talk to me like that. Can't let him talk to me whatever way he likes. Fuck him!"

The barber has had his say. Now he returns to my head. The long-limbed teen, confident the cops are gone, sways out into the 90-degree heat, his loose-fitting pants dangling off his waist, a beeper on his belt.

When my hair is finished I go outside, and there he is—on a pay phone making sweeping gestures with his hands, talking loud. I know there's a crew of knuckleheads who work this phone, and he's obviously one of them. I walk past thinking about my man two weeks before and wondering if I did the right thing.

VILLAGE VOICE, 1991

# WHITE LINES THAT BIND
## Two Generations in the Cocaine Trade

### MERLE'S STORY

Five years ago, Clarence Merle Robinson came into the now-defunct Harlem restaurant Thomforde's to talk about his not parking cars, serving as a security guard, or working at any of the smalltime jobs that filled his days, retirement from the cocaine trade. Then Merle always looked as clean as short money allowed. On this day he wore a dapper summer straw, a blue-striped seersucker suit, and white shoes with nylon socks. Around his eyes were lines, souvenirs of a life packed with far too many all-night stands. Yet, when he laughed—snickered, really—you could see the face of a giddy little kid just below the wrinkles.

Arriving in New York from North Carolina in 1956 with wife Marianne and a child on the way, Merle was able to obtain a post office job because he was a Korean War veteran. Merle should have been set for the next 25 years. He could have bought a house in St. Albans or Hollis just as so many of his contemporaries did. By 1980 he would have been ripe for a pension. A pleasant but dull vision, one Merle still contemplated.

Except that one night, he thought it was 1957, a colleague took Merle up to Harlem after work and changed my man's life. "The first after-hours spot I went to was located on 122nd Street in Harlem and was called Cary's," he remembered fondly. "It was in the basement of a building. I came with a friend who was known there. They were very careful to see if you had any weapons before they let you in. There was a bar section and people were sitting and drinking and smoking reefer, which seemed to be the main feature of going to this type of place."

Hanging out in this cool world became an integral part of Merle's life. "I was always a fella out in the street as well as being a working man," he recalled. "So I became acquainted with all the ways people made their livelihood. I met all the hustlers and all the hustles." Five years of trying to split his time between Harlem night life and the seven-to-three of mail delivery gradually took its toll on his marriage. While Dwayne, born just after the Robinsons' arrival in New York, would grow into an easy-going, straight-arrow type, by the time his daughter Penny was born Merle and his wife were engaged in open warfare over his drinking, women, and general failure to bring home the bacon. Penny absorbed her mother's resentment of Merle's transgressions, and her personality took on a sharp vinegary edge. Even decked out in summer suit and best man-of-the-world demeanor, Merle found it painful to describe Penny's disdain. Marianne threw Merle out in 1962, though the divorce didn't become final for many years afterward.

The reason the divorce didn't come through wasn't any lingering doubt on Marianne's part. It was just damn hard for her to find her husband for most of the next two decades. On his own in New York City during the '60s, Merle was a chameleon. Sometimes he was Pete Smith of White Plains or Joe Robinson of the Grand Concourse. Every now and then, he was plain old Clarence Robinson of Far Rockaway. Merchant seaman, doorman, short-order cook, and one-time bar owner until a woman—not coincidentally, his business partner and then lover—shot at him, Merle could have been a model for "Papa Was a Rolling Stone." Stability? It came from late nights at the after-hours clubs of Harlem, where, dressed in his best, Merle made pleasant conversation and moved from sniffing cocaine to selling it.

Smiling coolly over his grits and eggs at Thomforde's, Merle declared, "I sold cocaine because it meant quick, easy money. I sold only cocaine. Exclusively. Never marijuana. Never anything else. Cocaine meant fast money. Nice clientele, clean clientele. Selling any other drug, you run into the scum of the earth and I didn't want to be bothered. With cocaine, you only deal with kings and queens and heads of state. Just worked with blacks, too. Never sold a grain to a white man. Nothing.

They were bad news to me, baby, especially when it comes to drugs.

"Because I usually had a regular job somewhere, I was never forced into dealing with heavy drugs. Cocaine was my gravy money. I'd spend a few hours every day selling it. But mostly I worked, so they came to me and not the other way. People called me because I had good stuff. I sold in bulk and didn't want to see $25 or $30 anytime. I bought my stuff wholesale, then sold it at up to 100 or 200 per cent profit. I always sold it in large amounts, never small. In Harlem, my deals ranged from $250 to about $300."

Listening to Merle, one saw the schism between his generation of predominantly Southern-born hustlers and the Harlem-bred kids coming up. To Merle, the young interlopers "were into the heavy drug scene" and insufficiently respectful of after-hours club decorum. In the way that older Harlemites fondly remember the style of the '40s, Merle viewed the early '60s to the mid-'70s period as a relaxed, profitable time to hustle. In his mind, those were the years "before Harlem got real mean."

Over the next hour, Merle rapped about "bag followers" he had known: "These girls like cocaine but have no money, so they hang with a dude until they sniff up his blow and then move on to the next sucker." Once, Merle told me, without a trace of remorse, "I had two women in bed with me and some coke on the night table and decided I'd rather have a blow than get blown." He cracked up over the guy who was trying to peddle a casket, carrying it on his back from club to club: "Guess he figured someone in the life might need one."

But the night he got caught in a police raid at an uptown spot with a quarter ounce in his coat lining was Merle's favorite story. "While I was in the precinct bullpen, I took a sniff 'cause I needed it," he bragged. He ended up snorting all the evidence. "They took us in front of a judge and he just bullshitted a bit and then dismissed us . . . By the way, that cocaine never made it to the precinct. A cop, maybe all of them, either gave it to someone to sell or sniffed it. Nothing unusual."

That evening, we hit a few spots: the Big Track, a Harlem gaming joint where there's action 24 hours a day; a bar near Esplanade Gardens where a thriving numbers operation was headquartered; and a ragged tenement building around the corner from the bar. Up two flights was an apartment with a red door. Merle knocked. A dark face peered through the peep hole. After being scrutinized, we were granted entry into a room awash in red. The lights were red; so was the carpet and the bar. "J.C." was the proprietor, a balding brown man in a brown suit and black turtleneck sweater. Together they talked about "good times" with the casual camaraderie of two middle-aged men much closer to the end of the good times than the beginning. Despite their unaffected '50s cool, there was a bit of melancholy mixed with their bravado.

Merle obviously enjoyed the world of these white powders. Why, then, I asked him as our night together ended, was he quitting? "Well, it is two things," he said thoughtfully. "Most important, my connection got busted and I could no longer get what I wanted. That really ended my career. See, that's why having a job was so valuable. I didn't need to go to somebody else 'cause it wasn't my entire livelihood. When you're in the street, you always need backup of some kind. Besides . . . " He paused. "I have been feeling some vibrations. Nothing certain. Just enough to make me feel nervous, and when you get nervous in the street you definitely have to go. That is no place to be nervous."

Perhaps instinctively, Merle knew that the days of boutique cocaine sales were ending. Like heroin and marijuana before it, cocaine had entered an era of mammoth multinational combines. Door-to-door distribution was being dominated by aggressive, cold-blooded city kids. What Merle didn't know was that his retirement was not permanent.

## PENNY AND BILL

Penny Robinson is not a gentle soul. Her face and body are thin. Her light skin seems paler than it should be. In the hot summer of 1985, Penny can't seem to get a tan. But there is blood in her body and if you come off wrong it rushes to her face. "What are you, a detective or something?" she says, looking at me, apparently angered by a question and amused by my discomfort. You never know what will set Penny off or when you'll become a target of her bitter humor. Her husband, Bill, is quite different. Good-natured, outgoing, yet undeniably shrewd. A broad-shouldered West Indian with large hands and a pleasant face laced with a few bruises, Bill is the pussycat of the family. Yet his charm can't camouflage a pragmatic malevolence quite necessary in his business. Bill's business is cocaine.

They met two years ago when Bill and his crew moved into an abandoned building down the block from Marianne's house. Folks on the block were freaked out by these lean and hungry dudes. Not Penny. It pisses her off for anyone to suggest this, but it is said that she has always had a weakness for men with the same kind of street-corner savvy as her father. Bill had coke, a small organization, and a couple of storefronts in their Bronx neighborhood. Penny had a head for numbers and an enthusiasm for street life, and she knew plenty of potential customers. Penny and Bill hit it right off, to the pain of Marianne and the surprise of Bill's comrades. Bill suddenly had a woman—one woman—because Penny didn't play that here-tonight-gone-in-the-morning shit. They got married, with Penny's baby daughter Gail part of the deal, and a partnership was born.

To Penny and Bill cocaine is not "gravy." It is the whole meal. Don't get me wrong—Penny and Bill aren't Nicky Barnes, or even Super Fly; they are industrious retailers who make a comfortable middle-class living at their trade. Penny and Bill survive off the fact that in 1985 every fool with a free weekend and his paycheck is a potential sale. The cozy world Merle traversed has nothing to do with them. They compete with other blacks, Puerto Ricans, and South Americans of various nationalities, so they have no time for sentimentality. This is business, they say. They are happy to be working a winning commodity.

Penny and Bill have real contempt for those who let drugs overpower their good sense. The sorry tale of a dealer who is in the process of freebasing his enterprise away makes them chuckle. To generate quick cash, he has sold them his car and two storefronts and seems well on his way to giving up his apartment building too. Instead of working, their erstwhile rival sits in his apartment basing his life away.

Penny denies it, but she knows the feeling. About a year and a half ago, she was hospitalized for "exhaustion" looking more like a ghost than she does now, a victim of her merchandise's seductive power. Bill's scars are physical. At one of his video-arcade drug stores last summer, Bill and two employees were closing up when a local competitor entered. The intruder raised his knife and, with a quickness Bill attributes to angel dust, slashed his two comrades on the arms and legs. Blood flew everywhere. Bill raced up the steps to the second floor with the attacker at his heels. Backed against a window, Bill absorbed a deep cut to his stomach before hurling himself through the glass. Holding his guts in place with one hand and running on what turned out to be a broken right leg, Bill hopped a wire fence to safety. Still doesn't know how he made it. Penny and Bill don't romanticize this incident. They simply vow that they'll never be surprised like that again.

But in the drug business, surprise can come in many packages. The latest is their relationship with Merle. It started last winter at Dwayne's 21st birthday party, when Merle talked his son-in-law into leaving and scoring some coke for him. Even Penny was shocked at that one. Merle and Bill had met several times before at the request of Marianne, who had thought, naively, that Merle's counsel could prevent Penny's deepening involvement in drug pushing. Instead of sage advice, Merle offered Penny and Bill his admiration. Bill, in particular, just ate it up. An amateur shrink might assume that in Merle, Bill had found an understanding father figure. Maybe. But their friendship was cemented not with understanding but with old-fashioned Harlem stroke: Merle told Bill that his organization and ambition marked him as "a general," a leader of men. Bill still talks about it.

Penny suspects that Merle—never "my father"—is running a serious head game on her husband. The years since 1980 have been hard for Merle, and a recent stint as a scab worker during the hotel strike may have been the final straw. So when Merle took them to dinner and offered to move some coke for them, Penny was "bugged out" but went along, somewhat fascinated by the notion of her father's coming to work for her. Unfortunately, this business relationship, like the Robinsons's family saga, was ill-fated. Instead of proving himself once again an effective drug dealer, Merle has found it easier to play upon his son-in-law's good will and borrow money. He simply wasn't able to reconnect with his old clients or develop new ones. The business just wasn't the way it used to be, and neither was Merle.

He retains that boyish snicker, and his raconteurial skills remain undiminished. Yet what was a hint of melancholy five years back has intensified. So many of the places and people he knew have disappeared or changed. His daughter and son-in-law are part of the young legions that now dominate street-level drug dealing. There is little room for an old hustler without capital in this new world. And unfortunately for Merle, there is no pension fund, either.

VILLAGE VOICE, 1985

*Names and certain other identifying details in this article have been changed.*

# POINT MAN IN THE SWAMPLAND

## Dwayne Washington and the

## Death of Schoolyard Basketball

**W**hatcha gonna do, Pearl? shouted a black man in a white sweater sitting three rows from the top of Madison Square Garden. He put up with the nosebleed to see the New Jersey Nets's Pearl—oops, *Dwayne Washington*—play his first pro game in the place he dominated in sundry Big East wars. As a Syracuse Orangeman and a Boys and Girls High Kangaroo, Pearl was the classic New York guard: dribbling with a choppy hip hop grace; arrogant enough to take Patrick and the Hoyas fist to fist; quick enough to blow by Mark Jackson on coast to coast drives; and chunky enough, at 6-2, to be bullish under the boards. But, as the Garden homeboys soon realized, that Pearl may be lost forever.

Dwayne Washington, would-be Syracuse senior, current Nets rookie, is sloppy with the ball, reacts too slowly to defensive pressure, and rarely looks to shoot. Part of the problem is that the other Nets seem to have forgotten him, but Washington's unwillingness to seek out the ball or move without it is just as responsible. Pearl finally woke up in the second half of this game, sending several crisp bounce passes through the Knicks' defense. But in the final minutes, when the Nets rallied to win by one, Washington was on the bench with a thigh cramp. A good percentage of the Garden crowd came specifically to see Pearl (psychologically, the Meadowlands is more than 15 minutes from New York) and they were *pissed*. Up in the green section 309 talk was that Pearl is (a) lazy, (b) overweight (hence the cramp), (c) scared to shoot, (d) too slow, which makes him look lazy. In what has been a sad year for homegrown black stars (the King Brothers, Walter Berry) Washington's start is especially disheartening.

Dwayne Washington is the most recent product of the storied New York streetball tradition. His alma mater, Boys High (home turf for Lenny Wilkens and Connie Hawkins) was, for years, the city's premier basketball school. One of the sustaining mystiques of black New York is embodied in the tale of Hawkins, the Bed-Sty boy who rose from Riis Park and the Rucker tournament into the world of sneaker commercials. The Hawk's story is the soul of streetball.

But the days when a visiting NBA star risked being stuffed by a local playground legend are long gone. The decline in the level of New York schoolyard ball began with the 1961 Garden riot following Boys versus Columbus High PSAL championship game, resulting in a ban on high school basketball that deprived streetball of an essential, a *ritual* showcase. Since then, ball in the Carolinas and California has ascended (it was always first class in the Midwest). Meanwhile, city parks have been allowed to decay (can't play ball without rims) and heroin—the bane of streetball—has been joined by coke and crack. The synergy of these elements has made the famous sign on 135th Street, "Harlem Plays the Best Ball in the Country," a fading memory.

The root of Pearl's problem may be the same thing that now stifles local basketball talent in general. For all the continuing jingoism about New York City players, the fact is that most recent generations are addicted to a form of basketball that becomes more debilitating as the player ages. The city game, half-court three-on-three, is a subgenre of roundball that emphasizes none of the skills essential to big-time basketball; no outlet passes, no fast breaks, few long chest passes, little crosscourt passing, no need to "see" the entire court.

The keys to the schoolyard game are leaping over—not boxing out—for rebounds; dribbling, not to set up teammates, but to create shots for yourself; and brute, banging strength used to overpower the competition by ripping the ball off the boards (or out of their hands) and backing opponents in with your butt. This style of ball is about physical boasting with the flair of L.L. Cool J. In fact, the language of streetball ("taking you to the hole," "in your face") preceded the verbal one-upmanship of rap music.

Bad street habits often remain uncorrected in the PSAL, where coaching has declined along with teaching. "Twenty years ago, every public school coach was a shark," explains basketball scout Howard Garfinkel. "Now, money and working conditions make coaching PSAL unattractive. So a lot of the best black players go to Catholic schools, where the better coaches are." In Garfinkel's judgment, Washington, who bulldozed his way through the PSAL with his stocky build, big ass, and strong arms, hasn't developed since his junior year in high school. But instead of blaming Boys coach Ron Brown or Syracuse's Jim Boeheim for Pearl's deficiencies, Garfinkel cites Washington's poor work habits.

Another factor, perhaps ultimately the most important, is the elevated position of the basketball player in the black community. Dwayne became "Pearl" because he was as slick, quick, and provocatively chocolate as Earl "the Pearl" Monroe. Any black player tagged with a nickname by "the bloods" is under full-court pressure *off* the court. At the Red Parrot, Bentley's, or the Rooftop, the hot nightspots of the fresh 'n' fly generation, the local black star is treated to anything he might desire. Pearl has a good record around black New York for turning "gifts" down, but the line between the shadow and the act can be blurry. Even a clean player (especially in New York) can easily slip into Michael Ray Richardson land because of social expectations and, often, simple boredom—between practices and games, a pro player's life is filled with stretches of down time in unfamiliar cities. On some level, all these pressures weigh on Washington.

Will Pearl ever shine in the NBA? Garfinkel predicts Washington will be no more than a journeyman pro, hanging on because of his passing and penetration, but limited by chronic weak outside shooting and defense. Jeff Coplon, the Voice's Nets writer, thinks "Pearl is one of the five best penetrators out of college this decade," and shouldn't be written off so quickly. He notes that, except for Magic Johnson and Isiah Thomas, no rookie point guard of recent vintage has dominated in the pros. Also, aimless perimeter passing and general tentativeness are part of Pearl's history (namely, his sophomore year at Syracuse) that he may again reverse. Everyone agrees that Washington's erratic shooting—a common weakness of city players—must improve. Without the ability to pop from 15 to 20 feet, he won't fare any better in the pros than Clinton great Butch Lee.

Slipping on the black lizard shoes essential to any truly fresh New Yorker, Pearl is reflective in the locker room. "I'm playing a much more conservative game," he admits. "I take the shot when it's there, but I'm really looking to feed teammates." When it's suggested that this reflects a loss of confidence Pearl counters, "No way. That's the worst thing you can do." Pearl feels his job is to "push the ball and penetrate" which, it must be said, my man hasn't been doing consistently. As for the legendary explosiveness, Pearl claims it's still there. "Everybody expects me to shoot, but I'm running the offense. When the team gets used to that, I'll look for the shot," he says matter-of-factly.

Out in the hallway, Net coach Dave Wohl is more judgmental. "Pearl starts off good and then goes into a lull. He'll just stand around out there and fall back into a college tempo." That last point really strikes a nerve although Pearl's lazy playing rhythm reminds me less of college ball than the sleazy thump of Run-D.M.C. and the pounding dribble of three-on-three. Sad to say, but in a league dominated by the frantic pace of Hollywood Lakers and the ball-moving basics of the farmboy Celtics, this homeboy was hoping for a brand new beat.

VILLAGE VOICE, 1987

# BROOKLYN BOUND

Between 1950 and 1957 alone, Brooklyn lost a total of 135,000 men, women, and children. They were buying the blarney about the suburbs, they were buying cars, they were moving out to the sticks. Filling the housing vacuum they left behind 100,000 new comers moved in, many of them black and Puerto Rican, many also seeking a better tomorrow, as their predecessors had. Another wave of resettlement for Brooklyn.

—ELLIOT WILLENSKY, *When Brooklyn Was the World: 1920–1957*

In the good old days, before Ebbets Field was an overpriced highrise, Brooklyn's tribalism was a cute national joke. All those Jews, Italians, Irish, and so forth in Flatbush, Bushwick, Red Hook, and beyond, all rubbing up against each other and speaking an endearing local patois that inspired hundreds of whimsical stories, a bunch of musicals, and TV's favorite proletarians— bus driver Ralph Kramden and his sewer-worker pal Ed Norton. Some of New York's best-known columnists—Pete and Denis Hamill, Mike McAlary, Jimmy Breslin—write (and think) with a Brooklyn accent, and nostalgia for the Dodger days runs deep among news editors. Not that the old Brooklyn doesn't exist anymore. Out in Bay Ridge, New Utrecht, and Bensonhurst, the people who remember that world get dewy-eyed over names like O'Dwyer and Furillo and Steingut.

In today's Brooklyn, the Irish, Italians, and Jews are players but no longer the whole game. Now they are forced to share Brooklyn with Jamaicans, Dominicans, Puerto Ricans, African Americans, Haitians, Iranians, and Koreans. And every year since the Dodgers bolted, the tribes of black, brown, and yellow peoples have swelled and shifted, moving from Bedford-Stuyvesant down through Crown Heights, East Flatbush, and Flatbush, west from East New York and Brownsville into Canarsie toward Mill Basin. Though the white media still haven't figured it out, New York's biggest ethnic celebration, not just in the borough, but in the city—yes, larger than St. Patrick's Day—is the West Indian Day parade every September. The residents of the remaining white homelands have responded to this new social mix by running away or watching ruefully as their European enclaves turn into Third World villages.

Now imagine the anxiety of a working-class Italian teen in Bensonhurst, getting bum-rushed culturally if not physically every day of his life. The mayor is a black guy the neighborhood voted overwhelmingly against. The Italian American governor is as sanctimonious and distant as a Franciscan monk, and everybody laughed when the Russians dissed D'Amato in Lithuania. Where are their dynamic role models? Who is addressing their high dropout rate and rising criminality? No one can excuse the violence directed at Yusuf Hawkins, nor the everyday anti–Third World bias that spews from the youth of this tribe. But the untreated racial hostility that burst free in Bensonhurst and Howard Beach was generated by a nagging, evil insecurity that is shrewdly articulated by Brooklyn's own Andrew "Dice" Clay. The most written-about Italian American in this city is not a politician, athlete, or pop star, but that man John Gotti. His lifestyle, as so relentlessly promoted by NBC's John Miller among others, conforms to a stereotype that's bedeviled Italian Americans since The Untouchables. Yet to many teens Gotti's turf control, both of Howard Beach and his nefarious empire, is a welcome proof of potency.

It doesn't take an apocalyptic worldview for the kid to envision a day when the local pizzerias will sell beef patties and a decision will have to be made—do I stay or do I go? The post–civil rights era history of Brooklyn's vast middle section suggests that the kid, a product of New York's uniformly poor school system and hampered by the same dearth of blue-collar jobs that stifles darker Brooklynites, will leave. But the ongoing media lynching of Bensonhurst in the wake of Yusuf Hawkins's murder is one very powerful reason for not punking out. The peers of Mondello and Fama, the good kids of the 'hood, represent a long, rich heritage in Brooklyn, but their lack of direction and fear of the future is a formula for yet more racist violence. Their pessimism about their future is justified, and that pessimism breeds hate.

The homies of Bensonhurst aren't the only residents struggling with the borough's constantly evolving culture. You could take a city bus from near where Hawkins was shot and get off in Flatbush within walking distance of where the community is protesting the mistreatment of a Haitian woman by the employees of a Korean grocery store. For whatever reason, the Brooklyn district attorney didn't feel he had enough evidence to indict them, so African and Caribbean Americans are trying to shut them down. In a nutshell, that's what's up. The boycott, basically a battle over one nasty incident, has blossomed into: (a) a lightning rod for anti-Asian racism, (b) an example of real, heartfelt community activism and (c) disappointment over the mayor's refusal to support an avowedly "black" agenda.

Blacks are hardly the only ones ambivalent about the Korean small-business invasion, but given this tribe's history of economic exploitation by outsiders, it's proper to see the boycotters making a larger statement about economic control. To some degree that's how it's perceived in the black community and by the media—attempts to turn the boycott into an Al Sharpton sequel called the Sonny Carson Show failed because the situation is controlled by local leaders. And there is another, equally profound story emerging in Flatbush, one that will bedevil the mayor throughout his term. For the black and hispanic tribes that elected him, David Dinkins is a test case for assimilation. His "mosaic" rhetoric aside, brothers and sisters are looking for him to be their champion and, right now, the perception is that he's siding with the Koreans. Not good. Black Brooklyn wants Dinkins to show that beneath the suits, the noncommittal stare, and the rambling non sequiturs masquerading as answers, he's down with the tribe that spawned him.

A friend from Chicago recalls that when Harold Washington won

City Hall, "within a week all the worst streets in the black part of town were repaved. That sent a tangible message to all of us that the city was under new management." On a recent trip to D.C. I found plenty of natives ready to argue that Marion Barry was not merely the victim of a $50 million smear campaign funded by the Justice Department, but damn near Marion X. At the very least he was, in their eyes, the only African American politician in town that the white establishment feared. The Chicago storyteller may have exaggerated and the folks in D.C. may be misguided, yet all spoke of a passion for Washington and Barry born of each mayor's intense identification with his black residents and vice versa.

Even during the campaign Dinkins generated little passion; looking back, is there any question that it was Hawkins's murder that galvanized voters sitting on the fence? Now those who elected him are waiting for "their" mayor to show he's ready to pay his bill. In the case of the abused Caribbean woman, they feel he still owes them. Those who thought an African American mayor would cool the city's confrontational atmosphere were dreaming. In fact, Dinkins's mayoralty provides the nationalists with a golden opportunity to critique integration. Any black mayor in a northern metropolitan area is the scion of several generations of black political struggle and infighting, aided by decades of white flight. Integrationists hope that, by example, the black mayor will show that democracy can pay dividends for the children of the African diaspora. For nationalists, or simply the cynical and disinterested, a Milquetoast black leader proves that electoral politics are a waste, that the energy used to elect Dinkins should have been applied to protest and grass roots organizing. Right now Dinkins resembles a mayor black in pigmentation only—Los Angeles's Tom Bradley. Never having pressed an agenda for black empowerment, Bradley lacks the moral authority to address, for instance, the thousands of gang-bangers raised up under his regime. To those lost boys Bradley is a joke. Dinkins doesn't have to become one. But he's yet to convince the black tribes of Brooklyn that he is their chieftain.

There is, of course, another tribe centerstage in this urban ethnicity play. For the Korean merchant class in particular and New York's Asian community in general, the boycott is a front-page coming-out party. Obviously it hasn't been pleasant—the anger directed at them is ugly. The new jacks who beat three innocent Vietnamese in Flatbush straight up need their asses whipped, as do the angry brothers who ripped off an Asian merchant in downtown Brooklyn after the Mondello verdict. With further trials centered on tribalism coming this summer—more Bensonhurst, more Howard Beach, and eventually Central Park—expect Asian merchants to serve as scapegoats for criminality masquerading as blows against economic exploitation. The culprits will be sad by-products of the "cold gettin' money" mentality that passed for capitalism in some quarters long before rappers made it rhyme.

To turn this around the Koreans are gonna have to become total participants in Flatbush, East Flatbush, and all the neighborhoods where they are now leading small businessmen. Some African Americans seem to begrudge them their ability to open and sustain business in black neighborhoods, where redlining and racism have kept them from doing the same. This jealousy is justified, but it's also a cop-out. Their criticism should be directed toward making the Koreans accountable to their customers. Unlike the Jews, whose storefronts they (along with Arabs) have taken over in working-class black and hispanic areas, the Koreans, both one-on-one and as a group, have displayed little interest in networking with their new neighbors. Often they live up to every nasty stereotype that's been promulgated about them since they appeared in Brooklyn less than a decade ago. Incidents involving disrespect for black customers by Asian merchants aren't new. Nor are boycotts of their stores. But the black tribes of Flatbush are saying they're not gonna take it anymore. The only way for the level of anger to be lowered isn't for the Korean merchants to circle their wagons, but to extend themselves and, through employment and philanthropy, give some of the money back. Otherwise the hate will continue to fester.

As of now, however, the black activists, the youths of Bensonhurst, and the merchants of Flatbush are warring tribes whose antagonism flows through the city, united only by hostility and geography. Spike Lee brought them front and center a summer too soon. Somewhere in Brooklyn, on Eastern Parkway or on Twentieth Avenue or on Kings Highway, there is a Mookie. The question Brooklyn must ask is not simply whether he'll throw a garbage can, but in whose tribal homeland will the window be?

VILLAGE VOICE, 1990

# PHOTO CREDITS

## ABOUT THE AUTHOR

NELSON GEORGE is the author of seven books on black culture and music including *Where Did Our Love Go?*, *Elevating the Game,* and *The Death of Rhythm & Blues,* which was nominated for a National Book Critics Circle Award. A graduate of St. John's University, George was *Billboard*'s black music editor for seven years before becoming a regular columnist for the *Village Voice* in 1989. He is the coauthor of the films *Strictly Business* and *CB4.* Nelson George was born and raised in Brooklyn, New York.